The Siege of New Orleans

CHARLES B. BROOKS

The Siege of New Orleans

SEATTLE : 1961

University of Washington Press

TO BETTY

"Many [women] have been occasions of infinite goodness to their men, and sometime broken them of many errors."
Castiglione

✲ ✲

Preface

THE VICTORY of Americans over British near the city of New Orleans on January 8, 1815, is deserving of note because of the great discrepancy in casualties—over two thousand British and only seventy-one American. Whether or not America gained anything by the victory is still debated by historians. The fact that the battle was fought after the signing of the treaty of peace was the final irony in a war containing many ironies, and the campaign of which this battle was the climax had several ironies of its own. It is also interesting to Americans for other reasons: in it the man who was later to become one of the most colorful and controversial presidents achieved national prominence; Jean Lafitte and the Baratarian privateers played a role; and the prize at stake was one of America's most fascinating cities, gateway to the vast territory that America had acquired a dozen years earlier in a surprising deal with Napoleon.

The significance of this campaign has been effectively discussed in relation to various phases of history—to nineteenth-century American politics, as in Henry Adams' work; to the career of Jackson, as in the biographies of Buell, Bassett, and Marquis James; to the War of 1812, as in the history of that war by Francis F. Beirne; to the history of the British army, as in Fortescue's monumental work on that subject. But the story of the campaign has not been told in detail for its own sake since 1857, when Alexander Walker wrote *Jackson and New Orleans*. Certain accounts emphasizing the role of particular groups have appeared, and Stanley

Clisby Arthur, following Walker closely, wrote an account for the official program of Louisiana's centennial celebration of the event. In retelling the story, I have used material that has been made available since Walker's time by several excellent editors, translators, and scholars. I have also tried to convey the experiences of individuals in this campaign by drawing heavily upon eyewitness accounts.

I am grateful to many libraries and librarians for their generosity and courtesy. I wish especially to mention Mrs. Maude Carlson of the Long Beach State College library, who has efficiently and skillfully located materials for me. I received excellent criticism and suggestions from Professors Martin Ridge and A. P. Nasatir of San Diego State College. And I owe a special debt to Professor Bertrand Evans of the University of California for encouragement and guidance at various stages of my work.

C.B.B.

☼ ☼

Contents

Contents

☼ ☼

Maps

_____

The Siege of New Orleans

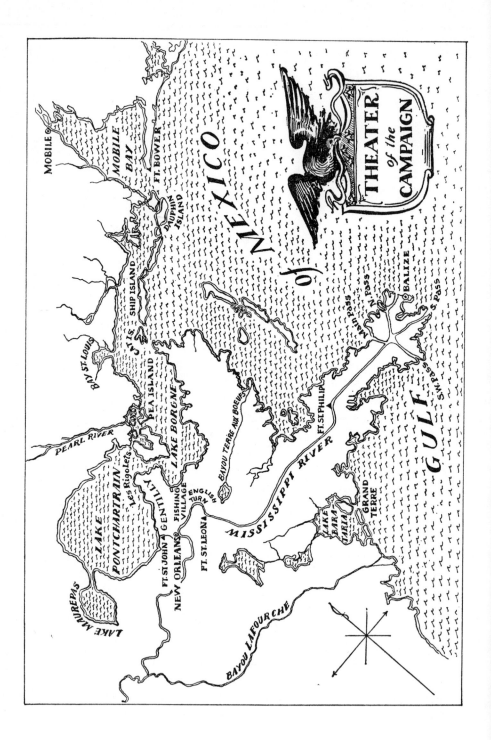

✿ ✿

ONE

Soldiers in the Peninsular War

ON THE thirty-first of March, 1814, the Emperor of Russia and the Duke of Wellington entered the city of Paris, ending, temporarily, the war of the Allies against Napoleon.

The 85th Regiment, buck volunteers (light infantry), was besieging Bayonne. On April 28 the soldiers, watching the Napoleonic tricolor descend the flagstaff above the fort and the white flag of the Bourbons rise in its place, raised a mighty shout. In a moment they were out of the trenches, dancing, singing, pushing, shouting. Young Lieutenant George Gleig, however, and his friend Captain Charles Grey, after respectfully raising their voices in the victory cheer, withdrew from the yelling throngs and sat down with their feelings. Many minutes passed before they had more than desultory remarks to exchange. For them the drilling, the marching, the camping, the deploying for action, the occasional clashes with the enemy, the plotting or digging of entrenchments—for them the war had had as much excitement as hardship. They had no special understanding of the soldier's mind; his cursing, his boisterousness, his evasiveness, his hardness they could at best only ignore, and, as long as their men showed discipline enough on the marches and in the attacks to bring the officers no discredit, they were content not to penetrate too deeply the soldier's motives. Now they persuaded themselves that they understood perfectly well the desire of this grimy lot to return to their grimy homes and grimy families in England, but share that desire they could not.[1]

They were young (Lieutenant Gleig was eighteen). They had no engaging prospects to return home to. They had worn their epaulets only a short time, not long enough to dull their visions of brilliant tactical maneuvers, rapid advancement up the ranks, and honor from the country and the ladies. A return home meant only the disbanding of the troops with consequent reduction to half pay for the officers. And they had no civilian professions that could give them nearly the status or prospect that the army offered.

So, when they had nursed their wishes in secret long enough, they began to exchange hopeful surmises about further action. There were always, of course, little rebellions to be quelled in isolated parts of the far-flung empire—India, Malay, Africa—ridiculous little actions that ended always in victory and nicely decorated an officer's record ("The general wishes to recommend to the attention of His Excellency the brave and skillful conduct of Lieutenant Gleig, who led a detachment on a spirited penetration of dense undergrowth to surround the rebel forces"). But the War Office had ample garrisons to quell such uprisings, and there was little hope that the 85th would be chosen for such an assignment.

Naturally, then, the ambitious youths came to talk of the American war. It had been much discussed in camp of late as the troops waited for news of Napoleon's surrender—discussed eagerly or cautiously by the officers, sullenly by the men. There was general agreement that it was annoying, viciously pursued by the Americans, and conducted by the British with amazing disorder. The haphazard thrusts by land and sea that had come to nothing, the isolated outbreaks like those of the Indians in the West and Southwest that had failed for lack of concerted effort, and the various meaningless butcheries here and there were unbecoming to a noble empire. For two years the anarchic Americans, with their loose federation of bickering local groups, with their armies of short-term volunteers and local militia, ill-clothed, ill-armed, ill-fed, ill-trained, with their government ever shifting in composition as the legislators begged for support of the popular vote at two-, four-, or six-year intervals—for two years these colonists had kept the British army and navy at bay. At a time when the English were defending the cause of liberty, protecting the people of the world from the tyranny of an ambitious dictator, these overseas offspring, these heirs of the great British traditions, these prodigal sons who were squandering their inheritance in a luxuriant new world had vindictively and ungenerously pestered their fatherland. Surely now the time had come to chastise them in the stern, orderly manner in which a mighty, civilized, cultured, liberal nation was capable of acting. America must learn that war was not to be declared with impunity upon Great Britain.[2]

Here was a chance. The great army that had pushed Napoleon's troops from Spain into France was the logical choice for a quick, decisive blow at America; or at least a part of it would likely go, and the 85th was less decimated by the European war than many another regiment. Perhaps it was only wishful thinking, but the imaginations of Lieutenant Gleig and Captain Grey reached out across the great ocean to the mysterious continent beyond.

But for the moment they could only hope and wait and feed their voracious curiosities by visiting Bayonne and tramping the countryside to study the ditches, the breastworks, the stockades, and the fortifications where they had lately fought. They hiked over these together, Gleig admiring his friend's litheness, Grey admiring Gleig's talent for close observation.[3]

The 7th Regiment, royal fusiliers (officially "South Britain fusiliers"),[4] received the news of the fall of Paris at Toulouse, having scarcely recovered from a fierce battle fought on April 10. Jack Cooper, sergeant, greeted the information with none of the reticence of officers Gleig and Grey. It was nearly the end of his seven-year enlistment, and he had lost all of the exuberance with which at nineteen he had joined this regiment. He remembered his first retching attack of a common military disease less than six months after joining. He remembered an Irish lad's receiving a thousand lashes for desertion. He remembered the violent seasickness he had experienced on the voyage to Lisbon five years previously. He remembered the brazen plundering of Portugal by the soldiers and the two to five hundred lashes they received when caught. He remembered a man, flogged for stealing silver candlesticks from a church, whose back became festered with maggots. He remembered drunken revelry in camp, sixty-mile marches in twenty-four hours, sleeping on the ground in a greatcoat with his legs thrust into the sleeves. He remembered floggings administered to the beat of drums, ten taps between each stroke. He remembered a sheep's head, a rare delicacy given him by his brother of the 43rd Regiment, stolen while he was looking for a pot to cook it in. He remembered selling blankets, shirts, and shoes to buy bread, coffee, and wine to supplement his miserable rations. He remembered sentry duty at night when he had to stand or sit in high wet grass and bushes. He remembered the skirmish at Redinha, the skirmish at Campo Mayor, the battle of Albuhera, the skirmish at Aldea Ponte, the siege of Badajoz, the battle of Vitoria, the skirmishes in the Pyrenees, the battle of Vera, the battle of Orthez, the battle of Toulouse. He remembered attacking across plains in waves of parallel lines, attacking up steel hillsides, storming through hedges. He remembered storming a breach at Badajoz: the first line ran forward to throw grass bags into the ditch and ladders from the ditch to the breach; the second line charged over the ditch, down the ladders, and up the breach, only to find the gap filled by a beam full of sword blades; and the third line came on to push the men in front against the blades. He remembered the mad plunder of the town afterward.

Skirmishes, attacks, marches, bivouacs he remembered. He remembered meals of boiled meat so strong the stench staggered him. He remembered the company formed and marched to watch the execution of captured deserters, and then marched in single file past the bodies. He remembered a morose sergeant (who had always been his bitter enemy) shot in the spine, and how he no longer seemed to be an enemy. He remembered, at Orthez, how his squad, firing from behind a house, discovered wine in the house, and how the order was subsequently "drink and fire." He remembered men shot down at his elbow. He remembered sleeping, at Albuhera, on a tuft of rushes surrounded by mud and corpses. He remembered a wounded man, stripped by plundering soldiers, crawling about stark naked. (He touched his belt; he had had it only a few days, having taken it, on the battlefield, from a man of the 42nd who seemed to have no further need of it, though he was still breathing.)

He remembered a German woman at Redinha trudging behind her husband in the line of attack with a heavy load of equipment and provisions on her back. He remembered a soldier's wife killed at Salamanca while giving drink to a wounded man. He remembered a soldier's wife following the march of her husband's company with two greyhounds, slipping into deep water while fording a river, dragged out by the dogs. He remembered, at Toulouse, a shell bursting near a loaded donkey driven by a soldier's wife, scaring both donkey and wife, but not driving them away. He remembered his friend Sergeant Bishop, who had married an Irish lass after her previous husband, a drummer, had left with his regiment for foreign duty; four years she had been with Bishop and the 7th on the Peninsula. He remembered when she was caught stealing and publicly flogged on her naked behind. Subsequently she had left Bishop to live with a colonel of another regiment, and Bishop, at Pamplona the previous summer, had been severely wounded.[5]

Memories to cherish in later life, perhaps, but he wanted no more of them. His seven years would be up in a few months, and Sergeant Cooper could think only of being in England when his discharge was handed to him. His friend Corporal Fitzpatrick, who seemed to thrive on army life, joshed him about his eagerness to be released and spoke ironically of a glamorous voyage to the new world; in America, he said, every soldier would have three Indian wenches to serve him as though he were a lord. But Cooper wanted no more marches, bivouacs, attacks, floggings, nasty food, dysentery, dirty hospitals, and thieving companions. His seven years were almost up.

The 95th Regiment, rifle brigade, also marched into Toulouse as Marshal Soult departed. William Surtees, quartermaster of the 95th, had at thirty-four served in the army for seventeen years. He could claim a wider experience of military life than Lieutenant Gleig or Sergeant Cooper not only because he had served longer, but also because he had been both soldier and officer, having risen from the ranks.

Quartermaster Surtees remembered miseries as acute as those of Sergeant Cooper. He remembered fighting in Holland, where the troops trudged mile after mile through knee-deep mud intersected by flooding canals and ditches. He remembered night marches in rain so heavy that the water gushed out the bottom of his trousers as from a gutter on a house. He remembered marching to battle over a sandy beach; he remembered chasing the enemy from sand dune to sand dune for a day, and then retreating for a day from sand dune to sand dune before the same enemy. He remembered after firing 150 rounds being choked by gunpowder from biting off cartridges, and being black and blue from the recoil of the musket. He remembered as a green rookie having believed a report that the Duke of York would replace their knapsacks if the men discarded them during an advance; and he remembered that when he did so he had had to sleep unsheltered on the sand in heavy rain. He had pulled a corner of another soldier's blanket over his cheek to protect his face from the pelting rain, but during the night the soldier had awakened and snatched the blanket away.

His memories of ocean voyages were particularly distasteful. He was a poor sailor and seemed always to have been transported on the worst boats. But it was not only seasickness that he remembered. On one occasion the soldiers were sleeping between the ships' guns, while the sailors slung their hammocks above the soldiers. One night, while making his hammock, a burly sailor planted his foot on Surtees' cheek and stood there until he had finished. The young soldier did not know whether or not the sailor was aware that he was treading on a human head, but he chose to remain silent rather than have the shoe slip and peel the skin off his face.

But in spite of misery, Surtees had found military life congenial. His first enlistment over, he had re-enlisted, and this time in the rifle corps, reputed to be the most dangerous service in the army but consequently glamorous to an ambitious young soldier. He had watched others transgress and suffer: a soldier who stole plate from the officers' mess took eight hundred lashes at one standing without wincing; a former captain who had become pay-sergeant rather than live on half pay became financially involved through dissipation and blew out his brains; another former officer, who had enlisted after being forced by gambling debts to sell his commission, deserted, tried to cross the channel to join the French, and was caught, tried, convicted, and deported for life as a felon. But Surtees himself had worked hard and gradually risen in rank. As quartermaster sergeant he fought under Wellington in Denmark and then in Spain. There were more miseries: at night the soldiers often had to crowd into the corridors of convents like pigs in a sty; retreating from Astorga, the British had to destroy the magazine, and a large number of rum casks were staved and poured into the gutters—while thirsty soldiers dipped up the rum with their caps and drank it.

Surtees thrived, and in 1809 he returned to Spain as quartermaster of his regiment's 3rd Battalion. No longer did he have to share the misery of the soldiers or go into battle as an infantryman —as quartermaster he quartered with officers and witnessed the battles as an observer. But he still saw misery: he walked over the field after the battle listening to the groans of the dying. He stood near Wellington to watch the assault on Badajoz, seeing in the glare of battle the faces of French soldiers on the walls a mile away, listening to the strange muffled sound of guns that were pointed downward into the ditch. After that assault Surtees tried to have the wounded carried from the ditch into town, but the soldiers were bent on mad plunder, and when he persuaded men to help for a brief time they were so drunk that while carrying one man they would trample upon several others. He saw one rifleman sitting upon a hogshead of brandy in the middle of a street and forcing everyone who passed to drink from his messtin. After the battle of Salamanca he visited a barracks that had been used as a hospital by the French, and he saw that the burning roof had collapsed upon the helpless wounded. In camp near Rodrigo he watched when a grenadier of another regiment walked aside with a gay young woman who had deserted him, leaving him with several children, for a sergeant of the 95th; Surtees watched as their discussion became a quarrel and saw the grenadier suddenly draw his bayonet and plunge it into the woman's breast. After the battle of Vitoria, while he was trying to get to camp with the baggage, he was hampered by the plundering of the French wagon train— and he watched muleteers, women, and other camp followers vie with the soldiers to make off with supplies. Surtees had had close experience of human passion and violence.

One trait of the officers he was never able to share: bravado. He remembered two senior officers strolling along a path when a shell struck close at hand and lay for a moment hissing; the officers walked past it without even a glance, and the shell burst harmlessly. This to Surtees was "rather too brave." At Barossa Surtees saw a colonel of a Portuguese regiment ride slowly backward and forward among his attacking troops, ignoring the balls that whistled past and crying out, *"Que bela musica!";* this, thought Surtees, was "absurdly brave and conspicuous." At Badajoz a lieutenant who had just been made captain claimed the privilege of senior lieutenant and insisted on leading his regiment in the assault, feeling that if he did not it might be construed as cowardice; this, thought Surtees, was "too refined a sense of honor."

As quartermaster, Surtees had not had to compete in such bravado with the other officers, and he had not had to share the miseries of the soldiers. But he had suffered another kind of misery. For many months during the campaign he had been unable to get supplies to his regiment to sell them, and his creditors in London had become clamorous. Worry over his debts had nearly driven him mad and had successfully driven him to drink. Another might have suffered little from the latter problem, but Surtees had a Puritan conscience which finally awakened in him. He began to remember his dissipations as a soldier and to think of himself as the worst of sinners. The climax came the day after his thirty-first birthday when, following a vigorous wine party, he awoke with a ghastly fire in his bowels. Sure that it was the fire of hell, he hastened to Lisbon in search of a chaplain (unwilling to seek advice of the priests in Abrantes); but the clergyman's talk of "good deeds" failed to relieve either his stomach or his mind. His mental torture continued for several months, abating only when he had recovered physically and when, by obtaining the additional position of paymaster, he escaped from his debts. In 1813, when he was injured by the kick of a horse, he received more relief, physical and mental, from a priest than the Lisbon clergyman had been able to give him.

Thus Surtees had shared the miseries of army life with both officers and men. But he had one special misery of his own to remember—his marriage. In 1807, after the Danish campaign, he had taken leave to visit his parents, and he had married a childhood playmate. But army life and marriage were not congenial. After a few months together, he was ordered to Spain, and he put his pregnant wife into a coach to make the long journey home by herself. It was nearly a year before they were together again, and then it was only for a few weeks, while his battalion was training for another expedition. She was not a happy memory. She was his wife, and he worried, during the long months of absence, about her welfare. But the brief months of cohabiting had not been enough to establish a strong bond, and since their first child had died after six weeks, they had no children. She was also a frail, delicate girl who during their last stay together had suffered continually from a chest affliction, which according to her letters still persisted. The first months of marriage had been pleasant enough, but her health precluded any chance of her accompanying him to war; the second stay together had been strained, her letters were full of complaints, and he preferred now not to remember her at all.

The last few months of the Peninsular war seemed to Surtees to have been the happiest of his life. He had been constantly active, he had felt useful, he had made close friends among the regimental officers, he had been prosperous, and he had been part of an army advancing victoriously through enemy territory. He was apprehensive about returning to a peacetime England, an unhappy family, and a complaining wife.[6]

So the British troops in Europe celebrated the news of victory over Napoleon. And the War Office in London turned its attention to the pesky war across the ocean—considered, analyzed, planned, debated, and arranged the show of British might that would subdue the treacherous colonials. Where might the vast continent be attacked? A thrust from Canada had failed; a thrust through the lakes had failed; a liaison with the Indians had failed. There still remained the underbelly—a jab from the Indies straight to the heart, Washington, or a bold leap still lower at the nether entrance, New Orleans. The navy was ready for the move across the ocean. The army had to be assembled. Officers were discussed, troops were discussed, decisions were reached, orders were dispatched, and the great movement began.

☼ ☼

TWO

New Orleans

ACROSS the ocean, in America, William Henry Harrison in a huff resigned his commission in the army. In his place on May 28 Andrew Jackson was appointed Major General, United States Army, and assigned to the command of the Seventh Military District, with the task of defending Louisiana and the Gulf coast.[1]

On March 27, just before Wellington's entry into Paris, Jackson's soldiers had won the battle of Horseshoe Bend, finishing, except for scattered resistance, the Creek war. On April 14 William Weatherford, the half-blood who had provided the Creeks their greatest leadership, rode into Fort Jackson to present the general with a deer and a surrender. On April 21 Jackson disbanded his army of Tennessee volunteers. (The British army of invasion was gathering at Bordeaux.) [2]

‡‡‡

New Orleans, a city of about 18,000, was situated beside the Mississippi River, 120 miles from the mouth, on a bend which carried the river close to Lake Borgne and Lake Pontchartrain. There ocean commerce could reach it via either the river or the lakes. Above New Orleans the river stretched up to the developing colonies of Louisiana, Mississippi Territory, Illinois, and Missouri.

Its arms reached into the fur lands to the west, the Kentucky region, Tennessee, and even as far as Pennsylvania. Throughout the West, wherever men were hacking new settlements out of the great forest wildernesses, there were streams to carry their produce to the river; it came down the river to New Orleans and went from New Orleans to the rest of the world; and through New Orleans from the rest of the world came the supplies the West needed.[3]

The river was the center of life for the city. It brought commerce, and along its banks, above and below the city, the oldest families had their plantations. Above the city well beyond Natchez and below almost to the mouth, these plantations lined the river. As far as Lafourche above and the English Turn below, they were cultivated for a prosperous sugar industry. Further down river, below the English Turn, they produced cattle, rice, oranges, and vegetables as well as cane; and the further from the city they were, the less cleared they were of swamp forests and cane brakes. The river also supplied the city with its water. River water was carried in carts to the houses, stored in jars by the citizens, and filtered before being used. A few subscribers received it from a waterworks on the levee where slaves pumped it from the river.[4]

The French had established New Orleans as mistress of the colonies that they struggled for a hundred years to maintain in the Southwest. Later the Spanish had made it a link between their Mexican and Floridan empires. And finally the clamors of the West for free access to the sea had led to American acquisition. New Orleans was international in extraction. Whatever government reigned, the French had continued to immigrate—from France, from Canada, from the West Indies—so that "French" was an insufficient designation of a man's origins. If he was not a native of France he was a Creole of Louisiana or a Creole of Domingo or an Acadian. The colored, too, were "Creoles of color" if they were slaves of Frenchmen or if they were freemen from the Indies; and they were Negroes or mulattoes or quadroons or octoroons, depending on the mingling of white and colored in their ancestry. There were a sizable number of Germans who had lived for many years near the river above the city, in an area called the "German coast" after them, and who had become so Creole in habit and name that they were indistinguishable from the French. During Spanish times many Englishmen as well as Spaniards had settled in the territory.

And the river and the ocean had brought Portuguese, Italian, and Dutch to the city and the coast, not to mention the Indians who still lingered in their ancient habitat. New Orleans had mixed blood in its veins (a "heterogeneous mixture," Governor Claiborne harassedly called it).

The original town, some half-dozen blocks on each of three sides of the Place d'Armes, was almost solidly packed with buildings. In most of them the ground floor was used for stores and shops while living quarters were above. The roofs were flat, allowing men to walk from one housetop to another to visit their neighbors. The streets along which these homes were built were forty feet wide, unpaved except for a tile footwalk along one side and beside the footwalk a gutter made of timber. The gutters drained into the canal behind the town, which ran to Bayou St. John and thence to Lake Pontchartrain. From the lake via the bayou and the canal came the commerce of Pensacola, Mobile, and the coast between.[5]

The houses were mainly two-story brick, with arched gateways opening on flagstone walks that led to courtyard gardens. It had formerly been believed that the soft soil of the city could not support buildings taller than two stories, but a few enterprising citizens had disproved that notion, and now along the streets nearest the river there were several elegant three-story buildings.[6]

But the old town was crowded, and from the center, as the planters nearest the old town sold lots to the new immigrants, the spreading city, following the river's bend, was taking the form of a crescent. Below, Marigny was industriously sponsoring a new faubourg for Creoles. Above, the owners Gravier, Mme. Foucher, Saulet, Livaudais, Delogny, and the Ursuline nuns had subdivided their land and established faubourgs into which the American newcomers were rapidly moving. The Creoles jealously guarded the original city, but as commerce inexorably flowed from the riverside over the nearby streets (like the frequent floods that levees could not wholly contain), the French town became less and less desirable. Sheds, warehouses, markets, buildings, inns, taverns, coffeehouses, dens, brothels, barracks, stores, smithies, ballrooms, and theaters—near the river the city was crowded, noisy, dirty, and smelly, and even beyond the commercial section houses were close together to accommodate the many who needed or wanted to be near the city's heart. (President Jefferson, when the citizens were appalled by the recurrent ravages of yellow fever, suggested that the expanding suburbs should be thinly built: "In the middle and northern parts of Europe, where the sun rarely shines, they may safely build cities in solid blocks," he commented, but in America "men cannot be piled on one another with impunity." But the builders of the suburbs were piling men together in great heaps, and yellow fever continued to ravage.) Growth was too rapid to be checked; newly rich Americans—merchants, lawyers, speculators, gamblers—moved into old town, and wealthy French who were discouraged by the inroads of commerce moved further away. Immigration was continual, and it was not only Americans who came. There were Frenchmen fleeing the European war and Creoles fleeing the Caribbean war, refugees who crowded into what quarters were available and established themselves in modest situations by selling the jewelry that remained from once sizable fortunes. From Santo Domingo came some two thousand free colored, many of whom camped above the old town near the Common Ground, attracted other freedmen of the Southwest (in numbers there is safety; alone, a freeman could too easily be seized and enslaved), and established a thriving town of their own. By 1810 there were over 5,700 free colored in the state. To escape the crush and bustle of the city, further and further away went the wealthy to build their mansions.[7]

It was a city of mixed blood and a city of tensions. Creoles clashed with immigrant French, French with Spanish, Latin with German and English, European with American, white with colored, planter with merchant, resident with transient, sailor with boatman, civilian with military, official with smuggler, rich with poor. Older citizens looked askance at the crowds of newcomers, considering them little better than rabble and rascals, while ambitious newcomers sneered at the long-time residents as an "indolent, pleasure-loving race, devoid of enterprise and hard to move from the luxurious routine of their existence." Down the river, in time of peace, floated rafts, flatboats, and barges with the produce of the West; up the river came sailing vessels, and up the road from the lakes came wagons and carts with the produce of Europe and the East. In New Orleans the boatmen and the sailors, the merchants and entertainers met, mingled, haggled, and scrapped.

In other cities Sunday was a day of rest from the business of the week, but Sunday in New Orleans was the busiest day. Slaves and Negro servants were freed to work and play for themselves; the stores were open; cards, billiards, music, and dancing were common; people wore their best clothes; the red wine flowed, and gumbo, pork, and mutton dressed the tables. Gaiety, rivalry, growth, dreams, plots—a city of health, expanding, vigorous as the West that nourished it, a city of unhealth, sordid and diseased with the refuse of expansion, old as the culture of the old world that spawned it, new as the culture of the new world now impregnating it.[8]

Tensions were increased by the stagnation of business during the war. In 1814 sheds, warehouses, and levees were bulging with goods that could not move, and only blockade runners and privateers were carrying a trickle of commerce. On the wharves were 150,000 bales of cotton and 10,000 hogsheads of sugar. This city was the target of the contemplated British thrust.[9]

‡‡‡

Governor William C. C. Claiborne loved New Orleans with a fatherly regard in spite of the fretting, the anxiety, the anger, and the grief her conduct had often caused him.

He had first come to the city on the tide of growing prosperity. He was of a Virginia family that traced its residence in the state two hundred years back, but his father had been "destitute of application," as William's journalist brother Nathaniel liked delicately to phrase it, and had had little to offer his ambitious children but advice. At fifteen, with fifty dollars in his pocket, William had sailed to New York, contracting measles on the journey. After that his progress had been rapid. While doing copy work for a clerk to Congress he had read, listened to congressional debates, studied French, and spent his evenings in the conversation and company of ladies. At eighteen he went to Richmond to study law (when he was not waiting upon more ladies), and after three months he passed his examinations and obtained a license. From there he proceeded to the territory of Tennessee, where he practiced law for two years, served in the constitutional convention when Tennessee was admitted as a state, and received an appointment (he was twenty-two) as a judge of the supreme court of law and equity.

There was another rising lawyer in Tennessee, and when Andrew Jackson resigned from Congress to accept an appointment to the Senate, Claiborne ran for and won the vacated seat. He ran for re-election, won, and supported Jefferson against Burr for the presidency. As a reward Jefferson appointed him Governor of Mississippi Territory. His stay in Natchez had been highly successful, and when Louisiana was purchased, in 1803, Claiborne was appointed governor of this more promising territory. At twenty-nine he had accumulated a fortune of two thousand pounds. And in 1812, when Louisiana became a state, he was elected its first governor.

To New Orleans he brought a wife, Eliza Lewis of Nashville, and a daughter; but yellow fever claimed the lives of both. New Orleans had consolations for one who enjoyed the company of ladies, and he soon married one of New Orleans' Creoles, Clarisse Duralde. She bore him a son, but she too died of yellow fever. From this blow he also recovered, marrying Miss Bosque, a Spanish lady of considerable fortune, who bore him two more sons.[10]

For the ravages of the yellow fever he could forgive New Orleans, but to forgive her for the political embroilments which had come to him after a life of almost unruffled success he had to call upon deeper patience. He had found a population of French, Creole, and Spanish that resented the new government, that clung tenaciously to old customs and exclusiveness, and that wanted no newcomers in Louisiana. He had found also a horde of Americans pushing into the Territory and demanding property and political office. Complaints flooded his desk. Preference was being shown for American over French dances at the public balls; the halls of amusement were invaded by bayonets; appointments to office were wretched; scandalous orgies were committed in the streets. In 1804 at a ball on Conti Street American soldiers demanded the substitution of the Virginia reel and the jig for the waltz and the cotillion. Swords were drawn and battle seemed imminent when an attractive young Creole jumped upon a bench and cried out, "Sirs, we have been Spaniards for thirty years without dancing the fandango, and we don't wish to dance the jig." When her words were translated, the Americans submitted for the time being to her bravery and wit, but the truce was only temporary. Placards calling for insurrection appeared at corners, and crowds gathered to keep them from being removed—to clash with other crowds that pushed in to tear them down. In 1812, when the state was about to enter the Union, a bitter debate occurred over whether the name should be "Louisiana" or "Jefferson." The governor was laughed at for being dull and ungraceful.[11]

At first it was the French who seemed to be his great enemies, and Claiborne informed the President that they were kindly disposed but ignorant beings not susceptible to self-government. But when he sought the good will of the French by delaying the changeover of laws and governmental processes and by appointing Frenchmen to office, the incoming Americans loudly attacked and slandered him.[12]

These Americans were of many types. Some had done well elsewhere. Edward Livingston, for example, was a successful lawyer and politician from New York, whose brother Robert was pioneering in steamboating and had obtained a monopoly on landing steamboats at New Orleans. Edward, retreating from political scandal in New York, came to Louisiana when American lawyers were much needed because of the change to the new government. By often serving the old families, he acquired considerable land in lieu of fees. Because his manners were polished and he was acquainted with Lafayette, he soon became socially acceptable to the French. At a party he met Louise Davezac, a young widow who was a fourth generation Creole of the Caribbean islands but who had lost her fortune in the revolutions there and now supported herself and her young sister by embroidery and dressmaking. This courtship ended with a double wedding of international flavor at the Ursuline convent; the other couple was Louise's Creole cousin and the nephew of a Spanish marquis (Livingston himself was Scotch and Dutch). Thus Livingston formed alliances with the old population (as the governor himself did), but he also increased his fortune so rapidly that he earned a reputation of being rapacious. He especially outraged the Creoles by claiming a piece of alluvial land fronting the upper suburb, land which the citizens considered to be common property, and by trying to dig a canal there. This involved him in long-drawn-out litigation with the city.[13]

Somewhat different from Livingston was Thomas C. Nicholls, who came to New Orleans immediately after the purchase, learned

French and Spanish, became a lawyer, made friends with the governor, and turned these accomplishments into success. He married a New York girl, a Protestant like himself, and rose rapidly socially and financially without forming any alliances with the old inhabitants. John McDonough came from Baltimore, bought land, made fictitious sales which he announced in the newspapers, and gradually by such tactics lured real purchasers and soon built a fortune.[14]

There were others like these: there were political speculators who badgered Claiborne for favors; there were men who had been failures elsewhere and would be failures anywhere but who hid their failure under contempt for the Creoles; and there were ordinary men with ordinary prejudices who considered Latins, in spite of their long incumbency in this territory, to be intruders. Interests so strongly clashed and antipathies were so deeply rooted that Claiborne, unable to satisfy anyone, soon felt isolated.

An American army officer, having eloped with a Creole girl, came to Claiborne to be married. For the girl not to marry, the governor thought, would be ruinous to her honor, so he performed the ceremony—only to be sharply attacked by the Creoles for abetting the outrage. Over and over again any action induced wrath.

The French, too, were ever ready to settle quarrels with a duel. Micajah Lewis, Claiborne's secretary and brother-in-law, resented an attack in a newspaper upon his dead sister, searched out the journalist to remonstrate, met his adversary at the dueling ground, and died at the second fire.[15]

But the clashes were not always between French and American. The Ursuline nuns complained of indecent attacks upon them on the stage of the theatre. A dispute arose among the Catholics between two priests, an Irishman and a Spaniard, who both claimed to be vicar-general of Louisiana, and for months the dispute dragged on while the governor pleaded in vain his lack of authority. When a crew of sailors, answering the cries for help of a slave girl, rescued her from a whipping administered by her master, the planters complained bitterly of such interference with their rights. Sailors of different nations clashed in a bloody battle on the levee. Planters shrieked of injustice when the slave trade was abolished. After the revolution at Santo Domingo, Claiborne attempted to forbid the immigration of free colored, but those already in New Orleans successfully harbored the newcomers. Then when Napoleon invaded Spain and the Cubans began to persecute the refugees there, Claiborne's problem was aggravated by a new mass immigration of these Creole colored. A statute fining them twenty dollars for every week they remained in the territory drove a few up the river and a few up the coast, but the majority merely melted into the great colored population. Orleanians and upstate Louisianans argued over their respective militia quotas. Tenants and landlords bickered over extravagant rents. A rebellious gang of slaves marched down the river toward the city, burning plantations and impressing more slaves, until soldiers and hastily called militia surrounded them, routed them, killed sixty-six in the battle, and hanged the rest. There was the question of the colored militia, which had been organized by the Spanish and wanted to continue to serve the country. White citizens protested that arming the free colored would be dangerous if they should support a slave revolt, but to deny them the rights that Spain had given them would be the best way to create disaffection. Claiborne left the decision to the secretary of war, who ordered that the corps be continued but not increased. But the whites were not satisfied, and only after the colored militia had helped quell a slave insurrection in 1811 and a new Spanish governor had arrived in Pensacola with colored troops did the legislature authorize a colored corps. Week after week, year after year, the bitter wrangles continued in the bustling, growing, prosperous city.[16]

One of the governor's bitterest memories was of the pirates who harbored at Grande Terre, on the coast some hundred miles away, preyed on commerce in the Gulf, and marketed their wares in the city. No efforts of his could dislodge them. When he appealed to the older citizens for help, they looked askance, unable to discover any wrong in piracy or smuggling—many were related to pirates, many were friendly with them, many had uncles or fathers who had made their fortunes that way. And the newer residents were scarcely more helpful, since the pirates, during the embargo, brought the city almost its only commerce. When soldiers were alert in the city, the pirates would smuggle their goods to points where bayous flowed into the river, and the people of the city always seemed to know where to find them. In October, 1813, a revenue officer seized contraband goods, and a band of armed pirates attacked him, wounded one of his assistants, and recaptured the goods. In January of 1814, when a slave auction was held at Grande Terre, a revenue inspector took twelve men to try to stop it; he was attacked, two of his men were wounded, and he himself was killed. Claiborne was determined to smash the pirates and to bring their leaders, Jean and Paul Lafitte, to justice.[17]

He had trouble, too, with overzealous lovers of liberty. There were constant plots and attempts to seize Spanish territory across the Sabine. One such abortive plot was hatched in March of 1814 by a doctor named Robinson, a Mexican named Toledo, and a Frenchman named Humbert, who had fought in the French Revolution and emigrated to Louisiana when exiled by Napoleon. Louisiana had been enlarged by such men four years before, when they stirred up the inhabitants of West Florida to rebel and apply for the protection of the American government. Because that incident had given the British ammunition for their propaganda against America, the governor now had to attempt to quell any plots against Spanish territory. (He applauded, though, when General Jackson marched to Pensacola to chastise the Spanish garrison for harboring the British.) [18]

Bickering, quarreling, attacks—but Claiborne had prospered, and the people had elected him governor. He had, by 1814, the good will, if not the respect, of most of the leaders of most of the different groups. But bringing these groups into any kind of concerted action seemed impossible. They hated each other too heartily.

In December, 1813, the President requisitioned U.S. troops from the state militias. Claiborne issued orders to execute the Louisiana requisition. In the interior counties his orders were promptly obeyed, and the Second Division of militia assembled, armed, and marched to the city. But in the city there was grumbling. The citizens feared that they would be left unprotected while their young men went off to Mobile to fight Indians. Denouncing Claiborne, they refused to obey his call. In February the Second Division arrived, learned of the situation, protested against serving unless the First Division also served, and offered to help the governor enforce obedience. The citizens, shouting in wrath at the offer, reached for their guns. To restore harmony Claiborne discharged the Second Division, leaving the President's requisition unfilled. (At about the same time, Andrew Jackson's West Tennesseans, disgusted with their poor rations, announced their intention of quitting the Creek war; when Jackson lined up the East Tennesseans, bayonets fixed, in their path, the West Tennesseans returned to their posts.)

In April news arrived of the fall of Napoleon, followed immediately by rumors of a great projected British invasion of Louisiana.[19]

✵ ✵

THREE

The British Army Moves

ON MAY 15 the 85th Regiment finally received its orders. As the troops marched through Bayonne with band playing and colors flying while women waved handkerchiefs from windows, young Lieutenant Gleig stepped firmly to the music and looked forward proudly at the bright red coats of the soldiers before him. Off they went with vigor, spirit, and admirable discipline across France. It was a peacetime march now, without the fear and tense expectancy or the forced speed of a march to battle, and the people they passed among at least acquiesced in their presence and perhaps welcomed their departure. Gleig and Grey could relax and satisfy their curiosity about the countryside. As they crossed wide, flat, treeless plains they noticed wonderingly, here and there, men walking on six foot stilts; it seemed a childish pastime, but, investigating, they discovered that these were shepherds who, because there were no trees to climb, used the stilts to locate wandering sheep. After some days the bare plains gave place to forests, and then the forests to beautiful vineyards. Finally the spires, towers, and buildings of Bordeaux loomed in the distance. On all the sights the young officers feasted their eyes, feeling that they were seeing the world. Then on the twenty-seventh they received orders to dispose of their horses.[1]

On the twenty-eighth they proceeded to the port of embarkation, where the regiment learned of its orders: to America. The officers were careful to hide their joy and expectancy from the men, but their spirits were high. On the thirty-first the regiment boarded the sixty-four-gun H.M.S. *Diadem.* The sight from the decks was inspiring—a proud fleet of trim vessels lay sedately at anchor in the river. The largest, most imposing of the ships was the *Royal Oak,* a seventy-four, flying the flag of Admiral Malcolm, fleet commander; aboard it was forty-year-old Major General Alexander Ross, entrusted with the command of the invading forces, his staff, and a brigade of artillery. There was another sixty-four, the *Dictator,* armed, like the *Diadem, en flûte,* and carrying part of the 44th East Essex Regiment as well as the engineers attached to the expedition. There were several frigates: the *Trave* and the *Weser,* carrying the 4th, the king's own royal regiment; the *Thames,* carrying part of the 44th; and the *Pomone* and the *Menelaus,* carrying various detachments. There were two bomb vessels, the *Meteor* and the *Devastation,* a couple of gun brigs, and several storeships and transports.[2]

Of the three regiments in this expedition, the 85th and the 44th were fresh regiments little eroded by the Peninsular war, but the 4th, the king's own, was a battle-marked veteran. For five years the men of this regiment had marched and fought with Wellington, sharing his frustrations and triumphs. Before that they had seen action in some of the endless campaigns in India. Nor were they visiting the new world for the first time, for in 1793 the regiment had won laurels at the subjugation of the islands of St. Pierre, Miquelon, and Newfoundland. It had a distinguished record to preserve, and the young officers of the 85th felt a tinge of envy when, visiting the frigates which bore the 4th, they noticed the easy self-confidence of its officers.[3]

On June 2, hoisting sail, the ships stood toward the sea. By dark they had cleared the river, and Gleig looked out over the wide waste of water that stretched as far as he could see. The long journey had begun.[4]

Meanwhile the 7th Regiment, royal fusiliers, was also marching. It too marched triumphantly through a city where it had lately fought, but Sergeant Cooper had no curiosity about the fortifications, no eye for sights, and no longing for glory. He thought only of the end of his seven years' enlistment and his forthcoming liberation from service. He too stepped firmly to the music and looked forward at the uniforms, but with a different sentiment from Gleig's. The tall caps had to be polished to a high shine, and they threatened at every moment to topple off; the stiff leather collars had to be varnished, and they rubbed the neck; the wings of cloth and wool on the shoulders had to be combed and trimmed; the jacket buttons had to shine brightly, and the jackets squeezed the stomach tightly; the lace on breast and cuffs had to be constantly scrubbed; the white breeches and black gaiters fitted tightly about hips and legs; and everywhere there were loops, loops, loops—loops to the gaiters, loops to the jacket, loops to the cross belt, loops to the wings. To Cooper the uniforms signified not glory but sweat and misery.

The 7th stopped at Condom for six weeks, waiting for the generals to solve the bottlenecks and plan the movements of the various troops out of Europe. There Sergeant Cooper and Corporal Fitzpatrick spent three weeks in the hospital, and Cooper wondered, after being waited upon for three weeks by veiled ladies, if the hospital might be a nunnery. On sunny days he watched babies playing near the building; Corporal Fitzpatrick waggishly said they were the children of the friars.

Rejoining their regiment, they at last set off again, marching across a wide, flat, treeless pasture land. Sergeant Cooper noticed men walking on stilts, thought to himself that they were strange, but made no attempt to find out more about them. Over the flat land the soldiers tramped, through forests they tramped, and across vineyards they tramped (appropriating, when they could, jugs of wine). Through Bordeaux they tramped, and they joined the thousands of troops awaiting passage by the Garonne.[5]

Not all the troops in the marching army found the journey as tedious as did Sergeant Cooper. The young officers of the 43rd, quartered in comfortable chateaux, found the ladies of Languedoc friendly and charming and enjoyed a gay round of festivities and dancing. On the last lap of the journey to Garonne, after dismounting, they walked arm in arm with some of these ladies. Crowds of women lined the banks of the river to wave good-bye to the departing troops, and one woman suddenly jumped into the water, swam to the boat carrying the sergeant she loved, and climbed into it, having thus determined to leave her homeland for his. Captain Cooke of the 43rd found the tableau touching: "There was kissing in the valleys, and kissing upon the hills, and in short, there was embracing, kissing, and counterkissing, from Toulouse to Bordeaux." [6]

On June 13 the 7th royal fusiliers embarked upon the transport *Anderson,* which carried them to Verdun roads, where they transferred to H.M.S. *Clarence,* 74. Although Lieutenant Gleig had found the *Diadem* comfortable enough for a regiment crossing an ocean (at least accommodations for officers seemed ample), Sergeant Cooper had another grumble about the army to enjoy as he watched officers, soldiers, women, children, and baggage bundled aboard the *Clarence.* But he had one favor to be thankful for: the destination of the 7th was England, and on June 27 he watched with grim pleasure as the ship rode into Plymouth sound. From there the regiment marched to Portsmouth. While Fitzpatrick and others collected back pay and began a wild homecoming celebration, Sergeant Cooper impatiently counted the days until his enlistment would end. If he had known the trick which destiny and the War Office would play upon him, perhaps he would have shot himself, or at least drunk himself, like the others, into insensibility. [7]

On June 3 the 95th rifles, fording the Garonne, marched toward Bordeaux. At Bazas Quartermaster Surtees watched the departure of the Portuguese for their homeland. Accompanying them was a regiment of Spanish and Portuguese women who had followed the army throughout the campaign and now took leave of the soldiers. There was much shedding of tears on both sides at this melancholy event. [8]

On July 8 the 95th embarked for Plymouth, and on the eighteenth they arrived. Surtees journeyed to London to arrange the battalion affairs and to replenish his wardrobe. He had heard that the battalion was secretly ordered on foreign service, probably to America, but, not knowing where, he prepared himself for both warm and cold climates. [9]

Meanwhile the 4th, the 44th, and the 85th rode the sea. Boldly and dashingly the well-ordered squadron raced toward the new world. Lieutenant Gleig and Captain Grey had little to satisfy their greed for observation but sea and sky. On the twentieth they reached São Miguel in the Azores, where they studied the mountainous but not rugged or barren island, gazed curiously at the numerous religious houses, spent a night with the mayor of Vila Franca and admired his English, and crossed the island on borrowed asses, studying the narrow track winding around cliffs under overhanging trees, and admiring the fig and orange orchards. They rested at a hotel in Ponta Delgada kept by an Englishwoman, poked about the streets of the town, noticed that the nuns were beggars ("It is as expensive to flirt with a nun in Ponta Delgada as with a belle in London," the smugly Protestant Gleig reported), and wished passionately to climb the island's volcano but discovered regretfully that there was no time. After the fleet had been well provisioned it stood again to sea, passing beyond sight of São Miguel on the twenty-seventh (just as Sergeant Cooper's regiment reached Plymouth).[10]

Thus the British Empire flexed its muscles and grinned across the ocean at the mistress of the Mississippi. Admiral Malcolm's squadron carried the advance—General Ross and three regiments. Following close behind was a smaller squadron, four frigates and some transports, carrying three more regiments, the 21st Royal Scots (officially "North Britain," as the 7th was the "South Britain," fusiliers), the 29th, and the 62nd. The latter two regiments would divorce from the party after a rendezvous in Bermuda and proceed to Canada to reinforce Sir George Prevost for a thrust at the head of America. The 21st would join General Ross in a thrust at the heart, Washington and Baltimore.[11]

The 21st was an ancient regiment, first organized in 1678 when most of the British troops still carried the matchlock musket, or perhaps merely pikes, and it was considered desirable to have a regiment of Scotsmen armed mainly with the new fusil or flintlock. It was originally, and had been ever since, recruited mainly from lowlanders. In 1694 it had been numbered "21st," to the chagrin of its officers, who felt that it should be 4th and certainly ahead of the 7th fusiliers, not organized until 1685; but the board which had numbered the regiments had considered only the first arrival of a corps in England, and the Royal Scots had not arrived until 1688. It had fought under Marlborough and had been in the battle of Blenheim. It had fought, too, under Burgoyne in America, and after the defeat at Saratoga it had been virtually disbanded until reorganized by new recruiting in 1781. In the 1790's it had suffered miserably in the fruitless West Indian wars. In 1803, on garrison duty in Dublin, it had put down an insurrection, "one of those sordid Irish affairs which the British soldier has always detested—a fight with a crazy and childish rabble." In 1806, at London, it had paraded for Lord Nelson's funeral. It had fought on the fringe of the Napoleonic wars—at Alexandria, Sicily, and Italy. Two of its companies had joined Wellington in Spain for the last battles of the Peninsular campaign. Thus the 21st had an ancient record to preserve.[12]

Meanwhile another wave of troops was being readied to cross the ocean while Ross was occupied in Maryland. Two noble regiments would form the backbone of this second force. The 93rd highlanders, organized in 1803, mustered one thousand sturdy Scotsmen with a sprinkling of Irish and English. They had seen action in 1805 in an expedition against the Cape of Good Hope, and since then they had drilled and trained to a high degree of precision. Now they were waiting at Plymouth. With them was a battalion of the 95th rifle corps, one of the busiest regiments in the Peninsular war. In 1807 the 95th had stormed Monte Video; the next year at Obidos, Portugal, it had stormed a windmill and routed the enemy, but in an overzealous pursuit had been outflanked and had fought its way out of the trap; in 1811 it had driven the French from the castle and town at Pombal; then, at Redinha, it had assaulted up wooded slopes to clear the woods while the main army was charging across the plain; the following month at Sabugal it had seized a small eminence and charged up a steep wooded hill in a bayonet attack so rapidly conducted that it had captured several French guns. ("This," reported Wellington, "was one of the most glorious actions that British troops were ever engaged in.") The following year it had participated in the attack on the redoubt at San Francisco.

With the haughty 93rd and the veteran 95th would sail a part of the 14th Regiment, Duchess of York's own light dragoons (dismounted). The dragoons, too, were veterans of the Peninsula. At the French passage of the Douro, they had gone upstream of the troops defending the right and had attacked successfully the rear guard, though they did not receive enough support to press the retreating French; at Salamanca they had forced the extreme right of the French army; at Huebra they had covered Wellington's retreat; and at the fourth combat on the Nive they had charged valiantly, though unsuccessfully, across a bridge. This was the second wave of the troops to be assembled in the West Indies. They would sail under the command of young Major General John Keane, who would serve as General Ross's second in command.[13]

Waiting in the islands to reinforce these British troops were two native regiments, the 1st and 5th West India. These troops would form the force for the final thrust of the invasion, the thrust at New Orleans by the 4th, 44th, 85th, 21st, 93rd, and 95th regiments, the 1st and 5th West India regiments, and the 14th light dragoons, with engineers, sailors, marines, artillery, rockets, and sappers and miners. It seemed a formidable force of well-disciplined troops, some hardy veterans and some fresh and eager to match the laurels of the others. More troops could be sent later as a third wave to reinforce the invading army in its march up the river after New Orleans had been ravaged—veteran troops such as the 7th royal fusiliers, who had fought at Busaco, Redinha, Campo Mayor, Albuhera (where the 7th had been practically annihilated), Aldea Ponte, Badajoz, Vitoria, Pamplona, Vera, Orthez, and Toulouse; the 40th Somersetshire, companions of the 7th in much of this action; and the 43rd Monmouth (light infantry), another active veteran of the Peninsular campaign. Ready to command this third wave of troops was Major General John Lambert. Commander of the expedition, it was planned, would be Lieutenant General Lord Hill, Wellington's second in command.[14]

That was the British plan: Ross to direct the first campaign, attacking Washington and Baltimore with his first four regiments while awaiting the arrival of the others; Keane to bring the highlanders and rifles, and Hill to lead these, supported by the two native regiments, against New Orleans; Lambert to bring three more regiments to swell the invading ranks after the capture of the New Orleans jewel. Meanwhile Sir George Prevost, with reinforcements, would penetrate from Canada, and with such a well-organized plan soundly administered, America would soon be humbled. It was hoped that still more troops could be sent and that Lord Hill could direct a concerted American war; but conditions in Europe were too unsettled to know yet how much could be done. For the moment the plan was to capture the Lakes and the mouth of the river. Then, if European conditions made peace with America advisable, Britain would have two vital prizes to use in the bargaining.[15]

So Admiral Malcolm's squadron plied merrily during June and July across the broad Atlantic, followed by a second squadron; at Plymouth the 93rd, the 95th, and the dragoons waited; and in nearby camps the 7th, 40th, and 43rd celebrated their return to England, and the seven-year men greedily awaited their discharges.

☼ ☼

FOUR

Troops and Leaders

AMERICA prepared its reception. On the nation's proudest day,
July 4, Secretary of War John Armstrong issued a new militia quota
to provide the citizen army which would welcome the British
veterans. Georgia was to provide three regiments and one battalion, Kentucky was to provide five regiments and one battalion,
Tennessee was to provide two regiments and one battalion, Mississippi Territory was to provide one battalion, and Louisiana was
to provide one regiment.[1]

The order wended its slow way across the various frontiers and
wildernesses to the state governors, who, when they finally received
it, acted to carry it out. Through the summer there was only waiting and fretting. General Jackson, commanding the Seventh Military District, was busy with the frustrating task of arranging a
treaty of peace with the Indians, who knew they had lost many
devastating battles but hardly understood the meaning of war or
the formalities of treaties of surrender, who knew they could not
conduct another strenuous battle against the white invaders but
hardly understood why they should relinquish the vast tracts of
their domain demanded by the land-hungry whites, who could not
act together in battle nor be brought together as a "nation" for
signing treaties. The summer dwindled away for Jackson in this
pursuit, while in Mobile, in Natchez, and in New Orleans citizens

waited for some word from him, conversed excitedly about rumored invasions, professed their loyalty, and squabbled about what should be done. In Mobile and in New Orleans a handful of regular troops drilled in their garrisons. At Pittsburgh a contractor embarked with a fleet of barges carrying five thousand stands of arms, ammunition, tents, and other equipment for New Orleans; he had permission to carry other goods and stop as often as he wished to trade with the inhabitants of the river towns and villages.[2]

New Orleans sweated through the humid summer days and occasional downpours. A trickle of commerce passed lazily up and down the river, but the wharves and levees remained glutted with cotton, sugar, and other goods that could not move to eastern and foreign markets. Sailors of all nations slept, drank, and fought in the hovels along the river front. Slaves lazily toiled on the plantations lining the river above, below, and across from the city. Citizens gathered at the coffeehouses for desultory discussion; ladies sat near the windows to fan themselves, strolled slowly through the markets, or occasionally visited one another. Small companies of variously uniformed men met irregularly to be trained by citizen officers with little military knowledge or sharpness. The governor read the journals, attended to his correspondence, listened to complaints and gossip, fretted about the state of the city's defenses, worried about the loyalty of the citizens, and visited various ladies for tea. About the only excitement was the government's halfhearted attempt to bring Jean and Pierre Lafitte to justice. The United States district attorney, John Grymes, had resigned his office to defend the Lafittes, and it was reported that he and Edward Livingston were to receive twenty thousand dollars each for this defense. New Orleans lazed through its heavy summer, its activity, commercial, agricultural, and social, almost at a standstill. Even duels were at a minimum. Even the gamblers and harlots play-worked lackadaisically. July passed.[3]

‡‡‡

Meanwhile Admiral Malcolm's fleet was enjoying a gay crossing. Gleig and Grey spent their time hiking around the deck or standing at the rail to gaze curiously at the waterspouts, the flying fish, and the dolphins. They watched a sailor harpoon a dolphin and noticed how, as it died, the fish changed from blue to purple to green. They were eager enough for experience to come on deck during squalls and thunderstorms and whirlwinds to study the seas and the skies. A long ocean voyage could be a dreary thing for eager adventurers unless they were determined to enjoy every incident.

From time to time there were balls and other entertainments. One morning the *Royal Oak* signaled an invitation for the officers of the fleet to visit, and when they boarded it that evening they found that a stage with a green curtain had been built on the quarter-deck, while flags were hung all around from the poop to the mainmast and lamps were suspended from the rigging and shrouds. The crew crowded the booms, yards, and forepart of the deck, while from the mainmast to the stage there were benches for what Gleig liked to call "the more genteel part of the audience." At seven o'clock the curtain rose for a performance by the ship's officers of *The Apprentice*, with *The Mayor of Garret* as an afterpiece. Afterward the deck was cleared for dancing to the music of the ship's band. Admiral Malcolm opened the ball with Mrs. Mullins, wife of Lieutenant Colonel the Honorable Thomas Mullins, an officer of the 44th. In spite of the shortage of ladies, the officers, by dancing with each other, enjoyed a gay facsimile of a ball until well after midnight.

The ships' captains had good libraries, too, and they freely loaned books to those who wished to read. In good weather the ships kept close together, and there was frequent visiting among them. So the days passed rapidly enough until finally, on the twenty-fourth, the cry of land was roared from the mainmast. Eagerly young Gleig and Grey looked out at the low cedar-covered shores and chalky rocks of Bermuda. By dark the fleet had anchored. While the fleet waited here, Grey and Gleig spent their days climbing hills, visiting caves, or rowing to other islands.[4]

At Bermuda the fleet was joined by the *Tonnant*, a stunning eighty captured from the French by Lord Nelson at Aboquir. It carried Vice Admiral Sir Alexander Cochrane, henceforth to command the naval forces in the invasion, and Rear Admiral Sir Edward Codrington. At Bermuda too General Ross's force was augmented by the arrival of the Royal Scots Regiment. The ships took on stores of provisions, fresh water, ammunition, and clothing.

And on August 3 Admiral Cochrane and General Ross embarked their expedition for the invasion of America. The British Empire was ready to chastise its rash young kinsman.[5]

The Duke of Wellington, when consulted about an expedition against New Orleans, had expressed doubts concerning its advisability. He protested that since there was no good landing place the transports would be so far from the point of embarkation that supply lines would be dangerously long. When Admiral Cochrane brushed aside these complaints with talk of flat-bottomed boats and of the value of New Orleans as a prize, the duke became suspicious that it was to be more an expedition of plunder than one of military value. Consequently Lord Hill was not given the assignment. Instead the expedition was wholly entrusted to General Ross, who, at forty, was a promising leader. Cooperating with Ross was Vice Admiral Sir Alexander Cochrane, Knight of the Bath, a rugged veteran of naval wars who knew thoroughly the islands and waters of the Gulf and who knew equally well how to storm fortresses with his sailors and marines. Ross listened respectfully to the admiral's stories of fierce battles and to his lavishly offered advice for storming America's cities; and quietly Ross laid his own plans.[6]

Commander of the second wave of troops was Major General John Keane, young like Ross but much less experienced. He had been appointed to a company in the 124th foot in 1794; he had been on half pay from 1795 to 1799, when he finally obtained a company in the 44th (one of the regiments now with Ross). In the campaign in Egypt he had served as aide-de-camp to Major General Lord Cavan. In 1802 he had obtained a majority in the 60th Regiment. He had served on the staff in the Mediterranean for a year, when he returned to England. In 1803 he had been appointed lieutenant colonel of the 13th foot, which he commanded at Martinique and at the siege of Ft. Dessaix. In 1806 he had married the second daughter of General Sir John Smith. In 1812 he had been appointed colonel. In April, 1813, he had joined Wellington's army, heading a brigade from Vitoria to Toulouse. On June 4, 1814, he had been appointed major general. He outranked only seventeen generals, all of whose dates of rank were the same as his. He had led his regiment on a spirited charge up a mountainside at Casal Nova, but of independent leadership he had had little experience. Now he looked forward eagerly to his chance in the new invasion, when he would have greater responsibility than as part of the massive army that operated on the Peninsula. He could envision a brilliant career opening before him.[7]

Commander of the third wave of troops was to be Major General John Lambert, who outranked young Keane. He had been appointed ensign in the 1st foot guards in 1791. He had served in Flanders, at the siege of Valenciennes, at Lincelles, and at the siege of Dunkirk. In 1793 he had been appointed lieutenant and captain, and in 1794, adjutant. He had served with the guards in Ireland during the rebellion (Humbert, French leader of that abortive rebellion, was awaiting him at New Orleans, desirous of settling an old score). He had been adjutant to the 3rd Battalion in the expedition to the Helder. In 1801 he had become lieutenant colonel and in 1810, colonel. In 1812 he had joined Wellington's army at Salamanca. On June 4, 1813, a year before Keane, he had been appointed major general, and he had commanded a brigade from the Nivelle to Toulouse. His experience was somewhat greater than Keane's, though it had been principally administrative rather than tactical. For him, too, the chance of future greatness was opening up. Thus the brilliant and experienced Ross would have two eager young generals to support him.[8]

‡‡‡

And whom did America have on the receiving line to welcome the visitors?

As commander of the Seventh Military District, forty-five-year-old Major General Andrew Jackson was entrusted with protection of the coast between the Spanish territories of Florida and Mexico. As a boy Jackson had seen action in a few skirmishes during the Revolution and had been captured by the British. Afterward he had moved to Tennessee to make his fortune as a frontier lawyer. He had dueled, gambled, and stumped his way to prominence. He had helped form the new state, scandalized friends by marrying a woman before her divorce was quite final, and served as congressman and senator. In 1802 he won election as major general commanding the Tennessee militia. In November, 1812, in response to a call from the governor for volunteer troops to defend New Orleans, he raised and mustered into the service of the United

States some two thousand men. These men he took in flatboats down the Cumberland to the Mississippi and down the Mississippi to Natchez, while a cavalry force under his friend Colonel Coffee made the trip by land. He announced his readiness to seize the Spanish towns of Pensacola, Mobile, and Fort Augustine; but General Wilkinson, then commanding the military district, did not know how to employ such impetuosity, and after a month at Natchez Jackson was ordered to disband his troops. Since there were no provisions for the return to Tennessee, Jackson drew twenty days' rations from the commissary and pledged his own credit for the wagons and pack horses he needed. Although the governor willingly relieved him of the financial responsibility he had incurred, Jackson's first attempt to serve in the war thus ended in frustration. During the rugged march back to Tennessee he had earned the title "Old Hickory." [9]

For a few months thereafter Jackson confined his military service to duels and street fights, but the Creek war brought him another chance, and off he went in October, 1813 (still sick from a wound received in a brawl), to sweep through the forests to the south in command of five thousand new recruits. His strategy was simple— engage the enemy only when all the odds possible were on his side, move straight, surround quickly, and exterminate the foe. With that strategy he defeated the Indians at Tallushatchee, Talladega, Emuckfau Creek, and finally Horseshoe Bend. The victories were not difficult, but the campaign was a nightmare; he had trouble getting supplies, his men mutinied over the terms of their enlistments, and the projected pincers movement from Georgia and Mississippi Territory failed. But his own courage, determination, stubbornness, energy, quickness to act, and strong personality overrode all difficulties. He commandeered provisions and equipment, used part of his army to prevent the desertion of the rest, executed a young mutineer as an example to others, dined with his men on acorn mush when there was no food, readily lectured his superiors on their duties, and thus gave America one of the few campaigns in this slovenly war that it could rejoice about.[10]

Now, in 1814, the general had only a handful of regular troops scattered over his district. For naval support he had a few gunboats, with Commander Daniel T. Patterson, serving his second tour of duty there, in charge of the naval station at New Orleans, and some promising younger officers—Thomas apCatesby Jones, John D. Henley, Isaac McKeever—commanding the ships. He had to depend mainly upon hastily raised militia, and for subordinate leaders he had to depend for the most part upon civilians. He had two Tennessee frontiersmen. John Coffee, married to a niece of Jackson's wife, had commanded the cavalry on the expedition to Natchez and had ably led part of Jackson's troops against the Creeks. Young William Carroll, who had come to Nashville recently from Pennsylvania, had acted as brigade inspector at Natchez and had also led troops in the Indian battles. Major Howell Tatum, who had recently joined Jackson as topographical engineer, had been an officer during the Revolution and a lawyer in West Tennessee for about as long as Jackson.[11]

One of the leaders of the Kentucky militia, John Adair, had once been a lieutenant colonel in the army before turning to politics and serving as a senator. Mississippi Territory had provided an able leader, a brother of the Louisiana governor, during the Creek war, but the hardships had left him wasted and sick, unable to leave Natchez. There was also a young Natchez planter named Hinds commanding a troop of dragoons made up of the pick of young manhood of Mississippi Territory. They had been active in warfare with the Creeks around Mobile and had infuriated General Flournoy with their hauteur and self-confidence. Hinds himself was a slender, handsome young man who had married the daughter of one of the social leaders of the Territory and through her become acquainted with the Jacksons.[12]

Louisiana had Governor Claiborne as commander in chief of the militia, a man who had heard stories of the Revolution from his father and liked to fancy himself a budding military genius. Commanding the two divisions of militia were James Villeré, New Orleans planter, and Philemon Thomas of Baton Rouge. There were other citizens who, because of their domination of the city's economic and social life, might prove to be leaders. There was Edward Livingston, the suave lawyer whom Claiborne implacably hated. There was Bernard Marigny, thirty-year-old descendant of ancestors who had served in the French campaigns against the English since the time of Bienville—one of whom had commanded the fort near Mobile as long ago as 1794. The Marignys had been in New Orleans almost since its birth; Bernard's father had built the greatest fortune in the city (and Bernard, with his generous living, was fast depleting it). Bernard had been educated in Pensacola and England (and Paris, which he visited constantly while in England). He had married, first, the daughter of a wealthy Philadelphian, thus allying himself with America, and second, the daughter of the former Spanish Intendant, Morales, contributing through his alliances to the heterogeneous mixture of the vigorous city (his son would later marry Claiborne's daughter).

There were other wealthy planters who had lived here over half a century—Denis De la Ronde, whose plantation was named "Versailles," as Marigny's was named "Fontainebleau"; Ignace de Lino de Chalmette, aging relative of Marigny; Augustin Macarty, neighbor of Chalmette, descendant of an Irish family that had moved to France in the seventeenth century to escape English persecution and found its way thence to Louisiana in 1730; Alexander Declouet ("a good man, honest, but with small intelligence," according to the elegant conversationalist Marigny); Michel Fortier and David B. Morgan. There was Magloire Guichard, Speaker of the House, an old man who had suffered considerable losses at Santo Domingo. There was Philip Louaillier, brilliant, outspoken, one of the most forceful members of the legislature; Dominic Hall, federal judge, noted for his incorruptibility but also for his reserved, austere manners and social exclusiveness; Jean Blanque, wealthy banker, descendant of an old family, a sturdy man with an oval face, black beard and eyes, aquiline nose, polished manners, and a readiness to draw sword or pistol; St. Gême, a giant naturalized Frenchman who loved to hunt, knew the countryside, and had earned a high place in Creole society by marrying the widow Dreux; Dr. Flood, referred to jocularly as "that big, fat Dr. Flood" by the Creoles, one of whom he had married; adventurous "General" Humbert, defeated by the English in the French invasion of Ireland; Reuben Kemper of Pinckneyville, constant plotter of rebellions in Spanish possessions; eager young men like John Plauché, Pierre Lacoste, and Gabriel Villeré.

There was Vincent Nolte, a German born in Italy, who had come to New Orleans as agent for a Dutch mercantile house, then set up in business for himself. There were also the Baratarian pirates, led by Jean and Paul Lafitte, Dominique You, and Beluche. There were miscellaneous groups of citizens, such as the fishermen who lived by Lake Borgne—Maringuier, old Luiz, Francisco, Graviella, Antonio el Italiano, Antonio el mayorquin, Antonio el Portuguez, Manuelilo, El Campechano, Garcia. There were Spanish planters, German farmers, slaves, free colored, unemployed sailors. Who would prove loyal and who would prove able no one could tell. Military experience was noticeably lacking (but what had experienced soldiers accomplished in other campaigns of the war?).[13]

On August 9, having signed the treaty of peace with the Creeks (giving half of the Creek territory to the land-hungry Tennesseans and Georgians), Jackson left the forests for Mobile to organize his defenses. He had intended to open headquarters at New Orleans, but hearing that a British expedition had landed at the mouth of the Apalachicola, he determined that Mobile would be the target and busied himself with the defenses of that town. Dispatches from Havana informed him that twenty-five thousand troops had arrived at Bermuda, and a rumor from Pensacola had it that the Emperor of Russia had offered fifty thousand choice soldiers for the conquest of Louisiana.[14]

On August 14 General Ross's troops sighted the coast of America on their way to Washington and Baltimore.[15]

☆ ☆

FIVE

Visit to Lafitte

As HIS Majesty's sloop of war *Sophia* tacked and came to anchor, Captain Nicholas Lockyer looked out at the coast of Louisiana. To the right, stretching eastward, was the isle of Grande Terre; to the left, stretching westward, was Grand Isle; and ahead was the pass which led into Barataria bay and thence, via many devious waterways, to the city of New Orleans, the ultimate prize, some hundred miles away. The island to the west was low, flat, and narrow, though it gradually widened in the distance. Beyond a narrow beach it was covered with tall grass, and at intervals it sported stubby cypresses. Grande Terre had a higher headland, cutting off the view of the waters beyond it in that direction. Ahead was a sheet of water shimmering in the blazing August sun, with still a third island in its midst, one with a great mound of earth near its edge. And in the far distance, right, left, and straight ahead, was a flat stretch of land with a few trees and various ribbons of water.[1]

To the left was a vessel that Lockyer's sloop had fired upon and forced aground. Though he had come to negotiate peace, Lockyer had begun with a hostile gesture. This harbor, with its access to the precious city, would best be won by diplomacy, but like the city itself it seemed rather to invite assault.

Lockyer was fortified for his negotiations with letters which Colonel Nicholls and Captain Percy, commanding respectively the

army and the navy of the British advance expedition now in Pensacola, had addressed to the pirate Lafitte (not "pirate," though—
the word might offend, if such an outlaw could be offended; he
and his men were privateers, plundering legally, as they claimed,
under commissions from Cartagena). The letters clearly enough
set forth the British offer, an offer which a desperate group of
Frenchmen, outlawed and pursued by the United States, would
scarcely decline. They opened a way for the pirates to become honorable, and even wealthy, citizens. Lafitte himself would be commissioned captain in the British navy, and after the conquest of
Louisiana he and each of his men—in proportion, of course, to
their respective ranks—would be given lands in the new British
colony. Military honor, lands, the security of property already held,
and "the blessings of the British constitution"—what more could
desperadoes wish? Colonel Nicholls' letter also reminded Lafitte
that France (the only nation which could possibly claim the patriotism of these men) was now at peace with Great Britain, leaving
only one enemy in the world, the United States; and it closed with
a sly warning which the bluff Irishman had gleefully penned: "We
have a powerful reenforcement on its way here, and I hope to cut
out some other work for the Americans than oppressing the inhabitants of Louisiana." [2]

Captain Lockyer's orders from Captain Percy were clear up to
a point: proceed to Barataria, communicate with the chief persons
there, urge them to accept the British offer; if successful, "concert
such measures for the annoyance of the enemy as you judge best
from circumstances," and effect a junction between the pirate fleet
and the fleet at Pensacola; if they decline to act offensively against
the United States, persuade them to a strict neutrality, demanding
that they refrain from hostilities against Spain; and "at all events
yourself join me with the utmost despatch" at Pensacola. Only
one loophole: in the event of delay, how to act? But it seemed
inconceivable that these French marauders would not eagerly turn
their instinct for plunder against the government that had usurped
Louisiana from France.[3]

It was a mission somewhat different, for an ambitious young
officer, from the usual skillful maneuvering and determined bravery of skirmishes upon the sea. Firing upon the vessel at the entrance to the pass had seemed more natural. But it was, neverthe-

less, a good road to advancement. Success would place him in temporary command of a squadron and would open opportunities for future exploits. Lockyer ordered the lowering of the *Sophia*'s pinnace and prepared himself for his courtship of the pirates.

‡‡‡

The pinnace had scarcely entered the pass when it met a small boat coming out. Lockyer drew alongside the other, waiting for some greeting from the man in it; but the stranger, a tall, sunburned, pleasant-looking man, also waited, looking with a searching glance at the young British captain. "John Lafitte?" Lockyer asked at last, but the stranger only shrugged his shoulders. The captain mopped his perspiring brow with a kerchief and listened to the water gently lapping against the boats, the only sound to be heard in the still summer air. The men waited, glancing at their captain. The stranger waited, staring at the visitor. At last Lockyer produced his packet of letters, held it out, and, keeping his voice as curt as possible, directed that it be delivered personally to Lafitte. The stranger made no move, not even to look at the packet.[4]

Then the young captain heard at his elbow a voice translating his remarks into French. It was the interpreter who had been brought along for the purpose, but this sudden strange language startled the captain. The stranger, however, smiled graciously, accepted the packet of letters, and made a courteous reply. After a brief exchange of questions and answers, the interpreter turned to Lockyer to explain that the stranger was inviting them to enter the harbor and speak personally to Lafitte.

The *Sophia* guarded the pass, and to the west, still aground, was the boat which she had disabled. The stranger seemed gracious. So, through the interpreter, Lockyer bade the stranger direct them, and together, rounding the headland of Grande Terre, they made for land. As they approached the landing the stranger suddenly broke the silence again with a soft, hurried speech. Lockyer glanced at the interpreter, who then explained that this man himself was Jean Lafitte and that Lafitte wished Lockyer's party to keep their mission secret from the other privateers.

As they landed, Lockyer looked uneasily at a crowd gathered on the shore—and met hostile glares. He listened apprehensively as

Lafitte addressed the crowd, seeming to argue; the crowd pressed closer and closer about the British visitors, some shouting, some jeering—and Lockyer had the uncomfortable feeling that only the protection of this pirate chief could gain him the mercy of that unruly mob. One rough-looking man, who answered to the name "Dominique" and who seemed to be the leader of the crowd in the argument with Lafitte, gave Lockyer especially menacing glances. Anxiously Lockyer sought information from his interpreter, who, from his imperfect knowledge of the strange French jargon that these desperadoes used, could report only that there was talk of spies, chains, prison, and ransom.

Lafitte forced his way through the crowd with the visitors following—pushing and stumbling—to the safety of a simple but sturdy house, apparently Lafitte's. There Lafitte left them while he retired with the packet of letters to another room. Outside could be heard the jeers and laughter of a hostile mob; but inside there was a gracious host, noncommittal, when he rejoined them, but more gracious than ever.

Lockyer warmed to his task. He could but enlarge upon the proposals of Nicholls and Percy, not add to them, but Lafitte seemed not like a pirate at all, but rather a gentleman, a peer, a man appreciative of Lockyer's own ethics and values. Talking to him was easy, and Lockyer enhanced the formal language of the letters with all the verbal warmth at his command. France and Britain at peace; a united effort on their part to hamper the preying of the privateers upon Spanish shipping; the profit in piracy, with the termination of hostilities, would disappear; what more desirable than to become honorable citizens of a great and expanding nation? From America the privateers—indeed, all the French of Louisiana—could hope for nothing but persecution. To America the privateers and the French could owe no allegiance. Now Britain, not America, was the ally of France. Now the time had come for all the foreign of Louisiana—French, Spanish, German, Portuguese, Italian, British—to join together to liberate themselves from a faithless, imbecile government and enjoy under the British constitution the protection of property, laws, peace, and tranquility. Great Britain had strained every nerve in defense of the liberties of the world; the bravest of her sons had fought and bled in that sacred cause; she had spent millions of her treasury to pull down one of the most formidable and dangerous tyrants that ever disgraced the form of man; when groaning Europe was almost in her last gasp, Britons alone showed an undaunted front—and at that moment basely did the American assassins endeavor to stab her in the back. But now the tyrant was down, Europe was happy and free, and Britain, renovated from the bloody but successful struggle, had turned to avenge the unprovoked insult. After the experience of twenty-one years, could the Europeans of the Southwest any longer support these brawlers for liberty who called their mob rule "freedom"? [5]

The privateers, with their knowledge of the treacherous countryside, could be of invaluable service as the British pushed into New Orleans and up the river, and they could expect reward and honor for that service. The alternative was degradation, for success was certain—Louisiana, torn with dissension among French, Spanish, plantation, and Kentuckian elements, could offer little resistance; the slaves, offered emancipation by the British, would rise in insurrection; with France no longer diverting Britain's interest, two powerful armies, one pushing north from the Gulf and one south from Canada, would unite to strangle the impotent, factious American democracy. Failure to join this glorious enterprise would leave the privateers outside the pale, pursued, thwarted, helpless. Cooperation would bring military honor and high civil position in the new British colony.

Outside a hostile mob; inside a gracious host. What could Lafitte expect personally? First, aid in releasing his brother from the New Orleans jail. A commission as Captain in the British service, with excellent prospects for promotion. And thirty thousand dollars, payable, at his option, in Pensacola or New Orleans.

Lafitte needed time. He glanced significantly out the window. It would not be easy to mold that hostility into acceptance. Then, pleading business, he left the visitors to sweat and pace the floor fretfully as the hours of the afternoon dragged stiflingly by. Outside were the treeless wastes and the hostile faces—laughing, jeering—of the mob. Hours passed, and Lafitte did not return. The sun sank and night closed in, damp, hot, oppressive. The noises of the mob gradually died away, and the pirate camp became still.

Lockyer tried the door; it was locked. The crowd had dispersed, but outside each window was a burly privateer, armed.

Through the interpreter Lockyer called for Lafitte. A guard answered, mockingly, that he had not returned. Had the privateers mutinied? What perverted sense of loyalty could make them resist the handsome British proposition—had they wedded their interest to the dethroned despot, or to the impotent government which had cast them from its bosom? Why should they hesitate to betray either, when the new suitor proffered freedom and glory?

It was too hot for any but fitful sleep. Then, with morning, Lafitte returned, dapper and gracious though seemingly nervous, adorned with graceful manners. Such a man (so skillful on the sea, as his marauding had amply proved, and so much better fitted than Lockyer diplomatically for such a task as this one) could achieve great honor in the British navy. Now he begged a day or two to consider the offer. He seemed deeply stirred by it, but his men were obviously unprepared for a sudden move. Outside were the treeless wastes, the overbearing heat, and the hostile crowd; Lockyer willingly followed Lafitte to the pinnace and left him to settle the issue with his men as best he could.

‡‡‡

How could Lafitte deny the British entreaty? One aspect of the argument seemed clear: with France out of the war and the British fleet concentrating in the Gulf for a drive upon New Orleans, there was little future for privateering. Barataria, too, would not long remain a safe haven. Lafitte had been wrangling for years with the governor of Louisiana, who had vowed to ruin him, had offered large rewards, and had spied upon him and sought vainly to trap him in New Orleans (and had successfully trapped his brother Pierre). One American military commander had cooperated with the governor by sending expeditions to Barataria—expeditions which Lafitte avoided by temporarily withdrawing to the west. Until now Lafitte had had the support of the dominant French population of Louisiana, but westerners—Americans—were rapidly migrating to New Orleans, and in the present crisis even the French were disinclined to support the smugglers. Now a new military commander was close at hand, sure to be drawn to New Orleans by the British approach, not, like his predecessor, inept, but a man of determination and action who with a few bold strokes had stamped out the uprising of the Creek Indians in Mississippi Territory. If Jackson acceded to the governor's demand that the privateers be once and for all cleared out, Lafitte could expect a harsher blow than any he had previously thwarted. The future for privateering was cloudy.

The best escape seemed surely to be an attempt to return within the law, to become accepted and acceptable citizens, and the best way of gaining acceptance and of protecting the property and wealth already accumulated was to perform notable patriotic service. But why not America as well as Britain? What more notable service than to apprise the city's guardians of the British designs and to offer them the very military services which the British desired?

So, while the *Sophia* lay in waiting at the mouth of the pass and Lockyer fretted, sweated, and fumed, Lafitte forwarded the British letters to Governor Claiborne and made his own advances for a courteous, open reception into the bosom of the city which he had had to enjoy surreptitiously for so long. "Though proscribed by my adoptive country," he announced magnanimously, "I will never let slip any occasion of serving her or of proving that she has never ceased to be dear to me." The advantages to him of the British offer were clear; his disclosure was clear proof of his patriotic devotion; and he asked only that the governor "restore to this state several citizens who perhaps in your eyes have lost that sacred title," permitting them, as citizens, to join in the defense of the continent (and absolving them from any crimes hitherto committed).[6]

To Lockyer Lafitte wrote to ask for fifteen days before giving an answer. Three men, Lafitte said, had stirred the Baratarians against the British, and these three must be disposed of. The least troublesome could be sent to town, and the other two could be sent elsewhere in about a week. Another week would be required to get his affairs in order. He added a diplomatic appeal to the vanity of an ambitious young officer: "You have inspired me with more confidence than the admiral, your superior officer, could have done himself; with you alone I wish to deal." [7]

The *Sophia* waited. Lockyer had his orders: enlist the aid of the Baratarians, and rejoin Captain Percy's fleet with the utmost dispatch. The orders said nothing of a possible delay. The *Sophia* waited, but from the harbor came no sign that the Baratarians were aware of its presence.

Governor Claiborne could not easily forget the past or predict the future, but Lafitte's offer shook his serenity. He was urged by prominent Creoles to accept it, and the possibility that the Baratarians—and perhaps many other French—might aid the British staggered him. On the other hand, they had notoriously abused the law which was sacred to him, he had vowed to crush them, and General Jackson had denounced them vigorously. What would the unswerving general think of a sudden shift of policy by the governor? Indecisively the governor worried and fretted. Meanwhile Pierre Lafitte mysteriously vanished from the New Orleans jail.[8]

The *Sophia* waited. Two weeks passed while the Baratarians remained aloof. "Join me with the utmost despatch," read Lockyer's orders. Perhaps Lockyer should return in the pinnace to the harbor—to the hot, dreary, treeless wastes; to the hostile, menacing crowd.

Hoisting its sails, the *Sophia* headed toward Pensacola. Nicholas Lockyer's dreams of brilliant naval success had to be postponed.

☼ ☼

SIX

Mobile, Washington, and Baltimore

JEAN Blanque, wealthy Creole merchant, delivered Lafitte's dispatches to Governor Claiborne. The governor read, reacted, fretted, and consulted his friends. The Creole social leaders were clear in their advice—accept Lafitte's offer. The navy commander, Patterson, was equally firm—pirates were neither to be believed nor to be condoned. The governor sat down and penned a letter to General Jackson, detailing the transactions and skillfully expressing his doubts about the privateers. He would then have waited for instructions, but Commander Patterson had already organized a raid on Grande Terre and insisted on carrying it out. The governor and all the city were on edge about the threatened invasion; and so incapable of acting in concert were they, with each group suspicious of the aims and loyalties of the others, that their inability to act in one way strengthened their nervous desire to act in another. At last, with hesitant approval from the governor, Commander Patterson set out with a force determined to eradicate the Baratarian stronghold.[1]

With seventy troops aboard under Colonel Ross, Patterson slipped down the river from the city during the night of September 11, meanwhile sending his gunboats from Lake Pontchartrain to the pilot station at Balize. There the troops were transferred to the gunboats, and on the fifteenth they crossed the bar of the southwest pass and sailed for Grande Terre, arriving the next morning. Only as they approached were they observed by the Baratarians, who hastily tried to form their ships in line of battle. Two of the gunboats grounded while trying to enter the harbor, but the other four, the schooner *Seahorse,* two barges, and a ship's cutter, continued the attack. The Baratarians broke without firing, cutting loose some of the boats and setting fire to the others. Patterson's sailors extinguished what fires they could. One fine schooner which mounted a twelve-pound cannon and four smaller guns was saved by the quick action of Lieutenant Thomas apCatesby Jones, who boarded with his men and brought the fire under control. After this skirmish, Patterson had the buildings burned, located and burned the telegraph posts along the coast, took what merchandise he could, and returned to the city.[2]

Meanwhile Villeré's New Orleans militia met irregularly, trained, and grumbled about the possibility of being sent to Mobile for service. The wealthy young men of the Orleans Battalion paraded their brilliant uniforms. And some expert riflemen formed a volunteer company with Beale, a native of Virginia with a reputation as an outstanding marksman, as captain.[3]

The free colored were anxious to increase the size of their corps, but the white citizens objected strenuously to having colored troops at all. Arming the colored and permitting them to serve shoulder to shoulder with whites, they felt, was a way of inviting a terrible rebellion. They scoffed at the idea that arming them would make them loyal—"Nothing short of placing them in every way upon a footing with white citizens," they said, "could conciliate their affections." Training in the use of arms and the pride that would result from serving their country would make them dangerous in future years. The governor fretted and sat down to pen a letter to General Jackson, reporting the offer of the colored citizens and the objections of the white.[4]

A letter was intercepted from a certain Colonel Colliel, formerly a Spanish officer, to Captain Morales in Pensacola, stating that the city was weakly defended. Colliel was an old man and (more vital) the father-in-law of Dussuau De la Croix, one of the wealthiest of the sugar planters and a director of the bank. Claiborne fretted and reported the incident to General Jackson. He confided also his distrust of the loyalty of the citizens of New Orleans: "I am not seconded with that ardent zeal which in my opinion the crisis demands. . . . I am not at the head of a united and willing people." Then he ordered the legislature to convene in special session to consider the city's problems.[5]

The officer in charge of the New Orleans department reported to Jackson the state of the city's defenses. Down the river, Fort St. Philip had twenty-eight twenty-four-pound cannon and some brass pieces, but its barracks were old and decayed and might easily be fired with enemy shells or rockets. In the fortification at the English Turn, there were no platforms for mounting cannon, no magazine, and no barracks. At Fort St. Charles in the city, the platforms were rotten and the parapets and glacis decaying, but the fort was not worth repairing because, being now in the middle of a growing city, it would be of little use against an invader. Fort St. John on Lake Pontchartrain, a small brick work, was out of repair, and the pickets in its rear had fallen down.[6]

In the French quarter, at the coffeehouses, and at the dinner tables and the intimate gatherings in the homes so effectually isolated from the outside world by wrought-iron balconied fronts and barred windows, the Creoles talked of defense. Discussion of impending doom supplanted the lively topics of previous years—complaints about the vulgarity, the brazenness, the lack of manners, the rapaciousness, the rootlessness, the inconsistencies of the Americans who were prying into plantations, industry, and society; fears about the growing disorder of the city, the sprouting colored town, the garish suburbs, the rowdy levees; rumors of strange rites in the woods and swamps after dark; quarrels about the disputed jurisdiction of rival parish priests; gossip of liaisons and matches, plans for balls, hopes for plays, anticipation of goods due from Europe (the social whirl had been suspended for the season, as commerce had ceased for the duration of the war); criticism of the governor's actions and the obtuseness of upstate legislators. Now the talk was only of the British, the hated British, their greed and their lust, their rapacities in the Peninsula and in eastern cities of the United States, their boorishness as military governors. The prospect of conquest by the British wiped from their minds any discontent they had felt for Americans. But the task of defense seemed hopeless, with no army to fight, with only ignorant frontiersmen and Indian warriors to depend on, and with no leader to direct. The governor? Well, he was honest, he was brave, but he was hardly a man to raise the populace in a common, spirited effort. The countryside seemed the epitome of chaos, and no one could do more than express his distress.[7]

In American homes the conversation was more vigorous but similar in tenor. What chance was there for victory, when the countryside was so predominantly foreign, with the Spanish, who were allies of the English, the Germans, who were too dense to respect liberty, the stuffy French, who were too cowardly to fight anyone? With no one to depend on, what chance had a small group of Americans? To many of these Americans, growing evidence of French anti-British sentiment and willingness to fight was unwelcome. To them the war was like a family squabble; they would not submit to the domination of their elder Anglo-Saxon brothers, but they resented the interference of such outsiders as the French. Hatred of the British was political only, while a racial and cultural gap separated them from the French. Abner Duncan spoke contemptuously of the "Frogs." [8]

On the river front, too, they talked, banteringly and ruggedly but with a note of grimness. The city was defenseless, and there was no one to organize defenses.

But General Jackson answered Governor Claiborne's letters. The Baratarian "brigands," he announced, must be crushed. Colonel Colliel should be expelled from the city. He issued a proclamation to the free colored of Louisiana, welcoming their participation in "the glorious struggle for national rights" in which the country was engaged; calling them "sons of freedom," "Americans," and "adopted children"; expressing his confidence that their intelligent minds would not be seduced by the false British representations; assuring them of a bounty equal to what the white soldiers received; and telling them that they would not "by being associated with white men in the same corps be exposed to improper comparisons or unjust sarcasm." He issued also a proclamation to the Louisianans, calling on them for vigorous action. And he ordered the Louisiana militia to be assembled and mustered into the service of the United States. The governor hastened to carry out these wishes, but he withheld publication of the proclamation to the colored until he had had a chance to express more strongly to Jackson the objections of the planters.[9]

And Edward Livingston, the suave lawyer, called on certain prominent social leaders and with their help convened a meeting of citizens at Tremoulet's coffeehouse. "We owe ourselves," he told them, "to disavow the unfounded and calumnious insinuations of the English that there is disaffection among Louisiana citizens. We owe ourselves to show the rest of the United States that we are not unworthy of a place among them." Under his direction the citizens formed a Committee of Public Safety to cooperate with the authorities, suggest means of defense, and call forth the energies of the country to repel invasion (and to preserve private property while men were serving in the field). The roster of the committee read like a social register: Edward Livingston, Pierre Foucher, Dussuau De la Croix, Benjamin Morgan, G. M. Ogden, D. Bouligny, Jean Noel Destrehan, Jean Blanque, and Augustin Macarty.[10]

The committee prepared to investigate the state of the city's defenses, to organize a corps of older men to protect private property, to consult with the governor and the legislature, and to communicate its opinions to the general. To Jackson it wrote that the natural strength of the country would render it impregnable if protected by a small force—two thousand men at the English Turn with gunboats, a good fort at Chef Menteur, a good fort on Bayou Terre aux Boeufs, a good fort at Petites Coquilles, one thousand men at Bayou Lafourche, a good fort and a few gunboats at Barataria, one thousand men across the river from the city, and a good fort at Balize. Unfortunately, because of the large slave population, these soldiers would have to come from Jackson, not Louisiana. With the communication Edward Livingston sent a bottle of claret that the Baratarians had given him. Jackson thanked Livingston, but to his confidants he remarked, "My whole force couldn't satisfy their demands." [11]

The city began to primp for its visitor. And Governor Claiborne wondered if, as commander in chief of the militia, he might not be the one who should be called to the field to direct the glorious defense. Jackson's health, he had heard, was somewhat impaired. If the general were disabled, who would then command? Though he had no military experience, he knew that Jackson too had had little until fortune had sent him against the Creeks. The governor's brother also had commanded successfully in that cam-

paign. Could he himself not translate with equal skill his civil
successes into military ones? This notion he chose not to communicate to his acquaintances, but in a letter to the President he
diffidently mentioned it.[12]

‡‡‡

For the time being, New Orleans was far from the scene of
conflict. General Ross's forces were moving toward Washington;
a smaller force was in Pensacola under Colonel Nicholls, training
fugitive Creek Indians; and Jackson was gathering an army at
Mobile. Jackson had little thought for the city by the river. To
him Florida and the newly acquired Indian land between Florida
and Tennessee were more important. He longed to take Pensacola
from the Spanish as his predecessor Wilkinson had taken Mobile.
To the secretary of war he wrote for permission to carry arms
into Florida. To the governor of Florida he wrote complaining
about the British activity among the Indians. When the governor
replied that he could do nothing to hinder the British and criticized Jackson for sheltering the Baratarian pirates who preyed upon
Spanish commerce, Jackson changed demand to threat: he was
taking action against the Baratarians, and the Spanish should do
so against the Indians, "for whom your Christian bowels seem to
sympathize and bleed so freely. . . . Your Excellency will be
pleased in future not to view me as a diplomatic character, unless
proclaimed by the mouths of my cannon." [13]

On September 12 four British ships appeared at the entrance
to Mobile bay—the *Hermes,* the *Carron,* the *Sophia* (Captain
Lockyer), and the *Childers.* Guarding the bay at the tip of a long
sand spit was newly erected Fort Bowyer, fortified with 20 guns
and a company of 160 men under Major Lawrence. Anchoring
six miles from the fort, the ships landed a company of marines
and a large band of Indians, who tried to erect earthworks but
were driven back by the long guns of the fort. On the fifteenth
the four ships moved into position to attack the fort.[14]

Perhaps New Orleans would be spared a visit. If Prevost captured the Lakes and Ross captured Washington and Baltimore,
the campaign might concentrate upon crushing the young republic
in the East. If Colonel Nicholls captured Mobile, he might, with a

revived army of Creeks, move across the wilderness to Natchez or Walnut Hills, cutting off New Orleans. When the British opened fire upon Fort Bowyer, on the afternoon of September 15, Jackson and his small force at Mobile waited breathlessly for the result.

The small band at the fort returned the fire of the British ships. They were favored by the narrowness of the channel, which permitted only the *Hermes* and the *Sophia* to get into easy distance. Then after an hour of firing a shot cut the cable of the *Hermes,* which drifted under the American guns. As it was raked by heavy fire, the crew forsook the deck, and the ship grounded on a sandbank. Captain Percy fired the ship, abandoned it, and transferred his wounded to the *Sophia.* Captain Lockyer's ship, badly mauled, struggled out of range, and the invading force sailed for Pensacola. For the second time Nicholas Lockyer had experienced failure in his affair with Americans.[15]

Having received word of the attack, Jackson had dispatched Captain Laval from Mobile with reinforcements. But Laval's ship had been unable to reach the fort, and when in the setting sun flames were seen, an argument developed as to what was burning. Captain Laval thought it was the tents of the fort, while one of the pilots claimed it was an attacking vessel. At 11:00 P.M. there was a tremendous explosion. Captain Laval hastened back to Mobile to report the destruction of the fort's magazine. But early on the seventeenth came word of a noble American victory.[16]

The British had suffered casualties of thirty-one killed and forty wounded; Major Lawrence had lost four killed and five wounded. The first defense of the southern coast from the British invasion had been successful.[17]

‡‡‡

At Plymouth, England, the 93rd and 95th regiments boarded ships in mid-September. Quartermaster Surtees boarded the frigate *Fox* with the commanding officer, the staff, three companies of his regiment, and the immense stock of provisions that he had collected for the voyage. But he had scarcely stepped aboard when the order to weigh was given, so there was no time to stow the provisions properly, and as they raced seaward the stock shifted and rolled in confusion about the deck. In the channel they met a series of adverse gales which slowed progress and upset Surtees' queasy stomach. And the quartermaster found himself squeezed into a cabin with twenty-three others.

The *Fox*, losing the rest of the fleet, sailed on alone. It was rumored among the army officers that the captain had purposely lost the other ships to see if he could chase the American privateer *Wasp*, which had been ravaging commerce in these waters. Such an enterprise seemed to the soldiers like a cow's trying to catch a hare.

When they reached Madeira, they found the rest of the fleet waiting. The officers of the other two companies of the 95th had playfully erased the names of those on the *Fox* from the army list as defunct, a jest which aroused ill feeling among some of Surtees' comrades. But they bought a cask of wine which they found delightful and soon sailed again, catching the trade winds to waft them to the new world.[18]

‡‡‡

General Ross and Admiral Cochrane, with the 4th, 21st, 44th, and 85th regiments, and parties of engineers, artillery, sailors, and marines, swept up the Potomac, brushing aside sporadic resistance, scattered the American forces at Bladensburg, marched to Washington, and set fire to barracks, storehouses, and public buildings. Lieutenant George De Lacy Evans, deputy quartermaster general, who had had horses shot out from under him at Bayonne and Toulouse, had two more horses shot out from under him at Bladensburg; but with two hundred infantrymen he seized the Congress House in Washington. As the 85th was marching up, the men saw the red skies and heard the explosions of powder magazines and the crash of falling roofs. Lieutenant Gleig, noticing the brilliant sky and the red glow of the road, marveled at the spectacle. "Except for the burning of St. Sebastian's," he mused, "I don't recollect to have witnessed a scene more striking or more sublime." At the President's house, some of the 21st Regiment discovered a banquet prepared but untasted; they promptly ate it. Many soldiers, becoming sick after the looting, claimed to have been poisoned by American whisky. Lieutenant Furlong of the 21st was less impressed by the spectacle than Gleig: "I must confess," he wrote in his diary,

"I felt sorrow when witnessing such magnificent buildings demolished." [19]

Lieutenant Gleig had also some sage military observations to exchange with his friend Grey, based on the experience of the preceding few days. Americans seemed to be marksmen, trained, no doubt, from boyhood, but their skill was of little use because militia could never hold up against regular troops. The habit of acting in concert, confidence in one's companions, and rapidity and good order of movements were alone of real service in battle. [20]

Withdrawing from Washington, Ross and Cochrane moved toward Baltimore. They were prosecuting the campaign vigorously, working well together, and generally demonstrating that the War Office had chosen the right leaders. In a skirmish at North Point with retreating Americans, their troops won another victory.

But this one was costly, for General Ross, riding forward toward the action, unexpectedly came upon a party of American marksmen. Into the arms of his aide, a twenty-five-year-old Scotsman named Duncan McDougall, who claimed descent from the Laird of the Isles, General Ross fell dead. (Major General John Keane, with the 93rd highlanders, the 95th rifles, and the 14th dragoons, had sailed from England, expecting to be second in command under the brilliant Ross.) [21]

Colonel Brooke of the 44th assumed command. He wondered if it would not be wise to withdraw the troops, but Admiral Cochrane glared so disapprovingly that he marched the army on toward Baltimore. Suddenly he discovered resistance—an American army entrenched on a ridge of hills near the river, supported by heavy artillery. That night was particularly dark; a heavy rain fell; and the admiral found the river too low for his ships to move to the support of the army. So Colonel Brooke retreated, and the expedition prepared to sail for Jamaica for a rendezvous with the second wave of troops. This thrust had ended as frustratingly and indecisively as all the other clashes of the war. The commander was dead; but the nation's capital, at least, had been terrorized, and a larger force was gathering as the Empire cocked its eye toward New Orleans. [22]

September wore away.

☼ ☼

SEVEN

The British Approach

NERVOUS expectancy grew in New Orleans. Merchants reported letters from correspondents in the Indies and Europe that spoke of a massive British fleet and army converging upon Jamaica. Jackson reported dispatches from Ireland that announced the departure from England of some ten or twelve thousand troops. The talk was all of war and the need for concerted action.[1]

Commander Patterson returned to the city, having leveled the fortifications at Grande Terre and sent the Baratarians scurrying to other places, bayou villages further west, the German coast, the hidden quarters of the city. The governor exultantly announced this success to Jackson, but French and Creoles grumbled that such a move at such a time seemed unwise.[2]

They grumbled too about a proclamation from Jackson denouncing the British and calling upon Louisianans for united support. Jackson had called the British "slaves," and the French felt that it was an unjust accusation. They seemed to read in the general's bitter language an implication that everyone but Americans was a "slave," the Louisianans being, at best, only "emancipated slaves." Since they had been given little choice of their own government, they wondered how much freer American citizens were than British.[3]

Jackson's proclamation to the free colored, when Claiborne at last published it, aroused them even more. It put the colored on too nearly equal a footing with white men. They could not see how native mulattoes could be "sons of freedom," how colored refugees from Santo Domingo could be "adopted children," or how any colored could be legitimately called "Americans," "fellow-citizens," and "countrymen." Two members of the Committee of Safety waited upon the governor to protest the arming of these people.[4]

The governor dutifully reported these grumblings to the general, but Jackson blithely ignored them. "I was aware of the jealousy of the citizens," he wrote back. "The colored may when danger appears be moved in the rear to some point where they will be kept from doing us an injury. If their pride and merit entitle them to confidence, they can be employed against the enemy." Michael Fortier drilled and trained his colored battalion.[5]

Drafting of the militia was delayed when some of the native French claimed exemption on the ground that they were not American citizens. The governor ruled that any resident of Louisiana at the time of the purchase was an American citizen, and in this matter his opinion, supported by the native Creoles, prevailed. By mid-October Philemon Thomas' Baton Rouge militia was ready to march to the city, and Villeré's New Orleans militia was formed and training, exercising twice a week. There were also two troops of volunteer cavalry and one company of volunteer riflemen (Beale's Creole sharpshooters). New Orleans now had two thousand soldiers close at hand, but no one knew very well what to do with them.[6]

Around the waterfront idled large numbers of sailors, stranded in the city by the stagnation of ocean commerce. They lounged about the streets and buildings and saloons, jabbering in a dozen languages, making citizens self-conscious about their half-ridiculous attempts to play soldier. Mingling among them were the Spanish and Portuguese fishermen who came daily from the lakes up the bayous with their catches. In other sections of the city large numbers of laborers and free colored were equally idled by the stagnation of business and equally talkative and critical. On the nearby plantations the planters strove futilely to find work for their slaves. The city was noisy and restless, though nothing constructive seemed to be going on. Officials and wealthy looked nervously out of their windows at the doings. It was rumored and believed that a British officer had come up the river, spent several days in the city unnoticed among the restless throngs, and even danced at one of the balls.[7]

Claiborne wrote voluminously to the general, finding in letters an outlet for his doubts and uncertainties. "I think with you that our country is filled with spies and traitors," and "Among the faithful Louisianans there is a despondency which palsies my preparations." One day he would complain that there were too many "on whose friendly disposition towards the American Government I cannot depend," and the next he would announce that the Louisianans were "a virtuous, a gallant people" inspired by confidence in the general. Edward Livingston also complained: "There are some," he wrote Jackson, "[who] hang like a dead weight upon the zeal of the well disposed and paralyze their efforts." He repeated the need for five thousand men and several strong forts.[8]

‡‡‡

Jackson still believed that Mobile would be the point of attack. He did not consider, in spite of his logistical experience during the Creek campaign, the great difficulty of supporting an army moving overland from Mobile to the river. Nor did he realize the avidity with which Admiral Cochrane and his civilian friends from the West Indies dreamed of those rich stores in New Orleans. He left New Orleans to its own resources while he worried about Colonel Nicholls' small force in Pensacola.[9]

General Coffee arrived from Tennessee with 2,800 soldiers, and on October 25 Jackson marched from Mobile with an army of 4,000. On November 6, after reaching Pensacola, he sent a demand that Fort Barrancas be placed in his hands within an hour. The governor fired upon the flag of truce. Early the next morning Jackson struck. A small column made a feint from the west along the beach, where the British ships were waiting, while the main body, detouring rapidly to the east, entered the town. The British ships were surprised by the maneuver, and before they could shift to meet the new attack the governor had surrendered. That night, while Jackson was waiting for the fort to be delivered to him,

Colonel Nicholls loaded his men and supplies aboard the ships, blew up the fort, and sailed away.[10]

When Jackson returned to Mobile, he found the call for his presence in New Orleans too urgent to be ignored any longer. Assigning a regiment of regulars to operate against the hostile Indians around Mobile and two regiments and the Georgia militia to defend Mobile, on November 21, with the Tennessee militia, he left at last for the city by the river.[11]

In New Orleans, the militia generals argued about who should command the brigade. The French citizens threw stones at the house of the consul of Louis XVIII. The legislature convened, heard a spirited address by the governor, and began to wrangle about the measures of defense that had been proposed. Some of the merchants, cut off from foreign trade, purchased small craft to scoot along the coast to Pensacola carrying flour, wine, liquor, and cotton. Vincent Nolte bought cotton in New Orleans for ten cents a pound which he sold in Pensacola for twenty-two cents, and he bought wool blankets in Pensacola for six dollars which he sold in New Orleans for eleven dollars; war, he discovered, was not wholly tragic.[12]

‡‡‡

Sergeant Cooper waited patiently for the end of his enlistment. At last the order arrived to discharge all seven-year men; but it was followed immediately by an order for the 7th fusiliers to embark on a secret expedition, and Colonel Blakeney was so busy loading troops and baggage aboard transports that he would not listen to the pleas of Cooper and the others to make out the discharges. The sergeant kept after the clerk, who continually promised immediate action. There was nothing to worry about, he and the company officers kept assuring the sergeant. Of course they would not sail on a long voyage without first releasing those whose terms of service had expired. The army was too efficient to make such an error.

So the sergeant could only wait. He gave a comrade who was going ashore half a crown to buy him some bread and spirits, but the rascal never came back.[13]

The fleet readied. Three regiments were aboard: the 7th fusiliers, the 40th Somersetshire, and the 43rd Monmouth, destined to support the regiments already headed for America. Captain Cooke of the 43rd had a different experience from Sergeant Cooper's. After embarking he became violently ill, and during the night he passed a gallstone. He was sent ashore, and as his illness abated he fretted that he must be left behind.[14]

The ships waited only for a change in the wind, and Sergeant Cooper waited only for his discharge. He and the other seven-year men haunted the clerks, who at last produced the documents. Wanting now was only the colonel's signature, but he was ashore. Sergeant Cooper stood at the rail, looking glumly out at the fleet. Corporal Fitzpatrick was at his side, giving encouragement by suggesting that the colonel was probably drunk and the fleet would sail without him. At last Cooper spied an approaching boat that might be the colonel's. Then another boat passed, carrying seven-year men of the 43rd Regiment who were headed for home, and the sergeant saw his brother waving at him.

"Are you for Bernard Castle?" his brother shouted.

"I only want my paper," Cooper shouted back. "As soon as I get it, I'll join you."

"I'll wait for you," his brother promised. (It might prove a long wait.)

The colonel arrived aboard. When Cooper and his buddies pressed about him, demanding his signature, he gave them a cold stare and pointed out to sea. Following his gesture with their eyes, they saw, flapping at the masthead of the *Vengeur*, 74, their convoy, a Blue Peter. The wind had changed; the anchors were being raised; the ships were in motion. The colonel hurried off to his quarters, and Sergeant Cooper and his friends gave vent to the heartiest curses they knew. Corporal Fitzpatrick told them they would be glad once they saw the Indian wenches in America.

Hearing that the fleet was moving, Captain Cooke jumped from his sickbed, hastily packed his gear, rushed to the beach, and paid an exorbitant price for a boat to take him to his ship. He was helped by his comrades aboard the brig *Helen* as its sails were unfurling to catch the wind.[15]

As they sailed along the coast of Cornwall, Sergeant Cooper hoped they would put in at Cork, where he could be released. But they put to sea, and when they were off the Lizard, Fitzpatrick pointed out that the course was too southerly for Cork. The next morning Cooper found by the compass that they were sailing south by west. He cursed the compass. They passed Gibraltar; he cursed Gibraltar. A heavy gale tossed them mercilessly, and he cursed the gale. They passed Madeira, and he cursed Madeira.[16]

The third wave of troops was on its way to New Orleans.

Meanwhile the first wave, without its general, headed for Jamaica. The ships carrying the 85th, having separated from the rest of the fleet, sailed through a gale. Lieutenant Gleig and Captain Grey watched the rolling sea and the dark sky. They watched the masts lean and lean until it seemed they would dip their tops into the waves. They went to their cabins and watched the waves splash against the windows. They went to bed, holding themselves in their berths by clinging to the bedposts. They watched stools, books, and trunks float along the floor from one side of the cabin to the other, pause for a moment, and then float back again.

When it was over they went on deck and heard that two small schooners had gone down. And now the air was still, and the sails hung limply from the masts. The sea continued to roll, but now gently and monotonously, so that the motion of the boat, not propelled by any wind, was more regular and annoying than ever. The next day, though, when a fair breeze came up, they felt a new exhilaration, until they became aware of a heavy, oppressive heat. Even the shade of awnings provided no relief. Each day was more sultry than the previous. The slightest activity was impossible. But Lieutenant Gleig carefully jotted in his precious little notebook every detail of his voyage. Storm, calm, heat—each was a new experience to be cherished by an adventurous young man.

On October 25 the boat crossed the Tropic of Cancer and received a visit from Neptune and his wife ("a clever active seaman," Gleig noted, "dressed up grotesquely in party-coloured rags, adorned with a long beard of spun-yard, armed with a tri-pronged harpoon," played Neptune, while another, wearing a hideous mask, was the wife, and a troop of sea-gods and nymphs attended). The young officers watched curiously as Neptune's company placed at the foot of the mast a tub of sea water covered by a piece of canvas; while four attendants held the canvas tightly, an initiate sat upon the tub, answered questions, and took oaths; then Neptune shaved him, using a bucket of grease and slops for lather, a dirty paintbrush for brush, and a rusty broken hoop for a razor; if an initiate protested against the ceremony, a bucket of sea water was poured over him, and when the shaving was done he was plunged into the tub. Lieutenant Gleig, though he thought it was a barbarous amusement, noticed that it was agreeable to the crew.

On the twenty-eighth the two officers gazed upon Santo Domingo and Cuba, marveling at the glorious shores. They noticed too the numerous waterspouts around the ship. On the twenty-ninth they watched as a shark followed the ship. They watched the sailors bait a strong hook with salt pork, catch the shark, and swing it on the deck. With the others, when the shark rolled wildly about, lashing with its tail and biting everything in its reach, they dashed madly from the quarter-deck. A sailor chopped off the shark's tail with an ax, split it open, cut it up, and distributed it among the bystanders. To the officers' cabin came the tail, which, though others bragged about the delicacy, Gleig thought was tasteless.

At night they sat for hours under a broad, full, cloudless sky, savoring the coolness after the heavy heat of the day. They looked at the clear moon and the rippleless ocean, and they listened to the dash of little waves against the ship's side and the rushing noise of the bow.

On the thirty-first they were chased by a privateer, but when they aimed their cannons it beat a hasty retreat. And before dark that day they saw in the distance the blue mountains of Jamaica. During the following two days they saw the hills give way to gentle slopes and green knolls and become perfectly level as they reached Port Royal. Gleig and Grey took a barge to Kingston, where they found streets lined with dirty wooden houses, but also excellent inns. The heat was so intense that they could not keep cool even indoors.[17]

Then there were balls and entertainments where the officers and wives aboard ship could meet and mingle with "the beauty and fashion" of the island. But Gleig had an old friend on the island, and he left the gaiety of the fleet for a brief visit to the Blue Mountains. He traveled through open, fertile country covered with fields of cane and coffee; at night, at a tavern at the foot of the mountains, he studied the fireflies dancing about like sparks from the anvil of a smith beating a bar of red-hot iron; he ascended the mountains, looking up at the hills towering into the sky, covered with rich green forests of coconut, plantain, pine, lime, cashew, and wild coffee, trees loaded with fruits and blossoms; he looked down at deep, almost bottomless ravines. He descended into a valley where a river dashed so recklessly that crossing was dangerous. And always his eyes were wide open, taking in everything. He saw clusters of Negro huts made with the limbs of trees thatched with straw, windowless, with two, three, or four doors, built on terraces in the sides of the hill. At noon he stopped at a neat little cottage with a view of a glen, mountains beyond the glen, and a bay in the distance—the cottage of his friend.

And so Lieutenant Gleig investigated, touring various sugar and coffee plantations, visiting the hospitals for slaves. He remarked how lazy and indolent were the free Negroes and how well cared for were the slaves (his superiors were officially denouncing slavery, hoping to woo the Louisiana colored to an insurrection). He noticed also how beautiful and shapely were some of the Negresses. And reluctantly he returned through rich cornfields and graceful forests to Kingston to rejoin the expedition. On November 17 they put to sea, and on November 19 they reached Negril Bay for the great rendezvous.

Already a large fleet had gathered. The 85th rejoined the 4th, 44th, and 21st regiments, back from Baltimore. The shores of the bay were covered with the tents of officers who were enjoying a rest from shipboard life and with stores and newly built flat-bottomed barges which were to be loaded on the ships. This point of the island, however, was not thickly populated, so there was little of the fraternizing which the 85th had found at Port Royal. Instead officers and soldiers grumbled about inconveniences. There was no high-ranking officer to inspire discipline. The loss of General Ross was lamented, and rumors passed around that the invasion was no longer secret. Some blamed Colonel Nicholls, who had attacked Mobile, sojourned at Pensacola, and approached the Baratarians, for writing incautious letters and publishing unnecessary proclamations; and others blamed various officers for conversing too openly with strangers in the Indies.[18]

Through October the second wave of troops had pleasantly crossed the ocean, enjoying a gentle, steady breeze. They too had crossed the Tropic of Cancer, and most of the ships had been visited by Neptune; but the captain of the *Fox* had discourteously dismissed the god, much to the chagrin of Quartermaster Surtees and his companions. At Bridgetown in the Barbadoes they had sailed close to a prison ship from whose deck an American prisoner had shouted, "So you've come to attack our country, have you? I hope you've brought your coffins." [19]

On November 21 they spied Jamaica, and on the twenty-fourth the *Tonnant* and the *Royal Oak,* preceding the squadron, entered Negril Bay. A new spirit of security and expectation spread among the troops already there. Aboard the *Tonnant,* with Admiral Cochrane, was General Keane. Aboard the transports were the 93rd highlanders (proud, self-confident Scotsmen), the 95th rifles, the 14th dragoons (dismounted), the 1st and 5th West India, detachments of artillery, rockets, sappers and miners, and engineers, and numerous recruits for the regiments which had fought at Baltimore. The Royal Scots were strongly replenished by men from their 2nd Battalion who had experienced battle in the terrible unsuccessful assault upon Bergen-op-Zoom.

Soon the bay was covered with small boats as parties of officers flitted about to exchange visits—to renew former acquaintances, to exchange news and rumors, and to assert through social amenities the solidarity of the great British army. Gay was the rest of that day; and anyone who looked out over the bay at the gorgeous, massive, busy, festive fleet could not but feel a thrill of confidence. A handsome, powerful, graceful athlete was this about to go acourting to New Orleans.[20]

Admiral Cochrane spent the day receiving reports and checking on his orders and arrangements. All was in the best order. The fleet was amply supplied, the army was amply provided for, a large number of flat-bottomed boats had been built to serve in the shallow Louisiana waters, the whole movement for New Orleans was perfectly arranged.

But General Keane had much to do. His was now the responsibility for the invasion. It was not enough to remember the campaign in Egypt; to remember the battle of Maadie, when the French had fortified an old Roman camp, and the determined advance of the Earl of Cavan's troops had turned their right; the Earl had barked out orders that day, and Keane had only delivered them. It was not enough to remember the battle of Alexandria, the long line of British troops from the canal of Alexandria to the sea, the sudden attack by the enemy, the quick movement of the reserve to support the weakest point, the penetration of an enemy column through a British regiment and the recovery and bayonet charge of that regiment, the fierce bayonet-and-club battle in the old Roman ruins, and the great charge by a highland regiment which had broken the enemy; it was not enough to remember General Abercromby, wounded by a French dragoon, grabbing the dragoon's sword, falling with a musket ball in his hip, keeping the field until the battle ended; General Abercromby had formed the line, moved the reserves, and acted heroically, and Keane had only carried orders and watched. (Corporal Brown of the 21st could remember the Egyptian campaign too; he had jotted in his diary, "The only result . . . was a lowering of our prestige throughout the Mediterranean and a bad outbreak of ophthalmia among the troops.") There was no use dwelling on the Duke of Wellington's great Peninsular victories, for he, Keane, had only moved a regiment dutifully here and there to carry out orders. Nowhere in his memory was there brilliant independent strategical action. Nor would dreams do; his was the understudy's great stroke of good fortune, to step suddenly into the star's role; but dreams would not make him a great actor. About America and Louisiana he knew little, and it was high time to learn.[21]

One friend was close at hand—the 44th Regiment. It was as company officer in that regiment that he had gone to Egypt. The officers and men were different now, but he felt that the regiment was an old and a tried and true friend who could not let him down. The 44th had fought in Germany against the French, especially at the unsuccessful assault upon Bergen-op-Zoom, where their colonel had been killed and much of the regiment annihilated. The 21st, too, had been in the Egyptian campaign. Keane studied the records of the other regiments. That of the 4th was good; it had been in the thick of the fighting against Napoleon's troops on several occasions, and before that it had won laurels in actions in India and Canada. Still more impresssive was the record of the 95th rifles—battle after battle on the Peninsula had found them in the thick of fighting. Four of the regiments had fought well and harmoniously together at Washington and Baltimore. And the highland regiment, though boasting no brilliant record, was acclaimed a model of order and discipline, and its officers had impressed Keane on the voyage with their shrewdness and pride. For this expedition the highlanders had abandoned their traditional kilts and were dressed instead in tartan trews; but with the tartan trousers and their flat-topped, checkerboard, tasseled hats instead of the tall plumed infantry shakos, their appearance was strikingly different from that of the other regiments. The 95th rifle regiment was also distinctive with its green instead of red coats. And to swell the ranks were the two West India regiments, who, Keane thought, would prove especially adaptable to the near-tropical New Orleans weather.[22]

About the officers he could only guess from the reports of their conduct in the recent American campaign. Colonel Brooke had been a brigade commander under Ross in all of the actions, and though he had been unsuccessful as Ross's replacement, he had shown forcefulness as a subordinate. Colonel Thornton of the 85th had also shown ability, moving his troops with celerity and determination; he had been severely wounded at Bladensburg, but he was recovering satisfactorily and showing considerable spirit. Colonel Patterson of the 21st had commanded a brigade, but his brigade had been held mainly in reserve. The most-wounded officer of the campaign was Major Robert Rennie of the 21st, who seemed to have a penchant for getting his troops and himself into the thick of action; Rennie was a man to bear watching. Another who must be given careful consideration was Colonel the Honorable Thomas Mullins of the 44th; he was proud of his aristocratic connections, he had a forceful wife who was constantly bragging of her husband, and he had a stubborn disposition. The others —Colonel Baker of the dragoons, Colonel Dale of the highlanders, Major Mitchell of the rifles, Colonel C. W. Whitby of the 1st West India, and Colonel A. M. K. Hamilton of the 5th West India —Keane knew little about, except that they were officers of his majesty's forces who had deserved the confidence of their superiors enough to earn promotion.[23]

He could feel confidence in the officers and in the eight disciplined regiments under his command. He could feel equal confidence in the great British fleet and the able naval commander, Admiral Cochrane. And it was his duty to feel confidence in himself.

So, assuming command, he planned his dispositions. The advance would consist of the 85th and 95th rifles, under the command of Colonel Thornton. The first brigade would be under his own command and would consist of the 93rd highlanders and the two West India regiments. The second brigade, under Colonel Brooke, would be made up of the 4th, the 21st, and the 44th.[24]

What he most needed was information. How should the troops approach the city? Where could they land? Where could they establish a base for supplies? Who would oppose them? What kind of terrain would they fight on? His lack of knowledge weighed heavily upon the general.

On November 25 the *Tonnant* sailed from Negril Bay, carrying Admiral Cochrane and General Keane, preceding the fleet in order to concert the necessary measures and procure information for the intended operations. On the following day the rest of the fleet got underweigh. Upward of fifty ships shook loose their topsails, lifted their anchors, caught the breeze, and moved toward the open sea. By dark the fleet was out of sight. Jamaica rested still and hushed after the excitement of the rendezvous.[25]

Behind these troops, crossing the Atlantic, were the 7th, 40th, and 43rd regiments, commanded by Major General John Lambert, somewhat older and more experienced than General Keane. But the War Office, having now learned from the young Scotsman Duncan McDougall of the death of General Ross, chose not to leave the expedition up to these young generals. Another ship, the *Statira*, 38, left England and raced across the ocean after Lambert's troops. On it were two more generals. One was Major General Sir Samuel Gibbs, who, though he had been made general only on June 4, 1813, the same day as Lambert, was an old and practiced soldier. He had served, since entering the army in 1783, in Nova Scotia, Upper Canada, Gibraltar, and Corsica. At Ostend he had been taken prisoner. He had fought in the West Indies, at St. Martin's and Martinique. He had fought at the Cape of Good Hope, at Travancore, and at Java. In the war against Napoleon he had served with the Allies in Germany. To the New Orleans adventure he would bring a cool head and a varied experience.[26]

Accompanying him was Major General the Honorable Sir Edward M. Pakenham, second son of Baron Pakenham. After a perfunctory education Pakenham had, at sixteen, become captain in the 92nd foot regiment, and seven months later he had become major in the 33rd light dragoons. He had served in Ireland during the rebellion. In 1801, at twenty-three, he had commanded a regiment in the West Indies, where he was severely wounded. He had been appointed lieutenant colonel in the 7th royal fusiliers in 1805 and served with it at Copenhagen, Martinique, and Nova Scotia.

In spite of his youth and rapid rise, Pakenham had been popular in the army. One of the captured West Indian islands had presented him some silver cups as a token of esteem. The officers of the 1st Battalion of the 7th had placed his portrait in their mess and presented him with an expensive sword. Then, in 1806, his stock had risen still more when the Duke of Wellington had married Pakenham's sister Catherine. (Catherine had been scarred by smallpox, but the Duke had gallantly refused to be released from his engagement; the couple had not, however, been very congenial.)

Pakenham had joined Wellington in the Peninsula, where in 1810 he had been appointed deputy adjutant general. He had achieved glory at Salamanca when Wellington, suddenly perceiving a gap in the French army, had turned to him and said, "Now's your time, Ned"; for Pakenham had led the third division in the movement which brought victory. In a letter to the Horse Guards Wellington had written, "Pakenham may not be the brightest genius, but my partiality for him does not lead me astray when I tell you that he is one of the best we have." On June 4, 1812, he had become major general. He was a Knight of the Bath, and he wore a gold cross with clasps for Martinique, Busaco, Fuentes de Oñoro, Salamanca, the Pyrenees, the Nivelle, the Nive, Orthez, and Toulouse.

Pakenham would bring to the expedition the glitter of aristocracy and the magic of a connection with the great duke. Since he had been marked for advancement, a successful enterprise now would enhance his reputation enough that he could be quickly promoted. But how would a commander who was "not the brightest genius" fare against Andrew Jackson? [27]

With Pakenham, as aide, was Duncan McDougall, the young Scotsman who had received dead in his arms the first commander of the expedition. With him also were Lieutenant-Colonel Alexander Dickson to command the artillery and Lieutenant-Colonel John Fox Burgoyne to command the engineers. The latter was the eldest of four illegitimate children of Lieutenant General the Right Honorable John Burgoyne, who had lost an army to the Americans at Saratoga in 1777. Colonel Burgoyne had been educated by his cousin, the Earl of Derby, at Eton and the Royal Military Academy at Woolwich. He had been gazetted to the royal engineers in 1798, had served in several campaigns, and had risen steadily. He had blown up bridges and forts in the major battles of the Peninsula, and after the siege of Badajoz he had been promoted to lieutenant-colonel. The Portuguese had granted him the Order of the Tower and Sword.[28]

In Europe, the British cabinet worried about Prevost's defeat on the Lakes. They worried, too, about a new uprising in France and a rumored plot to seize the Duke of Wellington in Paris. They needed an excuse for withdrawing Wellington from France, and the American war, now reduced to an attack on New Orleans, provided an excuse. So they offered him command of the American campaign. "The Duke of Wellington," Castlereagh wrote, "would restore confidence to the army, place the military operations on a proper footing, and give us the best chance of peace." But the Duke refused. He would not by such an action reveal to the European nations that the British situation was bad or give the Americans occasion to brag about their importance. Besides, he said, "All the American armies of which I ever read would not beat out of a field of battle the troops that went from Bordeaux last summer." [29]

During November those troops converged upon New Orleans, while Jackson and his party rode through the pine wilderness northwest and west to the Pearl River and south from there to Madisonville on Lake Pontchartrain. At Madisonville Jackson took a packet for an all-day voyage across the lake to Fort St. John and up Bayou St. John to the village at the head of the canal. There he paused to spend the night.[30]

☼ ☼

EIGHT

Jackson and the British Arrive

ANDREW Jackson rode into New Orleans on the morning of December 1.[1]

He had been eagerly awaited. Governor Claiborne was thorougly disgusted with the legislature. As far as he could see, they did nothing but debate, bickering over whether each small expenditure should be borne by the state or the federal government. Members of the legislature and their friends felt the governor's frequently reiterated complaints to be unfair. They had named a Committee of Defense—Marigny, Rofignac, and Louaillier. They had requested all citizens with more than one gun to send in the extras, and many guns had been donated. They had given approval to a loan of twenty thousand dollars effected by the governor during the recess. They had appropriated that money and eleven thousand more to General Jackson to provide fortifications. True, they had not appropriated this money to the governor, but to the general; and they wondered if this were not the reason for the governor's pique. At any rate, throughout the city there was more discussion of the threatening situation than there was meaningful action.[2]

In the better homes, too, the women of New Orleans were thoroughly alarmed. All the talk was about the British outrages at Hampton. The women of Hampton, it was said, were universally abused, not only by the enemy soldiers, but also by the savage blacks, who had been thoroughly encouraged in their excesses. The image of these "outrages" was never clearly expressed. But the women sat about and discussed them vaguely in low tones, and each individual could conjure up her own image. To some it was only an image of horror, like a poisonous snake. To others it had the form of a dirty, grimy soldier or a leering Negro reaching out an arm. To others it was a man vaguely like a husband and an act that was a nuisance even with a husband. To some it was an imagined contact that was as much a thrill as a horror, and these had to express their fear with doubled ardor to encourage their faith in their own chastity. So the women reinforced one another's terror, and their worried voices goaded their men to even greater anxiety about the helplessness of the city. But dissension and distrust among the various groups of citizens was too deeply ingrained for concerted action. The German merchant Nolte was much more concerned over his quarrels with various American mercantile rivals than over the impending battle; he dueled, wrestled in the street, and published insulting articles in the newspapers. Instinctively the eager but helpless throngs looked to the general for leadership.[3]

Jackson arrived after a pressing eleven-day journey through the wilderness from Mobile. He had contracted dysentery, and his tall, naturally gaunt figure seemed even more gaunt. His cheeks were hollow, his face pale, his sandy hair beginning to gray. He sat erect on the saddle, but the muscles about his mouth twitched in his attempt to hide his pain. After he was escorted from Bayou St. John to the city and saluted by the guns of Fort St. Charles, many officials crowded about him. They were solicitous, and they were ready to withdraw to allow him rest. Everyone else in the city was putting off decisions; why should not the sick general? But they hesitated before retiring from his presence, and they searched the stern, thin face for a sign.[4]

He searched faces too, reading anxieties and personalities. Then, with a gesture of his hand, he brushed aside the idea of rest. And he took the governor, Edward Livingston, Commander Patterson of the navy, Colonel Ross of the regular troops in the vicinity, Major Latour, his engineer, and Major Robert Butler, his adjutant, and sat down in his office to be briefed.

New Orleans seemed desperately vulnerable. There were many gateways inviting entrance—Barataria, the Mississippi, Bayou Lafourche, Terre aux Boeufs, Lake Borgne or Lake Pontchartrain, the innumerable bayous from the Gulf or the lakes to the river. Which route the intruder would choose was impossible to discern.[5]

Claiborne had done what he could. He had stationed a company at Lafourche with one twelve-pound cannon. He had stationed another company at Barataria. Colonel Declouet's regiment of Baton Rouge militia he had stationed at the English Turn, where they could guard the river or move quickly to the city should another approach be used. He had stationed a small squad at Fort St. Philip further down the river. A company of mounted riflemen were at Terre aux Boeufs. The Feliciana cavalry were in the city, communicating frequently with the various other troops. Two troops of volunteer cavalry had been formed in the city (Cheveau and Ogden). But the governor was mainly concerned about the shifting composition of the troops; men would leave one company and enroll in another. And in the next breath he would suggest that the general grant a furlough to some officer whose mother was sick, or he would assure the general that some Creole, though he had a close relative in the Spanish army, was loyal. The legislature, he reported, had not yet done anything to damp the public ardor.[6]

Commander Patterson was brief and to the point. He had seven small boats on the lakes with which to watch the enemy and delay their approach—but he could not defend the mouth of the river without surrendering the lakes. He had two ships and a gunboat on the river, but they were not adequately manned. His armory was excellent, with a good many more cannon than he had boats to use them on. And he had noticed large numbers of experienced sailors of all nations idling about the streets. Colonel Ross was happy with his 44th Regiment; it now had five hundred men, the French and American soldiers were learning to understand each other's language, and it had performed well in the attack on Barataria.[7]

Major Latour had drawn up, as well as he could with inadequate information, maps of the countryside, from which the general could see approximately the situation of the city.[8]

Livingston calmly expressed his faith in the determination of all to defend their city and mentioned that the uniformed companies were anxious to demonstrate their good order for the general.

Until now Jackson's idea of the disposition of Louisianans had been formed mainly by the governor's letters, but since arriving he had met several of them. He had been invited to stay with Bernard Marigny, one of the most aristocratic of the Creoles. When the officers of the colored battalion called upon him, he found them to be great enthusiasts in the cause. He began to suspect the governor's ability; he accepted Livingston's offer to become a volunteer aide; and he ordered a review for the next day. He approved also Livingston's account of the Committee of Safety's plan for a corps of veterans to police the city and a corps of exempted fathers to serve as a fire company within the city. (Claiborne frowned when he noticed how the general warmed to the lawyer.) [9]

A committee from the legislature, accompanied by General Villeré, visited Jackson to complain about the proclamation against the Baratarians and to urge his acceptance into the army of these seasoned warriors. Though he received a different report of the pirates from the one the governor had given him, a firmly planted idea was difficult to unfix from the general's mind. Politely he informed the delegation that the Baratarians were being prosecuted by the civil officers of the United States, that many of them were in prison, and that he neither could nor would do anything in the matter. [10]

The next day the general officially assumed command of the New Orleans department. In the afternoon he reviewed the New Orleans uniformed companies in the Place d'Armes, with the citizens, crowding the streets and balconies to watch, displaying mass gaiety for the first time in months. Proudly and snappily the companies formed, saluted, and marched—the Carabiniers, Captain Plauché; the Hulans, Captain St. Gême; the Francs, Captain Hudry; the Louisiana Blues, a company of Irishmen under Captain Maunsel White; and the Chausseurs, Captain Guibert. Each company had chosen a uniform of a different color, and they presented a bright and cheerful sight, if not exactly an awesome display of force. The general praised them warmly. [11]

After the review he dined with the Livingstons, admired their wine, and met the fashionable ladies of the city. Then he went over the plans of the city's defenses with his engineers. [12]

The next day Jackson inspected the city, attempting to become familiar with the arena. Except along the river the city seemed to him to be surrounded by swamps. At Fort St. Charles, near the river at the edge of the old town, between the town and the new suburb of Marigny, he visited the two detachments of the 44th and 7th regulars, commanded by Colonel Ross and Major Peire. Below Marigny he crossed a dozen or so plantations. The crops had just been gathered, and the barns and warehouses were bulging with sugar, while some of the cane was piled in the fields, covered with a thin layer of fodder and dirt. All along the river there was a cultivated plain stretching from the river to thick woods and swamps. The width of the plain varied, but the trees were always within view—a comparatively small army could easily block that entire plain. From the levee, across the wide river in the distance could be seen another line of trees.[13]

At Macarty's plantation, four miles below the city, there was an ample house, two stories and an attic, from whose dormer windows a good view of the country might be had. Beyond that the plantations were much the same—Chalmette, Bienvenu, De la Ronde, Lacoste, Villeré, Jumonville. Each was composed of fields of cane stretching from the levee to the swamp; canals ran into the swamp from the river; ditches and fences crossed the fields, more or less, but not wholly, parallel; near the high road on each was a large galleried house, a cluster of outhouses, groves of trees, and a garden. Just over the levee flowed the wide, placid, brown river.[14]

The next day Jackson set out on a longer journey to investigate the defenses between the city and the river's mouth. And in the city there was a general marveling at his constant activity and a new feeling of security.

✝✝✝

In midocean the fleet carrying the 7th, 40th, and 43rd regiments ran into a storm. For once Sergeant Cooper reacted to nature, feeling that it reflected his own angry mood. While his friend Fitzpatrick was below drinking some rum which he had kept hidden, Cooper stayed on deck, reeling with the ship, clutching the collar of his greatcoat, and setting his jaw determinedly in the face of the cold spray. He watched a mountainous ridge of water to windward rolling toward the boat; felt the sudden jar as the wave struck the ship, sending it heeling half over; listened to the wind whistling in the rigging, the masts creaking, the ship groaning. Sometimes a wave struck the bow, washed roughly over the bulwark, and rushed along the deck.

Then followed warm weather. Listlessly he watched the strange fish in the waters—dolphins, flying fish, and porpoises, the sailors said. He watched a sailor harpoon a dolphin, but the fish jerked and broke the shaft. All one day a grampus gamboled around the vessels.[15]

On the *Helen,* eleven officers of the 43rd were crammed into a cabin eight by six feet large. Two extra cots had been moved into it, and three of them slept on the floor. To add to their discomfort, their provisions became lost or damaged; salt water trickled into the biscuit and flour barrels, corks blew out of the porter bottles, their pigs and sheep became diseased, and their exquisite Bordeaux wine soured. Captain Cooke and Staff Doctor Ryan played ninety-five games of chess.[16]

When they crossed the Tropic of Cancer, Neptune and his company visited the ship. Neptune, an old seaman "dressed in a whimsical manner," sat on a gun carriage, which was dragged by ropes along the gangway to the quarter-deck. A longboat was filled with salt water and a bucket with a compound of grease, tar, and sewage (Sergeant Cooper had another word for it). Neptune used a rusty iron hoop for a razor. Blindfolded seamen were seated on the thwarts of the longboat, lathered while answering questions (when they tried to answer they received the brush in their mouths), shaved, and pushed into the boat. Sailors also climbed the rigging to dump buckets of water on the soldiers. A few fights broke out here and there. Sergeant Cooper remained unamused. Captain Cooke escaped the ceremony with a gift of spirits to the sailors and turned away disgusted with the brutal affair.[17]

Every Sunday morning the regiments paraded on deck in heavy marching order, pushing and tripping in the small space available. Frequently salt water was distributed at the parade, and the men were forced to drink it by the pint. One old soldier said he couldn't swallow the stuff. He was given 150 lashes.

After passing Santo Domingo, they were becalmed. Some transports which attempted to go ahead of the convoy were fired at. At last they put in at Port Royal, where they waited. Every morning the soldiers expected to sail, but the ships lay there in the heat, and no one knew why. Then one day the frigate *Statira* sailed in, and from the bustle that followed they knew the wait was over. The news quickly passed among the men that aboard the *Statira* was the new commander in chief of the expedition, Major General the Honorable Sir E. M. Pakenham, brother-in-law of the Duke of Wellington.[18]

General Pakenham was calm and placid enough. He had enjoyed a smooth, fast voyage, and he knew he had impressed his subordinates with his affability and polite reserve at mess. He had studied the reports about his troops. They seemed ample. The 4th had performed well at Coruña, Castrejon, and Badajoz. The 7th had charged magnificently at a key moment at Albuera. The 95th rifles had been in the thick of fighting at Monte Video, Pombal, Redinha, Sabugal, and Merexem. The 40th had also served through most of the Peninsular campaign. The 21st, 44th, and 85th had not been so active on the continent, but they had faced American armies around Washington and Baltimore, and Duncan McDougall glowingly described the good order of the army in that campaign. The 93rd highlanders were inexperienced, but they were well thought of by the War Office. The 14th dragoons had skirmished with Napoleon's crack cavalry at the Douro, Ciudad Rodrigo, Salamanca, the Huebra, and the Nive. (They would have to be provided mounts, and Pakenham made a mental note that a foray must be organized first thing to round up horses.)

He looked at the record of the 43rd, waiting, with the 7th and 40th, at Port Royal. This regiment had been in the Indies before, in 1794, when it had fought on the islands of St. Lucie and Guadeloupe. On the Peninsula in 1808 it had attacked up a hill at Busaco. The next year it had fought at Redinha. At Sabugal it supported the 95th rifles, seized a small eminence, carried some French guns in a bayonet attack, and charged successfully up a hill. The following year it fought hard at Ciudad Rodrigo. At Badajoz it had assaulted Santa Marca bastion, fighting determinedly before being repulsed. At Castrejon it supported some exposed cavalry, holding its position until Wellington brought up reinforcements. At Huebra it covered Wellington's retreat across the river, keeping its skirmishers in position in spite of mist and rain. It had fought in the rugged mountains at Echallar and Ivantellis. At Arcangues it had attacked a strongly fortified house, one of a chain of posts across a valley. And at the second battle of the Nive its pickets had been attacked by the French, but the riflemen had hastened from the village to repel the enemy. Mountain, valley, river, city, forest, and field fighting the 43rd had experienced in hot weather and cold, dry and wet.[19]

Of course there were also the 1st and 5th West Indies regiments, especially equipped for tropical action.

It was a noble army, and its leaders were promising. Sam Gibbs was a battle-scarred veteran, slow in being promoted but rugged and vigorous, whose presence on the voyage Pakenham had felt as a steadying influence. He would be a sobering companion for the two youngsters, Keane and Lambert, whom the War Office had so recently promoted. About Keane Pakenham knew little, but he met Lambert at Port Royal and found him to be laconic, self-confident, poised; perhaps a little cautious, but he seemed to have sound judgment. And Pakenham could feel sure that anyone who had been honored by the British War Office with promotion to the rank of general was deserving of the highest trust.

The report from Baltimore about some of the younger officers was also encouraging. Colonel Brooke had stepped readily into the shoes of General Ross. The Honorable Lieutenant-Colonel Mullins had "with excellent order" led "that part of the right brigade under his command, while charging the enemy in line." Colonel Thornton of the 85th had been an able leader; though severely wounded, he had lately returned to duty. And Major Rennie of the 21st had shown particular spirit in leading his troops. The glorious record of the British Empire would undoubtedly be enhanced by the action of these troops and these leaders.[20]

And would Pakenham prove an able commander? Had he not been trained by the great Duke himself? He remembered the battle of Salamanca. It had been fought in a great oval basin, an amphitheatre with ranges of hills on each side, two miles long and a mile wide. The French were moving along the southern side. Pakenham's 3rd Division was on the right of the long Allied line when Wellington noticed that the enemy's left wing had become separated from the center. On Wellington's order Pakenham quickly moved his troops against the French left. The French opened their artillery, "but," as Wellington reported, "Pakenham bearing onwards through the skirmishers, broke their half-formed lines, and sent the whole in confusion upon the advancing supports." It was a glorious moment, watching his troops push relentlessly through the enemy; and a glorious moment when the duke congratulated him. That memory fused with a vision of just such another glorious attack driving a confused American army back through New Orleans.[21]

Salamanca had never quite been repeated. The following year Pakenham had commanded the 6th Division, in the absence of General Pack, at Vitoria and Sauroren, but his division never seemed to be sharply engaged. He had, however, carried out to the letter, in every instance, the Duke's orders.

General Lambert could also remember a glorious action under the Duke of Wellington. At Toulouse, in April of this year, 1814, the French had kept the English at bay until Lambert's brigade rushed forward with a tremendous shout to send the French flying back to higher ground. The brigade pushed on to win the summit, and the French shortly thereafter were routed.[22]

So, on December 10, these generals with their memories and visions sailed from Port Royal for New Orleans.

‡‡‡

Admiral Cochrane's fleet meanwhile raced toward America with General Keane and his eight regiments. The wind was good, and Lieutenant Greig and Captain Grey commented joyfully about the astonishing rapidity of the voyage. They talked also about New Orleans—a rich city, they had heard, rich and exciting, but oppressively hot. Day by day, however, the heavy Jamaican heat lessened, and they wondered if New Orleans would be as hot as they had heard.

They passed the island of Grand Cayman, where they traded some salt pork for turtles. Then there was only water to be seen until the shores of Cuba appeared. They coasted along within a few miles of the beach and studied the forested shore with its huge rocks sticking out of the water like baronial castles. This interesting shore soon disappeared, and again there was only sea and sky, sky and sea. Now they were in the Gulf, and there was a short, disagreeable swell with such a continuous motion that Gleig and Grey had to give up their walks along the deck. From their cabin windows they watched the water, noticing the vast amount and variety of seaweeds that covered the surface of the Gulf. They could tell by the motion of the weeds that there was a rapid current sweeping around Cuba toward Newfoundland. The weather became cooler and cooler. And though most of the British troops welcomed the change, the West Indians, equipped only for tropical life, began to shiver and complain. Tragedy struck on one of the boats when the wife of Major Douglas of the 21st came down with a fever and, after a few days of illness, died.[23]

Ahead, the *Tonnant* glided smoothly along while Admiral Cochrane described to General Keane the country they were about to attack.

To General Keane, New Orleans seemed desperately invulnerable. There was an immense line of coast from Lake Pontchartrain to the mouth of the river and westward to the river Tesche, but it was intersected by a mass of bays, inlets, rivers, and swamps; the flat coast was too swampy for the debarkation of troops, and the bays and inlets were blocked by shoals and bars. The great river had several mouths, but they were difficult to find and treacherous to navigate. The route from Barataria was via a tortuous series of lakes and bayous through terrible swamps. Any route to the river below the city would put the fleet under heavy fire as it moved upstream. The route via the lakes was shorter; but the shallow channel from Lake Borgne to Lake Pontchartrain was guarded by a fort, while another guarded the entrance from Lake Pontchartrain to Bayou St. John. The other possibility was to land beside Lake Borgne and follow some bayou that would bring the army to the river as close to the city as possible. That route Admiral Cochrane seemed to favor. Keane looked at the narrow neck of land between the river and the swamp that showed on the map, but the doughty admiral spoke constantly of British troops emerging from the swamp and storming up that neck of land to the city—as though it would be a romp.[24]

General Keane fretted. And on December 8 the *Tonnant* anchored off Chandeleur Island near the coast of Louisiana. Other ships followed, the seventy-fours dropping anchor at Chandeleur while the smaller vessels proceeded to Cat Island, and by December 12 the fleet had assembled.[25]

☼ ☼

NINE

Jackson Prepares and Watches

AT PARIS, Lord Castlereagh was heard to say, "I expect at this moment that most of the large seaport towns of America are laid in ashes; that we are in possession of New Orleans, and have command of all the rivers of the Mississippi Valley and the Lakes, and that the Americans are now little better than prisoners in their own country." [1]

The British fleet was anchored off the coast of Louisiana, some fifty miles from New Orleans. Within view was the low shoreline of America with dense woods reaching almost to the water's edge. Nearby were some barren, sandy, swampy islands. The weather was foggy, damp, and chilly. And General Keane talked to various men whom Admiral Cochrane had picked up at Pensacola, men who claimed knowledge of the countryside and the city. Meanwhile the troops chafed at their confinement on the ships and cursed the disagreeable weather. Colonel Nicholls appeared with some Creek Indians who carried American rifles. The British riflemen examined these guns, which were longer than their own and fired a smaller ball. They laughed contemptuously; these were hunting rifles that would scarcely do for battle.[2]

The seaport towns were not in ashes, the rivers were not in the command of Britain, and the Americans were not prisoners. But

Admiral Cochrane could look out at the awesome array of his great fleet: the *Tonnant,* eighty guns, Vice Admiral Cochrane and Rear Admiral Sir Edward Codrington aboard, Captain Kerr commanding; the *Royal Oak,* seventy-four, Rear Admiral Malcolm aboard, Captain Wroot commanding; the *Norge,* seventy-four, Captain Dashford; the *Bedford,* seventy-four, Captain Walker; the *Ramilies,* seventy-four, Captain Sir Thomas Hardy; the *Asia,* seventy-four, Captain Skeens; the *Dictator,* fifty-six, Captain Crofton; the *Diomede,* fifty, Captain Kippen; the *Gorgon,* forty-four, Captain R. B. Bowden; the *Belle Poule,* thirty-eight, Captain Baker; the *Trave,* thirty-eight, Captain Money; the *Wever,* thirty-eight, Captain Sullivan; the *Alceste,* thirty-eight, Captain Lawrence; the *Hydra,* thirty-eight, Captain Dezey; the *Fox,* thirty-six, Captain Willock; the *Cadmus,* thirty-six, Captain Longford; the *Seahorse,* thirty-five, Captain James Alexander Gordon; the *Armide,* thirty-three, Captain Sir Thomas Trowbridge; the *Thames,* thirty-two, Captain the Honorable C. L. Irby; the *Dover,* thirty-two, Captain Rogers; the *Bucephalus,* thirty-two, Captain D'Aith; the *Sophia,* eighteen, Captain Nicholas Lockyer; the *Calliope,* sixteen, Captain Codd; the *Anaconda,* sixteen, Captain Westphall; the *Borer,* fourteen, Captain Raulins; the *Manly,* fourteen, Captain Montressor; the *Meteor,* bomb, six guns, Captain Roberts; the *Volcano,* bomb, six guns, Captain Price; the *Aetna,* bomb, six guns, Captain Gardner; the *Pigan,* schooner, six guns, Captain Jackson; the *Jane,* cutter, Captain Speedwell; the *Pigmy,* schooner; the *Norfolk, Golden Fleece, Thames, Diane, Woodman, Active, Cyrus, Elizabeth, Kah, Daniel Woodruffe,* and *George,* transports; and a few others. He had a thousand guns on that great fleet of fifty ships.[3]

Another group looked out with confidence and pride at that great fleet and forgot the inconveniences of cramped living and depressing weather. They were the civilians who had been brought from the West Indies to take civil positions in the new government that would be established in Louisiana. They visited cheerfully with one another and with the officers and talked glowingly of the vast stores of merchandise that were rumored to be waiting on the docks of New Orleans. One merchant from Bermuda prattled happily of his prospects and watched joyfully the success of his five daughters with young bachelor officers. The group was large enough, with the various officers' wives who had accompanied their husbands (presided over by Lady Mullins), to give an air of social respectability to this military show and to keep the army's officers on good behavior and in good spirits. (The soldiers' wives were not so gay as they squeezed into their husbands' cramped quarters; they only helped to keep the soldiers grumbling.)[4]

The seaports were not in ashes, and the Americans were not prisoners, but no one expected that situation to be long in coming. General Keane's interviewees reported the city almost undefended, lying ripe for the plucking. French and Spanish residents were disaffected with the government and eager to try a new one; the people were disgusted with high taxes; the slaves were seething with unrest, ready to rush to the aid of the British liberators; the Americans were incapable of fighting together; and the defense of the whole had been entrusted to a frontier lawyer whose only experience was in backwoods fighting against savages. Reports of these interviews spread through the force, and the general feeling was a desire to get out of the cramped quarters and bad weather and hurry forward to the gay, rich city.[5]

But to General Keane, who had to plan and execute the visit, the prospect was not simple. New Orleans was fifty miles away. Soundings indicated that the fleet could move no closer to the lakes. That meant that an intermediate point had to be found for a base of operations, because it was too long a distance to move the army and its supplies in small boats. One of the sand spits that were called islands between the anchorage and the shores of Lake Borgne had to be selected, the army moved in stages to that island, a supply base established, and a route then chosen for the advance to the city.[6]

Also the *Sophia, Seahorse,* and *Armide,* having preceded the rest of the fleet to this anchorage, had been fired upon, as they passed down the channel within the chain of islands, by American gunboats. Nicholas Lockyer (the ambitious young commander disappointed in his negotiations with Lafitte) had reported the incident to Admiral Cochrane, who reported it to Keane and waited, watching with his haughty eyes, for a decision. Keane gave it. The admiral was to clear the American boats from the lake; Colonel Thornton was then to take the advance forward and, with the admiral's help, select the point of land near the Rigolet pass most favorable for landing troops.[7]

Then Keane sat back to wait with his army the result of these preliminary feelers.

‡‡‡

At New Orleans, General Jackson was playing a new role. Throughout the Creek war he had been always the aggressor, moving his army forward, choosing the points of attack, disposing his troops, attacking, moving forward. At Mobile he had been the defender, but he had played his role there by taking the offensive— by marching to Pensacola and driving the intruders away. Now there was nothing to attack. He could only wait until the British chose their route, and meanwhile he had to keep his troops ready though inactive.

Waiting was a frustrating business for a man of action, so, leaving the Louisiana troops at New Orleans and the English Turn to drill and practice firing, he journeyed, with his aides and engineers, down the river. Below New Orleans the river made a broad sweep from southeastward to northwestward before gradually bending south again. From the southeast point of this bend to the Gulf ran a bayou flanked by farms and villages, called the Terre aux Boeufs. This bayou was a possible approach, though its entrance from the Gulf was difficult to find and navigate. Choosing a spot on the bayou, Jackson ordered a battery erected.

At the other end of this bend (the English Turn), on the west bank, stood Fort St. Leon, and there the Baton Rouge militia was stationed. Because of the bend the overland route from this fort to the city was shorter than the river route, so the troops were available to resist an enemy approach up the river or to return to the city for action on the opposite bank. The fort, however, was poor, and Jackson ordered that earthworks be thrown up and batteries constructed.

A considerable distance down the river was Fort St. Philip, which must be the main defense of a river approach. It was on a slow turn of the river, where it could command the river for a considerable distance downstream. Along the south and east sides of the fort were bayous, so that it stood on a point of land, and along both sides of the river below it there were heavy swamp forests right up to the river's edge; because an army would have great difficulty landing and maneuvering on that terrain, the enemy's ships must decommission the fort to get by. Across the river there had once been another fort, but its batteries and buildings were now in ruins.

This was a strategic spot. After inspecting it, the general ordered that the wooden barracks within the fort be demolished to reduce the possibility of fire, that several additional guns be placed on the rampart and a thirty-two-pounder and a mortar in the covered way, and that two new batteries be constructed, one at the old fort across the river and one half a mile above the fort. He ordered Colonel Ross also to reinforce the small garrison. It was manned by 117 artillerymen under Captains Wollstonecraft, Murray, and Walsh. Ross was to detail two companies of the 7th Regiment to assist, and the general accepted the offer of thirty free colored and fifty-four white volunteers from the neighborhood. The fort would thus be defended by about four hundred men and some twenty-five or thirty guns.[8]

There was also the possibility, urged by the Committee of Safety, of fortifying the Balize, the pilot station near the mouth of the river. But Jackson's engineers reported that possibility inadvisable because there were no good locations for batteries that would command the passes. "A fortification in Siberia would be of as much service in defending the bar of the Mississippi" as would a battery at the Balize, they said.[9]

Jackson returned to the city, reconnoitering en route the passes from Lake Borgne to Lake Pontchartrain, Petites Coquilles, and the Rigolets; and he rode to the city along the Chef Menteur road over a high ridge of ground between the swamps of Lake Pontchartrain on one hand and the swamps of the river on the other, a ridge known as the plain of Gentilly. The pass at Petites Coquilles was 150 yards with only five feet on the bar, making it a good passage for barges but not for boats. The road began at the pass a mile above Lake Borgne and ran beside Bayou Sauvage with swamps close by on each side. It ran to the bridge on Bayou St. John above the city, a distance of twenty miles. These were other possible approaches—the fleet could pass via Petites Coquilles or the Rigolets from Lake Borgne to Lake Pontchartrain, and thence via Bayou St. John to the city; guarding against this approach was Fort St. John at the mouth of the bayou. Or the army could land from

Lake Borgne and attack up the plain of Gentilly. Jackson ordered a battery to be erected on the Gentilly road to delay an approach up the plain.[10]

Back in the city, while his engineers, Major Lafon and Major Latour, were drawing up plans for the new batteries he had ordered, and his adjutant, Major Robert Butler, was seeing to the new dispositions of troops, Jackson reviewed the situation. Barataria was defended by a comparatively adequate force that could be brought up the bayous to the city in forty-eight hours; Bayou Lafourche was guarded by a small detachment; Fort St. Philip would be well fortified, if time permitted, to guard the river, and a stand could be made at the English Turn if the fort fell; a battery was going up on the Terre aux Boeufs to impede progress from there; a good fort stood at Petites Coquilles, and Fort St. John guarded the bayou from Lake Pontchartrain; a battery was under construction to guard the Gentilly road. But there was still much to be done. He called in the governor and asked that the planters near the river provide slaves at the English Turn, Terre aux Boeufs, and Fort St. Philip to construct the new fortifications.

Three approaches seemed most likely—Lake Pontchartrain to Bayou St. John; Lake Borgne to Gentilly; or Lake Borgne to the river and up the river bank through the sugar plantations. Bayou St. John, if sufficient troops could be stationed at the fort, seemed fairly well defended. But the other two routes were vulnerable, and the army had to be ready to move quickly to either one. Part of the Louisiana militia was at the Turn, within easy reach of the city. Part, together with the New Orleans battalion and the 7th and 44th regulars, were in the city and could be swung to any of the three routes. The Feliciana dragoons Jackson ordered to Gentilly to watch that route. More could hardly be done before the arrival of the Tennessee and Kentucky forces.[11]

His topographical engineer, Major Tatum, tried his best to improve upon Latour's inadequate maps. Busily he queried townspeople and planters, but he found them amazingly vague. No one seemed to know the countryside beyond his own possessions, and many could not even describe their own lands accurately. Tatum wondered if their vagueness was deliberate—if they were afraid of revealing some secret smuggling passage from the lakes to the river.[12]

So the city and its environs were bustling with activity. Large numbers of slaves (there was little work for them now on the plantations) turned out to throw up breastsworks and redoubts and haul cannon; the troops drilled and practiced, singing as they marched about the city, and the citizens watched and cheered and sang with them; the ladies of the city began to organize and called on the governor and the general to provide them with something to do; the old men organized themselves into a veterans' unit, made plans for policing the city, and drilled along with the other soldiers; exempted men organized their fire battalion, made plans for fighting fires wherever in the city they might appear, and comforted themselves for their failure to volunteer for duty by thinking they had important tasks; people out near the coasts rode about, looking for British and organizing lines of communication to carry news to the city; and legislators assembled to proclaim their loyalty and to worry about their prerogatives. There was excitement, bustle, activity, and confidence.

Now everyone wanted to fight. Rofignac and Marigny, members of the legislature's Committee of Defense, consulted Judge Dominic Hall about the plight of the Baratarians. On the Judge's advice they persuaded the legislature to pass a resolution demanding that the procedures against the Baratarians be suspended for four months. When the resolution was passed, the Judge ordered the District Attorney of the United States to cease prosecution. Then Jean Lafitte called upon General Jackson.

The general remembered Claiborne's earlier denunciation of these men; he remembered that he himself had called them "lawless brigands," on the basis of the governor's information, in a proclamation. But Lafitte came with the recommendations of the prominent Creoles, Edward Livingston was by to plead for him, and Lafitte himself seemed quite a gentleman. Lafitte pointed out that his men were rugged fighters used to hardships and that they were experienced cannoneers. The general accepted his offer, promising the privateer that if the Baratarians fought well, he would recommend to the President that they be pardoned for their offenses. He sent Lafitte to help with the defenses being constructed at Barataria, but he asked him to return as soon as possible.[13]

A Captain Juzan offered to raise a battalion of Choctaw Indians in the vicinity. Jackson accepted. A Domingan colored refugee named Jean Baptiste Savary, formerly an officer of the French Republic, offered to raise a battalion of free colored among the Domingan refugees. Jackson accepted, appointing Savary a captain. This new colored battalion was quickly formed; Jackson gave command of it to Major Jean Daquin, a white émigré. He raised Fortier to command of the two battalions and made Pierre Lacoste, a prominent planter, commander of the original battalion. There were 280 men in Lacoste's unit and 150 in Daquin's. Colonel Fortier furnished these men at his own cost. When the assistant district paymaster questioned Jackson's authority to have Negroes in service, the general wrote him: "Be pleased to keep to yourself your opinions upon the policy of making payments to particular corps. It is enough for you to receive my order for the payment of the troops with the necessary muster rolls without inquiring whether the troops are white, black, or tea." There was never for long any question of authority. Jackson sent the colored troops to Gentilly.[14]

The most popular unit in the city was the New Orleans battalion, commanded by Major Plauché. The young men of the finest families eagerly pressed into its ranks, providing themselves with the colorful uniforms of the four companies. The merchant Vincent Nolte, though exempt by reason of a bad arm, enrolled in the Carabiniers, now captained (since the elevation of Plauché to battalion command) by the French bookseller Peter Roche.[15]

Down the river from Pittsburgh steamed a stern-wheeler, the *Enterprise,* captained by young Henry Shreve. He brought a supply of guns and ammunition, but more important, he brought a boat that could challenge the river current to carry supplies back and forth. Jackson commandeered Shreve's services for moving troops and supplies between points along the river.[16]

Thus troops were rapidly forming, and New Orleans was bustling with activity. But, thinking over the mixed nature of his army— a small group of regulars, the rest militia or volunteers—and listening to the polyglot commands as they drilled—English, French, Choctaw, French and English with colored accents, the peculiar Baratarian jargon—Jackson wished for the presence of his backwoodsmen from Tennessee. Coffee's troops were at Baton Rouge to cover any attempt of the British to cut off the city from above. Carroll was at Natchez, where he had paused on his march to allow his troops to relax and wash their clothes, and where he had found one of the barges from Pittsburgh (the other was still four hundred miles further up the river) and taken fourteen hundred stands of arms for his men. To Coffee Jackson wrote, "We may or may not have a fandango with Lord Hill in the Christmas holidays. If so you and your brave followers must participate in the frolic." [17]

Governor Claiborne watched the city frothing with activity under the general's directions and remembered how restless and indecisive it had been only a few weeks before. He noticed too that the general was too busy to confer with the governor most of the time and often issued orders without asking the advice of the civil leader. He began to mutter to his friends that Jackson was surrounded by enemies of the executive, like Edward Livingston, who were poisoning the general's ears. There were two other men, too, who were not satisfied with the situation. One was Judge Hall of the District Court of the United States; the other was Representative Louaillier of the legislature. Both had rigid conceptions of democracy, and both felt, as they observed the strong man who had come among them, certain misgivings about him. But the murmurs of these three were not enough to ruffle the newfound spirit of unity in the city.[18]

Excited and confident as the city now was, however, its vision was not sharp. Below it stretched over a hundred miles of swampland river to the Gulf and other swamps pierced by winding bayous. The ships that usually brought daily news up and down the river were idle or gone. The news that trickled in overland from the rest of the nation was too old to be useful. The city's eyes could see in only one direction—the lakes. On the lakes Commander Patterson had a schooner, a sloop, and five gunboats. The gunboats were No. 5, five guns, thirty-six men, commanded by Sailing Master John D. Ferris; No. 23, five guns, thirty-nine men, Lieutenant Isaac McKeever; No. 156, five guns, forty-one men, Lieutenant Thomas apCatesby Jones; No. 162, five guns, thirty-five men, Lieutenant Robert Spedden; and No. 163, three guns, thirty-one men, Sailing Master Ulrick. These, together with the sloop *Alligator*, a fishing smack converted into a tender and carrying one four-pound cannon and eight men (commander, Sailing Master Richard S. Sheppard), and a schooner, mounting one six-pounder and fourteen men (commander, Sailing Master Johnson), Patterson had sent, with Jones in charge, along the coast inside the islands to watch for the British.[19]

So the seven little boats ventured cautiously out, and hovering within an island they watched as the great British fleet came sailing in. When the *Sophia,* the *Seahorse,* and the *Armide* came along the run, Jones fired at them to discourage them and then sailed his little flotilla closer to the lakes. He sent word to his commander of the British arrival, but he held his post to watch further developments. Jones' plan was to keep between the British and the lakes until it became too dangerous, and then to cross the bar into Lake Borgne to contest possession of the lakes. The larger British vessels would be unable to get into the lakes, so the gunboats could harass the British when they tried to land the army and could keep close track of their movements. Also there was a small fort and magazine at Bay St. Louis which needed to be protected if possible, destroyed if discovered by the enemy.

On December 9 Jones ventured forward again with his little fleet to see what the British were doing. At daybreak the following day he discovered the enemy fleet in the channel between Cat and Ship islands. The gunboats wheeled about to make for Pass Mariana, where they provisioned from Bay St. Louis. After waiting a day they moved out again, this time to the eastern end of Cat Island, and they found the enemy fleet increased. On the thirteenth they returned to Bay St. Louis, and Jones sent the *Alligator* to report to Commander Patterson.

At 4:00 P.M. that day Jones discovered a fleet of enemy barges headed for Pass Christian. He sent his schooner to Bay St. Louis to remove what public stores it could and destroy the rest, while the gunboats retired closer to Petites Coquilles.[20]

So word reached Jackson and New Orleans that the enemy had arrived. The city held its breath, awaiting the next report from Lieutenant Thomas apCatesby Jones and his five gunboats.

Meanwhile Admiral Cochrane, too, waited for news, but his faith in his able, intrepid seamen was such that he hardly felt it necessary to hold his breath. He had gathered together the barges of his fleet and manned them with officers and sailors from various ships. The attacking force consisted of some forty barges mounting one carronade each of twelve, nineteen, or twenty-four caliber, one launch with a long brass twelve-pounder, one with a long brass nine-pounder, and three gigs. It was manned by some twelve hundred men and officers. Commanding was Captain Nicholas Lockyer of the *Sophia,* an eager and promising young officer, with Captain Montressor of the *Manly* and Captain Roberts of the *Meteor* to assist him. The navy, Cochrane assured General Keane, would quickly sweep clean the waters to smooth the way of the army for a quick journey to the heart of New Orleans.[21]

Lockyer had arranged his attacking force in three divisions, each to be commanded by one of the three captains. They left the fleet on the night of the twelfth and rowed steadily all night and all the next day until they sighted the enemy.

Lieutenant Jones had been watching. He had thought this fleet of barges was making toward Pass Christian to disembark troops, but at two in the afternoon on the thirteenth he saw them reach and pass that point, still rowing west. Now, realizing that this was an attack upon him, he ordered his gunboats to make with all speed for Petites Coquilles. But there was a steady west wind blowing, and as they sailed up the pass they discovered that the water was uncommonly low. Soundings lowered to eighteen inches less than the ships' draught and kept going down. Excitement grew among the crewmen as they realized they were about to be cut off. Feverishly they began to throw overboard all disposable articles. At 3:30 the flood tide commenced, and the boats began to move, but the barges were closing in. Now Jones spotted his schooner coming from Bay St. Louis. Lockyer also spotted it and dispatched some boats to cut it off. The other barges continued relentlessly toward the gunboats.

The schooner, after firing at the approaching barges to discourage them, returned to Bay St. Louis. There Sailing Master Johnson chose a position near two cannon on the bank. Seven enemy barges attacked, but he held them off for thirty minutes until they withdrew from range. Then he had his men blow up the schooner and set fire to the public storehouse. At 7:30 the explosion announced to Lieutenant Jones and Captain Lockyer what had happened.

Lockyer's barges rowed steadily on, while Jones' gunboats struggled to move over the shallow bar. At 1:00 A.M. on the fourteenth the wind died away, and the gunboats could go no farther.

They anchored at the west end of Malheureux Island to wait for daybreak. But when day did break, there was still a perfect calm, and there was a strong ebb tide flowing from the lakes. The enemy flotilla, Jones estimated, was nine miles away, but it was rapidly approaching. Jones called on board his boat the other four commanders, told them to form in a close line abreast across the channel, anchor by the stern with springs on the cables, trice up the boarding nets, and prepare to hold the line.

Lockyer saw the battle line form. The oars of his barges were dipping in the water in a slow rhythm, pushing the boats forward against the stiff current. The faces of the sailors were grimy, wet with sweat, grim. For thirty-six hours they had been rowing, and there were nine miles of hardy pulling yet to go. Lockyer glanced at the ripples of the swift current with mixed feelings. That current made the going rough, but it also blocked the retreat of the American ships.

Across the water, Lieutenant Jones's small force stood determinedly at their guns and looked out at the mass of barges.[22]

On the *Tonnant* and at the anchorage, Admiral Cochrane and General Keane and the British army waited. In New Orleans, Commander Patterson and General Jackson and the American citizens waited. In the Gulf, the *Statira* and its companions raced forward, General Pakenham, General Lambert, and General Gibbs waiting; and Sergeant Cooper stood on the deck of a transport and counted seventeen waterspouts in the distance.[23]

At Hartford, Connecticut, delegates of the New England states met in convention to complain about the war and to consider the possibility of making a separate peace with Great Britain.[24]

☼ ☼

TEN

The Battle on the Lakes

THE TIDE flowing out of the lakes was swift, but the air was perfectly still, and the sun rising in the sky forewarned of a hot day. Lieutenant Jones, on the deck of No. 156, glanced at his little fleet —Ulrick's 163, the smallest, with only three guns, was closest to him; then the others, 5, 162, and 23, Ferris, Spedden, and Isaac McKeever. The boarding nets were up, the men at the guns, and the commanders waiting, but the boats strained at their anchors as the current attempted to bear them away, and the line was irregular. Then Jones looked out again at the long line of black specks across the mirror of water. Relentlessly that line of specks approached.[1]

When Master's Mate George Parker tapped his arm, Jones glanced quickly in another direction. To the southeast he could see the little sloop *Alligator,* which had carried his reports to Commander Patterson, attempting to join the gunboats from Lake Borgne in spite of the calm. Again he fixed his attention on the approaching barges. He could see now that a group of the specks on his right had separated from the rest.

Captain Lockyer, having also seen the sloop, had directed Captain Roberts of the *Meteor* to take several barges against the newcomer. The rest slackened their speed to await the outcome. Lusty pulling carried Roberts' barges athwart the path of the sloop, whose little four-pounder tossed a couple of harmless balls. Then, seeing those barges approaching relentlessly with several hundred men ready to board, and glancing at his own crew of eight, Sailing Master Johnson surrendered. After Roberts sent aboard a crew to deliver the sloop and its crewmen to the fleet, he guided his barges again toward the main attack.

It was now midmorning. Lieutenant Jones estimated the distance of the attackers and decided his guns could not yet reach them. Captain Lockyer also estimated the distance; it seemed to him that he had just about reached gunshot. His men were sweaty, grimy, and tired from their long haul. He ordered the barges to come to a grapnel while the men breakfasted and the Roberts division rejoined the main force. He tested the current, finding it to be a strong three miles an hour.

In spite of the voracious appetite they had built up, the British sailors ate slowly while they stretched out as comfortably as possible in the cramped little barges, feeling strength return to throbbing muscles. Their glances were fixed on that row of five boats with cannon and netting, but they felt the shoulders or knees or thighs of tough comrades leaning against them, and they felt their own sweaty flesh. They had rowed steadily for thirty-six hours, but they were accustomed to hard work.

Across the water, Lieutenant Jones's small force stood grimly at their guns and looked out at the mass of barges. Jones also noted the time carefully by his watch and fixed it in his memory to make his report later to his commanding officer. The *Alligator* had been captured at 9:30. The enemy had halted its advance at 10:00. The minutes passed, and through his glass Jones watched the enemy take places in the barges. When the oars began to move again, Jones's watch read 10:30. He looked over at his line and frowned; the current had swept his own boat and Ulrick's No. 163 ahead of the other three, so that the line was no longer solid. 156 and 163 were perhaps a hundred yards ahead of 5, 162, and 23.

On came the barges. Jones ordered his men to fire. One of the cannon roared, and he watched as a spout of water shot up well ahead of the barges. The other gunboats took the signal, and four more cannon roared. The balls sent up their spouts far apart, some ahead and some beyond the barges, but all off the mark. The barges made too small targets to strike at such a distance. Firing continued rather slowly while the targets approached and grew.

Now the British tars pulled heftily, and the barges glided toward the enemy as balls hit the water or shells exploded around them. Some splashes were close enough to rock the boats and spray the men. The positions of the gunboats became clearer, and the attack took more specific shape. Lockyer's division made for No. 156, which had been pushed closest by the tide. Montressor's and Roberts' divisions singled out the other gunboat that had been swept forward. The barges opened fire to answer the enemy.

That happened, by Jones's watch, at 10:50. Cannon were roaring on both sides, balls and grape were whistling and splashing and occasionally splintering with a hit. Smoke rose and lingered in the still, warm air. The engagement became general.

Command could no longer be extended beyond a single barge. Lockyer saw the nearby barges, under Midshipman White of the *Seahorse* and Lieutenant Tatnall of the *Tonnant,* forging steadily ahead, and then concentrated on his own, which Lieutenant Pratt was directing. He received his first wound, sharp and biting but not enough to divert him from his mission. Lieutenant Pratt was struck much harder, but he too held his post. The explosions of the cannon and the churning of the water by the shells made progress erratic, but Lockyer yelled to his men to pull, and pull they did.

Jones's men worked feverishly, loading and firing rapidly as they saw barges gradually closing around them. The gunboats were larger targets than the barges, and there was scrambling and screaming as balls crashed sometimes into the decks. Ulrick's three guns were also busily tormenting the barges closing in on 163. The other three boats, though not yet attacked, kept up a steady firing.

Three barges forged ahead of the rest toward 156, and the cannoneers trained on them and found the target. Balls and grape struck among the men and silenced the guns. One rowed away, but two drifted helplessly, shipping water as they slowly sank. For a moment Jones smiled grimly, but four more barges advanced.

One of the sunk barges was that of Lieutenant Tatnall of the *Tonnant.* Tatnall swam to another attacking barge and climbed aboard. He was not one to give up easily; once he had escaped from a French prison dressed as a monk. Now, dripping and panting, he rested on his knee in the barge, glaring at the hull of the gunboat with the triangular net stretching up the rigging toward the top of the tall mast. Lockyer's barge near at hand was struck by grape, Lockyer taking his second wound and Lieutenant Pratt being flattened by his second. But the barges closed and the sailors jumped and clambered aboard the gunboat, cutting and crashing through the nets. Midshipman White led the assault, with Lieutenant Tatnall and Captain Lockyer close behind.

Lieutenant Jones had fallen, bleeding profusely from the left shoulder. He crawled from the deck, leaving George Parker and his forty men to grapple with the boarding British. But the British poured over the bulwark, and the battle was soon over. Jones managed to consult his watch. It was 12:10.

The other two divisions of barges had closed with Ulrick's gunboat, and a few minutes later that one too was conquered. Now British sailors manned the cannon and directed their fire against the three remaining gunboats while a dozen barges pressed against 162. Lieutenant Spedden's left arm was suddenly shattered at the elbow, and a moment later he was shot in the right shoulder. As he fell to the deck, his men surrendered to the boarding British. Sailing Master Ferris' No. 5 was next. After a good shot dismounted his best gun, the British soon swarmed aboard.

Isaac McKeever's No. 23 was the last. The cannon of four gunboats (still flying the American flag) raked his decks. Resistance was useless, and he surrendered.[2]

By Jones's watch, the time was 12:40. Commander Patterson's little fleet on the lakes, the eyes for Jackson's army, had been destroyed. Admiral Cochrane's promise to sweep clear the waters between Keane's army and the city had been fulfilled.

The British tars rested, nursed their wounds, and gathered together their prisoners. Captain Lockyer counted his losses. Dead were three midshipmen, thirteen sailors, and one marine. Wounded were one captain (Lockyer himself), four lieutenants (Lieutenant Pratt severely), one marine lieutenant, three master's mates, seven midshipmen, fifty seamen, and eleven marines. Ninety-four casualties. The American loss was almost as great, amounting to one third of their men, and including among the wounded three of the commanders, Lieutenants Jones, Spedden, and McKeever.[3]

‡‡‡

Nicholas Lockyer, in spite of his losses and his wounds, could view his prize with a certain grim satisfaction. It was only five small boats, not very formidable as an opponent for the great British fleet; but it was the eyes of the American army, and those small boats in the shallows of the lakes where the giant men of war could not tread could have badly harassed the invading troops. Lockyer could feel that he had settled an old score. His victory could salve the smart that he had nursed since his visit to Barataria.

After a brief rest the sailors began the long movement back up the channel to the anchorage. Some manned the rigging of the gunboats while others returned to the oars of the barges. A bright midday sun beat down upon these men who had rowed for some forty hours, fought a blistering battle, and now had to make the same long journey back. And when this journey was done, the army must be conveyed by the same method from the fleet to the city.

The battle had been fought in a channel surrounded by waste land, sandspits, swampy islands, and sandy, swampy coast, far from any habitation. Certain isolated villages were within sight of the smoke and sound of the cannon, but there were no apparent witnesses other than the participants. The outcome did not, however, go unnoticed. Some families at Bay St. Louis and Pass Christian knew from the blowing up of the schooner and the magazine that the battle was in progress, and they watched as the British barges returned with their prizes. One Frenchman wrote a letter to his sister in New Orleans, a panicky letter mentioning a vast British fleet, translating fears of British ravages upon the coast into reports, and calling upon the sister to flee New Orleans at once before the city went up in flames. Two others, an American and a free colored, set out in a fishing smack, once the British barges had passed, to run for the lakes, and to the colored man the Frenchman entrusted his letter.[4]

Other witnesses were Portuguese fishermen who hid their boat near an island just far enough away to understand the outcome of the battle and return with the news to their village on the shore of Lake Borgne. The men of this village fished the lakes and then took their fish to New Orleans by way of a bayou through the swamps to the river plantations, along canals from the swamps to the river, and up the highroad to the city. Though they were familiar sights to the planters whose canals they used and to the citizens who bought their wares in the market, they were hardly known otherwise. They intruded upon the consciousness of planters and citizens no more than cattle and much less than slaves. Yet they were men with a gay and thriving community of their own, alert to the activity of the coast, the river, and the city, and alive, through their contacts with the city and through occasional communication with their families in the old world, to world affairs.

Now the witnesses of the battle carried the news of a British victory to the village, and the men of the village, some thirty of them, debated the news excitedly. They might have carried it to the city. But their allegiance, isolated as they were from all the other groups in the countryside, was not strongly directed to America. With the dominant French group of the city they had no friendship and with the Americans they had no acquaintance. In the old world, France was a bitter enemy who had ravaged Portugal while Britain fought as an ally. Now, as the war left the far-off old country and pushed to their doorstep, the fishermen saw a confused, disorganized army of defense and an immense, imposing fleet of invasion. Ships they understood and loved, and this great array of beautiful ships riding at anchor outside the sound aroused their admiration. Their sympathy went to the British and their expectation to a British victory.[5]

Admiral Cochrane was not idle. He knew of the many racial groups that made up the population of this area, and though he was disappointed that the French had resisted so stubbornly, he still anticipated mass capitulation by the Spanish and the colored. He knew also the complex, treacherous Louisiana coast, and he had boats exploring and taking soundings. One of these exploring parties came upon one of the fishing smacks, found the fishermen friendly, and brought them to the admiral.

‡‡‡

Knowledge of the encounter on the lake had not yet reached New Orleans. Commander Patterson, knowing that the British fleet was anchored outside the coastal islands, was waiting for the enemy's next move to be reported by the gunboats when they retreated into Lake Pontchartrain. But he was not so sanguine as to expect his little fleet on the lakes to offer much resistance, and he wondered what he could do on the river when the enemy at last reached it. He had one well-armed schooner, the *Carolina,* that could trouble an army on the river bank, but one boat made a tiny force. He had a good arsenal across the river from the city with enough cannon to arm more boats. And he had his eye on one large ship in harbor, the *Louisiana,* which could be armed if it could be manned.

He approached Jackson again with a cherished plot of his. Almost daily he watched the many sailors of different nations loitering along the waterfront. Could they not be pressed into service to man a second ship on the river?

Jackson was beginning to form an estimate of the men under him. The defenses had been thoroughly planned, but the execution of the plans had not been accomplished as felicitously as the general had hoped. News from Fort St. Philip indicated that the new batteries above and across from the fort were hardly begun and that the fort itself was still unprepared for attack. Although the planters had answered the call for help readily enough with parties of slaves to do the work, reports to Jackson listed more complaints about difficulties than announcements of progress. The same was true of other fortifications. David Morgan's troops at the English Turn were eager enough for battle and smart enough in parade, but digging, hauling, and building did not entrance them. When the engineers Lafon and Latour were on hand to spur them on, progress was made on fortifications, but in their absence, Morgan seemed none too able to keep his men busy.[6]

The young Creoles were high-spirited and excitable, but it was the glitter of war that excited them. The ones serving as cavalry could be depended upon. They rode constantly hither and yon, keeping Jackson in excellent communication with all his outposts. Ogden's troop of horse proudly accompanied the general as a bodyguard. Messengers frequently appeared at headquarters, always wishing to deliver their messages personally to the general. Beale's rifle company was also proud enough of its independence from larger units to impress the general with its potential. The regiments of militia were more troublesome. The men were impatient with waiting in bivouac when their houses and families were close at hand, and there was frequent absenteeism and strong antagonisms between the various groups. Their knowledge of military maneuvering was also poor, and their effectiveness would depend largely upon their officers. Most of the officers carried their pride high and reacted with excessive sensitivity. Each commander had his own uniform; Claiborne wore an extremely high, stiff collar, heavy gold braid epaulets, a ribbon across his chest sporting a badge with a pelican on it, and a ruffled neckpiece of immaculately white linen; Plauché wore similarly heavy epaulets but a smaller collar, a coat buttoning down the side instead of the front with V-shaped velvet lapels, and a ribbon around his waist; De la Ronde wore an epaulet on the right shoulder only, a front-buttoned coat with bright lapels, and a tricolor hat. The neatness of their dress contrasted with the carelessness of Jackson's. Jackson wore a leather cap, a short blue Spanish cloak, and unpolished boots whose large tops swayed uneasily around his bony knees. Often the uniforms altered the personalities of the men. Lacoste, dryly humorous in society, became ridiculously pompous in uniform. But none took offense so readily as David Morgan at the Turn—an oval-faced gentleman with thick lips and a double chin—who was sure of his own importance, resented the suggestions of Jackson's engineers or adjutant, and acted only upon signed written orders from the general himself.[7]

Governor Claiborne was inconsistent. He seemed often resentful of some slight, he sometimes acted without consulting the general and other times brought trivial matters to the general's attention, he sometimes acted forcefully upon the general's requests and other times procrastinated unreasonably, and he was so often close at hand that the general felt spied upon. Of the other men at his elbow, there were five who attracted respect. Major Butler, the adjutant, kept records passionately and could inform Jackson on a moment's notice of the state of affairs throughout his command. The engineer Latour just as passionately produced detailed plans for fortifications while the engineer Tatum studied the country, drew maps, and complained about their inaccuracy. Edward Livingston, one of the volunteer aides, seemed to Jackson to be in much closer communication with all the important citizens of various groups, in spite of the bitter feelings some felt toward him, than did the governor. And Commander Patterson was a forthright man of action.

Patterson's plan for manning a ship with idled seamen appealed to Jackson. Just what the legal aspects were the general was not sure, and the lawyer Livingston recommended caution. So the general promised Patterson to work it out but advised him to wait. Meanwhile, summoning the governor, he suggested that Patterson's latest report on the strength of the British be transmitted to the legislature with a recommendation that the writ of habeas corpus be suspended for the duration of the emergency.

Since Claiborne was unhappy about the actions of the legislature during this session and had frequently complained to the general about their lack of support, this proposal suited him perfectly. Gleefully he lectured the legislators on the imminent peril and the need for every man in the state to expend all his energies on the impending battle. No one, not even a foreign seaman, could be allowed to remain idle. Those who were able to serve but did not do so voluntarily must be impressed. He requested immediate action on the suspension of the writ of habeas corpus.

When the measure was referred to the Committee of Ways and Means, Philip Louaillier, chairman of the committee, expressed his doubts to the others. He wondered if the state had the power to suspend the writ in federal courts even if it were desirable. He wondered if someone arrested by a United States navy or army commander could be relieved by a writ issued by a state court. If a state court had no power over federal authorities and the legislature had no power over federal courts, of what use would the measure be?

Someone suggested that Judge Hall of the United States District Court be consulted, so the committee suspended discussion to await his reply. Judge Hall quickly answered that in his opinion only Congress had the authority to withdraw the protection of the writ. He stated further that he would disregard any state legislation on the subject.

Why, then, asked Louaillier, should the state place itself in the undignified position of passing legislation in vain? Moreover, he was tired of the talk of sedition, disaffection, and treason which General Jackson and Governor Claiborne so frequently engaged in. He himself was sure that his constituents could be depended upon for unqualified support. If the protective writs were suspended, it would be an admission by the legislature that there were grounds for these apprehensions of disaffection. Better to express unqualified faith in the people. Perhaps General Jackson, whom all Louisianans held in respect, would be upset if his wishes in this matter were disregarded; but Louaillier recalled that President Jefferson had applied to Congress for a suspension of writs during the Burr conspiracy and had been refused. This was a safe precedent. Jackson could hardly complain of mistreatment where the great Jefferson had not.

The Committee of Ways and Means reported to the legislature that the measure was inexpedient. They suggested instead that six thousand dollars be placed at the disposal of Commander Patterson to induce sailors by bounties rather than to coerce them. The legislature passed this proposal of Louaillier's committee.[8]

Jackson fumed. He advised Patterson to accept this money, but to wait a few days before using it. The general had another plan in mind.

Meanwhile the fishing smack with the American and the colored man made its way along the coast, through the Rigolets, and across Lake Pontchartrain. There it reported to Major Hughes at Fort St. John. A messenger dashed off to Commander Patterson with news of the loss of the gunboats.[9]

✳ ✳

ELEVEN

Pea Island

THE SAILORS of Admiral Cochrane's fleet had begun the long
pull with the barges back from the anchorage to the lake, starting
a ferry service that would continue, with accommodations for only
two thousand at a time, until the entire army had been moved to
the new base of operations. Colonel Thornton's advance, the 85th
and 95th regiments and forty rocketmen, led the way.[1]

Many of the remaining troops, their families, and the civilians
had chosen to leave the cramped quarters of the ships in order to
camp as best they could on Cat Island. Departing troops had to take
their farewells of their wives, some perhaps forever. No one spoke
of the possibility of death. It was a vague presence, but each couple
felt that it would come only for others. That it would come to very
many was not thought of. The attack was envisioned as a foray,
a march up the river dispersing sporadic resistance, like the march
to Washington, culminating when the rich city of New Orleans
fell to the conquerors. Wives looked forward to a reunion in that
gay place of many legends. The privations of the sea voyage and the
stopover on this insect-ridden sandspit would give way to a marvel-
ous celebration in the city by the great river.

Single men equally anticipated that march into New Orleans,
city of the much-praised Creole belles, the exciting quadroons and

octoroons, the barrels of famed Kentucky bourbon, the fabled taverns and coffeehouses, the stores of fancy silks and cloths imported from around the world, the wharves glutted with valuable sugar and coffee cargoes. The cargoes would be of no immediate use to the troops, but any prize of war taken by the army, the men knew, would later be distributed as money. The Peninsular prize money, which amounted to some £800,000, though the troops had not yet received it, was to be distributed one sixteenth to Wellington, one sixteenth to be divided by the generals, one fourth by field officers, one eighth by captains, one eighth by subalterns, one eighth by sergeants, and one fourth by privates. A rich prize at New Orleans would give every man a welcome supplement to his scanty army pay.[2]

So as they huddled in the boats, packed together, unable to shift position, legs and shoulders aching to be moved, they grumbled little. They seemed to be taking an excursion; they were going somewhere rather than advancing to battle. The slogan which made the rounds was "beauty and booty!" Some of the coarser-textured spirits altered it to "lust and loot." One who did grumble was Quartermaster Surtees, who had never done well at plundering, who was now suffering his usual seasickness in the cramped quarters of the boat, and who disapprovingly noticed that the sailors were fortifying themselves with grog.[3]

There were others who were not reconciled to their misery by the thought of a lucrative conquest of New Orleans. Some felt that the navy's thumb was too deeply stuck into the pie. Oldtimers could remember dreadful campaigning in the West Indies for no purpose, apparently, other than prize money scarcely worth the suffering, heat, and disease that they had endured. Some felt that the fruitless attack upon Baltimore had been inspired by Admiral Cochrane's greed. And there were hardened veterans of many battles for whom army service, no matter what the prospects, was merely endurance. There were men who remembered pushing and shoving through the bayonet-lined breach at Badajoz. Corporal Brown of the 21st remembered the disease contracted by the regiment in Egypt, when over two hundred men were blind in both eyes, and upon disembarkation at Sicily the ones who could see a little led the way while the rest held the coattails of those ahead of them. Others remembered the assault at Bergen-op-Zoom—trudging through a horrible slough that clung to their legs like glue, so bad that some men became stuck and were trodden down in the darkness and smothered; pushing through the gate of the city, losing their way, moving recklessly along the ramparts of the fort while their ranks became decimated, and finally escaping through another gate. To many war was fevered swamps and hot sands, mob fighting in the Dublin slums, tramping through woods or assaulting ancient fortresses, skirmishing in the virgin forests of America, or waiting, the long, dull days of endless waiting or aimless moving.[4]

Gleig and Grey had experienced the New Orleans winter heat that they had heard about. But it was followed by a frosty night, and a rapid variety of weather succeeded. The sun would peek out warmly for a few hours, then clouds would gather, bringing a sudden rain, and at night a bracing frost would come. Sometimes stiff winds blew. The sailors, hampered in their journey by the shifts of weather as well as by their own fatigue, fell behind schedule. General Keane chafed at the delay. He was counting upon surprise to make his victory easy.[5]

As the base of operations Colonel Thornton chose Pea Island, formed by the mouths of the Pearl River as it flowed into Lake Borgne and named by Bienville because after camping there his sailors left behind a bag of peas. It answered Thornton's instructions as a point of land close to the Rigolets, and though it left much to be desired, it seemed no worse than the other marshy spots in the vicinity. There the advance disembarked, in a heavy rain, and attempted to settle as comfortably as possible while the boats returned for more troops. They had no tents, the boats having been too crowded with troops to bring supplies, and the island offered no shelter. On the edge of the water there were a few stunted firs, but inland there was only sand on the end where the troops landed and marshes at the other end. The 85th and 95th settled down and ate their evening meal of salt meat and hard ships' biscuits moistened with a small allowance of rum.[6]

The rain ceased as darkness closed in, but the respite was only briefly enjoyed until suddenly the air became bitterly cold. There was no fuel for fire. The men could only wrap themselves in blankets and coats and try to sleep away the night. Fortunately this first night they were weary enough from the cramped journey to succeed.

The next day, Friday, December 17, Lieutenant Gleig and Captain Grey, after beating themselves warm from the frosty night and breakfasting on the same kind of rations they had dined upon, set out to explore their new home. They made their way into the swamp, where with care they could find sandy spots between the pools of water. Seeing flocks of wild ducks and other birds in the water ahead of them, they kept their muskets loaded in the hope of dining better than on the previous day, but the birds moved away at their approach and finally vanished in an impassable morass. They found also in the pools of water many dormant alligators. Again they had rain followed by a cold night.[7]

‡‡‡

Commander Patterson announced to Jackson the loss of the gunboats. It was a heavy blow to the general, but seeing how crushed the usually brisk Patterson was, he kept his own pain out of his face.

The report was perhaps not reliable. The men who had brought it might easily be spies. But since the gunboats had not returned and had sent no message Patterson was convinced. The news could also hardly be withheld from the public. Either its importance must be minimized or everyone must be kept too busy to worry.

Patterson and Jackson looked at their maps. Without a navy on the lakes, nothing could be done either to hamper the British landing or to follow their movements.

The most likely approach was via one of the many bayous running from the lakes toward the river. The best would be Bayou St. John, but Fort Petites Coquilles guarded the pass into Lake Pontchartrain and Fort St. John guarded the entrance to the bayou. Jackson sent an urgent message to Captain Newman, artilleryman at Petites Coquilles, to defend the pass to the last man. He ordered Captain Henley of the navy, recommended by Patterson, to construct two new batteries at Fort St. John.[8]

It was possible also that if the British entered Lake Pontchartrain they could follow one of the bayous to the river above New Orleans, move on to Baton Rouge, and thus cut off the city. Or they might follow one of the bayous from Lake Borgne to the river below the city. These bayous, dangerous approaches, were too numerous to be adequately fortified. Calling in the governor, Jackson ordered him to obstruct every bayou from the lakes to the river.

The other approach, from Lake Borgne along the Gentilly plain to the rear of the city, was already fortified, but it would have to be carefully watched. Claiborne thought that this would be the route, while Major Tatum scoffed, certain that because the space between the swamps bordering the road was narrow and the road too soft for artillery, it would be the worst route.[9]

To General Coffee, camping at Baton Rouge, Jackson sent a message urging him to bring his troops to the city with all possible haste. Patterson, mindful of the men in his command, dispatched Thomas Shields, his purser, Doctor Morrell of the Marines, and Sailing Master Dealey to take a small ship under a flag of truce to the British that they might attend to the American wounded. Then Governor Claiborne, upon Jackson's recommendation, went before the legislature to announce the naval disaster and to request the legislature to adjourn. "The moment is certainly inauspicious," the governor said, "for that cool and mature deliberation which is essential to the formation of laws. Permit me, therefore, to suggest the propriety of adjourning the two Houses for fifteen or twenty days." [10]

This proposal was considered by Louaillier's committee. Adjournment not only seemed to Louaillier to be inexpedient, but in fact highly dangerous. Accidents might happen during this emergency when the interference of the legislature might be necessary. Moreover, if the members left the city for so short a time their mileage going and returning would increase the expenses of the state at a time when all resources were needed for the prosecution of the war. Louaillier opposed the idea of adjournment. The committee so reported, and the legislature so acted.[11]

It was the movement General Jackson had expected. He was especially delighted by the suggestion that the legislature might have to "interfere." Could that mean that if the loss of the city seemed imminent the legislature might capitulate? The possibility of such an action was a threat to the security of the United States. Jackson promised Patterson that he would be able to impress his seamen after the review of the troops which was scheduled for Sunday the eighteenth.

‡‡‡

The boat of truce, bearing Purser Shields and Doctor Morrell, discovered the British on Pea Island. Captain Gordon of the *Seahorse,* the navy commander, and Colonel Thornton, commander of the advance, were surprised by the intrusion and angry when they discovered that it was not a mere chance encounter but a planned visit. Since it was generally accepted by the invading troops that this expedition was a secret one which would catch the city completely off guard, no evidence that the Americans were aware of the British movements was welcome.

Shields and Morrell courteously requested permission to remove the wounded American seamen or at least give them attention. Gordon and Thornton frowned, consulted, hesitated, and finally sent the two men under guard to the fleet, where they were taken to Admiral Cochrane. The admiral, when they explained the object of their visit, was equally upset, but he did not hesitate. His answer to their request was an adamant no.

The doctor stiffened. "That's inhumane, Admiral."

The admiral returned, "We have able surgeons, sir, who will give the enemy as excellent treatment as they give our own wounded. We need no interference from American doctors."

Doctor Morrell could not meet the admiral's stern glance. "In that case, though I do so reluctantly, I will leave you."

"Oh, no!" The admiral's eyes sparkled. "I hope your reluctance is genuine, Doctor, because you must remain as our guest. It was a clever device of your commander to send you here to spy on us under this pretext. But Englishmen are not so gullible. You will remain with the fleet."

The doctor colored angrily. "You can't do that! I'm not spying; I haven't seen a thing; I came on a mission of humanity under a flag of truce—and if I can't see my patients, I'm entitled to leave."

But the admiral was cool and determined. "Truce or no truce, your visit was inopportune. You will remain with the fleet." This was a surprise attack, and nothing could be allowed to reduce the surprise.

So Purser Shields, Doctor Morrell, and Sailing Master Dealey were quartered upon the *Tonnant,* where, amidst the enemy, they must wait out the battle, hearing reports of it from the enemy point of view. They were not allowed to see the wounded seamen. On another ship, the *Gorgon,* Lieutenants Jones and Spedden lay helplessly in their sickbeds, unable to hear even reports from the enemy about the battle. They were cared for; Spedden had to suffer the ordeal of an amputation, and Jones had to suffer the terrible cries of his comrade. Then they lay ill, in the ghastly time-world of fever, reliving moments of the battle and of dream battle, the chronology torn apart and put together kaleidoscopically, un-til time and place gradually returned to the familiar. Their first discussions, as their health and spirits returned, were of time as they tried to determine what day it might be; their next discus-sions were of the battle, of bad luck and possible errors; and finally they worried about the situation at New Orleans and fretted about their own impotency. With difficulty Spedden kept his remaining hand, and Jones his eyes, off the stump where once a strong arm had been.[12]

On the ships and the island at the anchorage the soldiers and officers waited impatiently for their turn to move. Horror might lie ahead, but anything seemed preferable to the insects, the waste land, the cramped quarters, and the temporary nature of their present position. One officer jotted in his diary, "Suffered more from cold since landing in this place than I did in all my former campaigns." They wanted a camp on solid ground where they could establish a familiar environment. They wanted civilization, even hostile civilization, to be close, so they could at least rip some part of it away for their own use. They wanted to fight the battle to get it over with.[13]

The civilians and the wives had no change to look forward to for the time, so their impatience was less. At least for them this position was not so temporary, and they spread out as best they could, giving as permanent a tone as possible to their lives. Certain routines of eating and washing and visiting they established. The future civil officers were gay enough as they dreamed of their coming wealth, and they treated each other already with the social decorum that would exist when their offices became realized. Many of the wives had been through these separations close to the battle before. The older ones could comfort and educate the younger ones. Battles of the past could be fought again in memory, especially the battles of the Peninsular war, whose rigors and terrors and dangers grew for the benefit of those who had not been there.

Lady Mullins remained aboard ship, more comfortable now that its population had been lessened, friendly with the most promising of the future officials, condescending to the lesser officers' wives, full of her aristocratic connections, proud of her husband's brilliance, confident of his future promotion. Even when she returned to an aristocratic environment she would shine; she had once felt small where now she felt great, but when she returned she would have a glamorous campaign to wear upon her shoulders and an honored husband to display at her elbow.

Night and day Cochrane's sailors tugged at their oars, laboring through quick shifts of weather from heat to rain to frost, working while others only waited, ferrying troops and supplies some thirty miles from one desert island to another. On Pea Island the 85th and 95th ate their meager fare, cursed the weather, shivered through the nights, and fought boredom through the days. The 4th, 21st, and the 44th arrived and sought posts upon the sand to wait with the 85th and 95th. With nothing to do but quarrel, rivalries developed. The 4th and 95th argued about who had performed most nobly under Wellington. The 4th and 95th then joined in bragging about that war to the inexperienced 21st, 44th, and 85th. These three retaliated by speaking of the Baltimore campaign, and with the 4th bragged about their superior knowledge to the 95th, which had not yet fought Americans. The 44th and 21st, reaching back in memory, bragged of the Battle of Alexandria and their experience with General Keane in his early career. The highlanders of the 93rd, when they arrived, bandied words with the lowlanders of the 21st, the latter calling the former "bare-assed cattle stealers from the north"; and these two bodies of Scotsmen argued belligerently with the Irishmen so numerous in the 4th and 44th.[14]

General Keane and Admiral Cochrane came themselves to Pea Island on December 17 to superintend the establishment of this intermediate base of operations and to plan for the next move. To them came the friendly fishermen of Lake Borgne with their knowledge of the bayous around the city. From this forlorn spot on the lake New Orleans seemed only a legendary mistress; but they knew she existed, and the more she hid, the more desirable she became.[15]

‡‡‡

Around New Orleans the troops drilled, worked on fortifications, scouted, and waited. In the woods Captain Beale's riflemen sharpened their aim. Colonel Ross's regulars went into the swamps to fill in whatever streams they could find. Under the governor's orders, various planters along the river sent their slaves to fill in nearby bayous. The task was being done haphazardly, however, and Jackson's engineers reported as much to the general. Above the city Bayou Manchac, an important route from the lakes, had been blocked. But below the city there were many bayous hidden in the swamps, some only vaguely known to the inhabitants. Jackson consequently relieved Ross of the responsibility and gave it to Colonel De la Ronde and General Villeré, both of whom had plantations along the river and knew the ground well. But both also had troops to command, and confusion developed about who was to do what and how. Some minor streams and ditches and canals became blocked, but Bayou Sauvage still ran nobly up Gentilly, the Terre aux Boeufs bayou ran close to the Turn, and Bayou Bienvenu ran through the swamps with its tributaries connecting untouched to the canals of the river plantations—Macarty, Chalmette, Bienvenu, De la Ronde, Lacoste, Villeré, Jumonville.[16]

The citizens did what they could. The defense company and the fire company met, organized, and practiced. The legislators met, worried, made plans and alternative plans, considered proposals of the governor, and continually assured the general of their patriotism. The nuns made plans for nursing the wounded. The ladies met to make bandages, to sew clothes for the troops, to shiver at tales of British outrages, to wonder how they would evacuate if the worst happened. Old men watched the excitement and regretted their senility.

On Sunday the city poured its crowds into the Place d'Armes.

Creoles, merchants, and Americans crowded into the windows of the Cabildo, into the doorways of the cathedral, onto the balconies and the roofs of the buildings flanking the square. Laborers, sailors, and Negroes massed in the streets alongside the square. When the general and his staff appeared, great shouts and applause rang out. When the band marched on, playing lustily, the crowds sang, chanted, and shouted. And when the troops marched into the square a prolonged roar arose. In the balconies beautifully dressed ladies—some who had scarcely been shown before to the public—waved their delicate handkerchiefs. In the streets the women waved aloft colorful bandannas.[17]

Snappily the troops marched to the roll of the drums and lined up. The first and second regiments of Louisiana militia marched on, variously dressed and equipped but defiant. Then came Major Plauché's uniformed companies, the Carabiniers, the Hulans, the Francs, the Louisiana Blues, and the Chausseurs, carefully dressed and equipped, each company looking pitifully small because of its distinctive outfit; but the cheers for these sons, brothers, and lovers were delirious. Next was one of the battalions of free colored, and it was greeted by a great noise from the people in the streets. And last, proudest of all, came Beale's sharpshooters. In the small square this seemed a formidable force.

When the troops were assembled and the cheers had subsided, Jackson handed a prepared address to Livingston, who read it aloud. It praised the troops for their vigor and the citizens of Louisiana for their ardor and exertions. Louisiana might have been an easy prize had the dissident groups which made up its populace allowed their misunderstandings to rule. There were motives of disunion that might have operated on weak minds; but the citizens were strong enough to forget their differences of language and the prejudices of national pride. New Orleans would be saved untouched from the assault of the British.[18]

Those close enough to hear cheered the sentiments and reported them to their neighbors out of earshot, who cheered and reported to those still farther away, and though the words were much altered in transmission, the feeling of confidence and solidarity passed intact through the great crowd.

Then Jackson granted the troops leave to visit their families for the rest of the day. When they reported back, their commanders would have orders for stationing them.[19]

Finally, because of the dire emergency, Jackson declared martial law for New Orleans and environs. Every individual entering the city must report to the adjutant general's office. No one could leave the city without a permit signed by the general or one of his staff. No vessel could leave without a passport from the general or the naval commander. The street lamps would be extinguished at 9:00 P.M., and anyone on the streets afterward without a permit from the general's staff would be arrested.[20]

The troops marched in review and dispersed to join families and friends for a last visit. The crowd overran the square and gradually dispersed. In the excitement little attention was paid, at first, to the declaration of martial law. But Commander Patterson had his freedom to act. He commissioned Lieutenant Charles Thompson to gather a crew for service on the *Louisiana*. Thompson and a squad of marines went along the waterfront, choosing the sturdiest sailors they could find, ordering them to the ship (by signs when they could not speak the language), and promising a bounty.[21]

The city whiled away its last gay Sunday, visiting, drinking, socializing. The horizon of time had closed in, vision for the moment extending no further than the coming battle, bringing a spirit of relaxed freedom. Meanwhile, Jackson arranged his troops. One regiment of the militia he would send to the Gentilly road to reinforce Lacoste's battalion of free colored. The Feliciana dragoons he would also station there, so they would have the freedom of the plain to operate and so they could quickly bring news of a British approach. Two regiments would remain at New Orleans, and he ordered De la Ronde's 3rd Regiment to establish advance posts as far down as Jumonville's plantation. On Villeré's own plantation Jackson agreed to allow Villeré's son Gabriel to command, both to watch ground with which he was familiar and to look after his father's interests. Villeré he then ordered to the Acadian coast, where another regiment of militia had been raised and was waiting to be brought to the front. The militia regiments were rapidly increasing in size as men from back country settlements, boatmen from up river, and settlers from Mississippi Territory volunteered. One visitor from Massachusetts, though a Federalist opposed to this "unnecessary war," caught the excitement and joined. The regulars Jackson would leave at Fort St. Charles near the city, along with Beale's sharpshooters. Morgan's division of militia was at the English Turn to watch the Terre aux Boeufs approach. Morgan wanted more men, but Jackson was now convinced that that was an unlikely point of attack.[22]

Fort St. John seemed to him to be a likely point for the navy-minded British to seek. New batteries had been erected. To man them Jackson sent two newly formed artillery detachments—a company of Baratarians and some New Orleans volunteers. To command them he assigned Lafitte's ablest gunners, Dominique You, a rugged brute who caught Jackson's fancy, and Beluche. Serving in Dominique's company were Jean and Pierre Lafitte. Another company of Baratarians Jackson kept at Fort St. Charles. Also to Fort St. John he sent Plauché's uniformed companies.[23]

To Fort St. Philip, to speed the erection of fortifications, Commander Patterson dispatched Gunboat 65, Lieutenant Cunningham. Major Walter Overton of the regular army, who had just arrived on furlough from Nashville, offered his services, and Jackson sent him to take command of the fort down the river.[24]

The great front seemed well guarded: troops at Bayou Lafourche and Grande Terre; Overton and the artillerymen constructing Fort St. Philip; General Morgan and his militiamen at the English Turn, with a redoubt on Terre aux Boeufs; Chef Menteur guarded by a fort and a small detachment; the Gentilly road manned by Lacoste's colored, a regiment of militia, and the Feliciana dragoons; Fort St. John manned by Major Hughes's regulars, Dominique's and Beluche's artillery, and Plauché's men; Colonel Ross's regulars and three regiments of militia in or near the city, with advanced posts established on the plantations along the river. A division of militia guarded the Baton Rouge district, and a regiment was on the way from the Acadian coast. Marching down the river from Baton Rouge, soon to arrive, was General Coffee and a regiment of Jackson's dependables, the Tennessee volunteers, accompanied by Hinds's Mississippi dragoons; further up the river, now commandeering barges and flatboats to float down, was General Carroll and the other regiment of Tennesseans; and somewhere on the river in the wilderness above Natchez, though nothing had been heard from them, were the Kentucky troops of General Adair. Somewhere on the river, too, was a fleet of barges carrying the weapons and ammunition allotted by the President (less the ones taken by Carroll), making a slow journey as the contractor paused at every riverside village to trade with the frontiersmen who had enjoyed little commerce for the last several months.

To casual observers who had watched the parade in the square and who saw the constant stream of variously uniformed soldiers in and about the town and the frequent arrival and mustering in of new troops, it seemed that the general had gathered an imposing force for the defense of Louisiana. Even careful observers were fooled by the variety of uniform and the nervous shifting of units into overestimating the size of the army. Those who knew, the general and Commander Patterson and their staffs, and who had heard exaggerated reports of the size of the invasion, worried about the smallness of their force, but they did not voice their worry, and both the soldiers in the army and the civilians around the city continued to overestimate. Fifteen thousand came to be an accepted figure for the number of troops. Even people who knew that that must be double the actual size accepted this estimate because they wanted to believe it.[25]

Major Gabriel Villeré, at his father's plantation, mentioned that number to his men. One of them scoffed—ten thousand perhaps, but not fifteen. But young Villeré glared at him. "Fifteen thousand, and more arriving every day," he repeated, and fifteen thousand was tacitly agreed upon among his men as the proper figure.

At Pea Island, General Keane and Admiral Cochrane were much interested in the size of the defending army. They had queried the friends from Pensacola who had come along to share their knowledge of Louisiana, and these hopeful Pensacolans had assured them that there were scarcely any troops at New Orleans, while Colonel Nicholls continued to insist that the slaves and the European citizens would join the British cause. But developments had not borne out their optimism. The presence of a fleet of gunboats in the channel had indicated an awareness on the part of the Americans that an invasion was in progress. The captured sailors had admitted the presence of a constantly increasing army. The people along the coast made various guesses, but all of them seemed sure that the defenders were strong. Some believed that the entire American army had marched from the East. And there were no indications of any insurrections of citizens or slaves.

Doctor Morrell, when he had been allowed to nurse his frustration for a while, was invited to socialize with the admiral's staff, and he was cautiously queried in between the social amenities. The doctor, though he hid his grievance, was considerably peeved, and to make up for the inconveniences he was suffering he spoke confidently of fifteen thousand troops. He bragged too about the general in command, who was, he assured them, one of the greatest military geniuses the world had ever known. General Jackson knew at this very moment every plan that was passing through their minds, and he would have a few surprises awaiting them. They would find him a more formidable, shrewd, and resourceful opponent than the infamous Bonaparte himself.[26]

Keane and Cochrane were not readily fooled. They had expected to find a defenseless, bickering, confused, unprepared country, and they would not easily relinquish their dream. Eagerly they questioned the friendly lake fishermen who came to them. What did the fishermen know about the city's defenses?

The fishermen discussed this question in lively fashion among themselves, but the interpreter reported that they could not agree. One old fellow was convinced that the army was small; he had seen scattered troops, but no more. A young man, though, who had been daily to the city's wharves, was equally sure that there were troops everywhere, stumbling over each other for lack of enough space. The fishermen were also overly eager to please. When the admiral asked questions, they examined their hosts carefully and answered according to what they thought was wanted. They tentatively suggested a large army, and when that seemed to bother the admiral and the general, they reduced their estimate. Cochrane gave up the attempt in disgust, and Keane soon admitted that he knew no more than before. Without that knowledge of the city's state of preparedness, he was unsure how to act.

One point was clear, though. A place had to be selected for landing the army on the mainland and a route chosen for approaching the city. The easiest routes would be the best defended. The fishermen agreed that one route was unfortified and unwatched: the bayou from their village into the swamp, connecting with canals to the plantations of Jumonville, Villeré, and De la Ronde.

It seemed a dream approach. A massive swamp would hide the army in its progress from the lake to the river. The fishermen would be experienced guides who knew that route better than anyone in the defending army. The invaders would suddenly emerge from the swamp to the river plain a few miles below the city and would have good level ground from there to their destination. And around their river camp there would be rich farms to provide horses and forage.

General Keane chose Lieutenant Peddie of the quartermaster corps to accompany the fishermen and explore the projected route. Admiral Cochrane, never on the sidelines, chose the Honorable Captain Spencer, son of the Earl of Spencer and captain of the *Carron*, to explore with Peddie. Eagerly the fishermen departed to guide these two guests around their little domain.[27]

✯ ✯

TWELVE

The British Land

JOHN Coffee arrived with his regiment of Tennesseans and encamped on Avart's plantation some 5 miles above the city, having
covered 135 miles in a little over 3 days. He sent an aide hastening
to headquarters to apprise the general. The men around Jackson
could hardly fail to notice the new bounce in his step and the new
cheer in his voice as he received the news of Coffee's arrival; these
were old friends, men he understood well, while the ways of the
French who had hitherto predominated in his army were sometimes puzzling to him. Too impatient to wait, he rode up to the
camp. He greeted Coffee calmly, but he gazed with a twinkling eye
at the tall, massive frame of the Tennessean, and he gripped his
hand warmly. Coffee returned the greeting with an easy grace, as
though they had parted in Mobile only yesterday.[1]

To Jackson's query about the troops, Coffee replied that they
had had a fine journey and were ready for action. The men cheered
and hailed Jackson as he walked among them, while he waved in
return. They hardly looked like soldiers. Instead of the neat uniforms of the regulars, the gaudy uniforms of the city battalion,
or the Louisiana militia's makeshift outfits, which were clearly
imitations of uniforms, the Tennesseans were casually dressed to
go hunting in the woods. Most of their shirts were dark wool, but
there were different styles and individual fits. Most of the pants

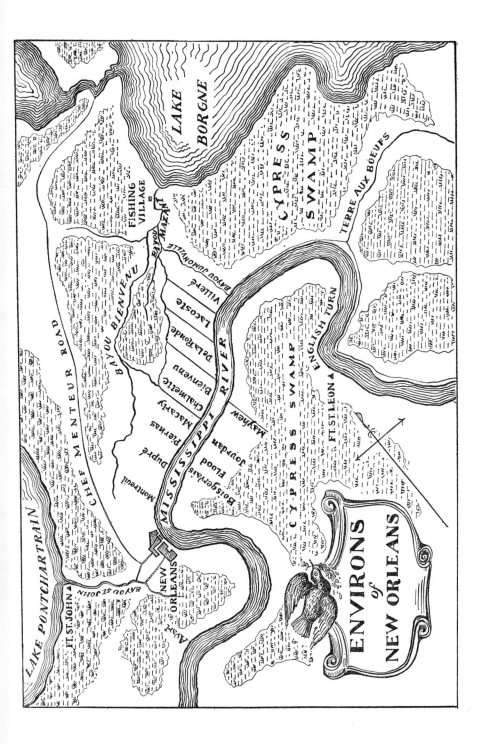

ENVIRONS
of
NEW ORLEANS

were homespun. They wore long, full coats that made them look like Quakers. Headdresses were slouching wool hats or raccoon or foxskin caps. They wore untanned deerskin belts with hunting knives and tomahawks and carried their prized long rifles. As they pitched their tents, prepared their meals, or lounged about, their dingy-colored clothes blended into the landscape instead of standing boldly forth from it like ordinary uniforms. They made no attempt to be military in bearing or speech. Except for the absence of women, the bivouac was more like a suddenly sprouted camp meeting than an army encampment. But Jackson, looking out at the hundreds of backwoods hunters spread irregularly over the fields, felt that at last he had something to fight with.[2]

Coffee accompanied the general and his aides back to headquarters. It was a strange group that rode through town—the gaunt general always pushing out in the lead; the smart, well-dressed lawyer Livingston keeping close at his elbow; the other volunteer aides, Americans, French, and Creole, jostling for position near the general; Humbert, the French exile from the Revolution and the Irish rebellion, sitting stiffly, keeping close behind; near Humbert, Don Juan de Anaya, a Mexican field marshal who had offered his services; then the gigantic, thoroughly relaxed Coffee; and finally Reuben Kemper, ragged, unkempt, and making no attempt to stay close to the others.[3]

From the window of a house where he was visiting, Governor Claiborne saw them pass. He had not learned of the Tennessee arrival until after Jackson had set out for the camp. Now to one of his aides he remarked that the general seldom consulted him; that Jackson had taken into his confidence men whose main object would be to create a schism between the general and the governor; and that it hardly seemed wise to rest the fate of Louisiana upon the loyalty of such men.[4]

There was grumbling in various houses of the city. Some of the planters with lands close to the city worried about the ravages the war would cause; some merchants worried about the fate of their property if the battle should rage through town; and some of these expressed their fears to each other and wondered what they could do. A few felt that perhaps Jackson was too strong-minded, and the destruction, if the British prevailed, would be greater than necessary. One remarked that Jackson made war in the Russian fashion—that he would destroy everything rather than give up valuable prizes to the British. A few wondered timidly if surrender might not be less costly than war.[5]

Some of the Creole and French social leaders, especially the group close to Jean Blanque, the banker, and Magloire Guichard, who had fled the British at Santo Domingo, were wary of Jackson. They trusted his leadership, but he was too forthright and unyielding for them to trust his administrative ability. They were displeased with his declaration of martial law.

The legislator Louaillier, though he disapproved strongly of all talk of capitulation, declared positively that martial law was an unwarranted invasion of the people's rights. He would not recognize its validity, and he withheld privately, though not publicly, his approval of Jackson. America would be better off without such strong commanders, no matter what their military genius. For these views he had the support of Judge Hall of the federal court.

Most of the citizens, however, paid little attention to the martial law and took heart from the military activity and the constant presence of uniforms. To them there seemed to be soldiers everywhere, and they took at face value Jackson's assurance that the British would get no foothold upon Louisiana. The worries of some of the older Creoles did not bother the majority, who were too busily enjoying army life to pay attention. The proudest were the members of the uniformed companies, youth of the city's best families serving under company commanders who were all naturalized citizens, four Frenchmen and an Irishman. But almost as proud were Cheveau's and Ogden's cavalrymen, the Attakapas dragoons, and the Creole and Baratarian artillerymen. Many Creoles had important assignments: Lacoste, Daquin, and Savary (the last two Domingans) commanding the colored troops; Davezac (Domingan), one of the aides-de-camp; Villeré, commanding the 1st Division of militia, and De la Ronde, commanding a regiment; Lieutenant Colonel Peire (Domingan), commanding the 7th regulars; Joseph Bosque, commanding the artillery at Chef Menteur. Nor were the naturalized French any less involved—in addition to the company commanders of the city battalion there were Maurian and Fauché Colson on the staff, Dominique, the Lafittes, Cadet Bonteville, Garrigue Fleaujac, serving cannon; Lefevre, former soldier of Napoleon, serving the mortars; Cheveau and Jean Baptiste Vigne, commanding the cavalry; and "General" Humbert always accompanying Jackson. With a great majority of the able men in uniform, there could be little thought besides preparing for battle.[6]

Meanwhile the citizens, sharing the excitement of the moment, relaxed their usual social rigidity. Officers from the various out-of-town units were welcomed in the homes that customarily presented a forbidding front to the world. Some formed intimacies with the daughters of the houses. Sweethearts from the army received embraces more passionate than they might have ordinarily expected. Impromptu parties bloomed when some of the youths unexpectedly slipped into town.

In the less fashionable quarters there was even freer gaiety as the soldiers were heartily welcomed by townspeople. Some found love with women who were stimulated by anticipation, wonder, and fear. Many found moments of good cheer in the respite before battle.

‡‡‡

The British on Pea Island could only dream of gaiety as they waited in their bleak camp. Only the highlanders, recently arrived, were too proud to display annoyance at this miserable situation. All the troops were ashore but the two West India regiments, which the sailors were currently ferrying toward the base, the poor men as they huddled in the boats carrying on a kind of community dance of shivering limbs and chattering teeth.

Lieutenant Peddie and Captain Spencer sailed on the little fishing smack across the lake to the opposite shore, keeping alert to every mark of the environment. They turned into a bayou which Spencer, after testing the bar, declared navigable for boats of a hundred tons. Half a mile from the mouth of this bayou they found a village of huts. Other fishermen greeted them, talked excitedly to their escorts, and brought blue shirts and tarpaulins to disguise the officers as fishermen.[7]

Then they sailed up the bayou. From the village on they were in swampland, where the ground seemed to slope downward from the banks of the bayou instead of upward, and a short distance away the ground was obviously mushy. There were many large bogs. All the land was covered with reeds taller than a man. Occasionally smaller streams or ditches emerged from the reeds to join with the bayou.

They came to an intersection of Bayou Bienvenu (the fishermen called this bayou Catalan) with another bayou, which the boat entered. This one the fishermen called Bayou Mazant. To Peddie's queries they replied in broken English that Bienvenu went close to the city but became more and more exposed to the view of the Americans, while Mazant led to the river. The land was the same —marshes and reeds stretching menacingly away from the stream.

They passed another bayou, which joined this one and which led, according to the fishermen, to the Jumonville plantation. They passed a canal which led to Villeré's plantation. Then they turned into another canal. After a while occasional cypresses rose above the reeds, and soon they were in a cypress swamp. The air was perfectly still. Overhead moss hung from the branches of the cypresses like the hair of disheveled, weeping women.

Suddenly they emerged from the cypress swamp into the level open fields of De la Ronde's plantation. In the distance, perhaps a mile away, was a high bank stretching along the horizon. Toward this bank was a grove of trees and several houses. To the right and left in the distance near the bank were other groves and clusters of houses. Ditches and fences cut across the fields, which were covered with a stubble that at first looked as though reeds like those of the swamp had been cut down, but which the officers soon realized was the stubble of recently harvested sugar cane. There were scattered stacks of cane in the fields.

It was a refreshing sight of civilization, startling the officers with the suddenness with which it replaced the exotic wood. They walked along the canal, passing the houses and the grove of trees and reaching a road that paralleled the bank. There, seeing that they were unobserved, they climbed the bank.

Below them, its surface well above the fields of the plantation, flowed relentlessly the great dirty mass of the Mississippi River. In the distance was the levee on the other side.[8]

Lieutenant Peddie had found the spot he wanted. To this plantation he would bring the British army. Here beside the great river it could camp before moving up the road to the city. Tents could be pitched in the fields; there would be water and fuel; and the imposing mansion back from the road, nestled among the trees, would serve for the general's headquarters.

Peddie and Spencer returned as they had come. On the entire journey they had not seen a single American soldier.[9]

✝✝✝

When General Keane and Admiral Cochrane received the spies' report, General Keane entertained doubts about the wisdom of the plan. Peddie's route was admirable enough for getting the army to the river, but it would still not be in the city, and from the description of the countryside the route from there to the city would be along a bottleneck of land hemmed in by the river on one side and a morass on the other. Such a terrain impressed the general as being better for defense than offense.

But the admiral received the report enthusiastically. Here was a water route that would allow his sailors to dump the army practically at the doorstep of the city. The enemy had no ships to oppose the movement across the lakes and could not operate in the swamps to impede the movement to the river. It was unfortunate that the nature of the waters made it impossible for him to use his gorgeous fleet, but the barges would do. And once in the cultivated fields along the river the army would have only to storm in stalwart British fashion over the fields to the city. What could be easier than to storm an unfortified city defended by a motley array of discontented citizens and illiterate backwoodsmen? When Keane expressed his doubts, the admiral laughed and said he would take the city with his sailors if that was what the general wished.

The presence of the doughty admiral embarrassed Keane. He felt that his own inexperience was making him timid. It was high time to act, so he made his plans.

All the troops were on Pea Island except the 1st West India. There were barges enough to carry the advance and one other regiment, and Admiral Cochrane had brought up the captured gunboats and some small schooners that could carry two other regiments part of the way. Keane issued his order: The advance and the 4th Regiment were to be in readiness to embark on December 22 at 9:00 A.M., and the whole of the troops would move

· 124 ·

as soon thereafter as possible except the 5th West India, which would remain. The 21st and 44th would be embarked in the gunboats and other vessels and would come to off Chef Menteur Passage two hours before sunset, while the barges pushed ahead. The advance and the 4th would arrive at the landing point, the mouth of De la Ronde's canal, soon after dark on the twenty-second. The troops would land and establish themselves while the barges returned to receive the other regiments. Keane presumed that the 21st and 44th would be landed by an hour before daylight on the twenty-third, together with artillery and reserve ammunition, and the 93rd soon after. The whole would be formed as they arrived into a column of companies at quarter distance right in front and would throw out pickets. No fires were to be lighted after dark; strict silence was to be observed through the night of the twenty-second. Three-pounders would be attached to the advance, and the remainder of the artillery would be put on shore after the landing of the 4th Regiment. Lieutenant Peddie would guide the advance and superintend the landing. Lieutenant Evans would be attached to the 21st, 44th, and 93rd regiments in order to arrange them in the boats which would return from landing the advance. Strictest attention must be paid that the troops enter the canal in a regular succession of companies and regiments.[10]

Through the night the staff worked. The navy planned the embarkation, arranging the boats in a proper order to receive the troops. The army distributed the engineer, artillery, and rocket detachments to the different divisions of troops. Details were smoothed out, orders were prepared and delivered to commanders of boats and detachments. The soldiers huddling on the sandy island committed themselves to sleep. General Keane worried, napped, and dreamed fitfully.

‡‡‡

General Jackson asked for a report on his plan to block the bayous near the river. Above the city many had been filled in, but there was only confusion about what had been done below the city; no one seemed to know who was responsible for carrying out the orders. With his staff and aides the general restudied his maps. They showed an intricate system of bayous in the swampland between lake and river. One good stream approached close to the river above Terre aux Boeufs. Another flowed into Jumonville's plantation. Another flowed behind Villeré, Lacoste, and De la Ronde. And Bayou Bienvenu stretched up through the swamp to a point near the river. As the closest of the bayous, it was the most important.

The general followed Bayou Bienvenu with his finger and touched the spot where it entered Lake Borgne. What was there? Someone remembered that fishermen used that bayou and that they had a village somewhere near its mouth. That point must be watched.[11]

General Villeré's son at the Villeré plantation was ordered to watch the fishing village. He sent in a small boat a sergeant, eight privates, two mulattoes, and a Negro to establish a picket. They rowed up the canal to Bayou Mazant, up Bayou Mazant to Bayou Bienvenu, and along the bayou to the huts of the fishermen, which they found empty. Where the fishermen were they did not know, but the habits of these fishermen seemed strange anyway, so they shrugged it off. They continued to the mouth and in the twilight saw the lake stretching tranquilly to the limit of their vision. Returning to the fishing huts, they looked about at the reedy swamps all around. They seemed to be at the end of the earth, isolated from all human life. They dragged their canoe on the bank, chose one of the huts for their quarters, agreed on the schedule for guard duty, and in perfect confidence prepared to while away the night. War for them was a long way off.[12]

‡‡‡

The twenty-second dawned, damp, grey, and gloomy. The shivering West Indians curiously examined the ice that had formed on small pools. Then the soldiers ate their breakfasts, packed their heavy rolls, and formed for embarkation. The barges beached and the advance piled aboard, first the 85th, then the 95th, then the 4th (properly a part of the second division rather than the advance). The artillery detachment hauled aboard two of the barges two three-pound cannon for the use of the advance. In spite of the carefully worked out details, confusions developed. Squads boarded the wrong barges and had to be shifted to the right ones. Barges took the wrong position and had to be rearranged. Harried officers shouted orders, contradicted each other, consulted superiors. The nine o'clock deadline passed well before the barges had finally moved into the designated lines.[13]

Then the sailing vessels took aboard the 21st and 44th with a similar confusion increased by their attempt to maneuver in water too shallow for them. During the night the busy admiral had brought up still more vessels, and it was found that the 93rd could also be taken aboard.

By 11:30, all being ready, the expedition pushed off. The sailors heaved upon the oars to pull the barges across the water, while beside and behind them the other vessels sailed. The atmosphere became darker, damper, and gloomier, and soon rain fell. As the day wore on, the rain became heavier. Steadily it fell from the dark skies, showing no sign of relenting. The soldiers huddled together on the boats while the sailors pulled grimly.

In the afternoon the sailing vessels began to run aground. One by one they ended their journey, stuck to the bottom. Some struggled free and attempted different courses, but the outcome was inevitable in the shallow waters around Chef Menteur pass. The barges, however, steadily pushed on.[14]

Then the rains ceased. But the drenched soldiers had little respite, for the air became rapidly colder. Damp clothes stiffened with frost. Limbs trembled. With charcoal from their supplies the men built fires in the sterns of the barges and huddled together around the fires. It was a small and temporary comfort; as dark gathered, the fires had to be extinguished according to orders, and the men had to shiver in silence as the sailors steadily pulled them across the water.[15]

‡‡‡

Along the coast at the mouth of Terre aux Boeufs bayou someone sighted three British schooners, apparently trying to make their way through the reefs and shoals into the bayou. The word, after quickly passing among nervous residents of the region, reached the English Turn—the invasion was coming by way of Terre aux Boeufs.[16]

The militiamen reached for their guns and clamored to rush to the attack. David Morgan wondered what to do. At this strategic spot he had to watch the river and Terre aux Boeufs or be ready to double back to the city to fight at Bayou St. John or one of the other approaches. Terre aux Boeufs was one of the important points to cover, but Morgan had visions of the fleet's suddenly sailing around the bend of the river or of a messenger's galloping into camp with orders to march posthaste to the city. He wanted to be ready for any eventuality. If he committed the troops to one approach, he would be unprepared for the other two. So, as the soldiers pressed around him for direction, he fretted, figured, wondered, jumped up as though ready to command, and settled back again with lips pursed and fingers drumming on his knee. At last he sent the troops back to camp, warning them to be ready to move on a moment's notice, and sent a messenger to Jackson to announce that the British had invaded Terre aux Boeufs.

Above New Orleans Carroll's Tennessee regiment floated down the river, pulled over to the bank at Avart's plantation, and happily hailed the troops already encamped there. While they were disembarking and spreading over the fields, Carroll joined Coffee and Jackson at headquarters. He was welcomed by the general as warmly as Coffee had been. When he stood beside his friend Coffee he was dwarfed by the latter's huge form, but he was a stocky, compact man with an erect bearing and a superior air. He listened quietly while the general rapidly surveyed the situation for him, describing the various troops and their positions, guessing about the possible route of the invaders, and warning him that the attack could be momentarily expected. Carroll assured the general that, though they were tired, his troops were ready to move quickly.[17]

The Mississippi dragoons also arrived and galloped proudly through town. They cut a fine figure in their dark blue uniforms faced with scarlet and crossed by white saber belts, and men and women rushed to the balconies to cheer as they passed. The crinkling of the general's eyes and the twitching of his lips betrayed his satisfaction. His army was assembled, and beside him were trustworthy commanders—Coffee and Carroll, Ross, Hinds of the Mississippi dragoons, and Patterson. He was happy too because he felt certain that his wait was almost over. For him it was frustrating to wait. He wanted to act; he knew that there was a certain moment when preparations reached their peak, when waiting and training built up in troops an anticipation and precision that marked them for brilliant performance, and after which they staled; and he suspected that that moment had arrived. Right now the troops were set for a sudden, concerted, devastating movement. Another few days of waiting would unnerve them, make them restless and taut, jealous and suspicious of one another. Jackson longed for a chance to act, and by his calculations the British should be appearing, somewhere, any minute.[18]

At Petites Coquilles Captain Newman's little force anxiously watched for British. At Fort St. John the artillerymen of Lieutenant Wagner and Beluche, Dominique's Baratarians, and Plauché's men anxiously watched and waited. On the Gentilly plain Lacoste watched and waited while his men cleaned and recleaned their equipment and frequently scouted the countryside. On the Terre aux Boeufs bayou a squad of artillerymen nervously scanned the stream and the road ahead of their redoubt. At the English Turn the militiamen fretted for action while Morgan worried about what to do. In the city soldiers and citizens alike listened for news and rumors. Above the city the Tennesseans calmly rested. At Fort St. Philip Major Overton's artillerymen, reinforced by two companies of regulars, a company of volunteers, and Listeau's company of free colored, labored along with the plantation slaves to build, in the mud above and across from the fort, two batteries, to tear down the wooden barracks of the fort that might catch fire, to clear the fort of rubbish, and to mount new guns. At the fishing village Major Villeré's pickets lounged through a dull day, occasionally sending a detail in the canoe out into the lake; and at the plantation the rest of the major's detachment relaxed.[19]

Across the lake the sailors pulled the barges, and the soldiers shivered. From a schooner further out on the lake General Keane and Admiral Cochrane watched the slow movement of their force. In the Gulf another fleet sailed toward the coast, bearing the 7th and 40th regiments, while Sergeant Cooper watched with bored eyes the monotonous flow of the seaweed and listened to the jibes of Corporal Fitzpatrick. Ahead of this fleet raced the *Statira*, carrying General Pakenham and General Gibbs; Pakenham knew that the British should by this time have landed, and it was possible that the city had already fallen, but he hoped he would find Cochrane and Keane waiting for him to direct operations from the start. He hated to take over someone else's campaign if the army was committed to an unfavorable plan, and General Keane, he felt, was too inexperienced.[20]

The oars of the barges dipped rhythmically into the water. Lieutenant Gleig, shivering, sat silently in the darkness, uncomfortably close to his men, listening to the sound of the oars and the mutterings of the soldiers. Remembering the experiences of the last week, he realized that adventure could be miserable ("the reverse of agreeable" he would write in his notebook). Somewhere ahead there was dry land for a decent camp, and sometime in the future there would be the excitement of battle, but now there was cold, wet, and aching muscles. On another boat Quartermaster Surtees suffered from a severe pain in his side caused by remaining so long in a single position. The hours dragged wearily by.

At midnight the boats stopped and cast anchor. As they were close to the bank, Cochrane sent two barges ahead to reconnoiter. The soldiers on these barges sat tight-lipped with muskets ready, and the sailors pulled mutely upon their oars. Only the dipping oars and occasional whispers broke the stillness. At last in the darkness they spied the bank, and they turned to row along it in search of the bayou.[21]

In the fishing hut, eleven men of the detachment slept soundly, rolled in blankets on the beds and floors. One sentinel trod up and down and around among the other huts. He listened to the croaking of frogs and the rustle of the slight breeze among the giant reeds of the marsh. Occasionally, bored, he explored a little way into the marsh, testing the ground. There were uneven spots of solid ground among the mushy patches.

Suddenly a new sound, a sound of splashing, caught his attention. He hurried to the river bank. He could make out the dark lines of a boat coming up the bayou. He ran to the hut, leaped up the steps, one after another shook vigorously the sleeping men, and hoarsely announced, "The British are coming! The British are coming!" They were shocked into consciousness, jumped up, grabbed their guns, and rushed outside. They hid behind the hut while the two British barges rowed past. Then they rushed for their canoe, but the British spotted them, jumped from the barges, and hurriedly surrounded them. Four of the Americans bolted into the canebrake, but the other eight surrendered.[22]

The forward British barge waited at the village while the other returned into the lake to bring up the main force. Keane and Cochrane also came from their schooner in a gig. While the barges slowly filed up the bayou toward Canal De la Ronde, the admiral and the general questioned their prisoners.

They found them amazingly confident. Although some were reticent about answering questions, some willingly spoke of the large army around the city. Several, questioned separately, estimated the army at fifteen thousand—with more arriving daily.[23]

Keane worried. Although he was none too sure of the veracity of these prisoners, he was surprised by their unanimity and confidence. There was at least an excellent possibility that the defending army was a strong one. If so, a clash upon the narrow plain by the river might not dislodge it. Admiral Cochrane, however, scoffed. Even if it was a large army, it was only a medley of untrained men, a mob without discipline, order, or experience. The first strong British attack would explode that mob in all directions.

So Keane carried his worries forward. There was confusion now in the line of barges, which had come to a standstill. Word was passed back that they could not reach De la Ronde's canal. Keane made his way along the bank to the head of the column, at a narrow place in the bayou, to find that since Peddie's journey the water had fallen and the leading barge was stuck to the bottom. Canal De la Ronde was still a mile ahead, but Canal Villeré entered the bayou close at hand.

On both sides of the bayou Keane saw a great stretch of reeds with a narrow stretch of solid land. He ordered the barges to close up to form a bridge down the bayou. The troops would pass over that bridge from one barge to the next to this point, form on the solid ground, and proceed along the canal to the Villeré plantation, where they would camp. While they were forming on the bank, Captain Blanchard would take the engineers ahead to cut a path along the canal through the reeds and to bridge the streams which crossed their way.

In the early morning of Saturday the twenty-third the engineers laboriously cleared the passage, while the 85th, the 95th, and the 4th regiments one by one marched up the bridge of barges and formed along the bank of the bayou. It was a slow march, and day broke well before the troops had landed. Surtees, for one, was "right glad" to stretch his legs.

Blanchard's engineers chopped their way forward, piling up the reeds in particularly mushy spots to make them passable. The marsh extended for about a mile before the reeds gave way to the cypresses. Since there were several small streams running into the bayou, some of the engineers had to make their way forward to the wood to lop branches off the trees for building bridges. In the wood the going was easier, but there were many bogs to which reeds had to be brought for a basket road. Finally the engineers came to hard ground and saw before them the end of the wood, with cultivated fields stretching to the levee.

At last, in midmorning, the troops marched, making their way in single file over the makeshift road through the swamp. It was noon before the 85th and 95th had filed into the swamp and the 4th had formed along the bank to follow. Then the barges rowed and poled their way out of the bayous to the lake and headed back for the next division of troops, while Colonel Thornton's advance proceeded. Three of the escaped American pickets, having become lost and traversed a circle, stumbled out of the swamp to surrender; one still dragged himself through waist-deep mud and towering reeds, uncertain of his direction.

Throughout the march Colonel Thornton was calm and efficient, but General Keane's temper was short under the pressure of constant frustrations. His great desire was secrecy, a sudden surprise appearance by the river and a quick thrust to the city before the Americans knew what had happened. But all signs indicated that he was expected and that the city had prepared an elaborate reception. Now his plans for the landing were wholly awry. By daybreak he had expected his entire army to be formed at the mouth of canal De la Ronde, ready for a precise and orderly march. By noon they should have been on the plain, ready to storm to the city. But it was noon now. Only a third of his troops were landed. This third would have to move to the river and wait there for the rest. It would be another day before he could attack, and by then he would have been observed and the Americans would be ready.

As the 4th began the march into the swamp, Colonel Thornton's advance paused near the end of the wood. Scouts crept forward to observe, reporting back that there were apparently pickets in the mansion. While the rest of the line halted in the wood, the leading companies rushed across the field toward the mansion.[24]

In the mansion, Gabriel Villeré and some thirty men were lounging, talking of the coming attack as though it would always be coming but would never arrive. Gabriel's young brother Celestin was also present, casting admiring eyes at Gabriel's handsome uniform with its epaulets of a major and displaying a hero worship that inspired the older brother to behave with especial bravado and nonchalance.[25]

Hardly did the cry of "British!" ring out before the enemy was there, pouring into the house from all entrances. Gabriel and his men were caught flat-footed without even a chance to reach their guns. Not a shot was fired. Quickly the entire detachment was rounded up, and there they stood in the large parlor, helpless, ringed by armed guards, while the other enemy soldiers searched the house, took possession of the buildings of the plantation, and sent news of their success to their colonel. Gabriel's self-esteem was sadly deflated. Now his young brother's eyes, showing consternation and disappointment, seared instead of inspiring.

Gabriel attempted to relax, offered a cigar to the British sergeant, and tried a few jests with what nonchalance he could muster. There were guards at all the doors. Through the large windows of the room Gabriel could see over the galleries and lawns and through the trees. In one direction the grove reached to a rail fence near the canal. Near that fence, toward the swamp, though he could not see them, he knew there was a cluster of slave huts. In the fields on both sides of the canal there were stacks of sugar cane.

Gabriel's men were standing and sitting disconsolately. The guards, whose dirty and sweaty faces showed great weariness, stood by the doors at rest, apparently secure enough that they were more interested in the countryside than the prisoners. From outside there came the shouts of other soldiers, busily exploring. Inside, almost constantly on Gabriel, there were the hurt, frightened eyes of young Celestin.

Suddenly Gabriel moved, leaping across the room, hurling his body through the window. One leap carried him over the gallery rail to the ground. Swiftly he zigzagged through the trees and slave huts. He vaulted the rail fence, splashed through the canal, and headed for the nearest stack of cane. After the first moment of shocked surprise, a guard was on the gallery and a shot rang out. Then from various spots soldiers appeared, more shots rang out, and several of the British rushed after the fleeing prisoner. But Gabriel had a head start; he had no pack upon his back or clumsy musket in his hand; and he was well fed and rested, while his pursuers were hungry and tired. He made the cypress wood safely and trotted among the trees, sometimes splashing through pools and mudholes, toward town. The British, not knowing how far Colonel Thornton would want them to go, gave up the pursuit when they reached the swamp.

Colonel De la Ronde had ridden down the river that morning to inspect his outposts and his own grounds. He was at his house when Gabriel came out of the swamp with the news of the British arrival. In one of De la Ronde's boats they crossed the river; they borrowed horses from the planter De la Croix, and rode toward the city.

Captain Ducros with a detachment of men was at the Jumonville plantation, just below Villeré's, when the British arrived. His little detachment was obviously too small to resist the invaders, so they watched, prepared to withdraw toward Terre aux Boeufs if the enemy moved their way. From Terre aux Boeufs along the high road came Augustin Rousseau. Stopped by Ducros, Rousseau looked over the situation and decided he would like to make it to the city. Applying the spurs, he galloped down the road past Villeré's. The British, still not settled in their new position, were unprepared for this move, and they fired unsuccessfully at the galloping horse, Rousseau escaping out of their range. By the time he had passed Lacoste and De la Ronde and reached Bienvenu his horse was tired, but at Bienvenu he found a dragoon sick in bed. Borrowing the dragoon's horse, he headed toward the city.[26]

That morning General Jackson had ordered Major Latour and Major Tatum to ride to Terre aux Boeufs in order to check Morgan's report of a British landing at that point. At Bienvenu they met slaves from Lacoste's who excitedly shouted the news that the British were at Villeré's. Tatum turned to hasten to the city, while Latour proceeded cautiously to Lacoste's to investigate.[27]

The news spread quickly among the plantations above and below Villeré's. From below various persons crossed the river and hastened up the opposite bank, spreading the word as they went. From above others hastened up the highroad. In later years there would be claims and arguments about who first carried the alarm to the city, but at the moment the excitement was too great for anyone to fix in his memory just where and how he had heard. To Jackson's headquarters one messenger after another hastened.[28]

The general did not wait to determine who should get the credit. The moment for action was at hand. He ordered the troops to assemble immediately at Montreuil's plantation below the city— the regulars, the militia, and Daquin's colored battalion from Fort St. Charles and various camps across the river and near the town, the uniformed battalion from Fort St. John, and the Tennesseans from Avart's. At 1:55 the alarm gun boomed its warning.[29]

‡‡‡

Colonel Thornton's troops marched to Villeré's and spread over it to establish their camp. The 85th Regiment moved to Lacoste's plantation near the river while the 95th settled in Lacoste's gardens and huts with pickets posted as far as the wood. The little three-pounders which had been brought with the advance were placed near the Villeré mansion. A company was sent down the river to Jumonville's (the American detachment hastily departing before them) and extended across the plantation to the wood to form a rear guard. When the 4th arrived, it was encamped on Villeré's. Keane arrived, and he and Thornton established headquarters at the mansion.

Thornton felt that the troops should advance, after a short rest, toward the city, which was still some seven miles away. This seemed to the general too impetuous an action when he did not yet know what lay ahead of him and had several regiments still to be brought up. The present spot seemed to him a pleasant place to primp for the adventure.[30]

The 85th had marched smartly out of the swamp across the fields, marched happily, after the dismal nightmare of the past week, as though on parade. Company by company they marched along the canal to the highroad, turned right, marched until the whole regiment had made the turn. Then Major Gubbins, commanding while Colonel Thornton had charge of the division, halted them. The pickets were sent ahead, moving leisurely, while the rest stacked arms and established a camp.

Lieutenant Gleig joined Captain Grey, and together they crossed to the levee and climbed it. They stared at the noble river, a mile wide, pouring along. After a long glance at the river they turned to look at the plantation stretching some three-quarters of a mile to the cypress swamp. Near the highroad, about three hundred yards from the levee, was an old levee parallel to the new one. Between the levees was a small shallow pond, and around that pond the troops were settling down, bringing rails torn from fences in order to light fires. Beyond the road on a rise of ground was Lacoste's mansion and groves. To the right, beyond the canal, was a gabled house surrounded by a gallery, nestled among oaks and pecans, with a large grove of orange and lemon trees near and an avenue of trees leading from the gallery to the road—Villeré's mansion, where Thornton had established headquarters. To the left as they stood on the levee they saw the advance guard camping between the two levees near Lacoste's canal. Toward the wood the 95th was settling down, with pickets beside a ditch in advance.

Gleig and Grey sat on the levee, watched the fires leap up, watched the soldiers walk back and forth to the river for water, watched them spread out in all directions over the plantation, watched them return with hams and chickens and wine commandeered from the plantation larders, watched them cook. Soon there was laughing and singing. The two officers walked among the men, accepted the fragrant meat that was offered them, savoring it keenly after the meager fare they had been eating, drank from the wine bottles that were held out, laughed and sang with the rest. Afterward they stretched out on the ground, as many others were doing. Some of the men chose instead to climb the levee and plunge into the cool water of the river to wash away the grime of the march. A bright midday sun warmed them. Men of the 95th came across the fields to enjoy the swimming too.[31]

In contrast to the holiday mood of the British camp, the city was active. Troops gathered quickly at the fort, and as soon as a company was mustered it marched down the road to Montreuil's. From Avart's four miles above the city the Tennesseans came at a fast pace, first Coffee's regiment and then Carroll's, and in an hour's time they were marching through town. From Fort St. John, Plauché's uniformed companies hurried down the bayou and marched through the streets. By 2:30 the 7th regulars, a detachment of artillery with two field pieces, a detachment of marines, and Hinds's dragoons were formed on the road near Montreuil's, ready to go.[32]

Commander Patterson sent word that the *Carolina* was set for action. Jackson formulated his plan of attack: the dragoons and Coffee's regiment would lead, followed by Beale's rifles, Daquin's colored, the regulars, and the uniformed companies. Jackson still felt that this might be only a feint; Governor Claiborne harassed him on that score ("continually riding his hobby," Major Tatum scornfully thought). So he decided to protect the Gentilly road by sending the 1st Division of Louisiana militia to join the troops already there. Carroll's regiment he would also send to the Gentilly road, near the bayou St. John bridge above town. The *Carolina* would drop down the river, and the firing of its guns would be the signal for attack.[33]

While waiting for Coffee, Jackson sent some Feliciana cavalrymen to reconnoiter. The other troops advanced to Canal Rodriguez, between Chalmette's and Macarty's plantations, where from an attic window of Macarty's house Jackson had a view of the plantations ahead: Chalmette, Bienvenu, De la Ronde, Lacoste.

THIRTEEN

Jackson Attacks

IN MIDAFTERNOON five of the eager Feliciana dragoons rode across De la Ronde's plantation in search of the British position. The British pickets on Lacoste's saw them, quickly hid behind the fence between the two plantations, waited until the horsemen were almost upon them, and suddenly fired. One horse fell, its rider hurrying for cover. The other horsemen wheeled and fled.

Hearing the shots, a bugler in the camp sounded the alarm. Men leaped up, rushed out of the river, and ran from their scattered positions for their guns. In great confusion squads, platoons, and companies formed. Soldiers asked each other what was happening; officers tried to locate their positions in relation to other units; commanders discovered men from other units mixing with their own while their own men were unaccounted for. For several minutes there was consternation, wonder, and fear. But when word came from the pickets that it was only a squad of horsemen which had probably lost its way, tensions quickly relaxed. Again the men stacked their arms and returned to their napping, washing, eating, scavenging, and visiting, regaining their good humor. "Americans have never been known to attack," Lieutenant Gleig remarked to his friend Grey; "we need hardly expect them to do it now." Soon the confusion that had attended the alarm was forgotten and glee returned. Again the units became widely dispersed about the plantation and levee. Quartermaster Surtees went forward with a company of the 95th on picket duty. He had purchased an excellent turkey at Villeré's, and he and the company officers had a fine meal at a little house near their post. They washed the turkey down with some grog.

The Felicianans returned to Jackson with two men wounded, having lost one horse. Now Hinds's dragoons, with Colonel Haines, the inspector general, went forward to reconnoiter; but since Jackson was afraid the previous experience might already have alerted the British, the new detachment was ordered to be careful. They hid on De la Ronde's while Haines tried to see the British without much success. When he returned to headquarters he stammered his estimate of the attacking forces—about two hundred, he said. The engineer Latour, who had earlier approached closer and observed more carefully, just laughed; there had been sixteen to eighteen hundred according to his previous estimate.[1]

Carroll's troops and the Louisiana militia had marched toward Gentilly. The rest were formed on Macarty's plantation. Jackson sent orders to Patterson to open fire on the British from the *Carolina* about 7:30, thus signaling to the army to attack. Then he set the army in motion. Down the road across Chalmette plantation marched Coffee's Tennesseans, followed by Hinds's dragoons, Beale's riflemen, Daquin's colored, Colonel Ross's regulars, Plauché's uniformed companies, and a small band of Choctaws.[2]

Jackson waited at Macarty, watching with his glass the *Carolina* across the river. Watching him were Major Robert Butler, the adjutant; Colonel Haines, the inspector general; Major Latour, the engineer; the doctors Kerr and Hood, Captain Reid, Colonel De la Ronde, Pierre Lafitte, Major Villeré, and citizens Duplis and Davezac (Captain Thomas Butler, one of the aides, was in charge in the city; Livingston was with Patterson on the *Carolina;* and the other aides were on various missions). When he saw the boat weigh anchor, Jackson mounted and rode after the army, followed by the staff.[3]

They marched past Chalmette and Bienvenu. At De la Ronde they stopped to deploy. Jackson sent Coffee, Hinds, and Beale toward the swamp to attack the enemy right, with Denis De la Ronde and Pierre Lafitte as guides. The other troops he formed with the 7th regulars (Major Peire) as advance, a detachment of marines on the river bank, the 44th regulars (Captain Baker) to their left, then the artillery with two six-pounders (Colonel Mc-Rea and Lieutenant Spotts), Plauché's companies, Daquin's colored, and the Choctaws. The army was thus divided into two divisions, Jackson's to attack near the river while Coffee's attacked near the wood.[4]

The movement had been made in great silence. There were no sounds but the steps of the men and horses on the soft earth and the occasional low commands of officers. Jackson's troops waited for the signal, while Coffee's moved up the plantation toward the wood. At the ditch between De la Ronde's and Lacoste's, Coffee halted to await the signal. His troops were in advance of Jackson's because the British line ran diagonally from Villeré's canal near the wood to Lacoste's huts near the river.

Meanwhile the *Carolina* dropped quietly down the river with the current, the air being too still to fill the sails. Patterson and Captain Henley stood on deck with Livingston, who pointed out the landmarks as they neared Villeré's. As maneuvering would be difficult without wind, Patterson ordered the anchor to be dropped and a long cable to be attached so the boat could be pulled out of danger when necessary. Then, as the time fixed for the signal approached, the *Carolina* sheered toward the river bank.[5]

The Louisiana militia was marching along the Gentilly road toward the post already guarded by Lacoste's troops. Governor Claiborne entertained excited visions of the main British attack coming against him instead of Jackson, allowing him to be the great hero. But he was disturbed also by the thought that Jackson must know what he was doing, so those closest to Jackson had the best chance of heroism. He remarked to his aide Shaumburg that this might be a plot to keep him in the background. The aide protested that since the Gentilly road was a strategic point, Jackson would commit it only to someone he trusted; but Claiborne nursed his doubts and built in his mind stronger and stronger suspicions.[6]

News of the British landing reached the troops at the English Turn, and as they had done the preceding day, they pressed about General Morgan with urgent pleas to hurry to the front. General Morgan thought of his responsibility to watch the river and Terre aux Boeufs and to be ready to double back to the city. The thought

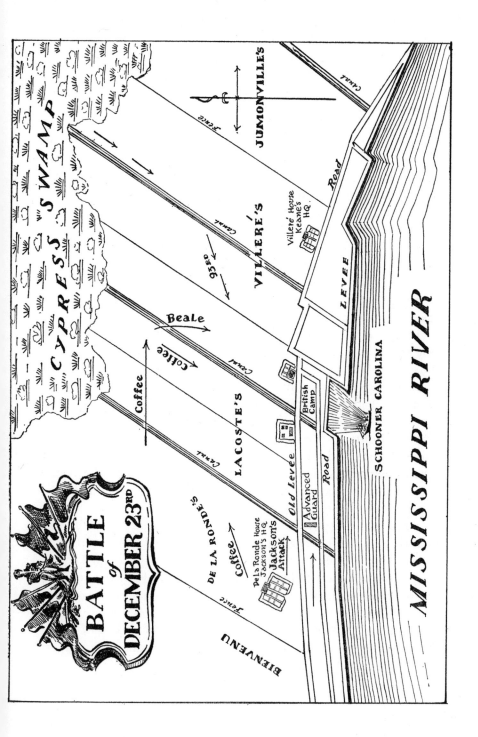

BATTLE of DECEMBER 23RD

CYPRESS SWAMP

JUMONVILLE'S

VILLERE'S

Villeré House
Keane's HQ.

Fence

Canal

95RD

Canal

Beale

Coffee

Coffee

LACOSTE'S

Canal

Coffee

DE LA RONDE'S

De La Ronde House
Jackson's HQ.

Jackson's Attack

BIENVENU

Fence

Canal

Old Levée

British Camp

Advanced Guard

Road

Road

LEVEE

SCHOONER CAROLINA

MISSISSIPPI RIVER

of taking definite action disturbed him because he might act wrongly, but his troops were not now to be denied. As he hesitated he could tell by their faces and voices that his men were losing confidence in him, and some seemed on the verge of disregarding his decision altogether and moving anyway. He hardly ordered them to march; rather he expressed himself ambiguously, and when they marched he set off with them as though he had made the decision. With Colonel Declouet's unit in advance, they headed up the river toward Jumonville's.[7]

In the swamp, the American who had escaped from the fishing village dragged himself from the canebrake to the "trembling prairies," patches of ground covered by tall grass amidst pools of stagnant water. Desperately tired and hungry, he rested in the grass, looking out at the massive swamp that surrounded him, wondering what way he should go. He pulled a few water plants and gnawed on their roots to assuage his hunger.

In the city people collected at various houses to await anxiously the outcome of the battle. Ladies tried to sew to keep their minds busy, but their hands shook at the task and they fidgeted nervously. They talked again in hushed voices of the outrages at Hampton. Someone had heard that the battle cry of the British was "beauty and booty." Some of the ladies displayed to others daggers which they had obtained from their husbands or fathers and hidden in their bosoms, and others, when they saw these, went to their kitchens to get knives. Some, however, laughed gently at the fears of the others and expressed confidence in General Jackson and the men who had gone to fight.

Some of the city's older residents, believing that the city's terrain was the best defense against invasion, felt that Jackson's attack was too rash an action. Their confidence in his judgment shaken, they wondered what would happen to the city if Jackson retreated. Mr. Skipwith of the legislature, after listening to some of these doubts, visited Captain Thomas Butler. Politely he asked the captain what Jackson's plan of defense might be if he were driven out of the city. The captain informed him that it was not his business. To Skipwith it was very much the business of a legislator, but to Butler it was an important military secret. Skipwith departed much disgruntled by his reception.[8]

In the terrible hours of waiting it was difficult to keep still and impossible to be alone. People took to the streets to hurry hither and yon in search of comfort and companionship. In the streets they were stopped by the patrols of the defense company, who protested their presence outside their homes, but because the patrols were uncertain what they should do, the citizens continued on their way with an admonishment that they ought to be indoors.

On Villeré's, as darkness gathered, large fires blazed merrily while soldiers, weary with the frustrations of the journey, felt alive for the first time in weeks. General Keane and Colonel Thornton, discussing their future plans, were almost the only ones who took thought of battle. Admiral Cochrane's barges passed the fishing village and reached the Villeré canal, and the 93rd highlanders and the 21st and 44th regiments leisurely disembarked.

Lieutenant Gleig and Captain Grey had built themselves a little conical hut of stakes and rails. At the door they had a fire going, they lounged in the doorway drinking a bottle of claret borrowed from the Villeré wine cellar, and they felt a pleasing drowsiness steal upon their limbs. They reminisced about the sights they had seen upon this journey to the New World, the ride over the hills of São Miguel, the begging nuns, the dolphins and sharks, the ceremony crossing the Tropic of Cancer, the gay parties at Port Royal, the seaweed on the Gulf. They thought of themselves as experienced world travelers, but they agreed that they were ready to return to England. Grey joshed Gleig about writing a book, while Gleig protested that there could be no book without greater action than had yet transpired. They spoke of rendezvousing periodically in future years to renew this comradeship that had been strengthened with each adventure—training, action in France, the long voyage, the fighting at Baltimore, the misery of Pea Island, and the dreams of glory at New Orleans.[9]

As some of the soldiers on the levee saw the boat coming down the river toward them, they speculated on whether it might be one of the British cruisers that had slipped past the forts to support the attack. A picket hailed the boat but received no answer. As the boat anchored and furled its sails, other pickets challenged, but no sound of a voice came across the water. Speculation grew; could it be an enemy? A few soldiers reached for their muskets. A picket fired, but still no answer came from the boat. More and more curious soldiers climbed the levee to watch. Now, its sails fastened, the boat swung toward the bank. Two or three more muskets fired. Soldiers around the campfires gazed wonderingly at those on the levee. Again a picket shouted a challenge.

The boat swung broadside. Commander Patterson spoke to Captain Henley, and Henley shouted in a loud voice that carried clearly in the still air to the ears of the British, "Now, boys, give it to them for the honor of America!" Immediately the starboard guns of the *Carolina* blazed with a deafening roar. As fast as the men could load they continued to fire.

Round and grapeshot raked the British camp. After the first moment of shocked paralysis, the soldiers scrambled wildly for their muskets. Briefly they attempted to form in regular units, while a few of the more level-headed tried to douse the fires. But as the balls and grape continued to rake them, there was a general dash for the cover of the levee. The artillerymen near the mansion attempted to answer the schooner's fire with some rockets which whistled and flared harmlessly in the air. But the boat's guns trained upon them, and in a few minutes the artillerymen had also taken cover. Along the bank the 85th was pinned to the levee, while the 4th was pinned to cover behind the buildings of the plantation. The 95th hurried to arms and formed in the field.[10]

A company of the American 7th regulars, led by Lieutenant McClelland, drove against the British pickets on the De la Ronde–Lacoste boundary. Behind them drove the rest of the 7th, with the 44th on their left and the marines on their right along the river.[11]

At the first sound of musketry in front, the pickets of the 95th had formed for battle. There was a railing perpendicular to the river in front of the little house where the officers had eaten. Quartermaster Surtees suggested forming behind this railing, but the lieutenant in charge, piqued at receiving advice from a noncombatant, formed the men on the road instead. This upset Surtees, who left these men to their fate in order to join the pickets of the 85th. After climbing a fence and entering a garden, he suddenly spied a body of Americans close at hand. Quickly he hid, and when they passed he crossed the garden rapidly. At the other end he met a sergeant of the 95th, and the two of them "took to their heels like heroes," running toward the main camp.[12]

The pickets fell back, while Colonel Thornton hastily joined his regiment, located what officers he could, and ordered them to get their men into the field to oppose the attack. The darkness was complete, clouds having suddenly obscured the stars and the crescent moon. Still the guns of the schooner thundered, but they were firing by guesswork, and the officers gradually impressed their men with the greater danger of the attacking army. Order was impossible, the companies having been hopelessly scattered along the levee. Officers gathered together what men they could, left the river bank, and hurried into the field.[13]

Gleig and Grey, still together, gathered some thirty men, forded the pond near the bank, added more men they found wandering about, and made their way at an angle across the field toward the action. They heard the rattle of musket and rifle fire in different directions, the steady booming of the schooner's guns, and the screams and groans of wounded. Their own horizon was a small one, a space of gloom interrupted by the dark shadows of canestacks. Occasionally they stumbled unexpectedly into and out of a ditch.

Ahead Gleig could make out a line of men approaching, and he caught Grey by the arm to stop him. "Enemy!" he said.

"That can't be the enemy," Grey returned. "It's another squad of the 85th." He shouted a challenge. The line of men, only barely visible, paused, but no answer to the challenge came.

"It's the enemy. Let's fire," said Gleig.

"No, no. We can't massacre our own men." Again Grey's challenge rang out sharply in the night air. This time a volley of musketry answered him. "They have us wrong," Grey said. He walked forward, waving his arm, shouting, "We're British! Don't fire! We're the 85th!" Several men cautiously followed him. Another volley rang out, and one of the men fell to the ground, clutching an injured arm. The others, except Grey, stopped and dropped to their knees.

Gleig, running forward, grabbed his friend again by the arm. "You fool, they're enemy!"

"They can't be."

"We'll, we'd better find out." Gleig dragged him to the shelter of a canestack, their men following. The two officers crept forward along the stack to the other edge and strained to see in the darkness. Although they could make out a few figures in a line in the field, it was impossible to tell the color of their uniforms. "They're Americans," Gleig said.

"They can't be," his friend repeated. "It's impossible for Americans to be this far forward. The battle's over there to our left, way across the field. Maybe this is a squad of the 95th coming down from the woods."

"Well, they're firing at us. You keep half the men behind this stack while I try to circle around them with the rest." Grey approved this plan.

So they parted. Gleig and his men cautiously withdrew toward the wood. Soon they found another squad of British coming from Villeré's, and with this reinforcement they turned upriver, climbed a fence, and stumbled across the field until suddenly a squad of the enemy was before them. Both sides fired, then closed, jabbing with bayonets, swinging rifles, and finally grappling. Gradually the enemy retreated.[14]

Thus it went. Throughout the fields near the river the Americans pushed against the British, gradually in the smoke and darkness losing contact with other units and engaging in scattered brawls. At first the British near the river fell back, but as they formed larger and larger units they stiffened, and a stalemate developed with each group of men on both sides isolated from the rest of its army.[15]

To individual units it seemed only a wild melee with the line of combat vaguely defined, the enemy suddenly appearing, exchanging fire, closing to battle with bayonets and fists, and one or the other group finally escaping in the darkness. To the commanders behind the lines, keeping messengers constantly on the go, there was somewhat more shape to the battle. Jackson saw his line advance, stop, move forward on the right near the river, recede on the left near the road under heavy British fire. Daquin's men, after a sharp advance, were attacked fiercely; Jackson rushed the 44th regulars to their support and pinned down the line at that point. Keane, too, after the first minutes of complete confusion, learned something of the state of his line. It was highly irregular, zigzagging across the plantation without any discernible order of battalions and companies, except for the 4th in the rear. Of the

American strength he was unsure, but his observers reported seeing so many different uniforms that he thought it great.[16]

Meanwhile Coffee's troops had advanced rapidly across Lacoste's plantation. The ground was so intersected by ditches that Hinds's dragoons, unable to ride in the darkness, were left behind with Coffee's horses, while the dismounted troops proceeded, Beale's riflemen near the swamp and the Tennesseans to their right. They pushed the enemy pickets back toward the main body. Then, hearing the vigorous fire near the river, Coffee wheeled his men at the boundary of Villeré's and advanced toward the river. Firing on this flank of the battle was much less than on the other, as both the Tennesseans and Beale's sharpshooters were careful of their targets. Occasionally they spotted British sentinels, whom they regularly picked off. Down the plantation they marched until, near Lacoste's slave huts, they reached the right flank of the enemy. From the cover of the huts the enemy opened fire, but the Tennesseans pushed on until the two units met in close battle. The British swung their muskets as clubs, but the backwoodsmen leaped upon them with knives and tomahawks. After a brisk defense the British retreated from the huts to Lacoste's grove, where new detachments from the river bank joined them.

Coffee paused to send word to Jackson of his position. His right was in Lacoste's slave huts, but in the wheeling movement his line had become considerably extended diagonally across Lacoste's and into Villeré's. Beale's riflemen, on the extreme left, had skirmished with squads of the 4th throughout the advance.[17]

Now a heavy fog descended upon the field, combining with the smoke and darkness to reduce vision until it was almost impossible to distinguish at a few yards friend from enemy. Extreme confusion developed. The battle line was irregular and formed by separate detachments. On Lacoste's near De la Ronde's between the river and the highroad, Jackson had a solid line and Thornton had collected enough of the 85th to oppose him with a solid line, but diagonally from that line to Lacoste's houses and grove there were various detachments. Behind the houses and grove Coffee's troops formed another line at right angles to Jackson's, with the 85th ahead of him and the 95th to his left.[18]

A strong squad of British attacked Jackson's guns on the highroad, but the marines and the 7th regulars hurried forward to oppose it. Jackson himself rode to the scene, urging on his men, and they pushed forward to repulse the attack. The artillerymen hauled the cannon out of danger.[19]

At the left of Jackson's line, the 44th and Plauché's men became separated, so that the left of the 44th extended in front of the right of the militia. In the darkness and fog the militiamen mistook the 44th for the enemy and fired a volley before the major hurried up to repair the error and restore the broken ends of the line.[20]

The 21st and 93rd highlanders had begun to arrive from the swamps and were joining the 95th in an effort to locate and oppose the left of the American line. Major Mitchell of the 95th, hastening between units of his regiment, saw a body of men approaching. He made out dark shirts which looked like the uniforms of the high-landers. He called out, "Are those the 93rd?" and someone answered, "Of course." He walked forward until suddenly an officer stepped up, clapped him on the shoulder, and announced, "You're my prisoner." Major Mitchell saw too late that he had mistaken hunting shirts for uniforms. Grumbling and cursing, he followed his guard toward the American camp. When an American officer offered him a change of linen to serve during his imprisonment, he replied haughtily, "My own baggage will be brought to me in a few days." [21]

Under orders from Jackson, Coffee wheeled his troops again and moved upriver toward the left of Jackson's division. This movement caught Coffee's own left by surprise, and Beale's rifle-men and certain detachments of Tennesseans lost contact with the rest. Colonel Dyer, attempting with the Tennesseans to restore contact, came upon a line of men that Dyer took to be Coffee's. He was challenged—"Who are you?" "The second division of Tennesseans," he called back. Suddenly, realizing by the silence that met his reply that he was amidst the enemy, he ordered his men to retire toward the swamp. As they retreated the British fired and rushed. Colonel Dyer's horse, felled by a musket ball, pinned the colonel to the ground. "Halt and fire!" he shouted. Quickly his men dropped to the ground and fired at the advancing British, checking them. Struggling free, Dyer managed to retreat with his men to the safety of the swamp.[22]

Captain Donelson had a similar experience. Finding his company isolated, he halted at the end of a large garden. After a long, tense wait for news from the rest of the army, he discovered a body of troops approaching. When they were hailed, their officer identified them as "General Coffee's men," but when they were allowed to come closer, the same officer suddenly commanded, "You damned Yankee rebels lay down your arms!" "Be damned if we do!" Donelson shouted back. His men fired immediately, and Donelson led them in a run to their right until they finally rejoined Colonel Williamson's regiment. He had lost three men killed and three captured.[23]

Beale was stranded by this retreat of the Tennesseans between him and Coffee's main body. His company advanced determinedly into the British camp near the Villeré slave huts, scattering various squads of the 4th, until Beale suddenly realized that he was isolated and surrounded. Then his men scattered in squads to fight their way out however they could. Some made it, but some were captured. One squad, after working toward the swamp until it was seemingly out of danger, found a line of men advancing through the fog. Thinking by their dark coats that they were Tennesseans, the sergeant called out, "Where's the first division?" The answer came in a heavy Scotch accent—"Here they are!" and the line of highlanders quickly surrounded the Americans.[24]

At Villeré's mansion General Keane paced the floor and listened to conflicting reports of advances and retreats, widely scattered skirmishes, hand to hand fighting with tomahawk-wielding backwoodsmen. The battlefield now seemed to him to be wholly disorganized, and he had not the slightest idea what orders might straighten it out. To an aide he exploded in exasperation, "What kind of fighting is this?"

Jackson's line was also so twisted that it was dangerous to try to move it forward in the darkness and fog. Coffee's division was exposed to the *Carolina*'s fire. Jackson knew too that British reinforcements were coming steadily from the swamp. So he ordered his troops to withdraw and camp for the night along De la Ronde's canal. Firing gradually subsided as first the right division and then Coffee's obeyed and formed a line behind the canal, with Hinds's dragoons covering the left flank. The *Carolina* ceased firing and pulled itself by its cable across the river.[25]

Morgan's militiamen, spurred by the roar of the battle to a rapid march, reached Jumonville's. As they approached Jumonville's canal, they came upon a British picket, which took cover behind the canal. Morgan ordered his men to form a line in the field behind a fence, a movement which caused considerable confusion. Then he puzzled over the situation. Darkness and fog made it difficult to ascertain the enemy's strength, and the sounds of the battle had now practically ceased. While his men lay on the ground awaiting orders, the officers discussing fruitlessly what to do, Morgan remained undecided whether to move on, remain, or go back.[26]

Quiet flowed over the field, leaving the British suddenly exhausted after the wild surge of the battle. Realizing that the attackers had withdrawn, Colonel Thornton drew the 85th back to Villeré's and restored his companies to order along a line across the field that joined a similar line of the 95th and 93rd. On both sides the men settled down to sleep as best they could while pickets anxiously watched for a movement by the enemy.

Lieutenant Gleig had fought steadily in the field and among the huts, sometimes driving enemy detachments back and sometimes retreating himself. Now as the troops moved into their proper positions, he went in search of his friend Grey. For some time no one that he queried could help him, but at last he found an officer who directed him to the canestack where they had separated. Beside this stack Gleig found his friend, lying awkward and stiff, a pool of coagulated blood under his mangled head. Exhausted, drained emotionally as well as physically, Gleig sat on the ground, shivering. After a while he stretched out beside his dead comrade, trying to sleep while visions of bloody horrors danced through his mind.

The battlefield was quiet, but not the Villeré mansion. There all available candles burned while the wounded were carried in, dazed, unconscious, groaning, or screaming, and the doctors and their assistants worked busily to treat their wounds and make them as comfortable as possible. By 2:00 A.M. this task was completed, and all in the British camp who could were sleeping.[27]

At 3:00 A.M. General Morgan decided he had best return to his station at the English Turn. Some of his men were so tired that they fell out along the way, but the rest dragged themselves back along the river. At 4:00, after a long debate with himself about renewing the attack in the morning, Jackson decided not to play so deep a game of hazard. He consulted his engineers and decided to establish defenses at Macarty's two miles upriver. Arousing his troops, he returned to the Rodriguez canal, behind which a new line was formed from the river to the swamp. As the fog lifted, a sharp frost ensued.[28]

With dawn, Commander Patterson came on deck to see if the *Carolina* could be moved upriver. But he found a light breeze from north-northwest and a strong current which resisted Captain Henley's efforts to warp the boat upstream. An inspection showed that many musket balls had lodged in the bulwarks, masts, and topmasts, but little damage had been done to the hull, sails, or rigging. Since the boat could not be moved to safety, Patterson opened fire on the British camp, again forcing the soldiers to the shelter of the levee, buildings, and trees.[29]

Jackson counted his losses. Lieutenant McClelland of the regulars had been killed in the first assault. Lieutenant-Colonel Lauderdale, Captain Pace, and Lieutenant Brooks of Coffee's regiment had also been killed, together with 3 sergeants, 1 corporal, 15 privates, and 1 artilleryman. Wounded were Colonel Piatt, quartermaster, 3 of Coffee's colonels, 3 captains, 4 lieutenants, 1 ensign, 1 musician, 26 men of the 7th, 24 men of the 44th, 36 Tennesseans, 9 of Plauché's men, and 7 of Daquin's colored—24 killed, 115 wounded, and 74 officers and men of Coffee's division missing. Total casualties were 213.[30]

General Keane, on the basis of the fierceness of the battle, the number of American prisoners taken, and his estimate that the enemy force amounted to five thousand, guessed the American casualties at five hundred and so noted in his official report. His own losses included Captain Johnstone and Lieutenant Sutherland of the 4th, Captain Conran of the 21st, Captains Grey and Harris of the 85th killed, along with 2 artillerymen, 3 men of the 4th, 2 of the 21st, 11 of the 85th, and 23 of the 95th. Wounded were Lieutenant De Lacy Evans, deputy assistant quartermaster general (who had so often had horses shot out from under him in battle), 11 other officers, 7 artillerymen, 14 men of the 4th, 11 of the 21st, 63 of the 85th, 1 of the 93rd, and 59 of the 95th—46 killed, 167 wounded, and 64 officers and men missing, including Major Mitchell of the 95th. Total casualties were 277.[31]

In the frosty dawn Lieutenant Gleig arose and returned to his company. As he wandered through the field in the early light he looked at the dead strewn about in grotesque postures with ghastly wounds caused by blows and gashes. He had seen death before, but always from bullets that had caught the victims by surprise. Now faces were distorted by hate, rage, and pain. They lay on the ground, friends and enemies, in little heaps where struggles had suddenly erupted.

Choosing three men, he returned to the canestack, where when he again saw Grey he felt a pain that had been suspended during the first shock of the preceding night. Now he could not help weeping, and tears continued to blur his vision as his men carried Grey's body to the Villeré garden and buried it in a shallow grave. Then Gleig visited the mansion, walking among the wounded crowding the rooms, listening to their groans, curses, and prayers. Some lay motionless on their straw beds. Some struggled to move, shrieking with pain at the effort. Some were hysterical. One had been shot through the windpipe, and his breath had dilated him to such a size, with his eyes hidden by his cheeks, that his face had lost all resemblance to a human countenance. In one small room Gleig found several officers whom he knew. One, shot in the head, was gasping and insensible. Another, shot in the stomach with the ball lodging in his backbone, was intermittently screaming and gnawing his blanket.[32]

Outside again in the field, war turned Lieutenant Gleig's stomach.

☆ ☆

FOURTEEN

The Treaty of Ghent

Across the ocean, two groups of diplomats met on December 24 in the city of Ghent to sign in triplicate the treaty which would restore (upon principles of perfect reciprocity) peace, friendship, and good understanding between His Britannic Majesty and the United States of America.[1]

The negotiations had been long and frustrating. In September, 1813, Great Britain agreed to negotiate, and in January, 1814, America agreed. America sent to Ghent as her representatives John Quincy Adams, James A. Bayard, Henry Clay, Jonathan Russell, and Albert Gallatin, citizens of the several states. England sent the Right Honorable James Lord Gambier, Admiral of the White Squadron of His Majesty's fleet; Henry Goulburn, Esquire, Member of the Imperial Parliament and undersecretary of state; and William Adams, Esquire, Doctor of Civil Laws. But the citizens on the one hand and the lord and esquires on the other found that their views about justice and perfect reciprocity were far apart, and most of the year was frittered away in fruitless correspondence. While the British awaited news of victory in their Baltimore, Great Lakes, and New Orleans campaigns, they showed little inclination to relax their idea of justice, and the Americans were almost ready to give up in despair.[2]

But on November 10 the Americans, taking a plunge, submitted a prospective treaty of peace containing fifteen articles. It was proposed that all territory and possessions taken in the war by either party be restored to the other; that certain dates be fixed for the cessation of hostilities in various parts of the world, depending upon the difficulties of communication; that each party agree not to use Indians in any future wars; that each party exclude from naval or commercial service all seamen who were citizens of the other; that in future wars with a third party, vessels of a neutral sailing to a belligerent port without knowledge of a blockade should not be detained, and a blockade should not exist unless there were enough stationary ships near to make entrance an evident danger; that Britain indemnify the United States for illegal seizures of vessels during the French war; and that certain disputed boundaries be determined by three commissioners, one to be appointed by each nation and the other to be chosen by lot. The first of the disputed boundaries involved islands in Passamaquoddy Bay, and the second involved land around Lake Superior and Lake Huron.[3]

Since this document embodied the basic American demands, there was little chance of its acceptance, but at least it provided something to work on. During the dreary November days that followed, the American commissioners sat around impatiently, getting on each other's nerves. The British commissioners, they knew, could make no move without consulting their foreign office —they had no latitude for action, as did the Americans, but were present only as a kind of long-distance mouthpiece for the cabinet. The Americans, although they had difficulty agreeing with each other, were considerably freer to make decisions. So they waited, ready to go home if the reply should be too unfavorable.

But news from America had not been so sanguine as the British War Office had expected. First had come a report of the failure at Baltimore and the death of General Ross, and a few days later had come a report of the American victory on Lake Champlain. From France, too, came disconcerting evidence of a possible renewal of the European conflict. So the British replied. They returned the suggested treaty with marginal corrections—the framework, at least, they accepted. Some of the changes involved words: "persons or places" was to be changed to "places or persons"; "taken by either party from the other" was to be changed to "belonging to either party and taken by the other"; "immediately" for the cessation of hostilities was to be changed to "after the exchange of ratifications as hereinafter mentioned"; and to "forthwith restored" was to be added "as far as may be practicable." Instead of a commission of three to settle disputed boundaries, one to be chosen by lot, a commission of two was substituted, with any differences to be adjusted by the arbitration of some friendly sovereign or state. The articles about the use of Indians in war, impressment, illegal seizure, blockades, and indemnity were simply labeled "inadmissible." A new article was suggested, that prisoners of war pay debts contracted during captivity before being released. But one bombshell was tucked into the treaty: "It is further agreed, the subjects of his Britannic majesty shall, at all times, have access from his Britannic majesty's territories by land or inland navigation, into the aforesaid territories of the United States to the river Mississippi, with their goods, effects, and merchandise, and that his Britannic majesty's subjects shall have and enjoy the free navigation of the said river." Britain was to have free use of the great river. Henry Clay, the Westerner, roared in disapproval. He was ready to pack his bag immediately; but John Quincy Adams, the Easterner, saw nothing to be so concerned about. At least the framework of the treaty was there, and the negotiations could be kept alive. After considerable bickering, the delegation reached enough accord to return the document to the British with new proposals.[4]

They consented to the change of date for the cessation of hostilities, it being understood that measures would be adopted for a speedy exchange of ratifications. They agreed to the new article about prisoners and to the system of arbitration, suggesting that a time be fixed for the reaching of a decision by the commissioners. They "declined to insist" upon their suggestion about the Indians, or upon impressment, illegal seizure, and blockade, but they wished to discuss indemnity for vessels and property in port when war was declared. In omitting impressment and illegal seizure from the treaty, they wished it understood that the rights of both powers on the subject of seamen and the claims of citizens to indemnities for seizures should not be affected or impaired by the omission.

"In forbearing to insist," they wrote, "upon the discussion of subjects deeply involving interests important to their country, and upon which the undersigned view the proposals offered by them for consideration as founded on principles the most moderate and conciliatory, they give the strongest evidence of the anxious wish of their government that the negotiation should be brought to a happy issue." They requested a conference.

On November 30 the British commissioners sent a note in which they fixed a conference at the Chartreux at twelve o'clock, December 1. "The undersigned," they wrote, "request the American plenipotentiaries to accept the assurance of their high consideration." [5]

Through most of December the negotiations continued, sometimes in long sessions around a conference table at the Chartreux, sometimes in notes handed back and forth. They found at the first conference that there were a good many points they could agree on. Most of the British changes in wording the Americans were willing to accept. One the Americans objected to—territory, places, and possessions "belonging to either party and taken by the other," they felt, should read, as originally proposed, "taken by either party from the other." Although it seemed unimportant on the surface, a major issue was involved. There were certain islands that the British, having seized, would not return because the British would claim that these islands did not "belong" to the Americans; but if the treaty read "taken by one from the other" they would have to relinquish them because the Americans had been in possession even if their ownership could be questioned. The British saw no reason why they should give up possession of these islands until ownership was legally established. And so the commissioners hemmed and hawed about the wording until finally the British reserved the American proposal for consideration by their government.

The Americans were willing to accept the British plan for arbitrating disputed boundaries, but they suggested that a time limit for awarding a decision be established. This the British objected to. About the wording of these articles describing a commission for arbitration some discussion arose. The British had suggested, to save constant repetition, "as in many of the preceding articles contained." The Americans proposed "any" for "many." The British suggested "as in the latter part of the fourth article is contained." Agreed.

In naming the disputed boundaries to be arbitrated, the Americans had described one as involving ownership of some islands in "the bay of Passamaquoddy." The British had changed this to "the bay of Fundy." Now the Americans suggested that this be worded "several islands in the bay of Passamaquoddy, which is part of the bay of Fundy, and the island of Grand Menan, in the said bay of Fundy." Agreed.

In the article about the cessation of hostilities, blank spaces for the time limits in various parts of the world had to be filled in. The Americans proposed 15 days in the Channel, the North Seas, the Atlantic Ocean to the equator, and the Mediterranean; 2 months in the Atlantic to the latitude of the Cape of Good Hope; and 3 months elsewhere. The British proposed 12 days on the coasts of North America from 23° north latitude to 47° north latitude eastward to 65° west longitude; 30 days for the Atlantic east to the entrance of the British channel and south to the equator; 30 days for the Gulf of Mexico and the West Indies; 40 days for the British channel, the North Seas, and the Mediterranean; and 150 days elsewhere. The American commissioners reserved the British proposal for further consideration.

Then they attacked the British proposal for free navigation of the Mississippi River. John Quincy Adams, the New Englander, had a bombshell of his own to counter the one the British had dropped. He proposed that inhabitants of the United States should enjoy the liberty to take, dry, and cure fish in places within the jurisdiction of Great Britain. If this right to Canadian fisheries were granted to Americans, navigation of the Mississippi would be free and open to the subjects of Great Britain, and they would be allowed access to the river from some place selected within England's territories upon payment of the same duties payable on importation into the Atlantic states and conforming to the custom house regulations. This proposal the British reserved for consideration.

The only other issue was indemnification for ships in British ports at the outbreak of war. The Americans obstinately insisted on this indemnification, while the British obstinately resisted. On and on they wrangled.

On December 10 Lord Gambier had a new change in the wording of the preamble to suggest. Where the commissioners for each nation were listed, he wished "the right honorable James Lord Gambier, admiral of the White Squadron of his Majesty's fleet" to read instead "late admiral of the White, now admiral of the Red Squadron." The Americans agreed.

The British wished also to propose a new article on the slave trade, asserting that "the traffic in slaves is irreconcilable with the principles of humanity and justice," and that since both nations were desirous of continuing efforts to promote its entire abolition, both would exert every means to do so. They wished also to include in the treaty a provision that citizens of each nation could sue in the courts of the other for the recovery of estates, rights, properties, and securities due them by the laws of the country in whose courts they should sue. Both proposals were received by the Americans for consideration.

Then the Americans proposed a new time schedule for the cessation of hostilities: 12 days to 50° north latitude and 36° west longitude instead of 47° and 65° as proposed by the British; 30 days for the British and Irish channels in addition to the Atlantic and the Gulf as stipulated by the British; 40 days for the Baltic as well as the Mediterranean; 60 days for the Atlantic from the equator to the Cape of Good Hope; 90 days for the rest of the world south of the equator; and 120 instead of 150 days for other seas. This compromise the British agreed to.

They discussed again the fisheries and the navigation of the river. Now the British proposed that the Americans retain rights to the fisheries "in consideration of a fair equivalent" and that the British receive free navigation of the Mississippi "in consideration of a fair equivalent." They would not, that is, consider these two rights as equivalents of each other.

Much of the treaty was settled. Argument boiled down to a few key points, but as the number of debatable issues decreased, the obstinacy of each side on the other issues grew. And while they crawled slowly toward agreement, the two armies in Louisiana drew closer and closer together.

On December 14 the American commissioners sent a note explaining why they objected to altering "territory taken by either party from the other" to "territory belonging to either party and taken by the other." Such an alteration would allow one party to judge whether territory taken by him during the war did or did not belong to the other. That would be no way of establishing any permanent peace. The Americans would be willing to except the

Passamaquoddy islands from the immediate return of property if they did not fear that such an exception would be construed as an implied admission that Britain's claim was better. Therefore they prepared a new clause for the treaty, excepting those islands from the provisions of the original article but stating that this exception would not affect the American claim and that temporary possession could not be converted into permanent occupancy.

To the eighth article, about navigation of the Mississippi, use of Canadian fisheries, and "a fair equivalent," the Americans objected, suggesting that nothing at all be said about these subjects. The new article about the slave trade they were willing to accept. The article about citizens suing in the courts of the other seemed unnecessary.

They suggested that a time limit be established for deciding the issue of the Passamaquoddy islands. If the issue should not be settled by that time, they wanted the islands to return to the country in possession at the beginning of the war.

They were ready to agree in general terms about all other subjects not yet adjusted. The differences between the two parties were now small: possession of the Passamaquoddy islands, which the new proposal might settle; navigation of the Mississippi and use of the fisheries, which could easily be omitted; and an unimportant article about citizens suing for recovery of property.

On the twenty-second the British commissioners replied. They objected to establishing a time limit for the settlement of the Passamaquoddy dispute, feeling that the American government should be satisfied with a declaration that His Majesty's government intended to do everything possible to obtain a settlement without loss of time. They explained also that the article about navigation of the Mississippi and the use of the Canadian fisheries had been offered to attain the object of the amendment tendered by the Americans on the first (ignoring the fact that they had been the first to broach the question of navigating the river). They were willing to omit this article. Would the American commissioners meet with them on the morrow?

On the twenty-third the two nations again sat down at the conference table. The Americans professed themselves ready to accede to the propositions of the last note. Both parties agreed to certain alterations in wording: "after the exchange of the ratifications" became "as soon as the treaty shall have been ratified by both parties"; "whatsoever" became "without exception"; "taken by either party from the other" was restored with the addition of "excepting only the islands hereinafter mentioned"; "exert every means in their power" became "use their best endeavors." The various articles were renumbered. The British urged their proposed article about suits of law, but the Americans resisted, and it was omitted.

So on December 24 the treaty restoring between His Britannic Majesty and the United States of America (upon principles of perfect reciprocity) peace, friendship, and good understanding was signed in triplicate in behalf of the former by the Right Honorable James Lord Gambier, late Admiral of the White, now Admiral of the Red Squadron of His Majesty's fleet, Henry Goulburn, Esquire, Member of the Imperial Parliament and undersecretary of state, and William Adams, Esquire, Doctor of Civil Laws; and in behalf of the latter by John Q. Adams, James A. Bayard, Henry Clay, Jonathan Russell, and Albert Gallatin, citizens of the United States. Hostilities by sea and by land were to cease; territory, places, and possessions taken by either party from the other were to be restored with the exception of several islands in Passamaquoddy Bay and the island of Grand Menan in the Bay of Fundy; and archives, records, deeds, and papers were to be restored. After differing periods from 12 to 120 days from the date of the ratification by both parties, vessels and effects taken on the various seas of the world were to be restored. Prisoners of war were to be restored upon their paying the debts contracted during their captivity. Commissioners were to be appointed by each government to attempt to establish the boundary from the mouth of the River St. Croix to the Bay of Fundy, to survey the boundary from the source of the River St. Croix to the River Iroquois, to settle claims to the islands of the Great Lakes, and to determine the boundary from Lake Superior westward; upon the failure of these commissioners to agree, the disputes would be submitted to arbitration (but no time limit for agreement was mentioned). Expenses of these deliberations would be jointly defrayed, and if any islands changed hands as a result, previous grants of land would be valid. Both countries would end hostilities with Indians and restore possessions, rights, and privileges previous to 1811 if the Indians agreed to friendship. Both nations were to use their best endeavors to abolish the traffic in slaves. The ratifications of the treaty were to be exchanged at Washington with all practicable dispatch.[6]

The American commissioners formally declared that the rights of both parties on the subjects of impressed seamen and indemnifications for ships seized illegally were not to be affected or impaired by the omission of provisions in the treaty about them. War would cease, and the relationship of the two countries would become just what it was before the war began.

Mr. Baker, secretary to Lord Gambier, and Mr. Carroll, one of the secretaries of the American commissioners, embarked immediately in the British sloop of war *Favorite* to carry the treaty to London. Mr. Hughes, another secretary to the American commissioners, embarked for America with another copy in the schooner *Transit*.[7]

The war was over, and the combating armies must be so informed.

☼ ☼

FIFTEEN

Plans for Attack and Defense

GENERAL Keane awoke on December 24 as from a nightmare. But
lest he conclude that the horrors of the preceding night had only
been imagined, he had the evidence of reality about him. The
rooms of the mansion were crowded with the wounded, and the
dead were being deposited in graves about the garden and field.
Balls had dug holes in the ground all around, and shrapnel was
strewn about. Moreover, the schooner's guns boomed regularly,
keeping the men nervously scurrying for cover.

His plan to march quickly to the city seemed untenable, although
Colonel Thornton, who had been impressively active throughout
the battle, urged that it not be abandoned. The army was disorganized, and the condition of the city's defenses was unknown. To
Admiral Cochrane, Keane argued that Jackson must have gathered
a formidable army, just as the prisoners had claimed, or he would
not have attacked with such intrepidity; he would hardly have
risked the whole of his troops in one bold thrust. To penetrate the
city would take a carefully organized assault supported by heavy
artillery. As the *Carolina* continued to pound the camp with its
big guns, Keane looked disconsolately at his own puny three-
pounders.

Moreover, the 4th reported that it had learned from reconnaissance of the presence of some two thousand troops at the English

Turn, part of which had apparently failed the preceding evening to consummate a planned squeeze from below as well as above the English camp. Both flanks would have to be protected from another attack. Consequently Keane rearranged his line more parallel to the river, with each flank along a canal, the 93rd and 95th on Lacoste's and the 4th on Jumonville's, the 21st and 44th encamped between, and the 85th maintaining a position near the river bank. The 85th would still have to shelter itself as well as possible under the levee and among the buildings to avoid the *Carolina's* fire, but the rest of the line would be well back in the fields from the river.[1]

Admiral Cochrane's barges were ready to return for the two West India regiments. The wounded were carried aboard to be taken to the fleet and to make room at the hospital for future casualties. The admiral promised to bring up as soon as possible whatever artillery he could. He would also bring provisions to supplement those taken from nearby plantations. Much had been removed from the plantations before the British arrival, and Keane had been able to locate only enough horses for staff and commanding officers. His dragoons were still dismounted. For the time being Keane could only wait and keep a cautious eye on the untrustworthy Americans.[2]

The *Statira* reached the fleet, anchoring within Cat Island five miles above the line-of-battle ships and ten miles from the upper anchorage. Pakenham, Gibbs, Burgoyne, and Dickson proceeded in a gig to the inner anchorage, where they learned that the British had landed upon the Louisiana coast. They hastened on, passing the long line of ships which stretched from Cat to Pea Island and the low, flat coast with its thick pine woods and high reeds. By 10:00 P.M. they reached the *Anaconda*. Sir Thomas Hardy, aboard that ship, told them of the attack the night of the twenty-third. It was a fine moonlight night, clear and piercingly cold, and since Pakenham was anxious to proceed, they pressed ahead. Colonel Dickson marveled at the perseverance of the sailors, especially when a cutting breeze brought a hard freeze. At last they sighted the coast of Lake Borgne and ran along it until they spotted a pole among the high reeds from which a red flag waved. This marked the entrance to the creek. They proceeded up the creek between the great stretches of reeds until they reached the fishing village, where Admiral Cochrane's flag was attached to a high tree. It was

8:00 A.M. when they finally arrived here, and they were just in time for breakfast with the admiral.

At breakfast Admiral Cochrane told them of the terrible havoc caused by the *Carolina*. To Colonel Dickson's query he replied that he could bring up four eighteens speedily from the fleet. Dickson recommended that this be done. After breakfast the party proceeded up the creek toward the landing place and the camp. General Pakenham was in a great hurry to take command of the campaign.[3]

‡‡‡

Two miles up the river from Keane's camp, the Americans awoke on the twenty-fourth with a greater sense of accomplishment. They had done battle with the famed Peninsular heroes, held their own, struck a hard blow, and withdrawn with their strength scarcely impaired. This preliminary feeling out of the opponent left them with a confidence that they could master him.

Jackson had left the 7th regulars and the Mississippi dragoons at De la Ronde's to watch the enemy. The rest of the troops that had been engaged were encamped on Macarty's plantation behind the Rodriguez canal. The Macarty mansion was a large, roomy one nestled among evergreens, oaks, cedars, and pecans so plentiful that the house itself could be seen at only a short distance. It had more extensive and better kept gardens and orchards than most of the plantation homes. Around two stories were wide galleries, and above the second was a large dormer window which gave the general an extensive view of the plantations below, Chalmette and Bienvenu. At the canal, the swamp projected toward the river, narrowing the field to six hundred yards. Jackson succumbed to the charm of this spot, and when Hinds's dragoons, after a quick dash along the enemy front, reported that the British seemed to be preparing a camp rather than an attack, the general decided to build a strong defensive position here. "We won't abandon this position," he announced to the troops, "until we drive those redcoats into the river or the swamp." [4]

The troops were disposed along the bank of the Rodriguez canal, with Beale's rifle company (somewhat depleted after its misfortune of the night before) on the river bank, Plauché's battalion to

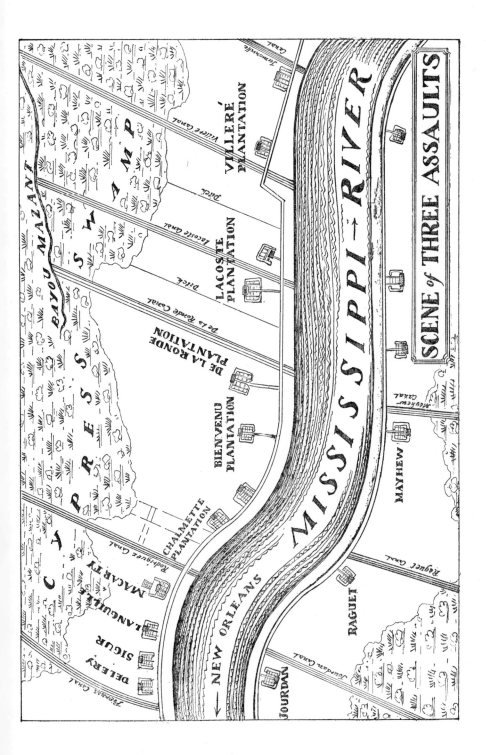

SCENE of THREE ASSAULTS

its left, then Daquin's colored, the 44th regulars, and on the left half toward the swamp Coffee's Tennesseans. When they had been lined up along the canal they received their orders: dig! Rifles were stacked, shovels and spades that had arrived from the city were taken up, and the men began to dig for the glory of their country, piling up a mound along the bank of the canal that would stand between the intruder and his wished-for haven.[5]

Near the right of the line the two four-pounders that had been used in the battle were mounted to command the highroad. Other artillery support could be added later and in the meantime be provided by the *Louisiana* and the *Carolina* on the river.[6]

In the city the previous night there had been many, hearing the reports of the guns, who entertained fears of the outcome of the battle, particularly after Mr. Skipwith divulged the refusal of Captain Butler to indicate Jackson's plans for the city in case of defeat. There was considerable talk of a great devastating bonfire that would send up in smoke all the property and possessions of the citizens. But as the night wore on and reports drifted in of successes (exaggerated favorably), most people took heart. By 4:00 A.M. an exempt citizen receiving prisoners in town could write an optimistic letter to a friend in New York predicting that Jackson would destroy the enemy in the morning. By sunrise the talk was all of the dashing attack, the bravery of the city volunteers, the accuracy of Beale's sharpshooters, the ferocity of the Tennesseans, and the cool, intrepid leadership of General Jackson. Jackson had stood by the cannons, fending off the British, until his soldiers rushed to his support. Coffee had walked along his line before an attack urging his men to prove that they could fight as well as they could boast, and they had done so. Every man had acted as if the fate of New Orleans depended upon his conduct alone. The colored troops, anxious for glory, had fought like desperadoes. Reuben Kemper, finding his men trapped by the enemy, had pretended to be a British officer, had ordered the enemy soldiers to follow him, and had led them to captivity. Plauché had ordered an attack which would have routed the British had not Colonel Ross inopportunely countermanded it. Coffee had been in a position to force a surrender had not the fog rolled in. One wag wrote to a friend about the battle, "The British were preparing to eat supper, but they got more COFFEE than they expected." Obviously, whatever might be the reason, whether because of the climate, the ease and independence of the environment, or the freedom of their political institutions, Americans possessed a faculty of fighting beyond the lot of other nations.[7]

The Ursuline nuns opened their convent and several Creoles opened their houses to the wounded, and the women of the city hastened to provide lint, linen, wine, and other provisions. Many free colored women tendered their service as nurses. Some of the wounded were captured British soldiers, and the officers were lodged with various citizens until Jackson ordered them back to the hospital. Louise Livingston, with her husband's aid, called upon the general to protest that the officer in her home might die if moved, and the general permitted her to keep him. Everyone wanted to help. Major Butler was surprised by an old planter whose hobby for many years had been astronomy and who diffidently offered, for lack of anything better, to lend the general the telescope with which he had studied Louisiana skies. Major Butler was at first doubtful that the general would want to watch stars, but when he looked through the scope and saw the extent of its magnifying powers, he accepted it. It was delivered to Macarty's and mounted in the dormer window, providing the general with an excellent eye for examining the enemy camp.[8]

On the *Carolina*, Commander Patterson was perhaps the most worried man in the defending army. Although his crew was having a happy time for the moment throwing balls into the British camp, Patterson knew that it was only a matter of time until the British would train guns on the boat, and the state of the wind and current made it impossible for him to move the boat upriver. To keep him company the *Louisiana*, newly manned by Lieutenant Thompson's crew of impressed seamen, dropped down to a position a mile above the *Carolina* and also fired on the British camp.[9]

At the English Turn, General Morgan's men, returning from their exhausting tramp through the mud and darkness, threw themselves on the ground to rest. Morgan nervously wiped his brow, thankful that he had regained his post without making a serious error. Later in the day those who had fallen out on the return march straggled in to report that close to the field where the detachment had spent the early morning hours was encamped a regiment of British. Morgan could hardly keep from trembling at his vision of the disaster his rash action might have brought. One of his officers, Colonel Declouet, likewise shivered at the thought of what might have happened to him.[10]

On the Gentilly road the Louisiana militia, hearing reports of the glorious battle, fretted that they had not shared in the glory. Governor Claiborne grumbled that he was being purposely kept in the background. Further down the road Lacoste's troops, not far from the lake, were on edge lest the British should shift the point of attack their way. Up the road, at the bayou bridge, Carroll's troops longed to join their fellow Tennesseans.[11]

The only action was the steady firing of the guns of the *Carolina* and *Louisiana*, the occasional demonstrations before the enemy by the Mississippi dragoons, the movements of the British troops to the new line designated by Keane, the steady movement over the lake of Cochrane's barges, and the digging of Jackson's troops.

At first the men dug slowly. The value of their task was not clear to them, and digging was scarcely a glamorous occupation. But gradually the report spread, originating with the Tennesseans who had strong faith in Jackson's judgment, that this mound of earth could save the city if it were thrown up high enough before the British attacked. The British army would amount to fifteen thousand crack troops when it was wholly organized; tremendous guns were to be brought from the fleet; Admiral Cochrane, the man who had burned Washington, a man callous of the cost in human lives of victory, had vowed to destroy New Orleans; it was a brilliant strategic maneuver of Jackson's to block this neck of land with a mound of earth. It was reported that a British prisoner had told Jackson the admiral had boasted he would eat Christmas dinner in New Orleans and Jackson had replied, "Perhaps so, but I shall preside at that feast." (When Cochrane heard of this reply, he retorted, "I shall not only eat Christmas dinner in New Orleans, but spend the Carnival there.") Men began to dig more spiritedly. Then as the mound went up irregularly, rivalry developed, first between soldiers working next to each other, then between units. The pile of earth a man was building came to be called his castle, and each strove to make his castle the greatest. As night fell the breastwork along the bank of the canal had grown to a height of three feet. The men laid down their shovels to make their beds as best they could in the mud behind the breastwork. Down the river on Villeré's the men also settled to sleep, more comfortable but less consoled by the thought that the day had been well spent. In the city there was some gaiety, but with most of the young men absent from home the gaiety was subdued.[12]

In the swamp the picket who had escaped from the fishing village plodded, floundered, and crawled his way in the grass and mud, trying to move in a single direction, often lying exhausted on a patch of ground, sometimes gnawing on roots or, in desperation, on a toad or lizard that he caught.

It was Christmas Eve.

‡‡‡

On Christmas morning, after an attempt to wash in the river in spite of the cannonading by the two vessels, and after the discovery that this was to be a day of inaction like the preceding one, Gleig and some of his fellow officers decided to pool whatever provisions they could collect in order to dine together. Around them the other soldiers were similarly planning what small Christmas cheer they could.[13]

At the anchorage it was just as difficult to celebrate. Reports from the battle had been discouraging, and a few wives had been made desolate by the arrival of wounded husbands or the news of husbands lost. Some found hope in the fact that the *Statira* had arrived and General Pakenham was on his way to take command. Perhaps now there would be a change. It was rumored that Admiral Cochrane would have his guns at the front in two days, and perhaps by the new year the colony could move from its miserable desert location.

On the brig *Helen,* crossing the Gulf, Captain Cooke and his fellow officers shivered with the unexpected cold and scraped together from their bad stock of provisions enough plums to make a plum pudding.[14]

While Pakenham and his party made their way over the boggy road that flanked the Villeré canal, Keane prepared the troops to receive their new commander. The companies formed unarmed in close order before their huts and tents, dressing by the regimental standards, which were held by ensigns. The colors of six of the regiments bore in the center, in gold roman numerals, the numbers of the regiments within wreaths of roses and thistles, with the union in the upper left corner. Matching the colors of the flags were the colors of the tall, pointed caps of the grenadier companies (except those of the 93rd, which were bearskin fur caps) and the coats of the regimental drummers. The 4th and the 21st, royal regiments, had special colors. The flag of the 4th had in the center the king's cipher on a red ground within a garter, with a crown over it; the union was in the upper left corner, and a gold lion was in each of the other corners; the ground of the flag was blue, and in the garter was printed the motto *"Honi soit qui mal y pense."* The flag of the 21st was also blue, sporting in the center a thistle within the circle of St. Andrew, a crown over the thistle, and smaller crowns in three corners, while the circle carried the motto *"Nemo me impune lacessit."* The ground of each flag was the color of the facings which the soldiers of the regiment wore upon their red coats—that of the 85th was, for example, yellow. And in contrast to the red coats of the other regiments were the green coats of the proud 95th riflemen. As Pakenham, accompanied by his staff and General Gibbs, rode smartly out of the swamp and across the field before this colorful line of troops, he was saluted by a flourish from each regimental bugler and by the drawn swords of the officers. The troops cheered him when he passed, and their cheer was caught up loudly by the 85th, near the river.

"The period is at hand," one officer commented, "for us to be relieved of our unpleasant situation and get into town." At headquarters, after politely receiving the command from Keane, Pakenham closeted himself with Gibbs, Keane, and Cochrane for the rest of the day.[15]

Gleig and his friends ate their Christmas dinner in one of Villeré's barns, attempting to be merry, wondering about future operations, and remembering reports of Pakenham's gallantry and efficiency on the Peninsula. Someone had heard that Pakenham had been promised an earl's coronet for the conquest of Louisiana. For a serenade they had the steady booming of the *Carolina*'s guns, and occasionally the barn rocked as a ball struck against the wall. They learned to judge subconsciously the time between the booming of the cannon and the sound of the ball's blow, and they would hold their breaths during those moments. On one occasion after the gun sounded, just when the ball should have struck, they heard a piercing scream. Rushing outside, they found a soldier writhing on the ground, his belly ripped apart. He was beyond repair, but they stretched him out and put a blanket over him. Gradually his screams subsided, but for an hour he continued to gasp for breath before sinking into death.[16]

A few slaves had appeared in the British camp requesting succor and offering to work. Their dress was uniform—a coarse blanket coat with loose sleeves and a hood, and shoes of undressed cowhide with the hair on the outside. Captain Hill of the artillery was moved by the pitiful plight of one young man who stumbled out of the swampy woods. He wore a collar of spikes around his neck, put there after an earlier unsuccessful attempt to escape his master in the city. Hill sent him to the blacksmith to have it removed.[17]

Quartermaster Surtees found the firing of the schooner extremely annoying. On one occasion he had just stepped out of the little hut where he was staying when an eighteen-pound ball rattled through the wall. On another, as he was approaching a house where some of the 85th were staying, he saw a ball plunge through the roof, and inside he discovered that it had driven clear through a corporal. He scarcely seemed able to move without being saluted by a shot.[18]

In most of the camp the prevailing feeling was one of expectancy; as soon as the generals laid their plans, the troops would march triumphantly into the city. But at the bivouac of the West Indian troops there was mainly despondency and apathy. A great many lay ill and helpless, and most of those who were not prostrated were torpid from the cold. Several had already died.[19]

At headquarters, General Keane explained his plan of attack, the difficulties of landing, the frustrations and delays, the over-sanguine expectations, and the unexpected actions of the enemy, but the more he talked the more he realized how inept it all made him appear, the more embarrassed he became about his report, and the more self-justification he offered. No one could have foreseen the bad weather or the low tide in the lake, no one could have known that the Americans would be so well prepared, no one could have predicted the troubles of the advance across the lake, no one could have guessed how terrible the terrain was by the maps and reports. No one could have supposed that an American general would attack. But to hindsight such as Pakenham's, foresight of just such events seemed natural, and Keane could tell what his superior was thinking. Throughout the interview Pakenham was perfectly charming, smiling, nodding his head at the younger general's statements, asking appropriate, gentle questions—but his smile was a set one, his eyes were unreceptive, and his very quietness betrayed disapproval.[20]

One thing Keane could hardly put into words—his nervousness at the presence and bearing of Admiral Cochrane. As Cochrane had carried out his own share of the invasion with great efficiency and success, he could hardly be blamed for any errors of the general, and with Cochrane sitting close at hand Keane would not have dared to protest. So he talked on and on, making himself look worse with every word.

When at last Keane had no more to say, Pakenham began, slowly and deliberately, to question minutely about the exact locations of the troops, the exact details of the city and environs, the exact state of the defenses. It became clear that he considered the Gentilly plain a much better route to the city than the river bank, and his questions indicated that he was considering a movement of the army from its present position to that one.[21]

It was then that Admiral Cochrane came to Keane's rescue. Certainly the navy could move the army if necessary, but the defending army could move faster, and although there might be more room for the British to maneuver, there would also be room for the enemy to use his cavalry, and the small British cavalry was as yet inadequately horsed. Cochrane's ferry service was moving admirably. In a short time he would have the artillery's guns brought from the fleet and would blast the enemy's boats from the river. If Pakenham needed more room, Cochrane could dig a canal from the bayou to the river to bring boats to carry the army across to the other bank. There had been enough dillydallying. One hearty thrust in the traditional English manner should scatter these farmers and backwoodsmen to the winds.

"If you wish," Cochrane said acidly, "I will take the city with my sailors and marines, and the army can bring up the baggage." [22]

It was Pakenham's turn to feel discomfited at the presence of the admiral. He was accustomed to politeness and indirection, not to sharp barbs. He began to feel that the honor of the British army rested upon him, that he owed it to the army to act with spirit and courage and good form without too nice a regard for strategy.

Bring up the guns, then. Silence those annoying boats on the river. Equalize the enemy's artillery, and the soldiers would storm the city.

‡‡‡

At Canal Rodriguez Christmas was celebrated by digging. Three times during the day Jackson rode along the line to inspect. It was rumored that he had not slept since the twenty-second. Steadily the men dug, steadily the great mound rose, stretching from the bank of the river almost to the swamp. Near the river a few cotton bales stacked nearby were thrown in on the theory that cotton could absorb bullets even better than earth. To strengthen the line Jackson ordered Carroll's troops to come from Gentilly and take position between Coffee on the left and the 44th regulars, in a spot where the mound was lower because the troops had been strung out thinner. Before the mound the canal, some ten feet wide, now carried a foot or so of water, and near the swamp the Tennesseans threw in thornbush to make passage more difficult.[23]

Now from town many citizens came down the river carrying their shovels. Not wanting to disrupt his line of troops, Jackson sent the citizens to Dupré's canal some two miles nearer the city to throw up another breastwork. If the British should dislodge him from his first line he would fall back to the second. Citizens as well as soldiers began to dig, planters sent gangs of slaves to dig, almost everyone was digging, old and young, and the breastworks grew, crossing the fields from the river to the swamp. They were uneven mounds, more or less straight, but thick in places and thin in others, high in places and low in others. Hour by hour, however, they grew.[24]

The position at the English Turn seemed weak, since the British were between that place and the city. Jackson ordered Morgan to leave a garrison of one hundred with his artillery at Fort St. Leon and to remove the rest of his division to a position across the river from the Rodriguez line. Willingly Morgan traded a position which had worried him with too many alternatives for one closer to his commanding general. At the point directly across the river from Jackson's line the field seemed to Morgan too narrow because the swamp there curved closer to the river; so he selected another point some distance downriver from Jackson, where the plain was much wider.[25]

Jackson kept a constant watch over his enemy. Frequently he scanned the fields with his telescope. Hinds's dragoons often rode out and returned with reports about the enemy's activity. General Humbert, too, discovered something he could do; in the morning he rode from headquarters to De la Ronde's plantation, carefully observed the enemy camp with his glass, and returned to report his observations minutely (in French, since he spoke no English; Livingston or Davezac translated) to his commander. The stiff, proper Frenchman amused Jackson, who agreed to let this be a daily activity and assigned a few Tennesseans to accompany Humbert as a bodyguard. From these reconnaissances Jackson learned of the arrival of a new British commander.[26]

Wishing to know more about the British supply route, Jackson sent Reuben Kemper to ride into the swamp and descend Bayou Bienvenu as far as possible. Kemper, after picking his way among the cypresses and pushing through the reeds to the bayou, followed along the bayou until he saw smoke. Making his way cautiously forward, he discovered one of Cochrane's barges coming up the stream while the sailors set fire to the reeds on its banks. (The admiral, never idle, had decided to clear a better path from the lake to the landing and to build a redoubt at the confluence of bayous Mazant and Bienvenu to protect the supply lines; he wanted the reeds ahead of this redoubt burned away to permit better observation.) Before Kemper could return with his news, Lacoste's own reconnaissance had brought a similar report to the troops at Gentilly, and Lacoste, interpreting this as a British move into the plain and fearing that he would be cut off, moved his troops three miles up the plain to Lafon's plantation. His message reached headquarters as a report that the British had landed at Chef Menteur. Jackson hastily sent an aide to check the report.[27]

He also ordered Major Nicks at the naval ordnance across the river from New Orleans to load his powder on a vessel and send it to Baton Rouge, keeping only what Commander Patterson needed for his guns. The river was high, and he ordered his engineer Latour to cut the levee, flooding the Chalmette plantation to provide a muddy field for the British to cross. He sent word for Morgan's engineer Lafon similarly to cut the levee below the British and flood Jumonville's, an operation that would have to be performed under enemy fire.

Down the river at Fort St. Philip, Major Overton's little garrison, with the help of hardworking plantation slaves, rapidly cleared the fort of all combustible debris and constructed new gun locations. The fort across the river remained incomplete; work stopped, upon the news of the British landing, in order that the main fort could first be put in order.

When Kemper reported the truth about the rumored invasion of Gentilly, Jackson sent two hundred of Coffee's men to reoccupy the position evacuated by Lacoste.

Throughout the day the *Carolina* and the *Louisiana* regularly pounded the British camp. The mounds beside the canals grew higher. New Orleans' defenses became stronger, while the British organized for a noble, well-ordered assault. During the night a few of the Tennesseans stole through the swampy wood to Lacoste's, crept up on the British pickets, and with some careful shooting killed several guards. On their return they informed their comrades that hunting was good.

The American picket from the fishing village dragged himself at last from the swamp into Lacoste's camp, where he fainted. He was carried into the city to be nursed back to health.[28]

On the twenty-sixth Lacoste begged Jackson that his men be permitted to join the line. Gentilly now seeming safe to the general, he ordered the 4th Regiment of Louisiana militia, with a detachment of artillery and two field pieces and a company of thirty Choctaws, to join the two hundred Tennesseans at the Chef Menteur battery; he ordered Lacoste to place his battalion on the Rodriguez line between Plauché and Daquin; and the 1st and 2nd regiments of Louisiana militia he ordered from Gentilly, the 1st moving in on the right of the line, and the 2nd going to De la Ronde's as an advance. Governor Claiborne, thus left without a command, returned crossly to the city, feeling that he had been deliberately squeezed out of his chance for heroism.[29]

Hinds took his cavalry along the edge of the wood to within five hundred yards of the British camp and set fire to the cane trash in the fields. There was a great blaze, but when it died down the British were ready to thank their enemies for nicely clearing the ground before them.[30]

Commander Patterson found the wind blowing a heavy gale from the northwest and the current sweeping down stronger than ever. The two boats consequently continued their serenade of the British camp.[31]

Mr. Skipwith and a committee of three from the legislature waited upon General Jackson to complain about Captain Butler's treatment of Skipwith the night of December 23 and to request the general to inform them of his plans in case of an enemy victory. They found the general preoccupied and irascible. Coldly he informed them, "If I thought the hair of my head knew my thoughts, I would cut it off or burn it." When they seemed discontent with this reply, he told them to inform the Senate that if he was unfortunate enough to be driven from his lines and retreat through New Orleans, they would have a warm session of it. Upon this he refused to enlarge, and the legislators returned to the city disgruntled and alarmed.[32]

In the British camp there was no bickering or complaint except for the curses that soldiers directed at the unrelenting cannonade. Pakenham rode forward to survey as best he could the terrain between him and the American line, while Colonel Dickson supervised the erection of a battery on Villeré's. Embrasures were cut in the levee, the ground was leveled for the guns, and a few pieces of paling were laid across as platforms where the ground was soft. Dickson also asked Pakenham to furnish the artillery with horses. The general issued an order that all regimental officers were to send in their horses, but the ones that were sent proved to be miserably unfit animals.[33]

That night while the army slept Cochrane's sailors worked feverishly, dragging up the canal two nine-pounders, two six-pounders, and two howitzers, and mounting them in the battery. But the sleep of the soldiers was only fitful. Parties of Tennesseans were slipping from the swamp to attack the pickets, and alarms were frequent. Lieutenant Gleig brooded over the savage nature of the enemy. In modern, civilized European warfare there were sacred rules; outposts were unmolested unless a direct attack was intended; French and English sentinels could be posted only twenty yards apart without bothering each other. But the Americans had no chivalry and thought of an enemy simply as an enemy; their conduct was an ungenerous return to barbarity; they were acting the part of assassins rather than soldiers, murdering in cold blood.

The British sent six Indians in search of cattle and horses, but the pickets on Jumonville's were not notified, and when the Indians returned they were fired upon. The mistake was finally rectified, and four of the Indians came to camp with about thirty horses they had found at Terre aux Boeufs. The whereabouts of the other two Indians could not be ascertained.[34]

Commander Patterson knew what was in store for his boats in the morning. When he was called to headquarters by Jackson, he exhorted Captain Henley to make every effort at daybreak to warp the *Carolina* upstream. Reluctantly he himself departed to confer with the general, whom he found worried both about the situation of the schooner and his own lack of artillery. He wanted Patterson to bring him guns during the next few days and to arm whatever merchant vessels he found in port.[35]

The waiting for action, with the enemy so close, was wearing on the nerves. In some Creole homes there was fear about the rapacities which Jackson's backwoodsmen might commit if they were driven from the city. Perhaps the Americans were more to be feared than the British. It was rumored that the British, instead of ravaging the plantations down the river for provisions, were paying more than the actual worth for what they took. Had not the general used language to Skipwith's committee which couched a threat to burn the city? In other homes and among the troops there was resentment of such suspicions, which were countered by suspicions that the older citizens might defect. James Bradford, the editor of one of the city's American newspapers who was now serving as a dragoon, claimed to have met under suspicious circumstances the speaker of the house down the river below the English camp. Some of Plauché's volunteers claimed that the legislators were meeting secretly every night to discuss how they might surrender. Sebastien Hiriart, a senator from Baton Rouge who was serving with the volunteers, claimed to have been at such a meeting and to have heard the speaker of the house accuse Jackson of intending to burn the city; and he said that Colonel Declouet, who had stayed in the meeting after Hiriart had left, had told him later that several members had expressed a desire to capitulate. Abner Duncan, an aide of the general who was notably antagonistic to the Creoles, substantiated these claims; he had heard from several legislators that an attempt to surrender would be made. General Morgan had heard it, and he and Colonel Declouet frequently expressed their fears to each other. Many of the Tennesseans, proud of their Anglo-Saxon heritage and unprepared by their frontier background to appreciate the culture of New Orleans, sneered at the French and Creoles, calling them a "soft race" who lived in a "luxurious lethargy" that was the next thing to a "perpetual siesta." The city was a "dreamland of tropical luxury" that could hardly be expected to produce dependable citizens and soldiers. The city soldiers responded by sneering at the Tennesseans' sloppy appearance and poor manners—the undisciplined frontiersmen, they feared, would take to the woods at the first British onslaught. The enmities of years came out too in the mutterings of the city soldiers about one another; Vincent Nolte and his Creole friends in the uniformed battalion laughed at the misfortune which Beale's riflemen had experienced on the twenty-third—Beale, Nolte announced, was only a great braggart (Beale was a friend of a man with whom Nolte had dueled). The men of the 1st Regiment of militia grumbled that the 2nd Regiment, now at the advanced post, was a worthless collection of odds and ends swept from the streets, wharfs, and alleys of New Orleans.[36]

But for the most part both soldiers and citizens were too weary from the heavy exertions of building the defenses to do anything but sleep. The soldiers lay in the mud behind the breastwork, while the citizens lay in their comfortable beds. Because of a sudden drop in the river, the water that had flooded the Chalmette plantation had flowed back to the river, leaving the ground soft but not wet. The night was frosty, hardening the ground along Villeré's canal to make it easier for the sailors to bring up the guns, but making a cold time of it for the sleeping soldiers.[37]

At 2:00 A.M. on the twenty-seventh, the British artillerymen lighted their furnace to heat shot. Somewhat later, on the *Carolina* and the *Louisiana*, the sailors of Captain Henley and Lieutenant Thompson hurried to their posts. The wind, still from the north-northwest, had dropped, the current was still strong, and Captain Henley found it impossible to warp his boat up the river.[38]

At 7:45, as soon as it was light enough to discover the schooner, the British guns opened. Henley answered with a twelve-pounder, but the second enemy shot lodged in the mainhold under some cables. Sailors scrambled down to try to dislodge it, but it had found a position beyond their reach. Smoke billowed from the hold. Other hotshot passed through the cabin, where powder was stored. The bulwarks were knocked down. The vessel was in danger of sinking, and the fire spread rapidly.

Reluctantly Henley ordered his men to abandon ship. Lowering the boats, they scrambled in them too hurriedly to carry with them any of their effects. They rowed quickly away. The British watched as smoke billowed first from midships, then from head and stern, until there was a mass of smoke from the entire hull.[39]

Lieutenant Thompson had been equally unsuccessful with warping the *Louisiana,* but when the British guns opened on the *Carolina,* he sent his men ashore with cables, and they tugged and heaved until the ship moved upstream. There was a pause, both among these men and among those rowing from the other ship, when the *Carolina* deafeningly exploded. The sailors from the sunken schooner joined the others, and as the British guns trained upon the *Louisiana* they towed it safely out of range.[40]

On Villeré's the men of the 85th scrambled up the levee and broke into wild cheers as they saw the *Carolina* blow up. To them this was a fine, gratifying sight. To Captain Henley and his sailors it was the violent death of a great friend.[41]

For the rest of the day Pakenham's troops hauled stores, ammunition, and heavy guns from the bayou where Cochrane's barges delivered them to the camp at Villeré's. They brought, also, some Congreve rocket units—"mouth-of-fire" launchers, long tubes supported by two bipods, the forward one longer than the rear one so that there was a fixed elevation. Pakenham arranged his attack: on the left General Keane would lead a column of the 85th, 93rd, 95th, and 1st West India; on the right General Gibbs would lead a column of the 21st, 44th, and 5th West India; the 14th, with Pakenham and his staff, would direct operations from the center of the line; the 4th would be in reserve near the wood. Pakenham ordered the troops to cook two days' meat in case the attack should develop into an extended pursuit of the enemy up the river.[42]

At the Rodriguez canal Jackson now had a strong breastwork

and behind it a good line of troops—Beale's rifles, the 7th regulars, the 1st Louisiana, Plauché's battalion, Lacoste's and Daquin's colored, the 44th regulars, Carroll's and Coffee's Tennesseans. He withdrew the 2nd Louisiana militia from De la Ronde's and placed it on the extreme left of the line, leaving Hinds's dragoons as the advance. Now, with Patterson's help, he strengthened his artillery, which previously had consisted of two field pieces covering the highroad, by adding two twenty-four-pounders and a thirty-two-pounder. Beluche's artillerymen were brought from Fort St. John to man one of the twenty-four-pounders; Dominique's Baratarians were ordered to follow in order to serve another; and when the crew of the *Carolina* returned to the line, a detachment was sent under Lieutenants Crawley and Norris to serve the thirty-two-pounder, Crawley supervising the construction of a platform upon which to mount it. The *Louisiana* took position near the river bank.[43]

In front of the breastwork was the canal. Beyond that, the plain of Chalmette, with the mansion, outhouses, and gardens near the river. Half a mile away the river bent gradually to the left, and the houses and groves of Bienvenu, De la Ronde, Lacoste, Villeré, and Jumonville (where the river bent to the right) could be seen, in daylight, in a line slanting off in the distance parallel to the slanting river. Because of that slant the river and the opposite bank could be seen straight ahead in the distance. At the left of the plain the woods also bent, but in an arc that carried them further and further away from the river. At Rodriguez the plain was less than half a mile wide, but about four hundred yards into Chalmette the arc began, making Bienvenu nearly two miles wide. Then the wood curved back again toward the river, leaving Lacoste's and Villeré's plantations about a mile wide. The far end of Chalmette was hidden from view by the curve of the wood. In the wood the ground became softer and softer with pools of water oozing up.

The plain before the line was cut by a number of ditches, but there were three large ones that would be especially important in an attack. At the fringe of the wood, perpendicular to the breastwork, a double ditch ran for some four hundred yards into Chalmette. Bordering it was a rail fence, and at the far end of the ditch the fence turned at right angles and went into the wood. About three hundred yards from the line this double ditch was crossed by another ditch that ran from the swamp to the levee, angling away from the breastwork so that its right end was fifty yards farther away than its left. And about one hundred yards beyond that was another, parallel to it, its left end (near the wood) about four hundred yards away, its right (at the levee) about a quarter of a mile away. Both ditches could shelter an attacking army, though for three hundred yards from the canal there would be little shelter.

In the left half of the plain a thick, tall sedge grass grew; it had been cut as far as the first parallel ditch, but it hid the second one from the view of the breastwork except in spots where clumps of bushes grew beside the ditch. In the right half was cane stubble, now considerably trampled down. The stubble was still thick on Bienvenu, and at De la Ronde's near the wood there was a large field of tall, uncut cane.[44]

During the night Colonel Dickson, who had been given most of the horses (poor specimens in the main), prepared his guns for the attack. They were dragged forward to Colonel Thornton's advanced picket. A three-pounder and half of Captain Lane's rocket brigade would move into the field to accompany Gibbs's column; three small mortars and the other half of Lane's rockets would march along the road with Keane; and two nine-pounders, two howitzers, and two six-pounders would move along the road behind Keane's column as reserve. Two sixes and a light howitzer were left at the Villeré river battery to prevent boats from passing up or down the river.[45]

During the night parties of Tennesseans annoyed the British pickets, and Hinds's dragoons periodically rode out for a demonstration. In spite of the serious business of the morrow, this raucous party lasted all night.[46]

‡‡‡

In New Orleans the people found sleep difficult. The pressures of interrupted routine, of an enemy on the doorstep, and of hostilities suppressed under a front of unity were beginning to fray nerves. For several days the rumble of guns had created an atmosphere of a threatening thunderstorm. Fathers worried about property, mothers worried about sons at the front, girls struggled with mysterious emotions. In some houses people lay awake in the darkness, pretending to each other that they were sleeping. In others they kept restless vigil by lamplight or firelight.

The fiasco of Morgan's march from the English Turn to Jumonville's and the tense situation in general had left Colonel Declouet shattered. Having come to town from Morgan's station, he wandered about the streets until he spotted a light in the house of Magloire Guichard, refugee of Santo Domingo and prominent legislator. Though the two were not on good terms, Declouet sought relief for his tortured nerves in Guichard's house, where he was received with some annoyance. After several attempts to get rid of his guest, Guichard finally picked up his candle and went to his bedroom, but Declouet followed. He sat by the fire, talking aimlessly of war, Jackson, and the legislature, while Guichard, ignoring him, undressed and finally climbed into bed. Only when the fire burned low and his host began to snore did Declouet go to the guest room to toss and turn through the night, dreaming of guns, bayonets, and a city in flames.[47]

✵ ✵

SIXTEEN

Advance and Repulse

WHEN THE first pink tinge of dawn appeared, the British bugles
sounded, calling the troops to arms. They woke to a bracing morning with frost lightly touching the grass and cane stubble and a
faint mist in the air. The troops mustered quickly and sharply,
forming into columns for the march. The generals and their staffs
came from the mansion, mounted their horses, and looked over
the assembled troops. General Keane rode to the left column and
General Gibbs to the right, while Pakenham remained between.
In the left column, Colonel Thornton and Colonel Dickson rode
with Keane and his aides, followed by the 85th, the 95th, Colonel
Dale's smart highlanders, and the 1st West India regiments. On the
right Colonel Patterson rode with General Gibbs and his aides,
followed by the 21st, 44th, and 5th West India regiments. Colonel
Mullins, at the head of the 44th, felt piqued that precedence had
been given to the 21st over his boys. He stood sullenly at the head
of his troops, wearing the round hat and the blue overcoat that
always distinguished him from the other officers. Colonel Brooke
of the 4th wore a blue overcoat but a cocked hat. Ahead of Mullins,
in charge of the first detachment of the 21st, Major Robert Rennie,
as he marched along skirting the wood, studied the cypress swamp,
wondering if it would not be possible to take troops through it,
where it curved toward the river, and flank the American position.[1]

At first the army had formed in silence, but as it marched and the men revived in the bracing air, they began to talk banteringly. Listening to their bawdy jests, Lieutenant Gleig's feeling of apartness from his men returned to him. In battle they answered to orders, but out of battle their crudeness was beyond his ken.[2]

Ahead of the marching army the American pickets fired and withdrew quickly. The troops crossed De la Ronde's plantation, Keane's column moving on the high road while Gibbs's moved over the field near the swamp. At Bienvenu they paused to wait for more light and to allow the artillerymen to drag forward and plant their guns. Before them stretched the field of stubble, with several ditches and fences crossing at different angles. Keane's column could see nothing else but the buildings and trees of Chalmette, where the road turned. Gibbs's column could see in the gloom the cypress wood projecting into the field.[3]

As the first muskets cracked, the American bugles called the defenders from their sleep to take position behind the breastwork. Lieutenant Crawley's sailors climbed to the platform to serve the thirty-two-pounder on the center of the line. Lieutenant Norris' sailors readied a nine-pounder on the left, and Beluche's volunteers prepared one of the twenty-four-pounders on the right, while, in the absence of the Baratarians, some inexperienced men of Plauché's battalion took charge of the other. Commander Patterson and Lieutenant Thompson readied the guns of the *Louisiana*.[4]

Jackson rode along the line, shouting encouragement to his men. On the left the Tennesseans shouted back that they expected a good haul from the day's hunting. On the right, hearing of the Tennesseans' confidence, Captain Beale's men promised to prove their superiority. The general seemed gay and secure; to no one did he betray his concern. Would this mound of earth stand against an army that had stormed the great forts of Europe? Would his men keep their nerve when a British army moved steadily upon them, or would they break under the first threat? He ordered his officers to keep alert, to watch every man and shout heartening words.

As the sun rose the mist quickly dispersed, the frost vanished, and a clear, bright day greeted the men in the field. Again the bugles sounded. Major Rennie's detachment formed on the right flank of Gibbs's column. Keane deployed the 95th rifles as a line of skirmishers across the field between the two columns. They marched, Gibbs's column tramping through the cane stubble, Keane's column following the road toward Chalmette's buildings, Rennie's flank detachment approaching the projection of the wood.[5]

Suddenly the *Louisiana*'s guns boomed. Keane's men set their jaws grimly, forgetting their jests, marching resolutely, tensing themselves for the shot. In a few moments they realized that they were not yet the targets. The balls were pounding the Chalmette buildings, splitting the trees in the garden, crashing through windows, knocking down chimneys, tearing through the roofs. A wisp of smoke curled out from a broken window, followed soon by other wisps—the buildings were being struck by hot shot. Soon the wisps grew into trails and then into clouds of black smoke pouring forth from the buildings. As the head of the column approached the turn in the road, one of the buildings burst into violent flames. Several others quickly followed, until all were blazing and crackling. Past the burning buildings marched the troops, and as they turned with the road they suddenly saw before them the mound of earth that protected the defending troops.[6]

At this moment Dominique You trotted into Jackson's camp, followed by his red-shirted Baratarians. As Jackson pointed the way, Dominique and his men hurried to their battery, shouldered aside the Creole militiamen, and took charge of the gun.[7]

‡‡‡

When Colonel Declouet met Magloire Guichard for breakfast, Declouet was still nervous and embarrassed and Guichard was still gruff and unfriendly. Guichard, to heckle his guest, referred to Morgan's march of December 23, laughing at its futility. "I wonder, Colonel," he said acidly, "that you did not consummate your attack upon the enemy rear. Perhaps you would have routed him."

Excitably Declouet pulled at his hair and mumbled an accusation that it was all Morgan's fault. Then, to free himself from that embarrassment, he said slyly, "I wonder why the legislature has not adjourned during this crisis. Why do you stay in session, Magloire?"

Coloring, Guichard said sharply, "There's nothing I'd like better than to adjourn. My private affairs are suffering because my time is so taken by the legislature. I lost everything at Santo Domingo, and it looks like I might lose what I've regained here."

Guichard rose from the table, bade his guest good-bye, and went to his room. From his desk he took a cigar, but as he was lighting it Declouet entered and sat near the fire. Leaning toward his host, Declouet spoke in a mysterious tone. "My friend, do you think the British intend to keep the country for themselves, and that they can?"

Guichard gave him a searching glance. "No," he said.

"How do people say they're treating the planters down the river? Have they committed any depredations?"

"People say they don't. Their policy is to pretend to be friendly protectors."

"We do more harm than they do, don't we? Don't the planters complain that our militia are killing the cattle and stealing?"

"Some do."

"What will happen if the British win?"

"The country will be lost. I've had experience with the British. They robbed me of everything." Guichard sat at his desk and prepared to work.

Declouet rose, stood musingly with his back to the fire, and finally asked again. "Why doesn't the legislature adjourn?"

"I don't know. You're constantly asking me why this, why that. Since we're asking questions, let me ask you why you didn't drive the British back on the twenty-third? You've exposed the country to be sacrificed."

There was a long pause before Declouet again mentioned the legislature. With great exasperation Guichard said, "You're mad. I'm tired of your questions."

"I don't mean you," said Declouet. "Nobody loves you more than I do. But some of those damned legislators are intriguers who want to see the country overturned. They have no reasons for not adjourning, that's my opinion."

Guichard jumped up. "You'll always be suspicious. The legislature is the sentinel of the people, and it has to be ready in a crisis to take such measures as the calamities of war might render necessary." He clapped his hat upon his head and stalked out of the house.

Declouet, his nerves still shaken, took a horse to ride toward the battle.[8]

†††

As Keane's column rounded the turn in the road just beyond the burning Chalmette buildings, the rifles on the right of Jackson's line cracked, and the twenty-fours and the guns of the *Louisiana* boomed. The first men in the column fell. The balls tore into the marching ranks. Smoke billowing from the buildings blinded the soldiers. As some broke ranks and sought shelter among the buildings, flames scorched them to send them reeling back. For a moment Lieutenant Gleig thrilled to the sublimity of the scene. But Keane, taken by surprise by the ferocity of the enemy fire, ordered his regiments to take cover in the field. In minutes the column ceased to exist. A semblance of a line formed in a shallow ditch stretching into the plantation, with companies and squads scattered in various other places about the plain.[9]

Dickson's rocket teams set to work with their launchers, one man shoving the rocket into the rear of the launcher, another lighting the fuse, each launcher shooting four times a minute. The rockets screamed upward with brilliant flaming trails—but the American gunners remained undaunted, and the rockets did little damage.[10]

On the right Gibbs's column was met by the fire of the Tennesseans (still beyond effective rifle range) and the thirty-two-pounder. Seeing Keane's column break, Gibbs also ordered his men to cover. Quickly they spread out along the large ditch four hundred yards from the breastwork. Some of them tried to return the American fire, but they were much too far away to do any damage. Rennie halted his men behind the projection of the woods.[11]

Dickson rushed his reserve guns forward along the road past the burning buildings, and the artillerymen opened as soon as they could. Two sixes and one nine fired on the enemy line, while the other nine and the howitzer opened against the *Louisiana*. Jackson's guns now trained on the British guns. For a few minutes the firing was furious on both sides. But the *Louisiana* found the range of a howitzer, its balls ripped into the artillerymen serving it, and a direct hit finally knocked it from its mounting. The artillerymen scurried to the field to the protection of a ditch. One after another the other guns were dismounted as their wheels or axles were shot away, and the artillerymen took cover amid the Chalmette ruins, garden hedges, or ditches. Quartermaster Surtees, observing from a ditch, saw a ball take off the head of an artillery sergeant, and the force of the blow sent the sergeant's hat spinning over the ditch.[12]

Behind the breastwork Jackson's soldiers lay securely, looking out at the cloud of smoke in the plain, listening to the raucous cannonade and the lusty shouts of the artillerymen, peering for British uniforms in the ditches, firing occasionally, watching spurts of dust as balls hit the mound; they were sweaty and grimy but secure and excited. Officers walked back and forth behind them, unnecessarily shouting encouragement. Round shot from the British cannon struck the mound or fell in the field behind the line. Major Carmick of the marines, while riding behind the line, was struck by a rocket which ripped limbs from his horse and wounded the major in arm and head. Since the safest positions on the battlefield were against that mound of earth, few men were inclined to move. By watching for the flashes of the guns, the men knew when to duck to escape the balls.[13]

Jackson watched from Macarty's dormer window, surveying the field with his glass or his telescope. One British gun was dismounted. Several of the field pieces had been deserted. The British fire was off the mark, and the British soldiers were pinned to the ground.

Pakenham, watching from the center of the field, saw his army lying on the ground while his artillerymen futilely struggled against the devastating fire of the enemy guns. General Keane and General Gibbs were on the ground with their men, looking out at a well-entrenched enemy and looking around at soldiers who were stunned by the punishment they had taken. Several artillerymen had been felled. A sailor and Captain Collins of the 1st West India were decapitated by a shot.[14]

Colonel Thornton sent orders among his officers to rally the 85th. On his order the regiment rose from its position in the field and advanced in a line, crossing the first large ditch and heading for the second. From the breastwork the rifle fire increased as the British moved within range, but they proceeded to the second ditch. Thornton could see, now, that there was a canal before the breastwork; he had no idea of its depth, but the ditch before him had water in it. Again he ordered his men down, and they leaped in, throwing themselves against the opposite bank, hiding in the rushes that grew on the bank, while the water covered their legs to the knees.[15]

On the right Major Robert Rennie studied the situation. He saw how formidable the breastwork was, but he saw also that it was smaller as it entered the swamp. Ahead of him, to the right of Gibbs's column, a double ditch ran at the edge of the wood to the breastwork. By passing along that ditch he would be protected from the American batteries by its bordering fence. Beckoning to his men, he led the way in a crouching run along the ditch.[16]

From the breastwork Coffee saw this movement. Quickly he extended his Tennesseans from the breastwork into the swamp, where they had to lie in the mud behind trees or clumps of reeds. At the edge of the swamp there was room for a few men to fire upon the advancing column, and they did so, crowding together to fire as solidly as possible. Rennie crossed both large ditches and approached to a point about 250 yards from the line. There he paused, hiding his men in the sedge grass. He sent men into the swamp to investigate the possibility of flanking the breastwork completely.[17]

‡‡‡

One of Jackson's aides, Abner Duncan, was on his way to the city with a message when he met Colonel Declouet, who excitedly hailed him. Declouet turned his horse and galloped beside Duncan. He shouted, "The legislature's about to surrender the country to the enemy!"

"What!" shouted Duncan.

"They're gathering at the statehouse. They're going to surrender. For God's sake tell General Jackson."

Now Duncan pulled his horse to a stop, Declouet following suit. The words only confirmed Duncan's own suspicions about the Creoles. "You're sure?" he asked.

Declouet was white and trembling. He nodded.

Excitedly Duncan wheeled his horse and spurred toward headquarters.[18]

‡‡‡

A few British guns still fired, but the British army was pinned
to the ground. Jackson's and Patterson's guns continued to pound
the troops in the field.

Rennie's scouts returned to report that the Americans had a
line of riflemen well into the swamp. Rennie's detachment was too
small for an effective attack, so he remained in the sedge grass,
protected by the fence from the American artillery.[19]

Jackson left Macarty's to ride behind the line toward Carroll.
As he was passing behind his troops at the breastwork, Abner
Duncan raced up to him, shouting excitedly.

"What's the matter?" the general asked sternly, pausing in his
journey.

Breathlessly Duncan told him, "I have a message that the legislature is about to give up the country to the enemy."

Jackson's haughty brow contracted darkly. "What's the governor
up to now? Did he write a letter?"

Under his searching glance Duncan wilted. "Well, no," he said.
Some soldiers watched the exchange.

"Then what is the source of your information?"

Duncan, suddenly calmed, realized that he had acted too precipi-
tously. Weakly he said, "A militia colonel."

Jackson could tell by the aide's reaction that the report was
unreliable. "That colonel should be immediately apprehended. If
the information proves false, he should be shot."

For a moment Duncan, envisioning himself before a firing squad,
was speechless, but as Jackson turned to leave, Duncan felt a need
to protect himself by saying more. "The governor expects orders
what to do," he said. Later he would be unable to explain how the
governor ever became involved.

Glaring coldly at him, Jackson said, "Tell the governor to make
inquiry. If the report is true, blow up the legislature."

He galloped off, while Abner Duncan nervously turned again
toward the city. The soldiers within earshot laughed at him.[20]

Two miles from the city Duncan met Colonel Fortier, an aide

of the governor's, and told him, "The governor is to place a strong guard at the door of the legislature and employ armed force to prevent it from meeting." He reported this as an order. Fortier carried it to the governor, who transmitted it to General Labatut of the veterans' unit, who promptly stationed guards at the state-house. The legislators were stopped upon the steps when they tried to enter.[21]

‡‡‡

Now Pakenham attempted to remove his army from its perilous position. One by one the units left their hiding places to hurry to the safety of De la Ronde's plantation, while the enemy guns trained on them to hasten their departure. The men of the 85th, farthest forward except for Rennie's detachment, kept their stations in the mud and water of the ditch, sweating from discomfiture, fear, and warmth. Rennie's men to the right lay behind the fence, answering the fire of the Tennesseans.[22]

Through Carroll, Jackson ordered Colonel Henderson to take a detachment into the swamp to dislodge the enemy from that fence. The plan was for Henderson to move well into the swamp and emerge from the wood beyond the second parallel ditch, where he would have a fence between him and the British detachment. Thus he could cut off that detachment while the batteries prevented the troops in the field from coming to the rescue. Henderson moved into the wood with two hundred Tennesseans.[23]

After most of the army had retreated, Colonel Dickson had to retrieve the deserted and broken guns. He assigned the task to Captain Troubridge of the navy and his seamen. Troubridge found that his men could sneak around the burning house to the road near the guns without being seen. After reaching this point, they dashed to the road, hooked on to a gun, and with a concerted effort dragged it away on one wheel and the point of the axle. They did not stop until they had gone four hundred yards to the turn in the road. But having succeeded once, they were expected on the next trip. All the American guns trained upon them as they dashed into the road the second time. Amidst the heavy fire they again hooked a gun and dragged it steadily up the road to safety.[24]

Captain Hill discovered a group of West Indian soldiers huddled together in an exposed position, heedless of the shot and shell striking around them. When he shouted to them to take cover, one of them merely shook his head and said in his broken English, "No, thank you, massa. Rather stay here and get killed. Never see the day go back to Jamaica, so me die now, thank you. No stand them damn cold and fog. No house to live in. No warm clothes. So poor nigger die like dog." [25]

Colonel Henderson, misjudging his distance while sloshing through the water of the swamp, moved back into the plain at the wrong spot. Instead of going four hundred yards and getting beyond the second ditch, he moved diagonally through the wood and emerged in full view of the hidden British. As he appeared with his men, Rennie's soldiers fired. Most of the Tennesseans scurried back into the swamp, leaving several men and Colonel Henderson lying on the field. Their commander gone, the survivors returned to the breastwork. But Rennie knew now that he could do little with the rest of the army retreating, so he withdrew his detachment. [26]

The battlefield was quiet except for the booming of the American cannon, which continued to harry the British units as they retreated. It was noon by the time the last of the 85th, moving from ditch to ditch, escaped from Chalmette to De la Ronde's. Soldiers were scattered over De la Ronde's, lying exhausted or carrying the wounded back to the hospital that had been established at Jumonville's. [27]

Jackson counted his losses. In each of Coffee's and Plauché's commands one private had been killed. In Carroll's, Colonel Henderson, one sergeant, and five privates had been killed. One major of marines, three of Plauché's volunteers, one lieutenant and three privates of Carroll's, and one of the sailors on the *Louisiana* had been wounded. Nine killed, nine wounded. Among the British some sixteen men were killed and forty-three wounded. The dead included Ensign Sir Frederick Eden of the 85th, a baronet, who had been struck down in the first firing along with five of his men. [28]

Once the men and guns had been brought to safety, the three British generals studied the field, taking reports from various officers, attempting to ascertain the exact strength of the American line and the exact nature of the terrain. For the bleak results of this battle, Pakenham had consolation in the faith that he now felt in two units and two young officers. The 85th and the 21st regiments had held up under fire, and Colonel Thornton and Major Rennie had displayed courage, determination, and ingenuity. The 4th and 95th, in spite of their brilliant records in the Peninsular war, had not followed up these two units with the spirit that the general could wish. The 44th had also taken readily to the ditches, and Colonel Mullins had not exposed himself to rally his men as the other commanders had done; but General Pakenham was reluctant to judge this nobleman too readily.

General Jackson had learned that his breastwork would serve nobly. He sent word to the governor to encourage the citizens to strengthen the Dupré line and to build still a third breastwork at Montreuil's canal, and he ordered his engineer Latour to build a breastwork between river and swamp on the other side of the river in case the British should cross rather than attempt another attack at the same place. He had also learned that his men could act coolly under fire. The Tennesseans had not flinched, and the Louisianans had held their posts. He was especially proud of the heavy and accurate fire of the artillerymen, and he visited the Baratarians, slapped the grinning Dominique lustily on the shoulder, and thanked the Lafittes politely. About the navy he need have no qualms. Crawley's and Norris' sailors had fired well, and the *Louisiana* had thrown eight hundred rounds into the midst of the enemy while receiving only a few hits.[29]

About some of his officers he felt less confidence. Colonel Henderson had suffered for his mistake, but his error showed that the inexperienced ones could not be relied upon for good tactical judgment. The aides, too, had become so excited that Jackson had had to deliver important commands in person rather than trust them to others. General Humbert had stayed staunchly close at hand, seeming unruffled, but his lack of English reduced his worth. Edward Livingston's shrewd judgment was of no special value during the actual fighting.

The general called Abner Duncan to him to learn more about the report that the legislature intended to surrender the country. Duncan repeated the report, naming Declouet as his source. The general scolded him soundly, telling him that even if it had been better substantiated than it was it should never have been delivered in the presence of troops. He sent him to Claiborne with instructions to reopen the statehouse unless there was real evidence of treachery.[30]

Before Jackson's temper had time to cool, Declouet appeared, still rattled. Through the interpreter Davezac he defended his actions, assuring the general that a legislator had called Jackson's war a Russian one that the legislature could not tolerate. Reluctantly under prodding he named Magloire Guichard as the legislator. He thought that most of the others agreed with Guichard.

"Who?"

"Well . . . the French side of the house. You know, those who vote with Blanque. The ones who just do whatever Blanque and Guichard say."

"Louaillier?"

"Well, no, not Louaillier. Sometimes Louaillier votes against the French. The others . . . Blanque's crowd. . . ."

He was too ridiculous even to be angry at. Disgustedly Jackson dismissed him. He had a war to worry about, and the legislature was the governor's business. But his faith in the support he could expect from the citizens, like his faith in his inexperienced officers, was shaken.[31]

The statehouse was reopened, and the repulse of the British quieted most of the fears that citizens had of Jackson's tactics. But animosities had been created that would never heal, and some of the legislators would never forgive Jackson or Claiborne for the affront to their dignity.

‡‡‡

In the evening the British army mustered and was ordered to camp on De la Ronde's. The 4th and 44th were stationed near the wood; the 21st to their left; the 85th and 93rd to their left, in a line that slanted toward the enemy; and the 95th between the chateau and the river. Quartermaster Surtees, having no inclination to be deprived of his rest, chose a small house half a mile behind his battalion. Little reed huts appeared as the soldiers provided themselves with shelter. Large detachments were sent along the river and the Terre aux Boeufs bayou to get supplies, the immediate plantations having been exhausted of provisions. Pickets were established on Bienvenu's. There would be more days of waiting.[32]

Behind the breastwork the Americans again settled down to a night in the mud. Spirits were high, and more soldiers than usual slipped away in the darkness to celebrate their success in the city. Along the waterfront the taverns and brothels assumed some of the gaiety of prewar days when the harbor had been filled with boats and barges, the wharves had been busy with commerce, and the rivermen of the West had met with the sailors of the world to feast after a journey through the wilderness or a voyage over the seas.

In more respectable homes there was less gaiety, but there was less tension too. Apparently the invader would be neither quickly victorious nor quickly dislodged, but the two successful engagements indicated that the city might escape capture, and as the enemy's presence became a familiar one certain routines of life under threat were established, calming disturbed emotions. Those who had grumbled loudest about their suspicions of Jackson now felt shamed and proclaimed their patriotism and faith the loudest —though Louaillier and Judge Hall, who had kept their discontent to themselves, remained firm in their conviction that he was too strong and stubborn a man to be a democratic leader.

At Villeré's, Pakenham sat down with his generals, his staff, and Admiral Cochrane to plan the next move.

‡‡‡

In London the Treaty of Ghent was ratified by the Prince Regent. Mr. Baker, secretary to Lord Gambier, and Mr. Carroll, the American secretary, set out in the sloop of war *Favorite* to carry the official copy to America. Mr. Hughes with another copy was already at sea in the schooner *Transit*.[33]

SEVENTEEN

Artillery Duel

WHAT COULD Pakenham try next? He and his generals could not rid their minds of the image of that breastwork and the galling fire that had been poured into the ranks of their unprotected troops. True, Rennie's demonstration near the swamp had proved the weakness of Jackson's left; Pakenham could take advantage of this knowledge in the next attack. Perhaps the whole army could move through the swamp, circling around the breastwork instead of moving over it. The general ordered his engineers to investigate the practicability of such a route. Perhaps, too, the army could cross the river and move up the opposite bank.

Admiral Cochrane did not favor any change of plans. The army was set for a move up the plain, and move up the plain it should. The thing to do was not to worry about bypassing the breastwork, but to eliminate it. The artillery's pieces having proved inadequate, let the navy's guns do the job. Already his sailors had widened part of the canal; the admiral could have enough guns brought from the fleet in three days to pulverize the breastwork.

When Pakenham questioned them about the practicability of this plan, his engineer, Colonel Burgoyne, and his chief of artillery, Colonel Dickson, opined that they could seriously breach the defense with big guns if they planted them closer to the line than on the first attempt and mounted them in good earthworks.

Pakenham ordered them to plan their batteries, instructed his generals to organize their troops for foraging duty, and requested the admiral to bring up his siege guns as soon as possible.[1]

‡‡‡

At Macarty's, General Humbert insisted on making his daily morning trip to reconnoiter the British lines. As escort, Jackson sent a squad of Coffee's mounted Tennesseans. They rode from the breastwork across Chalmette to Bienvenu, when suddenly they were fired upon by British pickets. Quickly the Tennesseans wheeled and rode back to the line, while Humbert sought cover and spied through his glass at the camp. When he returned to headquarters he stormed into Jackson's office to report the infamous conduct of the Tennesseans. After pacifying him with a promise of discipline, Jackson called the sergeant in charge and demanded why he and his men had fled. "Well, General," the sergeant drawled, "not understanding French and believing our commander was a man of sense, we construed his orders to retire out of the reach of the muskets, and so we just kind of countermarched." [2]

Already Jackson, acting on a suggestion of Jean Lafitte, had ordered the Tennesseans to extend the breastwork on the left, bending it back to reach well into the swamp. He would not again risk being flanked in that direction. The men were digging, working now in the deep mud of the swamp. As the mud would not pile up, they stacked two long rows of logs and piled the mud between. They cleared the underbrush out of the way for thirty or forty yards in front of their line to give the riflemen a clear view of any possible enemy. Jackson also withdrew the 1st Louisiana from the line to Piernas' canal to serve as a rear guard, watching the swamp for any flank movement. Two miles back the citizens were digging, jubilant that breastworks had proved so worthy, and a third mound was going up a mile from town. Across the river, under Latour's direction, a large party of slaves was digging heartily behind the Boisgervais canal, throwing up still another.[3]

General Morgan, having witnessed the effectiveness of the breastwork, was also eager to throw up such a line, but he could not decide upon the best position. The line Latour was building was considerably upriver from Jackson's Rodriguez position, and Morgan wished to be closer to his commander. He wondered if he should be exactly across the river, somewhat below, or somewhat above. While he remained undecided his men whiled away their time in camp.

Commander Patterson established a battery on the right bank opposite Rodriguez. In it he mounted a twenty-four-pounder and two twelve-pounders.[4]

‡‡‡

When the engineers reported the swamp impassable, Pakenham decided to trust to Cochrane's guns for his next attack. His men shared picket duty and foraging, paraded, sometimes bathed in the river, and tied cane into bundles to provide the army with fascines. The enemy, however, elevated the guns across the river and on the ship and pounded the British camp, driving the advance to cover behind the levee and the buildings. Again the peacefulness of the bivouac was broken by a steady cannonade.[5]

Detachments of Cochrane's sailors rummaged about the plantations, commandeering several large canoes and wagons and a few horses. In their movement they gradually wore various roads through the cane stubble. Others pulled on the oars of the barges, continuing the ferry service that had operated now for nearly two weeks. From the fleet they brought ten eighteen-pounders and four twenty-four-pounders to the bayou, where they were loaded into the canoes, one to each canoe, and dragged up the bayou and the canal to a point half a mile from the highroad; there they were loaded into the wagons and hauled up to the camp. Dickson's artillerymen labored to convert the carts found on the plantations into sling carts for the guns. At the picket house on Bienvenu's fatigue parties worked to build a battery, and on the highroad they built another. Colonel Dickson also explored the fields to choose a route for moving the heavy guns. He decided to take them along the highroad to De la Ronde's, then to move to the new road that crossed the fields in the middle of the plantations, and to take them along that road to the batteries that would be built the night before the attack.[6]

The admiral had other ideas as well. He sent a squadron of

ships to the mouth of the river, where it captured the little group of pilots who guided boats through the shoals and reeds and up to the city. If the present plan failed, the admiral might try to pass Fort St. Philip.

On the thirty-first another British fleet reached the mouth of the Mississippi, carrying General Lambert and the 7th, 40th, and 43rd regiments. It made its way up the sound, searching for Cochrane's anchorage. During the night such a dense fog gathered that the ships had to lay to. Not a breath of wind stirred.[7]

‡‡‡

Pakenham issued his order for the attack. Knowing now that Jackson's greatest artillery strength was toward the river, he would assault principally the enemy's left and center. During the night Colonel Burgoyne must push back the enemy pickets, mark out the batteries requested by Dickson, build them, lay the platforms, mount the guns, and bring up the ammunition. He would be given large details of soldiers to do the work. At daybreak the guns would open, first silencing the enemy's guns and then opening breaches in the breastwork. When the line was breached, the army would carry the enemy position. On the right General Gibbs would assault in a column of battalions with fifty-yard intervals between each. General Keane would similarly assault in the center. Not a shot should be fired, and nothing should impede the head of the columns until they had mastered the enemy's lines. Such troops as the enemy might hold upon the line should be charged by corps as quickly as possible upon entry. The leading regiments could attack by wings and the succeeding ones by battalions. When the enemy was shaken, a new formation would be made. False attacks should be made on both flanks, from the left of Keane's brigade (on the road) and from the right of Gibbs's (through the wood). Keane's demonstration should not amount to a committal unless an evidently favorable opportunity presented itself (excellent language, that sentence). On the right, a party of eighty British and one hundred blacks would enter the projection of the wood before day and endeavor by a small circuit to reach the enemy's left flank—this would be Gibbs's flank attack. If they should fall in with the enemy's outposts before the hour of assault, they should conceal themselves until the general attack and then attract attention by firing, bugling, etc., and if circumstances permitted, penetrate in the enemy's rear. Three companies of the 4th were to be in column of half-companies behind the projecting wood to prevent the enemy from sortieing from his left (the movement Henderson had tried to make on the twenty-eighth). This would secure a reserve to the flankers detached through the wood.[8]

Pakenham smiled at his excellently worked out plan and sat back to await the hour of its execution.

Dickson had planned four main batteries. One of them, at the Bienvenu picket house, was already completed and ready to fire at the shipping. Ahead of it on the highroad, past Chalmette's ruins, he planned a battery for two eighteens. In the field, left of the center, he planned a battery for two nines, three sixes, and two howitzers. Right of center, eight hundred yards from the enemy line, would be a battery for six eighteens and four twenty-fours. There would be a rocket detachment to the right of the Chalmette ruins and another to the left of the woods. And behind the left rocket detachment there would be a small battery for three mortars.

In the night strong working parties of soldiers and sailors hurried forward to construct these batteries. They worked feverishly, throwing up earthworks, dragging forward the guns, and mounting them. Confusion developed—guns arrived before the platforms were ready, working parties got lost in the darkness, and progress was generally much slower than planned. For the road battery, hogsheads of sugar filled with earth were used. Dickson was not satisfied, at 5:30 in the morning, with the results—the platforms were weak and the earthworks too low; but guns had been mounted that could throw a broadside of 350 pounds of metal. Daybreak was fast approaching, so the work had to be discontinued.[9]

A small detachment under Lieutenant Wright was sent into the wood to reconnoiter, but it unfortunately came upon a Tennessee hunting party, and Lieutenant Wright and five men were shot dead.[10]

The army formed in the darkness, marched forward, passed the pickets, and took position for the assault. Gibbs's and Keane's leading regiments lay down in the ditch before the batteries; the other regiments formed similarly in ditches on Bienvenu's. Keane's left flankers waited in the Bienvenu garden, and Gibbs's right flankers waited behind the wood.[11]

On the other side of the canal there was less activity and less worry. Carroll had completed the extension of the earthwork into the swamp, and except for the discomfort of wet beds in the soft earth behind the line, the troops felt secure. A new regiment arrived, brought from Acadia by Villeré, and encamped behind Line Dupré, Jackson's second line of defense. There were plenty of men, and there were now seven batteries behind the breastwork: Captain Humphreys of the artillery on the right; Lieutenant Norris' sailors; the Baratarians under Dominique and Beluche; Lieutenant Crawley's sailors; Colonel Perry's artillerymen; and two newly established batteries, one under Garrigue Fleaujac, a legislator who had volunteered, and one under Lieutenant Spotts. Across the river Commander Patterson's guns could provide a flanking fire.[12]

There was a general feeling of security. Jackson had ordered a parade on the Macarty plantation for daybreak, and this night there was considerable absenteeism as the soldiers celebrated in the city the departure of the old year and the arrival of the new.

‡‡‡

The first morning of 1815 arrived with a dense fog. The British soldiers lay on the ground unable to see anything but reeds in the field a short distance ahead. The artillerymen at the guns had no target but fog. A detachment moved into the swamp, picking its way cautiously a short distance, but otherwise the army lay ready but inactive.[13]

At the canal bugles called up the American soldiers, who formed in the field behind the line in spite of the fog. After mustering they waited, the officers hesitating to begin the parade when visibility was so poor. Some citizens found their way from the city in the fog and waited in Macarty's garden. The units were ready, Plauché's volunteers dressed smartly, the others dirty from their days behind the mound. Colorbearers, drummers, and the city band were in position. But no one could see.[14]

Finally, about nine o'clock, the fog thinned, and Jackson, not wanting to keep his men standing any longer, ordered the parade to begin. The drums rolled, the band played, and the regiments marched in review.[15]

The gunners and the soldiers of the 85th waited, the gunners searching for targets, the soldiers lying in the ditch ready to move when a breach was opened. Then with dramatic suddenness the fog lifted, bright sunshine revealing the fields of grass and cane stubble stretching some four hundred yards ahead, the earthwork beside the Rodriguez canal, and beyond the earthwork the colors and some of the figures of the parading regiments. On the highroad the artillerymen of the left battery searched the river for the *Louisiana,* but it had moved out of range. The two batteries on the right had their targets and opened fire, seventeen guns blasting in rapid succession. Beyond the earthwork there was a sudden wild scramble of troops pushing and shoving each other as they made for the breastwork. The British guns bellowed again, their balls pounding into the great mound.[16]

Then from across the river roared Patterson's battery. Pakenham's four guns on the left trained in that direction. A moment later Jackson's six batteries opened. On both sides there was a tremendous booming of cannon, and trains of smoke rose to meet the fog bank. The duel was on.

The British soldiers lay in position on the ground, watching for the first breach, fingering their muskets as they waited for the order to march. The detachment in the swamp picked its way through the mud and trees toward the line. Behind the breastwork, the muskets and rifles of the Americans rattled as the men sought targets in the British redoubts and in the ditches.

Pakenham's left battery seemed to make no headway against the guns across the river, while the enemy's balls struck close, sometimes roaring into the sugar casks, sometimes hitting resoundingly inside the redoubt. The barrels shifted and tumbled. On the right, scores of balls pounded into the breastwork, but they only stuck in the earth, while the enemy's shots tore holes in the redoubts.

The Macarty mansion took a terrible beating. Balls, rockets, and shells struck the walls. Bricks and splinters of wood flew in the air. Windows were smashed, and balls tore into the furniture in some of the rooms. Jackson and his staff, forced to leave, took cover in the garden.[17]

On the right of the line the cotton bales that had been placed on the breastwork burst into flames. Two caissons loaded with one hundred rounds blew up. The troops scattered, then returned to push the bales off the mound, but the smoke billowing from them blinded Humphreys' artillerymen. Finally Plauché's men went forward to push the burning bales into the river. From the cane field could be heard British troops breaking into loud cheers, but when Dominique and Humphreys changed their sights and sent balls roaring in that direction, the enemy soldiers quickly became silent.

A hit broke the carriage of Dominique's twenty-four. Another hit damaged the carriage of Crawley's thirty-two. Another broke the foretrain of one of Garrigue's twelves. But the other guns had the range of the redoubts, and the men could see their balls striking the enemy. It was the fiercest cannonade, Major Tatum felt, that he had ever witnessed, surpassing the siege of Charleston.

From pickets on the left came word of an enemy detachment in the wood. On orders from Jackson, Coffee sent a company to meet them.[18]

Across the river shells whistled close over Patterson's battery. Some balls broke through the breastwork and embrasures. But his guns kept up their fire.[19]

In the fields the British infantrymen waited, muskets ready, for a breach to be opened. The hours dragged by, the guns boomed monotonously, the men shifted about vainly seeking to relieve aching muscles.

Enemy shot tore into the British redoubts, dismounting or damaging several guns and striking several men. The barrels rolled in all directions, and many were splintered. There were holes and cave-ins in the earthwork of the other two redoubts. The sweating artillerymen loaded, fired, watched, and dove for cover as balls shrieked toward them. The enemy fire roared unabated, and the Rodriguez earthwork stood as stoutly as ever. Smoke from the firing rolled over the field to obscure the targets. Several guns were disabled; as the artillerymen became more and more discouraged and harassed, the fire from the other guns slackened.

Quartermaster Surtees, having chosen to observe from a redoubt, was extremely annoyed by the enemy's thirty-two-pounder, whose balls ricocheted off the main British battery into the redoubt. Surtees trained his glass on that gun and saw what looked like sailors manning it. He was impressed by one giant red-shirted mulatto who sponged out the gun after each shot. He also discovered that he could see the ball, a small black spot in the midst of a cloud of white smoke, each time it fired. He could then drop to the ground to avoid being hit when it ricocheted toward him.[20]

Still the infantrymen lay in the field, waiting for orders. They came: the army must hold its position to protect the guns until nightfall.

From the American line the cannon continued to roar, aiming now at the infantrymen exposed in the field. The 85th and 93rd, the most advanced regiments, dived for better cover into the nearest ditches, hiding in the reeds, wallowing in the mud, muscles aching from the tense positions they had to maintain. Miserably they waited for the long day to end.

The detachment in the swamp, hearing of the failure of the artillery, retreated to the dry ground behind the wood, where they joined the companies of the 4th that were to be their reserve.

Behind Jackson's breastwork the soldiers lolled, in high spirits, joshing each other while they watched the busy artillerymen. Lieutenant Humphreys stood quietly behind his battery, relaxed, chewing on a cigar, periodically barking, "Let her off." "Phlegmatic Humphreys," the soldiers named him. Lieutenant Spotts nervously jumped among his guns, never still. Dominique peered steadily into the field, watching where his shots fell, shouting continuously and fiercely to his men, occasionally roaring with laughter at a good hit. Lieutenant Norris stood calmly, hands behind his back, almost at attention. Lieutenant Crawley quietly watched his men, occasionally issuing an order. Garrigue the Frenchman leaped excitedly about, yelling enthusiastically at good hits in a voice that carried along the line.[21]

At noon the fire slackened to allow the guns to cool, an occasional shot keeping the enemy alert. The British soldiers had a few minutes to shift positions in the ditches, to breathe more freely. But as their spirits began to rise the guns opened furiously again, raking the ditches, and they tumbled back into the mud, cursing and praying. The British abandoned the two main batteries in the field, the artillerymen racing back across the field to cover. For a while the battery on the road continued, but then it too was abandoned. In midafternoon Jackson called off his cannonade.

Then the British troops had to lie in the ditches, aching with weariness, waiting for the dark. Rain fell, lightly at first but steadily increasing, wetting the soldiers to the skin. Behind the Rodriguez breastwork, the Americans warmed themselves with a supply of whisky Jackson had distributed.[22]

In the gloom Pakenham sent forward working parties to haul the guns back. There was still light enough to see them, and Patterson's guns fired, harassing them as they pulled and tugged. The rain having turned the fields to mud, the guns could only with lusty effort be budged.[23]

When dark finally came, the other soldiers left the ditches to help. A large part of the army worked on the guns, trudging through the mud, heaving and tugging, dragging them inch by inch through the field. The night was far gone before the cannon had been pulled to safety. Several badly damaged ones had been left behind.[24]

As the miserably weary soldiers rested, there was grumbling about the hideous situation in which they found themselves. There were murmurs that the commanders were hopeless blunderers and the whole enterprise was an abortion. Many soldiers, disgusted with their experience, slipped out of camp to seek refuge with the enemy. Officers spoke contemptuously (though furtively) of "Sir Alex" and his promises of an easy victory. One wrote home, "New Year's Day afforded us a sight of fireworks, pop guns, mortars, and rockets such as has been seldom witnessed even in Lord Wellington's great action in the Peninsula; however, this attempt was unsuccessful." [25]

Jackson had lost 8 privates killed in the batteries and 8 wounded; 1 private of the 7th regulars wounded; 1 private of the 44th regulars killed and 3 wounded; 1 of Coffee's sergeants killed and 2 men wounded; 3 of Plauché's volunteers wounded; 1 lieutenant, 1 sergeant, and 1 private of the colored troops wounded—11 men killed, 23 wounded.

Dickson's artillery had lost 1 officer, Lieutenant Ramsay, killed, 1 sergeant and 9 men killed, and 12 men wounded. Lieutenant Blakeney of the 44th was killed, along with 1 man of the 21st, 1 man of the 44th, 2 of the 85th, 1 sergeant and 3 men of the 93rd, 1 man of the 95th, and 4 men of the 5th West India. Wounded were 1 lieutenant and 4 men of the 21st, 3 men of the 44th, 2 lieutenants and 4 men of the 85th, 1 lieutenant and 10 men of the 93rd, 2 men of the 95th, and 2 men of the 5th West India—26 killed and 41 wounded.[26]

At the hospital on Jumonville's Lieutenant Gleig sat by the beds of his wounded friends Charlton and Boys. Boys's wound was slight enough that he could return to duty in a few days, but Charlton lay weak and gasping, struggling against a terrible pain. Gleig and Boys tried to joke about Charlton's returning to the anchorage and gave him messages to take to their friends if they should not survive the next assault, but the jokes were dispirited. Gleig, oppressed with a heavy weariness, could not rid his mind of the image of his friend Grey lying on the ground in a pool of blood. Nearby, Lieutenant Phaups of the 93rd lay unconscious, sinking into death. According to report, he and some other officers had tumbled during the cannonade into a shallow hollow, and since Phaups was the only married one in the group, it was decided he should lie at the bottom. But, raising his head to peer out, he was struck by a twelve-pound shot.[27]

At headquarters the generals and their staff officers sat glumly, unenthusiastically reviewing the battle, desultorily discussing possible future action. Admiral Cochrane had not joined them, and everyone was devoid of ideas. Colonel Dickson of the artillery and Colonel Burgoyne of the engineers, the officers who had been sure they could pulverize the breastwork with naval guns, sat apart from the rest, somewhat in disgrace. "Such a failure in this boasted arm," remarked one of the admirals, "was a blot on the artillery escutcheon." Colonel Dickson felt that the artillery was maligned, and that the failure was due to the clumsiness of sea-guns on the shore.[28]

In New Orleans lights burned far into the night. Citizens paid calls upon each other as though it were peacetime again. Soldiers from the lines visited, and many found welcome and gay celebrations in the homes of the city. People who had left town at the beginning of the invasion were drifting back to share the excitement of a war that no longer seemed dangerous—social leaders to their luxurious apartments, gamblers and prostitutes to their places on the waterfront where new customers brought in by the army awaited them. There was laughter at the ridiculousness of "Wellington's regulars" lying with their noses in the mud. New Orleans merrily burned away New Year's night while the weary, hungry intruders vainly sought shelter from the rain in the crude reed huts they had built on De la Ronde's. The proud British visitor ignominiously squatted in the mud while his once-desired mistress laughed raucously at his plight.

☼ ☼

EIGHTEEN

Preparing for the Great Assault

AT CAT Island, as the days dragged by, the civilians fretted at the delay. Since the battle on the lakes there had been no good news, only reports of unsuccessful skirmishes. Meanwhile they fought boredom on a corner of the bleak island or in crowded quarters on the ships. Lady Mullins, unhappy at the delay, would see only the most important of her friends. On the island the women dared not venture far from their tents for fear of snakes or alligators. Some of the officers' wives, unable to cope with the insects and sand, returned to the ships. A few wives, apprised of the deaths of their husbands, wept away the time. A few nursed wounded husbands, sympathetically sharing the pain as they watched their twisted features. Others, watching these, realized their own nearness to death and carried fear in their stomachs.

The American prisoners fretted in confinement, listened eagerly to the disgruntled talk of the sailors in order to learn news of the battle, and longed to join the great enterprise. A few from wealthy families were admitted to the British officers' mess, and one, who in New York before the war had known the captain of the ship where he was imprisoned, found himself an honored guest at a special feast. Certain captured British officers, quartered in different Louisiana homes, had also to fret, and as they heard the reports of British failures they had less consolation than the Americans.

Some remained gloomily aloof; others marveled at Creole hospitality. Major Mitchell, his pride wounded by his capture on the twenty-third, gradually thawed out in the presence of his host's two daughters, and when they were visited by soldiers from the line he acted as interpreter. A wounded British captain, rallying under the care of Mrs. Livingston, often attended the parties she gave for American officers.[1]

Still more troops arrived—General Thomas' division of Baton Rouge militia—and encamped at Dupré's. Word came that the Kentuckians were at Baton Rouge, but that many were unarmed, a report that Jackson greeted incredulously—"I've never seen a Kentuckian without a gun, a pack of cards, and a bottle of whisky." Across the river at the Boisgervais canal, the engineer Latour was building a neat, strong earthwork with a level glacis for troops, monotonously superior to the sloppy and irregular Rodriguez parapet. General Morgan complained to Jackson that Latour's line was too far back and he needed Latour's slaves for his own line, and Jackson promised to send them as soon as the Boisgervais defense was completed. He met Morgan's request for more men by sending him the 1st and 2nd Louisiana regiments, leaving the Acadians and the new Baton Rouge division with Villeré. Meanwhile Patterson sent more guns to strengthen the artillery at Rodriguez. General Adair appeared at headquarters to report that the Kentucky militia had reached Lafourche and could be at the line in a few days. Reuben Kemper made a long trip through the swamps, returning to assure Jackson that the British could not possibly get through them.[2]

Since there were still rumors and a strong possibility that the British would attempt to destroy Fort St. Philip and come up the river, Patterson was anxious to send another thirty-two-pounder and other supplies to the fort. Jackson called Henry Shreve, whose steamboat had been busily transporting material between the city and the camp, to headquarters. The stern general looked into the face of the stern young riverman.

"Captain Shreve, I understand that you're a man who always does what he undertakes. Can you pass the British batteries with your steamer to take supplies to Fort St. Philip?"

After a moment's reflection Shreve replied, "I can do it if you'll give me my own time."

Time was something Jackson did not like to give. Throughout his campaigns in the Indian forests he had been hampered by contractors who took too much time and too few risks. Was Shreve just such another? "What time do you require?" he asked.

"Twenty-four hours," said the captain.

Supplies were loaded onto the *Enterprise* in the afternoon, and in the evening it ran down to a position above the British batteries. Cotton bales were fastened with iron hooks to the side facing the guns and the wheel was carefully muffled. That night, during a dense fog, the boat proceeded under a slow head of steam, with the crew almost holding their breaths to avoid noise, and passed the batteries unobserved. It delivered its supplies to the fort, steamed back up the river, and in a similar manner repassed the batteries. This time it was discovered by the British, but it was far enough past the guns that with a burst of speed it steamed out of harm's way. Shreve now asked permission to join the ranks, and he was stationed at Humphreys' battery.[3]

Busily the Americans worked, steadily adding to their defenses everywhere, while Pakenham's army sat more or less idly on De la Ronde's, rapidly depleting the provisions on all the available plantations.

Pakenham, disconcerted by his two futile assaults, decided to wait for Lambert's reinforcements before trying again. Admiral Cochrane, however, could not merely wait. He dispatched a squadron for the Mississippi—the sloop of war *Herald*, the *Nymph*, the *Thistle*, the schooner *Pigmy* as tender, and the bomb vessels *Aetna* and *Meteor*, the last commanded by Captain Roberts, who had aided Nicholas Lockyer against the gunboats. Captured pilots would guide them through the river mouth, and if they could destroy the fort they would clear the river for more of the fleet.[4]

When Cochrane assured him that his sailors could widen the Villeré canal sufficiently to bring up boats to transport troops across the river, Pakenham considered attacking on the right bank instead of the left. But this was not the admiral's idea. He could take across enough troops to provide a diversion, but he protested the difficulty of ferrying the whole army. Reluctantly Pakenham resigned himself to another attempt at the breastwork.[5]

The *Vengeur* sailed into the anchorage, bearing General Lambert and leading the squadron that carried the 7th, 43rd, and 40th regiments. While General Lambert hastened to the front, his soldiers contacted the men at the base for news of the invasion. Their queries were answered with vociferous curses. The army had landed all right, but the Americans stole upon it on their hands and knees, Indian fashion. They were driven out in quick time, but the army had not been able to dislodge them from their holes. The disappointed soldiers at the base found relief in thus venting their bitter feelings, and the new arrivals felt a lift as they thought of themselves as the rescuers of their fellow regiments. Sergeant Cooper merely cursed his luck; he had hoped the battle would be over and his discharge forthcoming. He asked Corporal Fitzpatrick where the Indian wenches were, but Fitzpatrick was now more interested in the octoroons waiting for him at New Orleans.[6]

‡‡‡

The arrival of John Lambert, looking cool and fresh, heartened the other generals. John Keane began to forget the embarrassment of his failure and to regain his youthful ardor. Pakenham, receiving Lambert's assured report of the good condition of the new regiments and remembering the great assaults on the Peninsula that the 7th and 43rd had conducted, regained his poise and confidence. Sam Gibbs, naturally optimistic, sensed the new spirit of the others and became heartily friendly. All was not lost. Four regiments from Wellington's campaign were on hand, the 4th, 7th, 43rd, and 95th. Three others, the 21st, 44th, and 85th, had proved worthy in the Baltimore campaign, and one of these, the 85th, had been the most effective of all so far in the present campaign. In addition there were the 93rd, which at least presented a smart appearance in camp, and the two West Indias, which because of poor equipment had suffered from the weather but which had carried out their duties without complaint. With these great British regiments, the generals would make of New Orleans another Albuhera, Redinha, Sabugal, or perhaps even another Salamanca (the great charge of his troops across that valley Pakenham could never forget). The present attack, however, combined the qualities of an open battle and of fortress-storming; necessarily it must take its own individual form. It was up to the generals to design a form worthy of the troops who would bring it to life. The troops were trained, experienced, orderly, and precise; they needed only effective leadership.

Cochrane's sailors were again ferrying troops across the lake. By January 7 they would have two of the new regiments in position on the plain and a few days later the third. As the squadron designated for the river could hardly reach Fort St. Philip before the eighth and would then have to besiege the fort, Pakenham felt that he could not wait for its support. After New Orleans was carried the fleet could come up the river to help secure the conquest. He would make his final assault—no tentative thrust, but a do-or-die plunge—on the eighth. He would attack on both banks of the river, with the main attack here, a noble display of British power and valor that would eradicate the previous clumsinesses.

The demonstration across the river must not, however, be skimpy. Besides distracting the enemy's attention, it would capture the batteries that had provided such a devastating flank fire on January 1. This movement Pakenham would trust to the field officer who had shown the greatest aptitude for independent command, Colonel Thornton. In the main attack, Sam Gibbs would storm over the field on the right and John Keane would storm the center. The resourceful Robert Rennie would move along the highroad. General Lambert, commanding a strong reserve, would be ready to move wherever the enemy first showed weakness.[7]

There would be no waiting this time for the artillery to breach the line. The artillery, firing from the batteries constructed on the thirty-first, would be trusted to blast the enemy's guns while the infantry broke his courage. If no breach was made, the infantry would swarm over the canal and the earthwork, and to accomplish this fascines and scaling ladders would be provided. No guess-work this time; a carefully planned, prepared, and executed drive that would lay the city bare for conquest.

Since the navy was now occupied in ferrying the new troops, the army must widen the canal to make the river crossing possible. The road along the canal, weakened by the rains, had been made an impassable mess by heavy use, so it too must be repaired. The troops on the plain were divided into four detachments to labor one at a time on these projects, while other details worked to build ladders and fascines and stack them, at night, in a redoubt that had been built on the twenty-seventh and abandoned since then. This work reduced the idleness of the troops, who began to catch the confident spirit of the generals.[8]

Until now the adventure had not prospered. The visitor had first been disappointed in his expectation that he would find discontented retainers among the city's guardians who would secretly deliver him the prize. Though in the first skirmish on the lake he had broken the outer defenses, it had only been to find himself foundering in a terrible moat. He had struggled through that moat to the doorstep only to be delivered in the darkness a heavy surprise blow which left him temporarily dazed. After that he had tried twice to seize his victim, once walking boldly forward to be repulsed with a hearty slap, once attempting to club his way only to have the club rudely pushed from his hand. Now he would dress his finest, display proudly his best form, and awe his victim into submission.

So the soldiers labored, worried only by occasional rains, morning fogs, the excursions of Tennesseans and dragoons against the pickets, and the target practice which enemy guns sometimes leveled against the camp. The sailors labored, heaving on their oars, ferrying troops and supplies. Admiral Cochrane decided to save time and effort by having the new troops carry some of the ammunition. He had each soldier place a cannon ball in his haversack. These balls provided the soldiers with hard pillows when they tried to rest in the boats, pillows which dug into the bases of their skulls. When they reached the landing and marched up the road to camp, the balls shifted around, pulling at the muscles of their backs and shoulders. Sergeant Cooper grumbled that he would rather have two balls because they could at least be poised against each other.[9]

While they crossed the lake one boat, carrying a sergeant and sixteen privates, swamped, and only one man was able to swim to safety. The others were dragged under water by their heavy haversacks. When they came out of the swamps, they camped on De la Ronde's, the other troops having moved forward to Bienvenu's.[10]

At Hartford, Connecticut, the convention adjourned, having proposed a union of the New England states for their own defense. In Washington the government, staggering under its debts, was

near collapse. Opposition leaders waited confidently for news of
the fall of New Orleans that they might demand the resignation of
President Madison.[11]

‡‡‡

At Macarty's Jackson observed, through his telescope and the
reconnaissance of Hinds's dragoons, the extensive British preparations. He fretted at his inability to act. No more than small parties
could move through the swamp; there were no boats to attack the
supply lines on the lake; and he did not trust his motley army to
move from the earthwork into the plain for an attack. His enforced
inactivity made him nervous, but there was nothing to do but
wait. Meanwhile with Patterson's help he passed the time by
mounting new guns along the line.

He now had eight batteries. Covering the highroad, seventy
feet from the riverbank, Battery 1, Captain Humphreys, had two
brass twelve-pounders and a six-inch howitzer on field carriages; it
was served by the regular artillery and some of Plauché's volunteers. Ninety yards to its left, Battery 2, Lieutenant Norris, had
a twenty-four-pounder served by crewmen of the *Carolina;* this
gun was the most elevated above the soil. Fifty yards further, Battery 3 had two twenty-four-pounders, one served by Dominique's
Baratarians and one by Beluche's volunteers. Twenty yards from
this, Battery 4, Lieutenant Crawley, had a thirty-two-pounder
served by *Carolina* crewmen. One hundred and ninety yards separated this from Battery 5, Colonel Perry and Lieutenant Kerr,
which had two six-pounders served by regular artillerymen. Thirty-
six yards from it was Battery 6, Garrigue Fleaujac, a brass twelve-
pounder served by some of Plauché's men. Another long stretch
of one hundred and ninety yards separated Garrigue's gun from
Battery 7, Lieutenant Spotts and his artillerymen, which had a
long brass eighteen-pounder and a six-pounder. Finally, sixty yards
further, was Battery 8, mounting a small brass carronade, served
by some of Carroll's men and commanded by Corporal Cheveau.
In addition to these eight batteries Jackson had an unfinished redoubt near the bank in front of the line. He had disapproved of
that redoubt, but Major Peire and the engineers had persuaded
him to build it. Across the river, Patterson had enlarged his bat-

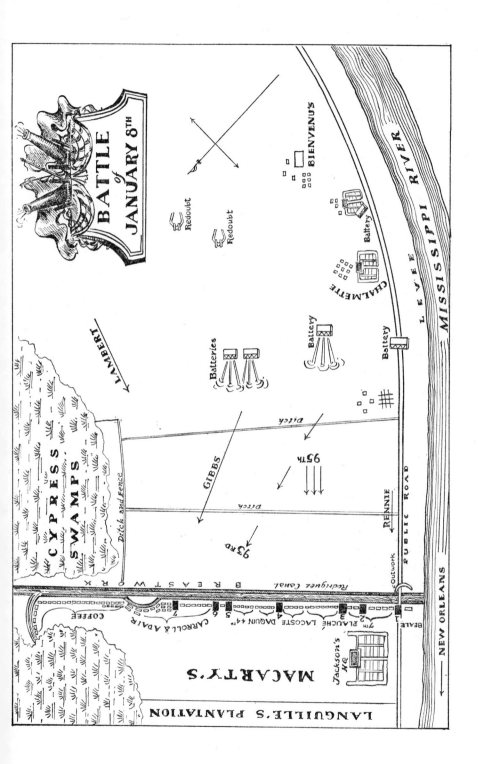

BATTLE of JANUARY 8TH

MISSISSIPPI RIVER

LEVEE

BIENVENU'S

Battery

CHALMETTE

Battery

Redoubt

Redoubt

Battery

Batteries

Battery

Battery

LAMBERT

CYPRESS SWAMPS

Ditch and fence

GIBBS

Ditch

Ditch

95th

93rd

RENNIE

PUBLIC ROAD

Outwork

Rodriguez Canal

BREASTWORK

COFFEE

CARROLL & ADAIR

7th FLAUCHE LACOSTE DAQUIN 44th

BEALE

Jackson's HQ

MACARTY'S

LANGUILLE'S PLANTATION

NEW ORLEANS

tery with two twenty-fours and four twelves, making altogether a formidable array of three twenty-fours and six twelves. He erected a second furnace to heat shot for these guns. Also he obtained for General Morgan two brass six-pound field pieces and one twelve-pounder to command the plain on the right bank.[12]

Between the highroad and the riverbank, Jackson's line was held by Beale's rifles. Between the 1st and 3rd batteries were Major Peire's 7th regulars. Between 3 and 4 were Plauché's volunteers and Lacoste's colored. To the left of Battery 4 were Daquin's colored, then the 44th regulars extending to Battery 5. The rest of the line, two thirds of the whole, was covered by Carroll's and Coffee's Tennesseans. Ogden's cavalry camped on Macarty's, and Hinds's dragoons on Delery's. Further back Villeré's militiamen camped as a reserve. Jackson had named Colonel Ross to command the right of the line and General Carroll to command the left.[13]

On the right bank of the river, engineer Latour, having completed his excellent Boisgervais breastwork, joined General Morgan and Commander Patterson to examine possible positions for Morgan's troops. They inspected the various nearby canals, Latour and Patterson suggesting the advantages and disadvantages of each, Morgan procrastinating. Morgan seemed to prefer Raguet's canal, but Latour objected that the plain was too wide at that point and the breastwork could never be finished in time. Finally Morgan asked Latour to make the decision. Latour selected a position between Raguet's and Jourdan's canals where the wood reached toward the river to leave only nine hundred yards of open ground. After making a rough draft of a plan for the earthwork, he left slaves to build it while he himself rejoined Jackson.

After Latour left, Morgan worried. There was no canal at the position Latour had chosen, and Morgan wanted his own line to be as much like Jackson's as possible. So he moved the slaves forward to Raguet's, which was some distance in advance of Rodriguez. First they built a bastion on the river for the twelve-pounder and a small redan on the right for the two sixes. Then, slowly, they began to throw a little dirt beside the canal. Morgan's troops lay idly on the ground paying little attention to their general, and the slaves soon caught their lackadaisical spirit.[14]

General Adair's Kentuckians, over two thousand of them, arrived at Dupré's plantation, the second line of defense; but Jackson was sorely disappointed when he inspected them. They were dressed in ragged clothes, inadequate for the cold, rainy weather and the muddy existence behind the breastwork and improper for a soldierly impression. Few of them carried guns. They had brought plenty of food, but only one cooking kettle for each eighty men. Jackson cursed the contractor from Pittsburgh who was somewhere up the river with the desperately needed weapons, possibly hiding at Natchez or Walnut Hills in fear of the battle; but the general was too preoccupied with other matters to give Adair any suggestions about locating guns. His displeasure was soon reported in town along with vivid accounts of the pitiful appearance of the Kentuckians. Solicitous comments passed among the townsladies, who soon met in groups to sew clothes. In the legislature Louaillier spurred his colleagues to appropriate six thousand dollars. Several merchants came forward with an additional six thousand and other Louisiana citizens with four thousand, providing Louaillier a total of sixteen thousand dollars to buy blankets and woolens for clothes. This spurred more women to join the sewing brigades, and blanket coats, waistcoats, pantaloons, and shirts soon poured into the army depot to be distributed to the Kentuckians. Meanwhile Adair hunted desperately for guns and managed to locate six hundred. Furnished with these, Colonel Slaughter's regiment was moved up to a position behind Carroll's troops. Only four hundred guns were left at the armory for the corps of veterans to police the city with. In the streets, while their mothers sewed, the boys of the town played soldier, drilling with make-believe muskets, building parapets where they could, conducting mock attacks.[15]

A rich widow wrote Governor Claiborne from Attakapas that she had sent four sons to serve in the line and would come herself whenever she was needed. A pretty Creole belle was reported to have told Major Mitchell, when he taunted her for praising the Tennesseans, "I'd rather be the wife of one of those hardy and coarsely clad but brave and honest men, who have marched through two thousand miles of wilderness to fight for the honor of their country, than wear an English coronet." (How many miles had the major traveled and how many hardships had he undergone to fight for the honor of his country?) Other belles similarly thrilled at the sight of the jaunty backwoodsmen, and some, cherishing the freedom from restraint which war allowed, formed secret attachments. There were also a few who became attracted to the manners of the captured Englishmen. Some of the attachments born of attraction to the mysteries of new ways would reach fruition in unusual unions. There would be delicately raised girls who would trade the excitements of the city to break land, heroically or bitterly, in the wilderness; men who would trade their sparse, rough, rigid backgrounds for New Orleans society, driving to success or sinking to dissipation; octoroons who would lose their color following stalwart husbands westward; Englishmen who would sink roots in the new world. A Creole girl fell in love with the tender hands of a young surgeon at the hospital, and the surgeon fell in love with the gentle sympathy with which she nursed his patients. A Tennessee lawyer fell in love with the attentions of a maid in the house where he was quartered, and she fell in love with the dashing cut of his officer's uniform. A shopkeeper's daughter fell in love with the pained, frightened eyes of a captured drummer, and he fell in love with her motherly attentions. A young prostitute fell in love with the tense seriousness of an officer who came to her for nightly relaxation, and he fell in love with her knowing devotion. A new mixture of blood, new harmonies, new tensions, new resolutions.[16]

Down the river at Fort St. Philip, Major Overton examined with pride the work of his men. Because of the terrible swamps, he had been unable to establish batteries across and above the fort, but the fort itself was ready. Everything combustible had been thrown out. Powder and ammunition had been stored in several well-covered magazines scattered around the fort. Overton had four batteries. At water level on the curtain of the fort were his two thirty-twos. The three bastions of the fort mounted several twenty-fours, a few eight-inch howitzers, and one thirteen-inch mortar (not ready for use). The left bastion was manned by fifty artillerymen under Captain Murray, the center by sixty-four under Captain Wollstonecraft, and the right, under Captain Walsh, by a company of the 7th Infantry. The crew of gunboat 65, which was warped into a bayou beside the fort, would serve the water battery under its commander, Lieutenant Cunningham. To help the gunners was another company of the 7th, a company of Louisiana volunteers, and a company of free colored. The total force was 406. They nailed the American flag to the standard, nailed under it, to taunt the enemy, the British colors, and swore never to surrender the fort.[17]

To Jackson all seemed ready. The troops behind the breastwork were cheerful, the guns set for action. He was annoyed by frequent false alarms that the British had appeared in unlikely places, alarms that had to be checked by the cavalry; he knew from Patterson that General Morgan's position was extremely weak; and he was worried that the unfinished redoubt in front of his line on the right might harbor an attacking party. But he was sure the British would strike at him head on, not across the river or anywhere else, and he trusted that they would not reach the redoubt.[18]

General Adair, having brought two thousand men all the way from Kentucky, hated to see his chance of glory dissipate for lack of arms. After much pleading with Mayor Girod and the Committee of Safety, he finally obtained a three-day loan of the four hundred guns still in the armory, provided that they were smuggled out after dark so the citizens would not know themselves defenseless. Another regiment was sent to support Carroll, leaving one thousand unarmed men still encamped at Dupré's. Jackson now had a strong reserve behind the line which could move quickly to the point of attack.[19]

On the seventh the two newly arrived British regiments were reviewed. They lined up smartly, these battle-hardened veterans of the Peninsula who were happy to be ashore after the long voyage and who had not yet experienced the frustrations of the campaign against the "city of the swamps." The 7th, a royal regiment, wore blue facings to their red coats; their flag had a rose in the center of the blue ground, with a garter around the rose and a crown over it and with a white horse in each of three corners. The motto on the garter was *"Honi soit qui mal y pense."* The 43rd had white facings and a white flag. The 7th had drummers, the 43rd buglers. The men of the 7th wore white tufts in their caps and carried light blue knapsacks; the men of the 43rd wore green tufts and carried black knapsacks. The sun shone brightly, and after the review the officers were in high spirits, ready for a brilliant victory.[20]

Meanwhile Cochrane's sailors brought fifty barges, pinnaces, and cutters up the bayou to the canal. They would be brought in the dark up the canal to the river, and before day they would transport

Colonel Thornton's detachment across the river. In the afternoon the various regiments paraded before their camps.[21]

Pakenham composed his order. Colonel Thornton's force on the right bank of the river would consist of the 85th, the 5th West India, four hundred marines, and two hundred seamen. For artillery support one of the barges mounting two nine-pounders and two howitzers would row up the river beside Thornton's column. This force would have to cross in two divisions, but it would land early enough to carry the enemy's works before daylight in order to turn his guns upon the enemy line as the main attack commenced.

In Keane's column would be the 95th rifles and 93rd highlanders. The 4th, the 21st Royal Scots, the 44th, and the 1st West India would form Gibbs's column. Lambert would keep the 7th royal fusiliers and the 43rd in reserve. A company each of the 7th, 43rd, 93rd, and 1st West India would form a detachment under Colonel (formerly Major) Rennie to advance along the highroad under cover of the levee, on the extreme left. A company of the 1st West India would skirt the wood to cover the extreme right. The dragoons with horses would serve Pakenham while those who were still dismounted would join the reserve as infantrymen.

The success of Thornton's movement would determine Keane's point of attack. He would move up the road that passed the center battery. If Thornton with the captured guns dislodged the enemy's right, Keane would move toward the river, and Rennie would follow him instead of remaining under the cover of the levee. But if the enemy held its ground, Keane should move right toward the other column, concentrating both attacks on the enemy's center.

Gibbs would strike the heaviest blow. His men would leave the road at the center (advance) battery, move to a position between the center and right batteries, form into a column of companies, and march over the plain. First would go the 44th, three hundred carrying the ladders and fascines while the rest, together with some companies of the 95th, provided a firing party. Those with the fascines would lead, their arms slung so they could carry their burdens; they would advance to the canal, throw in the fascines, and retire to join the firing party. Then the men with the ladders would cross the ditch on the fascines and throw their ladders against the earthwork. The rest of the column would cross the ditch, climb the ladders, and storm the enemy. No shots should be fired until the canal was reached. The enemy would be treated to the stunning sight of an unyielding, undaunted British army marching relentlessly upon him. As he wrote the order, General Pakenham thrilled to his glorious vision. A thought disturbed him, but confidently he wrote, "It will be impossible for the enemy to oblique the fire of his flanks sufficiently to enable his injuring the columns from his whole front when close up to his works."

When the position was carried, the flank battalions were to press the enemy's rear for half a mile or until they received further instructions. A detachment of sappers would accompany each column. While the troops were advancing, the artillery would fire over their heads to weaken the enemy's position.

Two specific commands were included in Pakenham's order. "The flank battalion under Lieutenant Colonel Rennie will carry the outwork battery on the enemy's right," and "The officer commanding the 44th regiment must ascertain where the fascines and ladders are this evening, so as there may be no delay in taking them forward tomorrow morning to the old batteries." Pakenham read over the finished order, thinking what a beautiful piece of work he had done. It remained only for his officers to execute it.[22]

Pakenham called his generals to copy the orders that pertained to them. The generals studied them and called the regimental commanders. Colonel Mullins, leaving his second in command, Colonel Debbeig, to complete the parade of the 44th, reported to General Gibbs. He copied the part of the order that related to his regiment: "The officer commanding the 44th regiment must ascertain where the fascines and ladders are this evening, so as there may be no delay in taking them forward tomorrow morning to the old batteries." While Mullins stared at these orders, General Gibbs explained to him the movement the 44th was to make.

Returning somewhat glumly to the hut which he shared with Debbeig, Colonel Mullins called his lieutenant colonels, Debbeig and Johnston, to him. With these officers he was not on good terms; Mullins and Debbeig, though they slept and ate together, scarcely spoke to each other beyond the line of duty, and Johnston was a good friend of Debbeig. Consequently Mullins sat in stony silence while Debbeig copied the orders. Then he sent Johnston, with a copy of the orders, to De la Ronde's house to find out from the engineers where the ladders and fascines were to be had.

Johnston returned in about half an hour to deliver a memorandum sent by the senior engineer officer. Without looking at the memo, Mullins stuffed it in his waistcoat pocket. "Where are the ladders and fascines, sir?" he asked.

"In the advance battery," Johnston replied. Then he reflected; had the engineer said "battery" or "redoubt"? One of the redoubts constructed for the battle of the twenty-eighth had been dismantled and had since been used as a picket station. Another unused redoubt was behind and to the right of this one, while considerably ahead of it were the batteries used on the first. Was it the advance redoubt that had been specified, or the battery that was in advance of that? He corrected himself. "I believe he said the advance battery. There will be an engineer there to distribute the equipment. It's written on that memo." [23]

Mullins merely glared at him, expressing with his haughty glance his scorn for such indecision. He waved the two officers out of the hut.

As the news spread, there was considerable grumbling among the men of the 44th—they were to be sent forward to slaughter with fascines and ladders and no chance even to fire. It was rumored that Colonel Mullins was as unhappy with the situation as the men were. While the rest of the army prepared its equipment, checked guns and ammunition, and talked about spending the next night in the brothels of New Orleans or the bedrooms of the Creoles, the men of the 44th grumbled, fretted, and argued.

Colonel Thornton climbed the levee to look at the great river flowing silently on its way. Without warning it had fallen so low that the canal was draining into it instead of away from it. As darkness gathered the sailors found the canal too low to float their boats. In answer to Thornton's plea, Admiral Cochrane built a dam to try to raise the water, but it did no good. The sailors had to pull and tug the boats through the mud.

Robert Rennie read and reread his order, worrying about that slow march his men must make into the enemy's fire. Colonel Dale of the 93rd, struck by a sudden melancholy, brought a watch and a letter to one of the doctors at the hospital, asking the doctor to deliver them to his wife. "I shall die at the head of my regiment," he said.[24]

Colonel Mullins called his officers to his tent to explain their orders to them. Among them was young Lieutenant Knight of the grenadier company, another officer with whom the colonel was on poor terms. A few days before, after a quarrel, Mullins had briefly placed Knight under arrest, and the lieutenant, like Debbeig and Johnston, could put an edge into his voice that suggested disrespect without overtly stating it. The days of frustrated waiting were taking their toll on the nerves of all these officers.

Mullins' mood, however, had altered. He seemed in a good humor as he spoke jauntily to them. After explaining in general the movements of the regiment, he addressed Knight brusquely. "You, sir, command the grenadiers. You'll have to take the ladders."

"That won't take me long," the lieutenant replied, the disrespectful edge showing in his voice. "They're in the redoubt." Knight knew well enough where the scaling equipment was, having been in charge of one of the fatigue parties that had placed them there.

Mullins bristled at the tone of voice. "We all know where they are, sir." That was enough to keep Knight from saying the words that might have cleared the confusion between "redoubt" and "battery." Instead the colonel unnecessarily explained that the men with the fascines would throw their burdens into the ditch and move aside, that Knight's men were to pass in front and plant the ladders against the breastwork, and that they were all then to storm with bayonets.

Then the colonel smiled. "No lying on the ground this time," he told his officers. "It's up and at them, no matter what. It seems a forlorn hope, but it'll be done even if the regiment must be sacrificed. The attack depends on us." He shook his head. "I think the 44th will catch it." He was in a good humor, and his words were meant to inspire his officers with the importance of their duties; but the speech fell on hostile ears. As the officers left the hut, they exchanged low words with each other about their commander's incompetence.[25]

The camp waited for the morrow. Far into the night labored Cochrane's sailors, tugging at the boats as the canal grudgingly gave way. Some of the newly constructed banks caved in under the plodding feet of the sailors. The cut in the levee was too shallow, and scarcely any water at all flowed in it. The sailors were sinking in mud up to their waists. Colonel Thornton watched fretfully as progress fell further and further behind schedule.[26]

Sergeant Cooper and a few of his seven-year buddies approached Coloney Blakeney to point out that their enlistments had expired and to request that they be excused from the morrow's battle. The colonel angrily ordered them to their tents, where Cooper found Fitzpatrick, drunk, railing at the seven-year men for their cowardice. Fitzpatrick's usual gaiety had dissipated, his belligerence betraying the fear he felt about the attack.[27]

Quartermaster Surtees accompanied his commanding officer and adjutant on an inspection of the ground over which the 95th must advance, locating the bridges which spanned various ditches. He was surprised not to see any other commanders doing the same. In camp he found the officers sure of success but apathetic. When he returned to his hut he had a feeling of deep depression. He lay down restlessly, unable to sleep but dreading the morrow. Occasionally the thought of his frail, complaining wife intruded comfortlessly.[28]

Lieutenant Gleig waited with the rest of the 85th for the boats to be brought to the river. The time for embarking passed while the sailors still struggled with the boats. Restlessly the men waited. Beyond the levee, the river flowed unceasingly, its current having increased to five miles an hour. Gleig and some of his friends agreed upon the messages which the survivors would carry to the families of those who perished.

Captain Cooke of the 43rd was preparing for a night's rest when he was ordered to join a working party at one of the batteries. With two hundred men he found his way to the battery, a dilapidated mud structure. The soldiers set to work to repair it, but only a thin layer of soil was usable; at a depth of less than a foot water oozed up to produce a mud that would not hold. Farther and farther from the battery they had to dig. Meanwhile others were laboriously dragging up the guns. Hours passed in this toil.[29]

Pakenham slept, nervous but dreaming of a brilliant victory. Near him Sam Gibbs slept soundly and unworried, John Keane lay awake fretting, and Lambert, who had not experienced the frustrations of the last several weeks, slept quietly. On the levee Colonel Thornton, waiting impatiently for the boats, paced nervously, watching the waters of the great river rush past.

‡‡‡

Behind the breastwork the men curled up to sleep, lying upon their arms, with the assurance that the great assault they had awaited would occur on the morrow. All day they had watched the steady activity in the British camp which warned them that the moment had arrived. Determined though they were, they were not so confident as a few days before; the previous thrusts had seemed tentative, but this one had been gathering during a week of constant preparation. They knew that new troops had arrived. No one went to town this night; few had the inclination, and to thwart those who might, Jackson had stationed strong pickets behind the line.[30]

Jackson remained awake late into the night. After receiving detailed reports on the state of their positions from all his officers, he had to visit along the entire line to observe for himself. He visited the unfinished redoubt, saw two guns mounted in it and a detachment of the 7th stationed to protect them. He received a report from Commander Patterson, who had reconnoitered along the other bank of the river and observed the operations of the enemy at the Villeré canal; Patterson had earlier recommended that Morgan establish a picket opposite the canal, and he now suggested that the troops on the right bank be reinforced. Morgan also sent an urgent plea for more troops, nervously announcing that the entire British army was ready to cross the river; and he worried about the weakness of Fort St. Leon, reporting that there was a question of authority. Jackson wrote back that the fort could be strengthened without weakening Morgan's position, adding, "This is not a moment in which the niceties of etiquette can be safely observed when the proper officers will not strictly and diligently perform their duties." But he also requested General Adair to send half of the Kentuckians still at Dupré's to join Morgan. They could withdraw for temporary use the guns in the armory. So Colonel Davis' Kentuckians set out in the dark to trudge up the river to the city and back down the other bank. They did not know that the guns which Jackson intended for them had already been smuggled to their companions on the line.[31]

Finally Jackson lay down to rest, only to be aroused at two in the morning by a messenger from Patterson. Morgan's picket had seen the enemy launching his barges in the river. Patterson wanted to know if he should send the *Louisiana* down to oppose the movement, thus withdrawing his men from the shore battery and risking the ship in a duel with the six eighteen-pounders which the enemy had mounted on the levee. As Patterson's reluctance to do so was evident, Jackson told him not to, suggesting instead that Morgan send the Kentuckians, upon their arrival, to oppose the British landing.[32]

Then, dismissing the idea of sleep, he walked into the brisk night air, strolling toward the river, looking at the quiet tents of the camp on Macarty's, the men sleeping behind the breastwork, the guards patrolling along it, the cannon with their noses pointed upward. At Battery 3 he found the Baratarians awake with coffee boiling in an iron pot over a small fire. Jackson stooped to smell. "That smells like better coffee than I get," he said. "Where do you get such fine coffee?" He glanced at Dominique. "Smuggle it?" Dominique grinned without replying and offered the general a cupful.

Thus fortified, Jackson strolled toward the swamp, speaking to the men who were awake. At the edge of the swamp he found General Coffee pacing restlessly. Then he retraced his steps as far as Battery 8, where he sat down upon a log to wait for the dawn.[33]

☼ ☼

NINETEEN

The Battle of New Orleans

THE APPROACH of dawn was obscured by the usual mist drifting across the land from the river.[1]

When Pakenham awoke at 5:00 A.M., the news was disconcerting. With incredible labor, far behind schedule, the sailors had finally dragged their flotilla into the river, allowing Thornton to proceed with half his force; but instead of being already on the march up the opposite bank, the other half still waited to be transported, while Thornton's group had only just left the camp. The enemy's guns across the water would not, therefore, be silenced by daybreak, the moment chosen for the assault. Moreover, Colonel Dickson reported his batteries still unfinished.[2]

Meanwhile the field was blanketed by fog. That might be a blessing, however, rather than a misfortune, if Thornton could move up before the fog dispersed. Perhaps, though delayed, the plan could still be carried out as designed.

At the camp of the 44th, the bugles sounded, and the soldiers shook the sleep from their eyes, rolled their heavy haversacks and slung them on their backs, picked up their muskets, and formed their ranks. In the darkness and fog little was visible. Officers came eerily out of the fog and disappeared again into it. Houses, ditches, roads, and redoubts did not exist visually. Lieutenant Phelan, returning with his company from picket duty, was unable to locate the rest of the regiment.

Captain Tapp of the engineers found his way to the redoubt where the fascines and ladders were scattered about. He stumbled around until he located a place to sit while waiting for the 44th to come for their equipment. After distributing it, he was to move forward with the attacking column to give directions at the ditch. Sitting alone in the foggy darkness he listened to the noises of the night and of the awakening army and shivered with the cold.

The 44th marched, following with difficulty one of the rough roads that had been beaten from the camp through the fields in front. The head of the column passed the redoubt, halting while Mullins tried to discover in the fog which path went to the center battery. Knight and Debbeig, at the rear of the column, stood near the redoubt. Only a few feet away sat Captain Tapp, dozing among the fascines and ladders. After ten minutes the column moved on.

Startled by the resumption of the march, Knight turned to Debbeig. "Mullins is forgetting the ladders and fascines."

Debbeig shrugged. "It's his own affair. There's no use trying to speak to that man."

Knight, however, called for a sergeant, and when one ran up the lieutenant told him to give the colonel his compliments, say he was forgetting the ladders and fascines, and inquire if Knight could take them with him.

The sergeant ran forward along the column and delivered his message to the colonel. "Be off, friend," Mullins told him gruffly. "Tell the lieutenant to go about his business." The sergeant returned to Knight with that message.

Halting his men at the advance battery, Mullins entered to look for the fascines and ladders. Colonel Debbeig now walked leisurely forward to the battery, where he found Mullins scolding Colonel Johnston for giving him false information. "You have the directions in your pocket, Colonel," Debbeig remarked. Mullins glared at him. "I have the command, sir," he said. Then, after venting his anger with a few curses, he ordered Debbeig to take three hundred men back to the redoubt for the scaling equipment. Debbeig's men set off at double quick march while Mullins and Johnston waited at the battery with the rest of the regiment.[3]

Now the other regiments were preparing. The men left their

huts, shivering in the cold, munching on dry biscuits (they had been forbidden to light fires). As they formed ranks they found the ground soft and the stubble dripping with dew. Keane arranged his column, the 95th extended as skirmishers, the 93rd behind, ready to move to the right or left. On the highroad Colonel Rennie walked rapidly back and forth along his own column, barking orders sharply, arranging his companies of the 7th, 43rd, 93rd, and 1st West India. In the field Sam Gibbs sat placidly on his horse while the 21st and 4th and the rest of the 1st West India formed. One of the West India companies fell in near the wood. Behind these forward brigades the 7th and 43rd, less the two companies in Rennie's column, fell in, while Lambert waited with Pakenham. At the batteries, the working parties put aside their tools, took up their guns, and set off for their regiments. The signal for attack would be the firing of a rocket.[4]

Silently the army moved into position, each company barely able to see the backs of the company ahead, the forward ranks watching objects gradually assume familiar shapes only a short distance in front. In the gloom the distance seemed much farther than usual. Near the Chalmette ruins Rennie halted his column. The 95th halted behind the ditch that fronted the center battery. Gibbs's column, right of the center battery, moved toward the position of the 44th. Lambert's reserve halted at the Bienvenu ditch a quarter of a mile behind Gibbs's men. The right flank column halted at the head of the double ditch that was perpendicular to the enemy line. In the darkness and fog the various units were mostly invisible from one another.[5]

Across the river, Thornton's force reached the bank, left the boats, and formed in column. The strong current of the river had swept them far downstream from their designated course. While the flotilla headed again across the river, the 85th and its accompanying detachments advanced, with a barge carrying the cannon rowing up the river beside them.[6]

At Rodriguez the American pickets quickly returned to the breastwork to report the British advance. As drums rolled out the call to arms, the men arose, slapped the stiffness from their limbs, and fixed a quick breakfast—bacon and cornbread, with coffee for the Creoles and grog for the backwoodsmen. Jackson was still near the center of the line, where he received reports from various detachments. He could see nothing ahead of the line but fog, and when Latour came up he asked the engineer when the fog would lift. "In about an hour," Latour said confidently.[7]

Across the river Patterson's furnace flared and his men stood at their posts beside the three twenty-fours and six twelves. Ahead of this battery, on the small earthwork beside Raguet's canal, Midshipman Philibert waited beside his twelve-pounder and Batique, captain of a merchant vessel, beside his two sixes. Along this line waited Morgan's infantrymen—the 1st Louisiana on the left, then the 2nd, then Declouet's regiment. Colonel Davis arrived with 170 bedraggled Kentuckians. They had found at the armory no guns other than some miscellaneous old muskets, so Davis had brought only part of his force. Weary from their ten-mile night hike, partly through ankle-deep mud, and poorly armed, they took a position at the right of the line, leaving a considerable space between them and the Louisianans. Only about half of the breastwork was completed; the Kentuckians were stationed along the bank of the old canal where by kneeling they could keep their heads behind cover.[8]

Morgan wondered if there was something more he should do. He had sent one hundred men under Captain Arnaud to oppose the landing across from Villeré. Should he send the Kentuckians to strengthen that group or make his main defense here? Jackson had told him to oppose the landing. Suddenly Morgan rode across to Davis to order the Kentuckians forward.

The Kentucky colonel, who had just arranged his men behind the bank, glared at his commander. "Forward!" he shouted incredulously. "General, these men are tired. They can't just move hither and yon on someone's whims. Look at this line you've got to protect—think that handful of men of yours can cover the whole thing?"

Morgan fidgeted, but at last he decided. "Send them forward. We can always bring them back again. Jackson's orders—oppose the landing."

Davis frowned, but as Morgan left him he ordered his men to join Arnaud's troops. The men grumbled, as they marched forward again, about their meaningless movements, the inadequacy of their arms, and the indecisiveness of their general.[9]

‡‡‡

To Villeré's Thornton's boats brought the news of the landing on the right bank far below the designated spot. Pakenham, frowning at this blemish in his beautiful plan, ordered the rest of Thornton's force to support Keane's column. He wondered if he should wait for Thornton to capture the guns before conducting his own assault. The fog was beginning to thin, and the troops were within rifle shot of the enemy.

On the right, the 21st Regiment reached the advance battery, where they found Mullins' men lying on the ground awaiting their equipment. Colonel Patterson ordered the 21st to lie down behind them.

News having reached General Gibbs that the 44th had moved off without the ladders and fascines, he rushed an aide to ascertain the truth of the report. At the redoubt Captain Tapp reported to the aide that the 44th had not arrived, but while they were talking Debbeig and his men ran up. Quickly but confusedly the men crowded into the redoubt, grabbed their burdens, and started forward, moving irregularly in their haste. Because the rest of the column had caught up, they had difficulty passing the troops to regain their position.

Pakenham, too, had heard of the mistake. Another blemish in his magnificent plan. But an aide reported that the 44th now had its equipment and must have regained its position at the head of the column. It was high time, because the fog was beginning to drift away under the pressure of a northwest breeze.[10]

‡‡‡

As the fog thinned, the field gradually opened to the view of both sides. Before the eyes of the British the grass and stubble field rolled to the canal and the breastwork, with two large and a few small ditches, their banks hidden by tall grass, in between. Before the eyes of the Americans the field stretched out, the swamp projecting into it on the left while on the right, surrounded by broken trees, stood the blackened ruins of the Chalmette buildings. On the riverbank and in the field the enemy troops were formed, their red coats colorfully dotting the landscape, the first line a quarter of a mile away, the second half a mile. Behind the first line of troops in the field were the enemy's batteries. It was an impressive sight—the invader poised motionless to strike.[11]

The mist dissipated, bringing the scene into sharper focus. Behind the troops Pakenham sat, several aides at his side. Impressed by his brilliant array of soldiers, he suppressed his annoyance at the failure of Thornton to reach the enemy's guns and the failure of the 44th to get their equipment. Admiringly he surveyed the field. Then he spoke to an aide, who galloped toward the right battery.

Behind the breastwork Jackson's men lay still, muskets and rifles ready to fire, staring at the gorgeous picture before them. Jackson climbed upon the parapet to observe; close at hand were Carroll and Adair. Suddenly a rocket whistled into the air, glowing fuzzily in the mist, a second one following quickly in another direction. Bugles blared a challenge, and the redcoats rose from the ditch and moved forward, one column approaching Battery 5 in the center, another approaching Garrigue's Battery 7 on the left.[12]

As Garrigue barked a command, his twelve-pounder bellowed. The corporal's carronade followed suit, then Spotts' long eighteen. Humphreys, Norris, and Dominique opened against the column on the road. The British batteries fired, their flashes showing rainbow colors in the mist, their balls and showers of grape passing over the heads of the men on the line. Crawley's thirty-two fired at the enemy's center battery. The smoke from the guns rose only sluggishly, thickening the gloom. From across the river Patterson's nine guns opened with resounding booms.[13]

Lieutenant Phelan, with his company, had finally located the 44th at the advance battery. He watched the balls of the British cannon striking the ground before the enemy line. As they struck a blue light seemed to spring up from the ground. When he called his colonel's attention to this beautiful phenomenon, he received in return a cold stare. Then Mullins ordered him to lead the column forward. Immediately Phelan moved along the road with his men, Mullins following with the straggling troops who were now coming up with the fascines.

But it was the wrong road. They were moving off to the right instead of the left. Ascertaining this, Gibbs hastily sent forward an order to reverse. Mullins passed on the order, but it did not reach Phelan, whose party continued to the right. The rest of the 44th faced about, but this put the ladders ahead of the fascines, and there was new confusion as the soldiers tried to readjust. They moved over the field in parallel columns instead of a single one. The 21st and the 4th moved straight ahead, Phelan's party on their right, while the rest of the 44th struggled to pass them on the left. The 44th was in groups now; some followed Mullins, some followed Knight, and some followed Captain Tapp of the engineers, but these officers scarcely knew one another's whereabouts, and the soldiers were uncertain just which way to go. Instead of two solid columns, the invaders were strung out across the plain in long lines.[14]

Captain Cooke was marching his detachment back from the battery they had repaired when he saw the signal rocket sputter overhead. Hearing the cannons open fire, he was momentarily at a loss what to do. Finally, turning the column toward the wood, he set off across the field. Most of the firing seemed to him to come from the wood—the reports so echoed from the trees that the wood seemed to be the direction of the attack.[15]

Behind the breastwork, General Adair could see that the deepest number of invading lines was headed for Carroll's position. When he ordered his Kentuckians forward, they pressed close behind the Tennesseans, making the ranks at this spot several deep. An old Tennessean, watching Jackson upon the parapet, suddenly burst into a camp song: "There's Gabriel standing by the gate. . . ." Carroll shouted to him, "Shut up, Sam! If the redcoats hear you they'll run away, and we want them to come on!"

Jackson came down from the parapet. "They're near enough now, gentlemen," he announced, and Carroll gave the order to fire. A tremendous crash rolled down the line of Carroll's troops. Immediately the next rank of soldiers pushed forward to fire a volley while the first rank fell back to load. The Kentuckians shouldered their way up, and as the men thus took turns firing and loading they produced an almost constant crash of rifle fire. Ahead of them in the advancing lines soldiers began to fall to the ground.[16]

Some of the sergeants of the 21st and 4th, not knowing whether to proceed or wait for the 44th to take the lead, ordered their squads to take cover, and as these soldiers scrambled into ditches or flattened out in the tall grass, the others around them followed suit.

The 95th marched steadily forward in a line, followed by the 93rd in column, but from the breastwork came the rolling crash of hundreds of muskets and rifles, mowing down the forward troops. Balls and grape from the guns ahead and across the river ripped into the ranks. Still they marched.

Across the river Colonel Thornton saw the signal rocket flare. At quick step, with one company in advance and the rest in column, he moved up the road, flanked by the barge on the river. Knowing how far behind schedule they were, the men marched rapidly.[17]

From the British and American batteries the cannon roared steadily, the British shot pounding into the earthwork or the ground beyond the line, the American shot striking in the redoubts, the field, and sometimes in the ranks of the advancing troops. Rhythmically punctuating this steady thunder were the rolling crashes of the volleys of muskets and rifles, and these crashes echoed melodiously from the woods. To the left Rennie's column, protected by the levee from Patterson's guns, continued in a solid column. Up the field, struggling in disorderly groups, came the 44th with the fascines and ladders, and as they gained the lead Gibbs rallied his men, the 21st, 4th, and 1st West India forming smartly. At this movement there was a pause in the firing of the Tennesseans, although the cannon continued to roar.[18]

Under the terrible punishment they had taken, the line of the 95th broke, the men hitting the ground amid the sedge grass, some of them crawling forward to the shelter of the large ditch closest to the canal. Behind them the column of the 93rd also halted and lay down.[19]

Rennie, seeing Keane's men break and his own front ranks raked by the cannon ahead of him and to the right, stopped his men, having them lie down close to the levee. To walk forward against this destructive fire was suicide, but if he gave the order to rush it would be an irrevocable decision, and he could succeed only if his small column was supported once it reached the breastwork. Would Keane come to his support? He allowed his men to rest a few minutes. Then he called, "All right, men, quick time!" Leaping up, he ran toward the American line, his men dashing behind him.

Gibbs's column moved again, scattered parties of the 44th with fascines and ladders leading, the 21st and 4th following, the right flankers moving along the fence that bordered the wood. As they moved a tremendous volley from the backwoodsmen met them, and Garrigue's and Cheveau's balls tore into the ranks of the column. On they marched, to be met by another resounding volley. Some of the soldiers of the 44th threw down their burdens, grabbed their muskets, and stopped to fire. As they did so, many soldiers in the other regiments also stopped to fire. Another ball from Garrigue ripped into the 21st, which obliqued toward the swamp to escape this devastating gun. Another volley from the breastwork decimated the column. Dozens of wounded now writhed screaming upon the ground. Dead men lay in grotesque positions, some with little purple spots in their heads widening as the blood oozed out.[20]

Rennie's column dashed up, the companies of the 43rd and 93rd moving into the outwork while the 7th and West India followed their colonel toward the parapet. A shell exploded on the levee, and as a shred of metal tore into his calf, Rennie stumbled but quickly regained his stride. There was only one plank lying across the canal between the outwork and the parapet, but Rennie ran across it and scrambled up the bank, his men following. Behind the breastwork Beale's men calmly moved back from the mound with rifles ready. Many of the onrushing troops had been shot in the advance, some missed the plank and fell into the canal, but the force was still strong as it scrambled up the parapet. The other companies rushed into the redoubt, the Americans having retreated across the ditch to the breastwork.[21]

As Rennie and his leading companions reached the top of the breastwork, some of Beale's rifles barked, and the Britishers tumbled to the ground, Rennie himself sprawling across the top of the bank. Another group was met by a similar fate, some falling back or sliding into those coming up. Now a detachment of marines ran forward to bayonet and club the next wave. The oncoming soldiers bumped into those ahead, many tumbling into the canal. From their right the militiamen sent a volley into the attackers, and those in the rear changed their course to plunge toward the redoubt. Though the redoubt was now in the possession of the British, they were uncertain what to do with it. They were exposed to fire from the breastwork, and with their commander gone, they huddled against the banks or in the ditches to cover themselves as best they could.[22]

According to orders Keane was to support Rennie if he reached the parapet or to support Gibbs if Thornton failed to take the guns across the river. Thornton had failed, but Rennie had reached the parapet, while Gibbs's column was staggering. After a long hesitation, Keane ordered the 93rd to support Gibbs. Colonel Dale formed his men and marched forward, obliquing toward Battery 7. The guns of Patterson, Crawley, Perry, and Garrigue trained on the highlanders; balls and grape showered the column, and rifle balls rapidly picked the men off. While marching steadily near the head of the column, Colonel Dale suddenly fell.

In the field, many of the men with the fascines and ladders had discarded their burdens, some to fire, some to take cover in the ditches or grass, and some to retreat. The 21st and 4th, obliquing across the plain, absorbed a tremendous fire from the Tennesseans and Kentuckians.

Behind the breastwork the frontiersmen set grimly to their task. In Carroll's part of the line, there was no longer an attempt to volley, but, as one soldier described it later, everyone "banged away on his own hook." Because of the crowded conditions, there was much jostling, each soldier moving back to load and then elbowing his way forward to fire. They talked, shouted, swore, joked. "I reckon those cannon are making a considerable noise," one would say, and another would curse the brass pieces to the right as "the noisiest kind of varmints to have for neighbors." Henry Spillman would look carefully over the breastwork, take deliberate aim, and crack away. Captain Patterson came running along, jumped on the breastwork, stooped to look through the smoky darkness, and shouted, "Shoot low, boys! shoot low! rake them, rake them! they're coming on their all fours!" Lieutenant Ashby, as busy as a nailer, dashed about and called out every now and then with an oath, "We'll pay you for the River Raisin! We'll give you something to remember the River Raisin!" Slukey Odd climbed the breastwork and peered coolly into the darkness; when Colonel Slaughter ordered him down, Slukey turned around, held up the flap of his old broad-brimmed hat with one hand to see who it was, and said, "Oh, never mind, Colonel, I don't want to waste my powder, and I'd like to know how I can shoot until I see something"; he aimed and fired before coming down. Other riflemen were climbing on the breastwork to aim, and officers ran busily along the line pulling them down.[23]

In Coffee's part of the line, which stretched into the swamp, those who were not obstructed by the wood fired regularly. All along the line the men concentrated on those advancing ranks, watching the foremost crumple to the ground and the others tread steadily around and over the fallen. From the head of the column almost to the rear, bodies were scattered over the field.

At the rear of the column bands of men were squatting on the ground or milling about. Many carried ladders and fascines, but many more of these were scattered around the field. There was a variety of orders, cries of "retreat" and "advance" and "oblique left" and "take cover." Into the midst of these men rode Sam Gibbs, cursing and shouting for them to go ahead. Some advanced with their burdens, others advanced only until his attention shifted, others surlily waited where they were.[24]

The column broke, some taking to ditches and some to the wood. The right flankers, who had kept abreast of the march, stopped. Seeing this, Gibbs rode forward, cursing the 44th and muttering that if he lived until the morrow he would hang Mullins to the highest tree in the swamp. As he rode he called to the troops to discard their heavy haversacks and charge again. One column was down, the other moving in spite of the devastation caused by the cannon and rifles at the center of Jackson's line.[25]

Captain Cooke, having spotted his regiment formed in a line near the wood, was crossing the field with his men, completely confused about what was taking place. To his left were great clouds of smoke, through which he could see the rapid sparkling of rifle fire and the flashes of cannon. From the clouds of smoke, also, groups of soldiers burst, running to the rear. He stopped one of these soldiers to ask, "Have the Americans attacked?" Breathing heavily, the soldier replied, "No, sir, we attacked," and then broke again in a run toward the rear.

Then the captain saw a fellow officer of the 43rd, Lieutenant Campbell, runing wildly about in circles, staggering, falling to the ground, and rising again. Cooke hurried over as the lieutenant collapsed on his knees. Campbell's uniform was ripped in several places; his leg was bleeding; in his hand he held the hilt of his sword, the blade having been ripped off; and there was a great gash in his forehead that had apparently blinded him. He fainted as Cooke took hold of him, and the captain called some men to carry him to the rear. The rest of his troops he formed to the left of his regiment, which was lying down at the edge of a ditch.[26]

‡‡‡

On the right bank of the river Captain Arnaud's men, retreating from Thornton, came upon the 170 Kentuckians at Mayhew's canal a mile ahead of Morgan's line. The Kentuckians had taken position behind Mayhew's sawmill and large boards, and Arnaud now placed his company to their right toward the wood. As Thornton's advance approached up the road, the defenders fired a volley. Thornton's advance quickly extended ranks across the field. While the boat on the river pelted the canal with grape, Thornton's line rushed. Morgan, watching from his position in the rear, suddenly panicked. He sent an aide to order a retreat. Many of Arnaud's men, not understanding English, wondered what the command was; when one reported it as *"sauve qui peut!"* Arnaud's company broke in a wild scramble for the woods. After two more volleys, the Kentuckians withdrew toward Raguet. Thornton's column marched on, listening to the roars of the guns and the crashes of the muskets and rifles across the river. Ahead of them they could see the constant flashes of Patterson's battery.[27]

The roar of the battle had reached the city, bringing the citizens from their beds and into groups to await nervously the result. Some, too excited to wait, mounted horses to ride toward the battle for news. Governor Claiborne arose, ate his breakfast, and rode to Fort St. Charles. In houses throughout the city the people listened and waited, some trying to busy themselves with housework, some pacing the floor, some going to the balconies as though outdoors they would know sooner, some breaking into tears under the tension. A disheveled woman ran about the streets, wildly clutching whatever men she saw to try to pull them to the ground with her, until finally a squad of the defense company got her into a house and forcibly held her in a chair. The fire company was at its stations, the defense company was helplessly patrolling.[28]

Under Gibbs's prodding, the men of the 21st, having laid aside their haversacks, formed and marched again, and more detachments of the 44th, nerving themselves to carry the fascines and ladders, accompanied them. Behind these troops the men of the 4th watched.

Unable to remain idle longer, General Lambert ordered his reserve forward, and the 7th and 43rd marched quickly from Bienvenu to follow the 21st. Again the rifles of the Tennesseans and Kentuckians opened their crashing volleys, each crash carrying down dozens of British soldiers.

Jackson pulled up his horse at Dominique's battery, where the guns were silent and the fiery Baratarian was cursing lustily. "Dominique!" shouted the general. "By the Eternal, what's the matter with your fire?"

"The powder's rotten," Dominique shouted back. "It's fit to shoot blackbirds, not redcoats."

Jackson sent an aide to tell the ordnance officer he would be shot in five minutes if Dominique complained again about his powder. As the general rode off, the pirate waved approval, and he and his men went back to the guns.

Great masses of soldiers lay on the road; the front company of the 93rd had been wiped out; the other companies tripped and stumbled over the bodies of their comrades. But on they came. The remnants of Rennie's force, helpless to advance from the outwork to the breastwork, decided to retreat. In scattered groups they departed, rushing up the road while raked from the rear.[29]

Behind the attack, in the center of the field, General Pakenham watched. He saw the terrible decimation of his center column and he saw the surgings and retreats of his right. Somehow his glorious vision had imagined the brilliant ranks of the army marching over the field and up the bank, but not the bodies strewn about the ground or flying in different directions as shells exploded, not the shrieks and sobbing of the wounded, not the crumpling of a line of men with the steady crashes of thousand-rifle volleys. General Pakenham panted and gasped. His eyes fixed on that right column, with the 7th and 43rd moving up from the rear while the 44th wandered in all directions. General Gibbs rode over to report sadly that he could not get the troops to follow him. Suddenly Pakenham spurred his horse to ride to the right, Duncan McDougall quickly following.[30]

Among the men of the 44th they rode, Pakenham shouting, "Shame, shame! Remember you're British!" Heading up the field toward the attack, he called, "This is the road you ought to take!"

He galloped some forty yards before a ball suddenly ripped into his horse, throwing the general to the ground. He rose to his knees, grasping an injured shoulder, unable for a moment to breathe. Duncan McDougall rode up, jumped down, and solicitously helped his commander to his feet. But Pakenham pushed him aside and leaped upon McDougall's horse. Again he galloped ahead, but he had gone only a few yards when his body was suddenly stiffened by another shot. As he tumbled again to the ground, McDougall ran forward and took the general in his arms. Even as he did so the young Scotsman remembered another occasion, a few months before, when he had held in his arms the dying General Ross, first commander of this unfortunate American expedition.[31]

Blood flowed from the general's neck and stomach. His eyes were closed, and he gasped for breath. Several men ran up to help Mc-Dougall carry him to the rear.[32]

‡‡‡

An aide remarked to Jackson, "That British officer certainly acted the hero at the last."

Jackson, about to spur off on one of his frequent rides along the line, paused for a moment. "When our intellect fails us, we have to become heroes." He rode off toward Carroll's troops.

‡‡‡

The column moved on. Not many of the 44th remained in front. Captain Tapp's detachment having dispersed, the captain joined Keane's column. Colonel Debbeig had received a scalp wound and walked back to the hospital. Colonel Johnston was also in the rear, looking for men of his regiment to send forward. Lieutenant Phelan had been wounded, and his party had immediately dispersed. Only Knight still had a good detachment, but it was dwindling rapidly as it pressed forward. Behind Knight's men marched the 21st, the 4th falling in behind it, the 7th and 43rd behind the 4th. On Jackson's line the frontiersmen fired and loaded and fired again. As they watched the troops coming steadily on, rank after rank crumpling to the ground, balls and grape ripping into the others, the tough frontiersmen fell silent. Tears rolled down the cheeks of some; others looked out through a film of tears; some sobbed, some shivered, some set their jaws grimly. The voices of officers trembled as they gave commands. Still the volleys thundered away.[33]

Jackson and Carroll, sitting together on their horses behind the line, watched the slaughter. "Magnificent, is it not, General?" Carroll remarked softly.

"Yes," said Jackson; "it's magnificent. But it isn't war." He whirled toward the other end of the line.[34]

On the right of his line many of the Louisianans found themselves too shaken by the sight to fire. Some stumbled away from the line to hide their faces in their hands. Some found their fingers frozen to the triggers of their muskets. Jackson rode by, shouting to them, rousing most of them out of their shock.

Pakenham, as he was carried to the rear, opened his eyes long enough to see the column of highlanders still moving. "Brave highlanders!" he whispered. Sam Gibbs rode among his men, shouting to them to go on, until he crumpled and slid from his horse. As he was carried to the rear, he was heard to be muttering curses. One of them seemed to be, "Damn Pakenham!" [35]

In the center John Keane sat upon his horse as his ranks filed by. His glance was fixed on the head of the column, which unrolled like a carpet over the bodies of the fallen. Over half of the highlanders had already been shot down. He watched them move on toward the earthwork, the front ranks falling, the next ranks passing over them. He saw the head of the column reach the canal, saw the foremost men fall and stumble into the water and mud, saw the column stop. A staff officer rode up to demand his attention. "General Pakenham is dead," the officer announced.

Keane, looking at his short column stopped in the field while shells continued to rip into it, gave the command to take cover. As the bugler sounded the command, the troops in the rear whirled and moved quickly backward, the front ranks racing and tumbling into the nearest ditches. Keane, watching as the column dissipated, suddenly felt a sharp sting in his neck, and a moment later he sank unconscious to the ground.[36]

Three generals down. Near the right battery Lambert grimly watched his column advance.

‡‡‡

Across the river Thornton's advance halted at an orange grove while the rest of the detachment marched up. Thornton ordered the 85th to extend files across the field, Major Gubbins to take two companies toward the wood, Captain Money to form his sailors in column on the road, and the marines to form as a reserve behind the 85th in the center of the field. When the formation was completed the bugle sounded the advance, the 85th moved forward on the left and in the center, and the sailors rushed up the road toward the battery near the river. A discharge of grape and canister from Philibert and Batique forced the sailors to reel back, but a moment later they rushed again.[37]

Seeing the attack begin, Commander Patterson ordered his men to turn their guns to meet it. Hastily the artillerymen tugged and shoved and realigned the cannon. Meanwhile General Morgan had ridden over to a position between the militia and the Kentuckians. "Wait till they're close," he shouted, "then fire, and kneel and load and fire again!" Restlessly he rode his horse back and forth over a short distance while the soldiers, kneeling behind the bank, glanced darkly at this nervous old man. As the enemy loped over the field toward them, the men fingered the triggers of their muskets and shifted their awkward positions. Some hundred and fifty yards away the enemy paused to fire a volley. "Fire!" Morgan suddenly shrieked, and along the line soldiers rose to fire. It was a broken volley with large gaps between the different units, and as the enemy advanced again they converged upon those gaps. "Every man for himself," called a backwoodsman, and of one accord the Kentuckians rose, faced about, and broke toward the rear.[38]

After staring for a moment in consternation, Morgan galloped toward the retreating Kentuckians, calling to the officers to bring the men back. Colonel Davis was jogging along with his men, and when Morgan told him to stop the men, Davis just shrugged and said, "I can't." Morgan rode among the fleeing men, who swerved to avoid his horse but kept on their undaunted way. "Kentuckians!" he shouted. "Remember your valor—your patriotism! Kentuckians! Your country has confidence in you! Is this how you requite it? Shame on you! Shame on you! You're not Kentuckians! You dastards! Shame on you! Kentuckians—shame!" Hoarsely, frantically he shouted as his horse danced among the fleeing men. But steadily, remorselessly they jogged on.

One Kentucky officer came to Morgan's assistance. Adjutant Stephens, wounded in the head, had fallen to the ground, but he recovered, and with his head streaming blood he now ran after the troops. "Shame on you, boys!" he called, taking up Morgan's cry. "Shame on you! Come, let's follow the general!"

Some of the men stopped and looked around. Heartened, Morgan turned his horse, drew his saber, and yelled, "Follow me!" He rode forward waving his sword, yelling, "Follow, follow!" for some fifty yards. Then, glancing back, he saw the entire force dashing rapidly in the other direction, and he stopped, alone on the field. To the left, the Louisianans, having seen the Kentuckians break, were also retreating. Midshipman Philibert and Batique had ordered their guns spiked. Should the general gallop headlong, alone, into the midst of the enemy, swinging his blade to cut down all before him until he should be brought down? The friendly voice of reason persuaded him to banish that heroic maneuver and follow his retreating troops.[39]

The retreat became general, many of the Kentuckians taking to the woods while the others mixed in disorder with fleeing Louisianans and artillerymen on the road. It was the kind of riotous break that General Jackson had feared from untrained, heterogeneous troops not welded together and inspired by an iron leader. Commander Patterson watched in astonishment as they fled past him. Turning his glass toward Raguet, he saw the enemy forming on the road for another advance. Reluctantly he ordered his crew to destroy the ammunition, spike the guns, and abandon the battery. Thus ceased Jackson's deadly flanking fire.[40]

In this skirmish the British had lost three men killed and forty wounded, including Colonel Thornton. The colonel did not think his wound serious, but his officers pressed him to take care of it, so, leaving Major Gubbins in charge, he set out with the other wounded for Villeré's.[41]

‡‡‡

On the left bank, one column still moved across the plain, approaching the earthwork. But the closer they came the more deadly became the fire of the Tennesseans. At last the soldiers in front could stand it no longer. The two leading companies of the 21st broke into a run, passing Knight's men. The company behind them paused to fire. This pause brought the rear companies to a halt, and not knowing what had happened, the rear companies of the 21st broke for the wood. The 4th, seeing the 21st flee, jumped into the perpendicular ditch.[42]

Behind the breastwork, Lieutenant Ashby saw the enemy plunge into the canal. He glanced wildly about for a gun but found none. So he picked up an empty barrel and flung it, then grabbed an iron bar, jumped on the earthwork, and yelled, "Have at them!" Some of his men climbed beside him to fire into the canal.

But a British soldier raised a sword to which a white handkerchief had been tied, the firing ceased, and the backwoodsmen helped the captured enemy to climb over the mound.

Carrying the flag of surrender was a British officer. A Tennessee soldier met him with a demand for his sword, but the officer hesitated, glaring at the unkempt soldier. Colonel Smiley hurried over, crying, "Give it up—give it up to him in a minute!" The officer held the sword in both hands, made a polite bow, and handed it over.

One neatly dressed young Englishman stood on the top of the breastwork and held out his hand for assistance. A Kentuckian took his musket, set it down, and gave him his hand. The youngster jumped lightly down and struggled to undo his cartridge box. Upon his clean white underjacket a red spot had begun to grow. "Are you wounded?" asked the Kentuckian. "Pretty badly, I fear," the youngster replied. An officer came up to help the Kentuckian take off the cartridge box. The youngster, now panting, begged them to leave him his canteen, which they did. Just then a Tennessean came along from the river with water in a tin coffeepot, and the young Britisher asked politely for a drink. He took the proffered coffeepot, swallowed two mouthfuls out of the spout, handed the pot back, and suddenly slumped to the ground. The Americans eased him against the bank. He gasped three times before dying.[43]

"It's no use going any further, sir," a sergeant said to Lieutenant Knight. "The whole is retreating."

Looking back, Knight saw most of the army a long way off, some making for the woods, some moving to the rear, some lying in ditches. At Knight's orders his men threw down their ladders and ran for the woods, where a great many of their comrades, including

Colonel Mullins, had already taken refuge. Afterward there would be intense argument, a number of men claiming that Mullins had approached as close to the ditch as Knight, while others claimed he was to be seen nowhere near the enemy lines; and who could successfully straighten out in his memory the confusion of that wild attack? [44]

Lambert ordered the 7th and 43rd to cover, an order which was passed among the men as "lie down to avoid the shower." They too took to ditches. As Sergeant Cooper hit the ground in a ditch, he felt someone fall across his legs. Looking over his shoulder, he saw his friend Fitzpatrick, blood smearing his face and running from his mouth.

Cooper shoved the corporal's body away. Examining it, he saw that Fitzpatrick had been shot in the forehead. His lips were twisted in a grin, perhaps at some jest he had made to the devil's dam. Sergeant Cooper removed the corporal's knapsack, opened it, and took some of the belongings.[45]

The cannon continued to roar. From the breastwork the musket and rifle fire continued, much slackened, as the Americans raked the ditches. A few of the English attempted to answer it.

Major Tylden, riding up to General Lambert, saluted. "Sir, General Pakenham is dead. General Gibbs has been taken back to the hospital. You are in command, sir."

Lambert, looking out at the bodies spread over the field, nodded silently. Then he rode to the house where Gibbs had established headquarters. There he met Admiral Cochrane. "What do you intend to do, General?" the admiral asked.

Lambert still envisioned the tragic field. He replied, "I do not think it prudent to renew the attack, Admiral."

"Why not? You saw Rennie make it. Rally the troops and we'll have this battle, General."

Avoiding the admiral's glance, Lambert looked out at the field. Everywhere there were bodies, with the remaining troops scattered in disorder. Ignoring the admiral, Lambert instructed Major Tylden to order the infantry to withdraw while the artillery continued to fire.[46]

‡‡‡

The troops on the right bank, led now by Major Gubbins, marched toward the city. The retreating Americans, winded, paused to rest at Jourdan's canal, where General Morgan thought he might make another stand; but when the enemy came in sight, Morgan's men fled again. Major Gubbins burned Jourdan's sawmill and marched steadily on. Again the Americans paused at Flood's canal, and here Captain Townsend of the militia got some seventy men to stand long enough to fire a volley, but when the British charged, the Americans again fled. Gubbins burned Flood's mill and marched on. By now General Morgan had galloped ahead. He found two detachments of dragoons, formed them at the bridge over the Boisgervais canal, and ordered them to cut down anyone who tried to pass. The retreating troops, coming upon this row of dragoons with drawn swords, and seeing Latour's imposing earthwork, consented to form for a new defense. They were mostly Louisianans, all but thirty-four of the Kentuckians having disappeared into the woods. When Gubbins reached this fortified position, he determined to rest his men until he heard news from across the river.[47]

On the left bank, Jackson and his staff watched the retreat by the blaze of the guns moving up the river. It was difficult to know how strong the enemy force on the other side was, and with the main force in the field before him, Jackson hated to weaken his own line. But he sent General Humbert with some of the militia from the Piernas canal. Delighted with his new command, Humbert led them at a smart pace toward the city. Jackson also sent Lafitte to advise Morgan about the possible canals and passages by which the enemy might penetrate the swamps to the city.[48]

Governor Claiborne had now arrived at Macarty's, where, keeping safely under cover, he attempted to learn just what had happened. Major Butler came up. "Morgan's been routed, Governor. Hadn't you better muster some men in town to reinforce him?"

Claiborne blinked. "There aren't any men in town. There are only old men there."

"Well, General Villeré has some men back of the lines. Let them go." Butler was hurried.

"Is this an order, Major Butler?" Claiborne asked.

The adjutant frowned. "Yes," he said gruffly as he rode away. Claiborne hastened to Villeré's encampment, but when he demanded men the planter stared at him. "Take my men!" he exclaimed. "I have no men to spare. Humbert's already taken half of them, and I'm guarding prisoners."

"I have orders from Jackson," the governor said, blushing.

"Well, I have orders from Jackson too, delivered personally. There are hundreds of prisoners here, and I've been posted to guard them."

"I want it clearly understood that I've delivered Jackson's order," said the governor, but Villeré had ceased to listen.

The governor returned to the city, where he found Humbert's troops, tired from their rapid march, waiting to be conveyed across the river. He busied himself locating boats for them, meanwhile sending his aide Shaumburg to reconnoiter.[49]

Lambert's troops hid in the woods or lay pinned to the ditches by the steady fire of the guns and the alert fire of riflemen. Some of the troops in the center made their escape, stopping to rest only when they reached De la Ronde's. On the right the 43rd withdrew squad by squad, each squad jumping up and retreating in a crouching run.[50]

Sergeant Cooper, looking around from his hiding place, saw a man on his right smashed to pieces by a cannon ball. A portion of the man's brains the size of a marble stuck to the sergeant's cap. Close at hand a man had his arm fractured near the shoulder so badly that it was taken out of its socket. A few yards behind one of the West Indians sat on the ground, the lower part of his face shot away, his eyes gone, the bones of his brow jagged and dripping blood. Near Cooper in the ditch lay one of the 43rd trying to hold in his bowels. Overhead showers of grape whizzed by like flocks of partridges.[51]

An officer of the 43rd, reclining on his side, was suddenly struck in the knees by grape. He rolled on his back, then raised himself, looked down at the blood gushing from his legs, and cried out, "Carry me away! I'm chilled to death!" As some soldiers picked him up and hurried toward the rear, he fainted.

Near Captain Cooke sat a colored soldier, moaning unintelligibly and scratching a hole in the earth. His face was a bloody mass with no features distinguishable. But a worse sight so fascinated Cooke that his glance was constantly attracted to it—some two hundred yards to the rear, amidst a pile of dead, lay a wounded soldier whose arm convulsively and regularly rose and fell. That strange arm, rising and falling in the midst of a pile of bodies, intrigued the captain and sickened him with horror. Cooke's misery was so great that the experience seemed like a horrible dream rather than reality.[52]

Quartermaster Surtees had posted himself well in the rear of the attack, determined, because he anticipated failure, to take no part in this action. He had not so good a view of things as he had had in past encounters. From stragglers and returning wounded he learned of various events. There was a moment of excitement when Rennie's column was reported to be in the outwork, but not long after that a lieutenant of the 43rd who had escaped from that predicament arrived to dispel the hope. Surtees mainly watched his own regiment with his glass. He saw it advance by fits and starts and finally take to a ditch. He saw the other regiments dissipated, leaving the 95th stranded.[53]

Back at Jumonville's the buildings were so crowded with the wounded who had been able to crawl back that the less seriously hurt had to sit outside. Mr. Robb, in charge, worked busily to get everyone cared for and bedded down, while the doctors dressed, cut, sawed, and bandaged.[54]

As the smoke cleared away, the Americans looked out at a field which at first seemed like a sea of blood until they realized that it was covered with redcoats. In places bodies lay in piles, and there were three rows of bodies, one near the levee, one near the swamp, and one in the center, corresponding to the attacking columns. The bodies were in many attitudes, some lying still in grotesque positions, some pitching and tumbling in agony, some laughing, some crying, some groaning, some screaming. There were heads, legs, and arms without bodies. Every now and then from behind a pile of the dead a body would suddenly rise and run off into the distance. One such soldier, a mulatto, after running some distance, stopped, gestured at the breastwork, then patted his rump. An American fired but missed, and the mulatto ran further, then paused to repeat the gesture. Then, as the Englishman again ran, a thin, cadaverous Tennessean known as Paleface shouldered his comrades aside, lay against the breastwork, ran his sight along the soldier's back and over his head, and fired. The soldier staggered forward a few steps and pitched down on his head some three hundred yards away.[55]

Some of the Americans went a short distance into the field to pick up muskets and take watches and other plunder from the bodies. One plunderer was wounded in the arm by British fire. Coffee's Tennesseans, appalled by the carnage, went into the field to bury some of the dead.[56]

In this situation the hours of the day dragged by. Colonel Thornton, when his wound was dressed, reported to Lambert. Asked if Major Gubbins could hold his position on the right bank, Thornton said he could. But Colonel Dickson of the artillery believed two thousand troops would be required to hold it. Colonel Burgoyne and Admiral Codrington urged that the attack be renewed, but the field and other staff officers demurred.[57]

The general found it difficult to think of anything but the dead and wounded strewn across Chalmette. Perhaps he could yet attack; perhaps Cochrane's ships would be able to pass the fort on the river; but his troops were decimated and demoralized, and he wanted first of all to bring the seriously wounded to the hospital and to bury the dead.[58]

He sent an aide forward with a white flag and a request for a cessation of hostilities while the field was cleared. Jackson sent Major Butler into the field to receive the message, which was signed "Lambert." He then demanded to know who Lambert was. Back came Lambert's messenger to British headquarters, and off he went with another message, signed now "John Lambert, Commander-in-chief of the British forces on particular service in America." In the interval Jackson had considered the proposition. He was worried about the right bank of the river; he had already dispatched troops that might be able to recapture the position; he needed that right bank in case the British attacked again. So when Lambert's messenger returned, Jackson sent by Major Butler a demand that the truce apply to the left bank only and only until noon of the following day, with each side agreeing to send no troops across the river. Back to Villeré's came Lambert's messenger. The general wondered what Jackson had in mind—he feared that the Americans were ready for a counterattack, and if he could not cross the river with reinforcements, Thornton's force would be stranded and perhaps captured. So he sent his messenger forward again, announcing that he would need until 10:00 A.M. the next day to consider. Then he sent Colonel Dickson to Major Gubbins with orders to retire.[59]

Shaumburg arrived at Boisgervais to find Morgan and the remnants of his troops sitting disconsolately behind the breastwork. When Shaumburg reported the governor's amazement at their conduct, one of them, glancing at Morgan, said, "Give us officers and we'll fight better."

General Humbert rode up, smartly saluted Morgan, and announced in French that he had orders from Jackson to destroy the enemy on the right bank. Morgan bristled. "Do you have that in writing, General?" he demanded. When Humbert stated that it was an oral command, Morgan said gruffly, "I will not relinquish the command without a written order."

Governor Claiborne arrived with Humbert's troops, and the three men debated fruitlessly who should be in charge. The militiamen behind the breastwork watched in glum silence. Finally, Morgan proving intractable, Claiborne and Humbert returned to the city.[60]

By now Major Gubbins had received the order to retire. Leaving Lieutenant Gleig with a picket to cover his rear, Gubbins marched off down the river. Gleig wondered what would happen if a strong enemy force suddenly marched from the city. As a protection, he took his men across the bridge, burned the chateau, and then burned the bridge. Having thus covered his retreat, he hurried after the main force, overtaking it at the embarkation.[61]

All day some of the British troops remained in the ditches. As dusk fell they retreated to De la Ronde's, harassed throughout by Jackson's batteries. When darkness came the British artillerymen withdrew their guns. Once more the invading army was in its camp.[62]

Jackson had lost 3 artillery privates killed and 1 wounded; 1 sergeant and 1 corporal of the 7th killed and 1 private wounded; 1 of Coffee's Tennesseans killed; 1 of Carroll's sergeants and 3 privates killed, 1 ensign, 1 sergeant, and 6 privates wounded; 1 of Adair's privates killed, 1 adjutant, 1 corporal, and 10 privates wounded; 1 private in the free colored battalion killed, 1 ensign, 3 sergeants, 1 corporal, and 8 privates wounded; 1 of Morgan's militiamen killed, and 2 sergeants and 2 privates wounded. Fourteen Kentuckians and 5 of Morgan's militiamen were still missing. In all 13 were killed, 39 wounded, and 19 missing; total casualties, 71.[63]

It would be long before the British could total up their losses, but when they did the list would be impressive. One general, Pakenham, killed; one, Gibbs, severely wounded, lying close to death in the hospital; another, Keane, severely wounded, but with a chance to survive. Of Pakenham's staff, 1 captain killed, 1 captain and 1 lieutenant (George De Lacy Evans, who had just recovered from a wound inflicted on the twenty-third) wounded. The artillery had lost 5 killed and 10 wounded. The engineers had 3 men wounded. The marines had lost 2 men killed and 1 captain, 2 lieutenants, 1 sergeant, and 12 men wounded. The navy had lost 2 men killed and 1 captain (Captain Money, wounded in the charge on Morgan's battery) and 18 men wounded. The 4th Regiment had 1 ensign, 2 sergeants, and 39 men killed; their commanding officer (Colonel Brooke), 1 major, 5 captains, 11 lieutenants, 4 ensigns, 1 adjutant, 9 sergeants, and 222 men wounded; and 1 lieutenant, 1 sergeant, and 53 men missing. The 7th had lost 1 major, 1 captain, 1 sergeant, and 38 men killed, and 2 captains, 1 lieutenant, 2 sergeants and 47 men wounded. The 21st had lost 1 major, 1 captain, 1 lieutenant, 2 sergeants, and 65 men killed; their commanding officer (Colonel Patterson) 1 major, 2 lieutenants, 6 sergeants, 1 drummer, and 144 men wounded; and 2 captains, 7 lieutenants, 8 sergeants, 2 drummers, and 217 men missing (most of them captured when they took cover in the canal). The 43rd had lost 2 sergeants, 1 drummer, and 8 men killed; 2 lieutenants, 3 sergeants, 3 drummers, and 34 men wounded; and 1 captain and 5 men missing. The 44th had lost 1 lieutenant, 1 ensign, 1 sergeant, and 32 men killed; 1 captain, 5 lieutenants, 3 ensigns, 5 sergeants, and 149 men wounded; and 1 lieutenant, 2 sergeants, 1 drummer, and 76 men missing. The 85th had lost 2 men killed; their commanding officer (Thornton), 1 lieutenant, 3 sergeants, 2 drummers, and 34 men wounded; and 1 man missing. The 95th had lost 1 sergeant and 10 men killed, and 2 captains, 5 lieutenants, 5 sergeants, and 89 men wounded. The 1st West India had lost 5 men killed; 1 captain, 2 lieutenants, 2 ensigns, 2 sergeants, and 16 men wounded; and 1 man missing. The 5th West India, hindmost of the reserves during the battle, had lost 1 sergeant wounded. Worst of all, the 93rd highlanders had lost their commanding officer (Colonel Dale), 2 captains, 2 sergeants, and 58 men killed; 4 captains, 5 lieutenants, 17 sergeants, 3 drummers, and 348 men wounded; and 3 lieutenants, 2 sergeants, 1 drummer, and 99 men missing. In the 4th, there were 351 casualties; in the 7th, 93; in the 21st, 463; in the 43rd, 59; in the 44th, 278; in the 85th, 44; in the 95th, 112; in the 1st West India, 29; in the 5th West India, 1; and in the 93rd, 545. In all, 13 officers and 278 soldiers were killed, 73 officers and 1,189 soldiers wounded, and 15 officers and 469 soldiers missing. The Americans had 71 casualties, the British 2,057. More of the wounded would die before morning.[64]

After the British had withdrawn, parties of Americans went to Chalmette to bring behind the lines the enemy wounded left on the field. Carts from nearby plantations and boats on the river carried them to the city—some forty carts and ten boats, all fully loaded. When the citizens saw cart after cart entering the city, many were profoundly shocked. They opened their homes as hospitals and volunteered as nurses. The celebration that night was a subdued one. The soldiers who came from the line were too weary and too moved to feel the same release from tension that their relatives and friends felt. From the swamps on the right bank stragglers sneaked in who were too ashamed to display themselves publicly.[65]

Before going to bed, General Lambert placed Colonel Mullins under arrest.

☼ ☼

TWENTY

Last Attempts, Retreat and Later Events

AT DAWN on January 9 several guns across the river roared, their shells reaching the British outposts on Bienvenu—Patterson had re-established his battery further up the river. They continued until ten o'clock, the time fixed upon for Lambert's reply to Jackson. In the British camp the soldiers sat sullenly near their huts, still dazed from the terrible experience of the preceding day. There were great gaps in the camp. The highlanders, when they walked about, kept their glances fixed on the ground so they would not see the rows of empty huts that had once housed their comrades. At De la Ronde's mansion almost every room was crowded with the wounded. The surgeons grimly ignored the shrieks of their patients as they deftly performed amputations. In one room was a large ghastly basket nearly filled with the still-stockinged legs of soldiers.[1]

At ten o'clock Lambert requested a six-hour suspension of hostilities on the left bank, and Jackson, already having reoccupied his position across the river, agreed.[2]

Detachments from both armies marched unarmed to Chalmette to clear the plain of the dead. A ditch was chosen to divide their labors. The American detachment of Tennesseans and Kentuckians, using the discarded scaling ladders as stretchers, delivered the bodies to the ditch, where they laid them in rows. The British working party then carried them to ditches on Bienvenu, deposited them, and filled the ditches. The corpses of officers were carried to Villeré's. General Coffee, upon receiving from Major Butler his instructions to deliver the corpses to the British, wrote back explaining that his men had already buried some of them. "Presuming the object was only to bury the dead, I have not raised those already buried." [3]

Mostly they worked in silence, but occasionally words passed among them. Lieutenant Gleig, visiting the field out of curiosity, saw an American officer, smoking a cigar, walking back and forth to count the dead with what seemed to Gleig "a look of savage exultation" and repeating over and over to the British that only eight Americans had been killed. An American soldier, more solicitous than that, attempted what he thought was a word of comfort—"I never saw the like of that!"—at which a British soldier sneered, "That's nowt, man; if you'd been wi' us in Spain, you would ha' seen summat for war!" Another American officer, when his own word of comfort was met by the British remark "Oh, this was a mere skirmish," replied sharply, "One more such skirmish and devilish few of you will ever get back home to tell the story." Nolte the merchant saw tears come into the eyes of the soldiers who received Major Whittaker's body. "Poor Whittaker," said one; "he was a worthy fellow." Colonel Dickson found the Americans "very civil." [4]

While working in the burial party, Sergeant Cooper stripped two bodies of their shirts. Though the shirts were bloody, they were in better condition than his own.[5]

‡‡‡

At 10:15 that morning Cochrane's river squadron rounded a bend and cast anchor two and a quarter miles below Fort St. Philip, the two bomb vessels in front, then the *Herald,* the *Nymph,* and the *Thistle,* and the *Pigmy* in the rear. At 11:30 two barges were sent forward for sounding, approaching to a mile and a half of the fort. Major Overton ordered Lieutenant Cunningham to open with the water battery, the thirty-twos boomed, and the shells fell close enough to drive the barges back. At 3:30 the bomb vessels opened with two thirteen-inch and two ten-inch sea mortars. As the guns of the fort were unable to reach far enough, Major Overton's force had to gird for a terrible beating. At first the shells sank in the soft mud of the fort, bursting under the ground, producing a steady tremulous motion.[6]

Back at Villeré's, Cochrane's sailors were again hard at work, dragging from the river to the canal the boats that had ferried Thornton's troops. After these boats were loaded with wounded, the sailors tugged and heaved them through the mud and low water to the bayou and rowed and sailed up the bayou and across the lake to the anchorage.[7]

The dead soldiers had been buried in ditches at Bienvenu, the officers in Villeré's garden. Pakenham, Rennie, and Gibbs (who had also succumbed) were disemboweled, placed in caskets of rum, and returned to the fleet.[8]

In camp the night of the ninth there was grumbling. The soldiers, believing that the battle had been a needless butchery, searched for scapegoats. Some thought General Keane had blundered by not advancing on the twenty-third or at least the twenty-fourth instead of waiting for the enemy to prepare an impenetrable defense. Some thought the artillery blundered by destroying the *Carolina* instead of the *Louisiana,* which was further upstream and could more easily make a getaway. Some thought Cochrane had done a sorry job of widening the canal. Some thought Pakenham should have waited for Thornton to seize the guns on the right bank. Some thought Lambert should have renewed the attack after Thornton's success. A great many, not caring what the individual errors were, felt that the commanders were incompetent. If only Rennie or perhaps Thornton had been in charge instead of Keane and Pakenham! A few clowns made great hits with their fellow soldiers by aping aristocratic manners that they thought were Pakenham's. Quartermaster Surtees felt that the whole army had underestimated the enemy, and that the Americans had proved to be superior marksmen both with cannon and rifles. A few felt that the whole expedition was a blunder misplanned and mismanaged by the navy; one suggested that Mullins was the wrong man to court-martial—Admiral Cochrane should be court-martialed and hanged from the yardarm of the *Tonnant.*[9]

The men of the 44th were ostracized by the men of the other regiments.

General Lambert's main concern was to get the army away. Though Cochrane still spoke of the time when his ships would demolish the fort down the river and sail to the city, Lambert listened to him so inattentively that the admiral visited him less and less. The 40th Regiment reached the shore of Lake Borgne, but Lambert sent it back without disembarking.[10]

In New Orleans the citizens, once the British wounded had been cared for and transported together with great numbers of prisoners to Baton Rouge by steamboat, could not contain their joy. Lights burned far into the night as gay celebrations took place. Jackson's troops kept a sharp watch at the lines, but great numbers of them returned to the city at night to enjoy the hospitality of a relieved populace.

A few people were unhappy. Morgan and Humbert grumbled about the command on the right bank until, learning that the troops would not serve under an unnaturalized foreigner, Jackson recalled Humbert. Governor Claiborne, nursing a grudge against the commander-in-chief, shut himself in the statehouse and communicated as seldom as possible with the military. Philip Louaillier felt that since the British had been beaten, martial law should be discontinued, but when he found that most citizens still worried about the presence of the British near the river, he held his silence. Declouet and Guichard were not speaking to each other since Guichard had accused Declouet of inventing the whole business about the legislature's planning to surrender the city. Jackson delivered a blistering denunciation of the Kentuckians for their retreat on the right bank—"While, by the blessing of heaven, one of the most brilliant victories was obtained by the troops under my immediate command, no words can express the mortification I felt at witnessing the scene exhibited on the opposite bank"; he accused them of "a spirit of insubordination"; and the Kentuckians protested that they were unfairly singled out, that they had been poorly armed and poorly led, and that the Louisianans were the ones who had first broken. A few individuals worried that Jackson's dispatches so often spoke of "my line," "my troops," "my battle." There were bickerings, but they could not decrease the ardor of the celebrants who felt such a magnificent release from such a terrible tension.[11]

At Fort St. Philip that night the British vessels moved closer in the darkness to the fort and fired into it with grape and round shot. Major Overton's men were forced to stay at their posts all night, though they had little chance of answering the fire.[12]

‡‡‡

The following days passed in much the same way. Occasionally Jackson's and Patterson's batteries would open for target practice on the British camp, worrying the British with a few shot and shell. The British troops grumbled away the time. To give them some occupation, Lambert ordered daily parades. Getting ready for parade one morning, Sergeant Cooper saw a man struck by a round shot. Another time he saw a man lying in a hut get both legs blown off. One day while he was fetching water he saw smoke rise from an enemy gun, and he hit the ground just in time for the ball to whistle past his head and sink into the boggy ground. One night a shell burst three feet from his hut, making a large hole but doing no harm. A ball dropped on a soldier's knapsack, driving it several feet into the soft earth. A ball plunged into a hut and knocked a kettle off a fire, spilling the soup. A shell exploded over a hut and cut off both feet of an officer sleeping inside. At night the Tennesseans still came on marauding parties to shoot down the pickets.[13]

To increase the discomfiture of the troops, heavy rains set in. There were lightning storms in the day that gave way to keen frosts at night. The picket posts became quagmires from heavy trampling. Fires could not be lighted, and the pickets had to shiver through the night on beds made of branches in the water of the posts.[14]

At the anchorage the grumbling was no less than at the camp. News of the terrible casualties struck with horror soldiers and civilians alike. Wives who had lost their husbands and would have to make alone the long journey home were inconsolable. There was ghastly wailing when the wounded arrived. Stunned as much as the bereaved wives was Lady Mullins, her dreams of triumph suddenly crushed when she heard that her husband had been branded a coward. She had to shut herself up, unable to bear the contemptuous looks of others or the accusing looks of the bereaved.

· 257 ·

Later she refused to believe the accusation, insisting that her husband had been maligned. A few friends defended her.

Dr. Dempster, returning with the wounded, had the disagreeable task of delivering Colonel Dale's watch and letter to his wife. There were many other men who, having made pacts with their friends, now faced the dread task of breaking the news. One officer, after having had both legs amputated and surviving a painful trip through the marsh and across the lake, died aboard ship.[15]

In the midst of this grumbling, John Keane, when he had recovered strength enough, set to work with the help of Assistant Quartermaster-General Major Charles Forrest on the journal of the campaign that he would present to Wellington. He had to explain away a failure. He listed the difficulties of the campaign. The first and most serious was the distance the army was removed from its supplies, over sixty miles in an intricate and uncertain navigation. A second was the impossibility of gaining intelligence; the inhabitants had abandoned their houses, no deserters came over, and the information of prisoners was vague and contradictory, that of Negroes trifling and unsatisfactory. The nature of the soil rendered operations dependent upon the weather. The enemy had unfortunately learned far in advance of the intended operations. The want of boats and small vessels rendered it impossible to land more than two thousand at a time, and it became an act "if not of necessity, of prudence" to wait for the remainder before advancing. The enemy's line was short, strongly flanked, and impossible to turn. The flank fire from his water batteries was devastating. The population of the country, which the British had been led to expect would receive them if not with open arms at least with an aspect of neutrality, formed instead the greater part of the opposing force, and captured letters and documents indicated that they clearly bore the British as little good will "as the people who were at the moment ruling them with martial law, and forcing them to carry arms with a degree of tyranny not excelled by the conscription." [16]

He fretted at the difficulty of communicating to someone unfamiliar with the country and the situation the utter impossibility of his task. The frustrations, uncertainties, and misfortunes he had felt so keenly he could not express. In spite of the long list of reasons, the fact remained: he had failed.

When Cochrane's barges had delivered their load of wounded to the fleet, they returned across the lake to fetch more wounded, the baggage, the guns, and the army's supplies.

Down the river, the British warships continued to pound Fort St. Philip. Except for two-hour rests at noon and sundown, their guns barked continuously, firing from beyond the range of the fort's batteries during the day and from closer at night. During the tenth and the eleventh, as on the ninth, the shells sank in the soft earth, keeping the fort shivering with their explosions but doing little damage. On the twelfth, however, the fuses were arranged so the shells burst in the air over the works, scattering fragments, and the defenders had to cover themselves as well as possible. The contractor's cabin in the fort was blown up, killing one man, but Overton had successfully cleaned the fort of all other dangerous buildings. A man on the right battery received a slight wound. In the center battery one man lost a leg. Several gun carriages were injured. One of the thirty-twos was struck five times, but it was readied for service after an hour's work. In the evening of the fourteenth Overton had his men bring timbers from the wood into the fort to form covers between the guns for better protection. The pounding of shells into the mud, combined with steady rains, made the interior of the fort almost a solid pool of water.

Whenever the British boats attempted to change position, Overton's batteries opened to prove that they could still destroy any ship that attempted to pass.[17]

After the night of the eleventh, the heavy firing at Fort St. Philip could occasionally be heard in the city, reminding the citizens that the campaign was not yet over. On the right bank of the river Jackson's engineer Lafon was building a strong earthwork at the place between Raguet's and Jourdan's originally selected by Latour. Patterson had mounted in his battery three twenty-fours and along Lafon's breastwork several twelves. Daily Jackson's batteries opened for target practice against the British camp.[18]

‡‡‡

On January 15, in the evening, a group of boats arrived above Fort St. Philip from New Orleans, bringing ammunition, supplies, and fuses for Overton's thirteen-inch mortar. They put in at the bank a mile above the fort, and on the sixteenth, the sun having peeked out, Overton's men carried these stores into the fort. They then set to work to prepare the mortar for action. On the seventeenth the enemy fire seemed less animated until, toward evening, Captain Wollstonecraft opened upon them with his mortar. Then the battle raged greater than ever. Wollstonecraft scored a hit on one of the bomb vessels that disabled it for several minutes. At dark the fire on both sides gradually ceased, silence falling upon the fort for the first time in nine days and shrouding the men in what seemed an unearthly calm. On the eighteenth Overton's men watched the enemy boats retreat down the river. The boats had thrown over one thousand heavy shells besides howitzer shells, round shot, and grape. Scarcely ten feet of the fort were untouched. Two men had been killed and seven wounded. Although the defenders had been nine days under arms and suffered sharply from loss of sleep and fatigue, Overton reported to Jackson, "The only thing to be regretted is that the enemy was too timid to give us an opportunity of destroying him." [19]

On the seventeenth, the last day of the bombardment down the river, General Lambert asked General Jackson for a conference between their representatives. Major Smith for the British and Edward Livingston for the Americans drew up articles for the exchange of prisoners. Cochrane would deliver his prisoners to the Rigolets; upon receipt of these, the Americans would send British prisoners equal in rank and number to the mouth of the river.[20]

Governor Claiborne meanwhile proclaimed himself commander of the Louisiana forces on the right bank, but General Morgan protested that he had orders from Jackson to consider himself free from Claiborne's jurisdiction. When the dispute was brought to Jackson's attention, he assigned six hundred men to Morgan and appointed Claiborne commander of the rest. The governor, discontented, rejected this solution and again retired into the statehouse.[21]

The next morning Lambert's troops began to move—first the prisoners, then the field pieces, then the infantry. One by one the regiments broke camp, formed ranks, and marched off briskly along the highroad to Villeré's canal, then along the canal and into the swamp on the road built of reeds by the engineers. As squad after squad tramped over the roads the reeds were pushed into the mud and water seeped up, until soon the road had disintegrated into swamp. The remaining regiments floundered knee-deep. Occasionally soldiers lost their footing and fell, wallowing helplessly until they could be dragged to their feet again. They carried their guns horizontally for balance. They turned along the bayou, where the road was the same. Step by step they dragged themselves through the swamp to the fishing village, where they arrived plastered from head to toe with mud. There they camped until boats arrived to return them to the anchorage. They were followed by many of the slaves who had left their masters to work in the British camp and who now begged not to be left behind. One of them told Captain Hill that if he returned, his master would lash his back raw and then rub it with pickles. Occasionally the slaves entertained the troops with dances. Quartermaster Surtees' Puritan conscience was shocked by the gyrations of the women.[22]

Through the night Lambert's regiments marched. The 85th arrived late at night at the fishing village, where they slept in their muddy clothes. The 7th marched last, forming the rear guard. As they struggled through the swamp, rumors passed among the men that many soldiers had sunk in mudholes, the swamp slowly closing over their heads while their comrades watched helplessly. At one terrible bog they had to wait several hours, lying in wet grass, while one squad at a time picked its way across on the roots of large plants. In the morning the troops arose cold and stiff and tried to make fires of reeds, which blazed up and were consumed in a moment.[23]

The 85th had reached the end of its supplies except for biscuits and a small quantity of rum. Lieutenant Gleig went in search of wild ducks. He reached a large lake, where he was able to shoot three ducks, but they dropped in the water twenty yards away. Although the day was piercingly cold and a thin coating of ice had formed on the pool, Gleig was so hungry that he finally plunged in and retrieved two of the birds. Some of the other officers also tried to shoot ducks, without much luck.[24]

On the eighteenth sixty-three American prisoners were returned by Cochrane to the Rigolets. On the nineteenth the American troops discovered the enemy camp empty except for eighty seriously wounded soldiers whom Lambert recommended to the humanity and generosity of Jackson. There was such cheering among the troops, such an excited feeling that the battle was over, that Jackson decided not to pursue the retreating army. He contented himself with sending Reuben Kemper and some of Hinds's dragoons to follow them. Kemper's detachment rode along Villeré's canal to Bayou Mazant, where they surprised and captured a picket of four men. They proceeded toward Bayou Bienvenu, but hearing what sounded like a large force ahead, they decided to go no farther.[25]

Dr. Morrell and Purser Shields, having returned with the American prisoners to Fort St. John, gathered a force of four boats and thirty-four men and set out to avenge the slight the British had practiced upon them by detaining them in spite of their flag of truce. At Petites Coquilles two more small boats and nineteen men joined their squadron. On the night of the twentieth they entered Lake Borgne. At eleven o'clock they discovered and captured a barge carrying thirty-eight dragoons (still dismounted), thirteen seamen, a lieutenant, and a master's mate. After delivering these prisoners to Petites Coquilles they continued daily sorties, but they did not again find Cochrane's boats so unprepared.[26]

On the second day that Lieutenant Gleig attempted to hunt ducks, he lost one of his last pair of wool stockings. After that he had to switch his lone stocking back and forth on his feet, keeping one foot at a time warm. Finally came the turn of the 85th to embark.

Last to embark was the 7th. Sergeant Cooper was squeezed with many of his comrades into the frigate *Fox*. A short distance into the lake the *Fox* was met by several boats carrying women who were seeking their husbands, most of them wives of the highlanders. When they failed to locate them on this last of all the boats, they wept and sobbed hopelessly. Some distance farther the *Fox* ran aground on a sandbank, and the soldiers had to wait for smaller craft to convey them the rest of the way. Sergeant Cooper saw a Swedish sailor slip over the bow of the vessel; he looked for him astern, but the sailor never rose.[27]

Lambert's army reached and encamped on Cat Island, and then moved, in February, to Dauphin Island, which had grass and groves of pines as well as sand. There they pitched tents and built huts. In one corner of the island the soldiers discovered a bed of oysters.

In the woods roamed cattle and hogs, which the soldiers soon slaughtered. In the central parts of the island there were deep pools of dark water where a number of alligators were seen. One night an alligator crawled into the hut of a soldier and his wife; feeling its weight upon her knees, the soldier's wife screamed, and it hastened back to the water. The next day a party went to the pool and shot at the animal every time its muzzle appeared above water until it finally crawled out of the pool to die. The 14th dragoons caught one young alligator and determined to take it home with them. There were also many snakes. One crawled down the back of a captain, who sprawled up the tent pole yelling fearfully until it was removed. Hunting snakes and alligators, fishing, cutting wood for the ships, parading regularly, and socializing, the troops began to recover from the nightmarish experience at the city, while part of the fleet went to Cuba for supplies.

On the *Alceste,* Lieutenant Forbes penned a letter to a friend in London, expressing thankfulness that after going for forty-four days without a change of linen and with only a blanket and greatcoat to protect him from rain, frost, and swampy ground, he was now sitting in the captain's cabin before a large fire; but he gloomily added, "Not only our prospects of prize money have vanished, but promotion also, which I fully expected would have followed success." [28]

The British army had withdrawn, less gallant than when it had arrived, leaving the mistress of the Mississippi unviolated. To salve somewhat the frustration of defeat, Lambert sent the 44th, 21st, and 4th on February 9 to Fort Bowyer. They established a strong line across the sandspit three hundred yards from the fort, as Colonel Nicholls' small force had tried unsuccessfully to do earlier, and planted strong batteries. Major Lawrence looked out at this formidable invader and decided to surrender. But news arrived from England of the end of the war, and the force returned to Dauphin Island.[29]

‡‡‡

At New Orleans, Jackson marched his army on January 23 (one month after the first engagement of the two armies) triumphantly to the city through lines of cheering citizens. The nearer they came to the town, the thicker the throngs became and the greater the resounding cheers. The population lined the streets, the balconies, the windows, and the tops of houses to see the heroes and to give vent to their uncontrollable joy.

Across the Place d'Armes, from the river entrance to the church door, two lines of Plauché's uniformed volunteers formed a wide avenue. Between these two lines, in the center of the square, a triumphal arch had been erected, supported by six columns. Standing at the right of the arch was a woman dressed as Justice and at the left a woman dressed as Liberty. Under the arch two young girls held crowns of laurels. From the arch to the cathedral, between the two lines of soldiers, were two lines of young ladies representing the states and territories, dressed in white with transparent veils and silver stars on their foreheads. Each had a state flag in her right hand and a basket of flowers trimmed with blue ribbons in her left. Behind each, on a lance stuck in the ground, was a shield naming the state represented. Streamers of flowers linked the lances, forming within the avenue of soldiers a lane from the arch of triumph to the church. Outside the avenue of soldiers, the square, the streets, and the buildings were mobbed by a great mass of people.

As the general and the army came into view, a deafening, delirious roar arose from the mob. The army halted at attention while the general entered the square, Plauché's soldiers holding aloft their bayonets and steeling themselves against the jostlings of the crowd surging behind them. While the band played lustily, its music almost drowned out by the roar of the crowd, the Hero of New Orleans marched down the avenue of bayonets to the triumphal arch. There, with Justice and Liberty beaming at him, he was met by Miss Louisiana, who took the crowns of laurels from the girls and placed them on his head (even though the tall general bowed, she had to stand on tiptoe and stretch). She murmured some congratulations which were lost in the cheers of the crowd before stepping back to let him pass down the lane of state queens. The beauties curtsied to him, waved their flags, and threw petals of flowers upon him. One impetuously stepped forward to kiss him upon the cheek. On the steps of the cathedral he turned to wave at the crowd, and the roars somehow became even louder.[30]

Abbé Dubourg, administrator apostolic of the diocese, came

forward, and after subduing the crowd by waving his arms, he addressed the general, speaking of grateful America re-echoing from shore to shore his splendid achievements and inscribing his name on her immortal rolls among those of her Washingtons, praising him for religiously acknowledging his debt to the signal interposition of providence, and calling him the man of God's right hand whom God had fitted out for the important commission of defending New Orleans. "We extol that fecundity of genius by which, under the most discouraging distress, you created unforeseen resources, raised, as it were, from the ground hosts of intrepid warriors, and provided every vulnerable point with ample means of defense. To Him we trace that instinctive superiority of mind which at once rallied around you universal confidence. . . ." The Abbé presented the general with another crown of laurel which he called "the prize of victory and the symbol of immortality." [31]

Graciously Jackson replied, shouting so the crowd could hear, "I receive the symbolical crown which piety has prepared. I receive it in the name of the brave men who have so effectually seconded my exertions. For myself, to have been instrumental in the deliverance of such a country is the greatest blessing that Heaven could confer." Then, as Jackson entered the church, the crowd roared again. All New Orleans seemed to raise from the square one great voice of mighty thanks.[32]

The barges from Pittsburgh finally arrived, and the contractor, proud that he had performed a patriotic service and that he had profited richly from the trip, delivered to the arsenal President Madison's supply of arms and ammunition for the defense of New Orleans.[33]

‡‡‡

Mr. Baker and Mr. Carroll arrived in New York with the treaty of peace on Saturday, February 11. Mr. Hughes arrived in Annapolis February 13. Hughes reached Washington first, Baker and Carroll soon following with the official copy. It was ratified by the Senate on the seventeenth and proclaimed on the eighteenth.[34]

News of the peace brought joy to Lambert's troops at Dauphin Island. The horrors of the battle had faded in the minds of most of the soldiers, though the danger of renewing it could quickly remind them. Those of the 93rd could not as easily forget, so great a number of their comrades were missing, and the bereaved women would grieve still longer. But the camp became gayer. A theater was built, and officers and men produced plays. The officers of the 7th, 43rd, and 14th dragoons attacked those of the 85th, 93rd, and 95th with pine cones in a mock battle that lasted several days.[35]

There was joyful personal news, too, which arrived along with the news of peace; General Lambert and General Keane had been appointed Knights Commanders of the Order of the Bath—for their services in Spain and France, not in New Orleans. Colonel Thornton had been made Knight Companion. General Gibbs and General Pakenham unfortunately could not know that they had been similarly honored, Gibbs as Knight Commander and Pakenham as Knight Grand Cross.[36]

Finally, on March 15, the troops began to embark for the long journey home. The campaign against New Orleans was over.[37]

‡‡‡

For many of the combatants life held adventures yet in store. General Lambert arrived in Europe in time to reach Waterloo, where he commanded a brigade supporting Picton's 5th Division. He had the satisfaction of being mentioned in Wellington's dispatches as having "conducted the movements of his brigade in the most able manner" and of being listed among the officers receiving thanks from the House of Lords. He also received the Order of St. Vladimir of Russia (Third Class) and the Order of Maximilian Joseph of Bavaria (Commander). John Keane recovered from his wounds sufficiently to join Wellington in Paris in July. He then went to Jamaica, where he administered the civil government as well as the army. Then, in India, he directed a campaign that was marked by a reckless expenditure of transport animals—and as a result he was raised to the peerage as Baron Keane. In 1844 he died of dropsy. Lambert followed Keane as commander in Jamaica. He became general in 1841 and died in 1847. The statues of Pakenham and Gibbs were placed on a pedestal in St. Paul's cathedral, with an inscription announcing that they fell in an assault on the enemy's works at New Orleans.[38]

Colonel Brooke of the 4th commanded a brigade at Waterloo. Colonel Burgoyne, the engineer who had planted the artillery batteries, missed Waterloo, but he rose steadily in the army. He was chairman of the board of public works in Ireland, inspector-general of fortifications, and Irish relief commissioner. In the Crimea he planted batteries for a futile pounding of strong earth-works similar to the one he had pounded futilely at New Orleans. He became baronet in 1856, Grand Officer of the Legion of Honor, Knight First Class of the Order of the Medjidie, D.C.L. from Oxford, and finally field marshal. George De Lacy Evans, twice wounded at New Orleans, had two horses killed under him at Waterloo. He rose through three steps in rank in six months' time. As a radical he was elected to Parliament. As commander of the British Legion he served brilliantly in Spain in 1836 and 1837. As lieutenant general he commanded a division in the Crimean War. He received the Grand Cross of the Bath and became a Grand Officer of the Legion of Honor, a Knight First Class of the Medjidie, and an honorary D.C.L. of Oxford. Admiral Cochrane, having covered himself with glory in the American war, retired with many honors and great self-satisfaction.[39]

Colonel Mullins returned to face court-martial. He was dismissed from the army for disobedience and neglect. Lady Mullins was troubled by violent headaches.[40]

The 4th, 7th, 43rd, and 40th regiments reached England in time to serve at Waterloo. The 95th followed but reached Ostend too late. The 21st, 44th, 85th, and 93rd, having suffered too heavy losses for immediate service, went to Ireland to relieve troops there for the great battle. The 21st—the Royal Scots—saw action in the Crimea, South Africa, and finally the Great War. The 44th later went to India, where it regained some of its lost honor. The 93rd for many years preserved in a glass case in the anteroom of the officers' mess the fragments of the colors they carried in the battle.[41]

Sergeant Cooper finally received his discharge at Spithead before his regiment departed for Ostend. Upon the recommendation of his company commander, brother of the bishop of Carlisle, he became a school teacher in Carlisle. In later years he vainly petitioned the government for a pension. Instead he received a medal with nine battle clasps—for Talavera, Busaco, Albuhera, Ciudad

Rodrigo, Badajoz, Vitoria, the Pyrenees, Orthez, and Toulouse, but none for New Orleans, a battle that the government did not care to commemorate. He died at the age of eighty-seven.[42]

Quartermaster Surtees, after Waterloo and a sojourn in Paris, went on leave to visit his family and his ailing wife. He took the frail girl with him to rejoin his regiment in Ireland, but she died in Dublin only three days after their arrival. Seeking comfort for this sad incident, he became very pious. But he too, in time, developed a severe chest affliction, and it bothered him during his later years of military service, especially after his regiment moved to Nova Scotia. It became severe enough that he obtained a medical discharge in 1827 and retired on full pay after twenty years of service.[43]

Lieutenant Gleig, sick of hostility, left the army upon his return to England. He traded war for peace, took orders, and served as chaplain of Chelsea Hospital for many years. In 1846 he became chaplain general of the British army. He could never forget the excitements of his journey across the ocean, the horrors of New Orleans, or the vision of his friend Grey lying in a pool of blood.[44]

The planters, merchants, and lawyers who had served in the Louisiana militia returned to their businesses, their fortunes, and their social stations, although some with plantations along the river had to overcome serious losses of cattle, provisions, and slaves. Later in life they had thrilling tales to tell their children and grandchildren about the exciting events when the British invaded their homeland. Judah Touro, millionaire merchant, told how on January 1, while carrying shot and shell from the magazine to Humphreys' battery, he was struck on the thigh by a twelve-pound shot; how his friend R. D. Shepherd, Patterson's aide, was coming with a message from the commander to Jackson when he found Touro in an old building behind Macarty's; how Shepherd put Touro in a cart, took him to the city, gave him brandy, and lodged him with some ladies to be nursed; how Shepherd was in high disfavor with Patterson for negligence until he made up for it by diligent service later. Many fabulous stories were passed down about the exciting campaign.[45]

John Plauché became lieutenant-governor of Louisiana in 1850 and died in 1860 on the eve of the Civil War. Walter Overton, hero of Fort St. Philip, served as congressman from Louisiana. William Carroll was governor of Tennessee in 1821–23 and 1830–35. John Adair was governor of Kentucky in 1820–24 and congressman in 1821–23. Colonel Slaughter capitalized on the glorious victory to become governor of Kentucky in 1816. Hinds served with Jackson in acquiring land from the Choctaws, served in Congress, and had a county in Mississippi named after him, as Jackson had a city.[46]

Dominique You died in New Orleans, poor enough to be buried at public expense, but with a tombstone that reminded citizens that he was an intrepid warrior on land as well as sea, having proved his valor in a hundred combats; that this modern Bayard, without reproach or fear, could have witnessed without trembling the destruction of the world. Beluche, the other Baratarian gunner, migrated to South America and became a commodore in the Bolivian navy. Jean Lafitte and many of his men moved westward to trouble and misfortune.[47]

Reuben Kemper returned to his schemes for extending the westward boundary of the United States across Texas. General Humbert, after a fruitless expedition into Mexico, grew old in poverty and became a well-known sight in the French market, where, ragged but stiffly proper, he described to any willing listener his great campaign in Ireland and his famous victory over the English at Chalmette. He died in 1823.[48]

Daniel Patterson continued to serve the navy, became captain early in 1815, navy commissioner 1828–32, commander of a squadron in the Mediterranean 1832–35, and commander of the Washington navy yard until he died in 1839. Edward Livingston became more and more prominent in New Orleans; he wrote a criminal code for the state while his wife became noted for her parties; he served in Congress in 1823 and the Senate in 1829; he became in 1833 American minister to the French court. His claims to lands along the Mississippi were not settled until after his death. Thomas Nicholls, a soldier in Plauché's battalion, became a judge, and his youngest son, Francis, became governor of Louisiana.[49]

The colored troops returned to their uncertain status as freemen. Some who had been wounded received small pensions, as did the children of the ones who had been killed. In years to come the veterans were sometimes honored by the city, and often they were ignored while the white men who had fought beside them got the glory. Among their own they were honored. They had been the first colored unit to serve in the United States Army. They had been in every engagement of the campaign. They had stood their ground as stanchly as any, suffering as many casualties. They had contributed significantly to the saving of the great city by the river, as their descendants have contributed significantly to its culture.[50]

Claiborne continued, as governor of Louisiana, to struggle to maintain concert between the hostile elements of his state. He became much concerned with vindicating his actions throughout the battle. Of Jackson he wrote, "I acknowledge that General Jackson has rendered important services nor do I deny him the possession of some great qualities; but the violence of his character casts a shade upon them all, and in this capital he has observed a course of conduct which cannot be easily excused." On November 23, 1817, at the age of forty, Claiborne died of a liver complaint.[51]

‡‡‡

Andrew Jackson returned to Tennessee to become a strong political leader and eventually President of the United States. But he carried from New Orleans more than the memory of a great military victory; he carried the experience of trying to govern a strong-willed people. For before his departure he found himself immersed in the broils which constantly raged in New Orleans.

After the departure of the British Army the Louisianans began to clamor for release from the army. They longed to hurry triumphantly to their nearby homes, to share their experiences with wives, mistresses, and relatives, to receive the glorious recognition they had earned. "Such is the character of the men of the South of Europe," wrote an apologist; "they love war, particularly against the English, but after battle they want to amuse themselves." For some the need to be released was urgent. "A number of unfortunate half starved women of Terre aux Boeufs," wrote the Abbé Du Bourg, "fall at your feet to redemand you their husbands." And "Dear Sir," wrote a deserter, "my wife was turned into the street by the landlord . . . and she wrote me to go home." A captain of volunteer dragoons requested that his men be allowed to return home lest they lose their next year's crop as they had already lost this one. Jackson, however, insisted on keeping his army intact as long as there was an enemy near the coast.[52]

With news of the treaty of peace the clamors of the soldiers were swelled by the clamors of the citizens to be free from martial law. Local jealousies, thinly buried during the struggle against a common enemy, suddenly erupted anew. The Tennesseans felt that as long as they had to remain in the field the Louisianans should do likewise. The Louisianans felt that the Tennesseans, far from home, could more easily endure a continued camp life. The Tennesseans reacted against the clamors of the militia by boasting that it was the Tennesseans who had won the battle while the citizens were trying to give up the city to the British. They scoffed at the idea that the artillery had had any effect; it was the sturdy backwoodsmen, not the motley crews from Louisiana, who won. To this the local Creoles reacted by accusing the Tennesseans of falsifying their accounts to perpetuate a fiction of Anglo-Saxon superiority.

In the heat of the discussion, stories of cowardice began to replace earlier stories of bravery. On the twenty-eighth Duncan and Duplessis had been seen lying flat on the ground behind Macarty's mansion. Governor Claiborne had been so frightened that he ignored orders to provide the batteries with ammunition until Jackson sent word, "If you don't send me balls and powder instantly, I shall chop off your head and ram it into one of the cannons." Livingston had carefully kept out of sight during all the engagements, and on the seventh had gone home upon a pretense of being ill; on the eighth he had sat restfully in his dressing gown upon his balcony. Abner Duncan had obtained for certain friends fraudulent orders that they were not to leave town no matter how urgent their wishes to go to the front.[53]

On February 22, after the arrival of the Charleston *Gazette* with news of the ratification of the treaty, the French militiamen applied to and received from the consul Tousard certificates releasing them from service. Jackson ordered Tousard out of the city and commanded all French subjects to retire at least as far as Baton Rouge. The French accused him loudly of arrogance and tyranny.[54]

Now Philip Louaillier judged the time ripe to make his protest. On March 3 he published a letter in the newspaper criticizing Jackson's order for the French subjects. Jackson had Louaillier arrested as a spy. Louaillier applied to Judge Hall of the district court for a writ of habeas corpus, which Judge Hall promptly granted—a writ upon which unfortunately the date was altered, giving rise to a claim of fraud. Jackson arrested Judge Hall for aiding, abetting, and exciting mutiny. In the legal skirmishing, Edward Livingston, who had long kept New Orleans stirred up by his actions, advised the general.[55]

A resolution was introduced into the legislature to present to the general an eight-hundred-dollar sword of honor. It passed the House, but by the time it reached the Senate it had become a focus for the squabble of Americans and Creoles. Opponents felt that the resolution approved the whole conduct of Jackson, including his action against Louaillier and Hall. Fulwar Skipwith had himself replaced as president in order to oppose the resolution, and the French and Creole senators rallied behind him. Meanwhile Americans jammed the galleries to support Jackson. But the Senate rejected the resolution and omitted Jackson's name from the list of those receiving thanks for conspicuous service at the battle.[56]

Louaillier was tried by a court-martial presided over by General Edmund Pendleton Gaines, who had earned recognition and promotion in the campaigns around the Lakes and who had just arrived to command the post of New Orleans. Louaillier protested against the jurisdiction of the army, and Gaines dismissed all charges except that of spy. Of that charge Louaillier was acquitted because he was not found lurking about the camp or fortifications. Jackson, reviewing the court's action, set aside the decision. He sent Judge Hall out of the city with orders not to return until official notification of peace was received.

On the thirteenth, having received official notification, Jackson released the militia with a speech of hearty praise, suspended his order for French subjects, and released Louaillier. On the fourteenth he delivered his farewell address to the army. On the twenty-first he was hailed before Judge Hall for contempt of court. After several skirmishes and delays, Jackson tendered a written answer to the charges, but the judge ruled that it could not be admitted. Jackson was ordered to appear Friday, March 31, to answer a list of interrogatories.[57]

By now the split was not entirely between American and French. One important group of French, the Baratarians, supported Jackson, and many others, their own complaints having dissolved, remembered his generalship and sympathized with him. Plauché, who had commanded the uniformed battalion, called the opposition "uneasy and turbulent persons" for whom Louaillier was the "organ." Davezac ("with squinting eye and golden epaulettes," according to an enemy) and De la Ronde likewise defended and advised the general. Mrs. Jackson arrived in town, and the Creole women, busily entertaining her with balls, concerts, and plays, wanted their husbands to forgive hers.

An immense crowd jammed the courthouse. Jackson refused, because his written defense had been barred, to receive or answer the interrogatories, and Judge Hall fined him one thousand dollars. Throwing down the money, Jackson marched amid cheers to his carriage, where he found that Dominique's men had removed the horses. The Baratarians dragged the carriage to the Exchange Coffee House, where they toasted the general's health, accused the judge of giving vent to personal feeling rather than serving public justice, and offered to repay the fine. Refusing this offer, Jackson announced, "Considering obedience to the laws, even when we think them unjustly applied, as the first duty of the citizen, I did not hesitate to comply with the sentence." He published his defense, including in it a sly reference to the judge's departure from the city during the battle: "Probably under an impression that the exercise of his functions would be useless, [he] absented himself from the place where his court was to be holden, and postponed its session during a regular term." As the British fleet was getting underweigh with the disappointed invaders, Jackson left the city with the cheers of the citizens resounding behind him, again acclaiming him the savior of New Orleans.[58]

Once again New Orleans was busy and gay with the excitements of peace. On March 16 Governor Claiborne could write, "Our harbor is again whitened with canvas; the levee is crowded with cotton, tobacco, and other articles for exportation; the merchant seems delighted with the prospect before him, and the agriculturist, in the high price for his products, finds new incitements to industry." [59]

For the last time, England and America had embraced in violence on the battlefield.

✧ ✧

Notes

CHAPTER ONE

1. George R. Gleig, *The Campaigns of the British Army at Washington and New Orleans* (London: John Murray, 1847), p. 2.

2. *Ibid.*, pp. 2–3. The final sentence is Gallatin's declaration to Monroe of the British design as quoted by A. T. Mahan, *Sea Power in Its Relations to the War of 1812* (Boston: Little, Brown & Co., 1905), II, 332.

3. Gleig, *The Campaigns of the British Army*, pp. 9–15.

4. John Buchan, *The History of the Royal Scots Fusiliers: 1678–1918* (London: Thos. Nelson & Sons, 1925), p. 63, is the authority for the 7th's official title.

5. These incidents are related in John Spencer Cooper, *Rough Notes of Seven Campaigns* (2nd ed.; Carlisle: G. & T. Coward, 1914), pp. 127 (news of fall of Paris), 3 (his sickness), 4 (the Irish lad), 5 (seasickness), 13–14 (plundering), 14 (silver candlesticks), 15 (drunken revelry), 25 (sixty-mile marches), 30 (sleeping), 14 (flogging to drum), 29 (the sheep's head), 37 (selling supplies), 45 (sentry duty), 55–57 (Redinha), 58–61 (Campo Mayor), 62–71 (Albuhera), 72–73 (Aldea Ponte), 78–86 (Badajoz), 89–95 (Vitoria), 96–98 (Pyrenees), 99–111 (Pamplona), 112–15 (Vera), 118–23 (Orthez), 124–35 (Toulouse), 55 (parallel lines), 64 (hillsides), 73 (hedges), 79–80 (storming the breach), 80 (plunder), 72 (boiled meat), 76–77 (execution of deserters), 100 (morose sergeant), 118–19 ("drink and fire"), 67 (sleeping and the naked man), 126 (the stolen belt), 55–56 (German woman), 125 (soldier's wife), 116 (two greyhounds), 126 (loaded donkey), 105–6 (Sergeant Bishop).

6. Surtees' experiences are related in William Surtees, *Twenty-five Years in the Rifle Brigade* (Edinburgh: William Blackwood, 1833), pp. 10–11 (Holland), 14 (night marches), 16 (Russian soldier), 16–27 (fight-

ing on sand dunes), 20–22 (firing and discarding knapsack), 72, 94, 97 (experiences of seasickness), 33–34 (stepped on by a sailor), 39–40 (enlisting in rifle corps), 43 (eight hundred lashes), 48 (suicide), 49 (deserter), 60–71 (Denmark), 73–95 (Spain), 75, 94 (sleeping in convents), 88 (retreat from Astorga), 123 (groans of dying), 138–39 (Badajoz), 144–45 (attending the wounded), 148 (drunken rifleman), 165 (French hospital), 158 (grenadier's wife), 209–10 (plunder of baggage train), 19–20, 121, 152 (bravado), 171–77, 184, 220 (drunkenness, priest), 73, 101 (his wife), 308–9 (end of the war).

CHAPTER TWO

1. Marquis James, *The Life of Andrew Jackson* (New York: Bobbs-Merrill Co., 1938), p. 175. John Spencer Bassett, *The Life of Andrew Jackson* (New York: Doubleday, Page & Co., 1911), I, 124. Andrew Jackson, *Correspondence of Andrew Jackson,* ed. John Spencer Bassett (Washington, D.C.: Carnegie Institution of Washington, 1927), II, 5.

2. Bassett, *The Life of Andrew Jackson,* I, 116. Benson J. Lossing, *The Pictorial Field-Book of the War of 1812* (New York: Harper & Bros., 1868), pp. 779–82. Mrs. Dunbar Rowland, *Andrew Jackson's Campaign against the British* (New York: Macmillan Co., 1926), pp. 207–9 (incident of the deer).

3. Bernard Marigny, "Reflections on the Campaign of General Andrew Jackson in Louisiana in 1814 and '15," *Louisiana Historical Quarterly,* VI, 78. Concerning population, Augustus C. Buell, in *History of Andrew Jackson* (New York: Chas. Scribner's Sons, 1904), I, 361, says 26,000, one half colored and 10,000 Creoles; total in Louisiana, 70,000. Vincent Nolte, in *The Memoirs of Vincent Nolte: Reminiscences in the Period of Anthony Adverse* (New York: G. Howard Watt, 1934), p. 86, says 16,000 in 1806, one third colored.

4. G. P. Whittington, "Dr. John Sibley of Natchitoches, 1757–1837," *Louisiana Historical Quarterly,* X, 476–79. Jackson, *Correspondence,* II, 51. Bassett, *The Life of Andrew Jackson,* I, 148. Reed McC. B. Adams, in "New Orleans and the War of 1812," *Louisiana Historical Quarterly,* XVI, 480, describes the waterworks.

5. John S. Kendall, "Old New Orleans Houses," *Louisiana Historical Quarterly,* XVII, 693. Whittington, "Dr. John Sibley," pp. 478–80.

6. Kendall, "Old New Orleans Houses," pp. 683, 693–95. François-Xavier Martin, *The History of Louisiana* (New Orleans: James A. Gresham, 1882), p. 11.

7. Grace King, *Creole Families of New Orleans* (New York: Macmillan Co., 1921), p. 43, and Meloncy C. Soniat, "The Faubourgs Forming the Upper Section of the City of New Orleans," *Louisiana Historical Quarterly,* XX, 193–99 (developing suburbs). Charles Gayarré, *History*

of Louisiana: The American Domination (New York: Wm. J. Widdleton, 1866), pp. 36–37 (Jefferson's comments). W. O. Hart, "Mrs. Louise Livingston, Wife of Edward Livingston," *Louisiana Historical Quarterly*, V, 352–53 (immigration of Creoles from the West Indies). Gayarré, *History of Louisiana*, p. 218 (immigration of free colored). Donald E. Everett, "Emigres and Militiamen: Free Persons of Color in New Orleans, 1803–15," *Journal of Negro History*, XXXVIII, 385, reports 1,977 colored from Cuba between May 19 and July 18, 1809; on p. 377, 5,700 is given as the free colored population in 1810.

8. Gayarré, *History of Louisiana, passim* (the city's tensions); e.g., pp. 25–26, 120, 197, 201, 209–10, 227. The description of the Creoles is that of James Parton, *Life of Andrew Jackson* (Boston: Houghton, Mifflin Co., 1860), II, 15. The description of Sunday is from Whittington, "Dr. John Sibley," pp. 480–83.

9. Parton, *Life of Andrew Jackson*, II, 14. J. W. Fortescue, *A History of the British Army* (London: Macmillan Co., 1920), X, 151, estimates that cotton and sugar crops in the city were worth £3,500,000 at the time of the invasion, and other merchandise was worth £500,000.

10. Nathaniel Claiborne, *Notes on the War in the South* (Richmond: Wm. Ramsay, 1819), pp. 91–111.

11. Gayarré, *History of Louisiana*, pp. 10–11. Marigny, "Reflections on the Campaign," pp. 78 (incident of the ball), 81 (debate about naming the state).

12. N. Claiborne, *Notes on the War in the South*, p. 110.

13. James, *The Life of Andrew Jackson*, p. 193. Parton, *Life of Andrew Jackson*, II, 19. Hart, "Mrs. Louise Livingston," pp. 352–53. Gayarré, *History of Louisiana*, pp. 185–90 *et al*. W. C. C. Claiborne, *Official Letter Books of W. C. C. Claiborne, 1801–16*, ed. Dunbar Rowland (Jackson, Miss.: State Department of Archives and History, 1917), VI, 54–55, 104–5, 259, *et al*.

14. "The Nicholls Family in Louisiana," *Louisiana Historical Quarterly*, VI, 7. Nolte, *Memoirs*, p. 87.

15. Gayarré, *History of Louisiana*, pp. 104–5.

16. *Ibid.*, pp. 112 (the nuns), 115 (the priests), 184–85 (the slave girl), 197 (sailors fighting), 214–18 (planters and the slave trade), 219–20 (free colored). Everett, "Emigres and Militiamen," pp. 380, 385–87 (free colored). Gayarré, *History of Louisiana*, pp. 202, 322–23 (militia quotas). Whittington, "Dr. John Sibley," pp. 479, 484, and Gayarré, "Historical Sketch of Pierre and Jean Lafitte," *Magazine of American History*, X, 284 (high rents). Gayarré, *History of Louisiana*, pp. 266–67 (slave rebellion). Everett, "Emigres and Militiamen," pp. 377, 389–92, 394–95 (colored militia).

17. W. C. C. Claiborne, *Official Letter Books*, VI, 279–80, 301. Gayarré, "Pierre and Jean Lafitte," pp. 286–88, 290. Gayarré, *History of Louisiana*, p. 312.

18. Gayarré, *History of Louisiana*, pp. 240–43, 319–20. Lossing, *The Pictorial Field-Book*, pp. 738–40. W. C. C. Claiborne, *Official Letter Books*, VI, 287.

19. Gayarré, *History of Louisiana*, pp. 320–23, 330. Bassett, *The Life of Andrew Jackson*, I, 101. Lossing, *The Pictorial Field-Book*, pp. 767–68.

CHAPTER THREE

1. George R. Gleig, *The Campaigns of the British Army at Washington and New Orleans* (London: John Murray, 1847), pp. 4, 15, 17–21.

2. *Ibid.*, pp. 21–22.

3. Richard Johns and P. H. Nicolas, *The Naval and Military Heroes of Great Britain or Calendar of Victory* (London: Henry G. Bohn, 1860), *passim.*

4. Gleig, *The Campaigns of the British Army*, p. 23.

5. These incidents from Cooper's journey are related in John Spencer Cooper, *Rough Notes of Seven Campaigns* (2nd ed.; Carlisle: G. & T. Coward, 1914), pp. 127–28, 158–59.

6. John Henry Cooke, *A Narrative of Events in the South of France and of the Attack on New Orleans* (London: T. & W. Boone, 1835), pp. 15–40.

7. Cooper, *Rough Notes*, pp. 128–29.

8. William Surtees, *Twenty-five Years in the Rifle Brigade* (Edinburgh: Wm. Blackwood, 1833), pp. 314–17.

9. *Ibid.*, p. 323.

10. Gleig, *The Campaigns of the British Army*, pp. 23–35.

11. John Buchan, *The History of the Royal Scots Fusiliers: 1678–1918* (London: Thos. Nelson and Sons, 1925), p. 63, is the authority for the official name of the 21st.

12. Buchan, *The History of the Royal Scots Fusiliers*, pp. 6–10 (origins), 36, note, and 23 (number), 49–55 (Blenheim), 122–29 (America), 135–43 (West Indies), 145 (Dublin), 146 (Lord Nelson), 150–59 (Napoleonic wars), 157–59 (Spain).

13. Alexander Walker, *Jackson and New Orleans* (New York: J. C. Derby, 1856), pp. 77–78 (93rd). Johns and Nicolas, *The Naval and Military Heroes of Great Britain, passim* (95th and 14th).

14. Johns and Nicolas, *The Naval and Military Heroes of Great Britain, passim*. For the assignment of Lord Hill, A. T. Mahan, *Sea Power in Its Relations to the War of 1812* (Boston: Little, Brown & Co., 1905), II, 385, and Henry Adams, *History of the United States of America during the Second Administration of James Madison* (New York: Chas. Scribner's Sons, 1904), II, 311, quoting a letter from Bathurst to Ross, July 30.

15. Mahan, *Sea Power*, II, 385.

CHAPTER FOUR

1. A. Lacarriere Latour, *Historical Memoir of the War in West Florida and Louisiana* (Philadelphia: John Conrad & Co., 1816), p. xvi.

2. John Spencer Bassett, *The Life of Andrew Jackson* (New York: Doubleday, Page & Co., 1911), I, 123–25. For the barges carrying arms, J. Fair Hardin, "The First Great River Captain," *Louisiana Historical Quarterly*, X, 27; Andrew Jackson, *Correspondence of Andrew Jackson*, ed. John Spencer Bassett (Washington: Carnegie Institution of Washington, 1927), II, 113, note (A. R. Woolley to Jackson, Nov. 8), 85, note (Monroe to Blount, Nov. 3).

3. Charles Gayarré, "Historical Sketch of Pierre and Jean Lafitte," *Magazine of American History*, X, 294–95 (the buccaneers' legal troubles).

4. George R. Gleig, *The Campaigns of the British Army at Washington and New Orleans* (London: John Murray, 1847), pp. 35–39.

5. *Ibid.*, pp. 45–46. Alexander Walker, *Jackson and New Orleans* (New York: J. C. Derby, 1856), p. 95 (*Tonnant* at Aboquir).

6. Field Marshal Arthur, Duke of Wellington, "Letter of the Duke of Wellington (May 22, 1815) on the Battle of New Orleans," *Louisiana Historical Quarterly*, IX, 8. Henry Adams, *History of the United States of America during the Second Administration of James Madison* (New York: Chas. Scribner's Sons, 1904), II, 312 (Croker to Cochrane, Aug. 10; Bathurst to Ross, Aug. 10).

7. *The Dictionary of National Biography*, X, 1154–55. John Philippart, *The Royal Military Calendar* (London: A. J. Valpy, 1815), II, 162.

8. *The Dictionary of National Biography*, XXII, 950–51. Philippart, *The Royal Military Calendar*, II, 112–13.

9. Bassett, *The Life of Andrew Jackson*, I, 19 (Jackson's marriage), I, 76 (commission). Marquis James, *The Life of Andrew Jackson* (New York: Bobbs-Merrill Co., 1938), pp. 148–50; Bassett, *The Life of Andrew Jackson*, I, 80–86; and Benson J. Lossing, *The Pictorial Field-Book of the War of 1812* (New York: Harper & Bros., 1868), pp. 743–44 (the Natchez incident). Marquis James, *The Life of Andrew Jackson*, p. 150 ("Old Hickory").

10. Bassett, *The Life of Andrew Jackson*, I, 88, 92–117; and Marquis James, *The Life of Andrew Jackson*, pp. 152–53 (street fights and the Creek War). Bassett, *The Life of Andrew Jackson*, I, 126 (Jackson's strategy).

11. Bassett, *The Life of Andrew Jackson*, I, 21 (Coffee), 67, and Lossing, *The Pictorial Field-Book*, p. 1043 (Carroll). "Major Howell Tatum's Journal," ed. John Spencer Bassett, *Smith College Studies in History*, VII, 5–6.

12. Lossing, *The Pictorial Field-Book,* p. 1045 (Adair). Mrs. Dunbar Rowland, *Andrew Jackson's Campaign against the British* (New York: Macmillan Co., 1926), pp. 219 (Claiborne), 9–24 (Hinds).

13. Bernard Marigny, "Reflections on the Campaign of General Andrew Jackson in Louisiana in 1814 and '15," *Louisiana Historical Quarterly,* VI, 84, and Grace King, *Creole Families of New Orleans* (New York: Macmillan Co., 1921), pp. 9–58 (Marigny), 313–22, 368–82 (Macarty). Marigny, "Reflections on the Campaign," p. 68 (Declouet). "Andrew Jackson and Judge D. A. Hall," *Louisiana Historical Quarterly,* V, 533 (Hall). Marigny, "Reflections on the Campaign," p. 80 (Jean Blanque), 74, and King, *Creole Families of New Orleans,* p. 444 (St. Gême). Marigny, "Reflections on the Campaign," p. 67 (Flood). Rowland, *Andrew Jackson's Campaign,* p. 369 (Kemper). Latour, *Historical Memoir,* pp. 82–83 (the fishermen). Vincent Nolte, *The Memoirs of Vincent Nolte: Reminiscences in the Period of Anthony Adverse* (New York: G. Howard Watt, 1934), pp. 82–85, 175–84 (Nolte).

14. Bassett, *The Life of Andrew Jackson,* I, 123–24 (Creek treaty), 126, 128 (Mobile). Jackson, *Correspondence,* II, 33–34 (Jackson to Blount, Aug. 27) (dispatches from Havana).

15. Gleig, *The Campaigns of the British Army,* p. 46.

CHAPTER FIVE

1. This chapter is based mainly upon the account of A. Lacarriere Latour, *Historical Memoir of the War in West Florida and Louisiana* (Philadelphia: John Conrad & Co., 1816), pp. 12–25.

2. Latour, *Historical Memoir,* appendix, pp. ix-xi (Nicholls to Lafitte, Aug. 31, and Capt. Percy unaddressed, Sept. 1).

3. *Ibid.,* p. xi.

4. Marquis James, *The Life of Andrew Jackson* (New York: Bobbs-Merrill Co., 1938), p. 185, describes Lafitte.

5. Latour, *Historical Memoir,* appendix, pp. vii–viii (Proclamation of Colonel Nicholls, Aug. 29, 1814).

6. *Ibid.,* pp. xii (Lafitte to Blanque, Sept. 4; a different translation is given by Marquis James); xiii–xiv (Lafitte to Claiborne).

7. *Ibid.,* pp. xi–xii (Lafitte to Lockyer, Sept. 4).

8. Charles Gayarré, "Historical Sketch of Pierre and Jean Lafitte," *Magazine of American History,* X, 297. Stanley Clisby Arthur, *The Story of the Battle of New Orleans* (New Orleans: Louisiana Historical Society, 1915), p. 37.

CHAPTER SIX

1. A. Lacarriere Latour, *Historical Memoir of the War in West Florida and Louisiana* (Philadelphia: John Conrad & Co., 1816), p. 22

(Blanque). Charles Gayarré, "Historical Sketch of Pierre and Jean Lafitte," *Magazine of American History*, X, 390; and Latour, *Historical Memoir*, p. 253 (the advice). Gayarré, "Pierre and Jean Lafitte," X, 391, and Latour, *Historical Memoir*, p. 253 (Patterson's expedition).

2. Andrew Jackson, *Correspondence of Andrew Jackson*, ed. John Spencer Bassett (Washington, D.C.: Carnegie Institution of Washington, 1927), II, 66–67 (Ross to Jackson, Oct. 3).

3. Jackson, *Correspondence*, II, 27 (Jackson to Claiborne, Aug. 22). Vincent Nolte, *The Memoirs of Vincent Nolte: Reminiscences in the Period of Anthony Adverse* (New York: G. Howard Watt, 1934), p. 206.

4. W. C. C. Claiborne, *Official Letter Books of W. C. C. Claiborne, 1801–16*, ed. Dunbar Rowland (Jackson, Miss.: State Department of Archives and History, 1917), VI, 295. Charles Gayarré, *History of Louisiana: The American Domination* (New York: Wm. J. Widdleton, 1866), pp. 355–56. Donald E. Everett, "Emigres and Militiamen: Free Persons of Color in New Orleans, 1803–15" *Journal of Negro History*, XXXVIII, 389, 392–93. Jackson, *Correspondence*, II, 76–77 (Claiborne to Jackson, Oct. 17).

5. François-Xavier Martin, *The History of Louisiana* (New Orleans: James A. Gresham, 1882), pp. 364, 368. W. C. C. Claiborne, *Official Letter Books*, VI, 293 (to Jackson, Oct. 28). "Andrew Jackson and Judge D. A. Hall," *Louisiana Historical Quarterly*, V, 556 (Claiborne to Jackson, Aug. 24). Latour, *Historical Memoir*, p. 51.

6. Jackson, *Correspondence*, II, 46–47 (MacRea to Jackson, Sept. 9).

7. Latour, *Historical Memoir*, introduction, p. xvi. Bernard Marigny, "Reflections on the Campaign of General Andrew Jackson in Louisiana in 1814–'15," *Louisiana Historical Quarterly*, VI, 63.

8. Marigny, "Reflections on the Campaign," p. 68.

9. Jackson, *Correspondence*, II, 56–57 (Jackson to Claiborne, Sept. 21). Latour, *Historical Memoir*, pp. xxxi–xxxii (proclamation to the free colored). Jackson, *Correspondence*, II, 57–58, and Latour, *Historical Memoir*, pp. xxix–xxx (proclamation to the Louisianans). Latour, *Historical Memoir*, pp. xx–xxi (General Orders, Sept. 5). Jackson, *Correspondence*, II, 76–77 (Claiborne to Jackson, Oct. 17).

10. Benson J. Lossing, *The Pictorial Field-Book of the War of 1812* (New York: Harper & Bros., 1868), p. 1023 (Sept. 16). Latour, *Historical Memoir*, pp. xxv–xxvii (Sept. 15).

11. Jackson, *Correspondence*, II, 51–54 (Committee of Safety to Jackson, Sept. 18), 81 (Jackson to Livingston, Oct. 23), 70 (Jackson to Monroe, Oct. 10).

12. W. C. C. Claiborne, *Official Letter Books*, VI, 321–23.

13. Jackson, *Correspondence*, II, 12–13 (Jackson to Armstrong, June 27). John Spencer Bassett, *The Life of Andrew Jackson* (New York: Doubleday, Page & Co., 1911), I, 128–30. Jackson, *Correspondence*, II, 20–21, 28–29, 36–40, 44–46 (Jackson to Manrique, Aug. 24 and Sept. 9; Manrique to Jackson, July 26 and Aug. 30).

14. Jackson, *Correspondence,* II, 50–51 (Jackson to Monroe, Sept. 17). Bassett, *The Life of Andrew Jackson,* I, 133.
15. Jackson, *Correspondence,* II, 50–51 (Jackson to Monroe, Sept. 17).
16. "Major Howell Tatum's Journal," ed. John Spencer Bassett, *Smith College Studies in History,* VII, 55–61. Jackson, *Correspondence,* II, 49–50 (Jackson to Col. Butler, Sept. 17).
17. Bassett, *The Life of Andrew Jackson,* I, 133–34.
18. William Surtees, *Twenty-five Years in the Rifle Brigade* (Edinburgh: Wm. Blackwood, 1833), pp. 324–27.
19. George R. Gleig, *The Campaigns of the British Army at Washington and New Orleans* (London: John Murray, 1847), pp. 47–70. *The Dictionary of National Biography,* VI, 926. Lossing, *The Pictorial Field-Book,* pp. 921–34. John Buchan, *The History of the Royal Scots Fusiliers: 1678–1918* (London: Thos. Nelson and Sons, 1925), p. 171.
20. Gleig, *The Campaigns of the British Army,* p. 83.
21. Lossing, *The Pictorial Field-Book,* pp. 950–51.
22. *Ibid.,* pp. 955–59. Buchan, *The Royal Scots Fusiliers,* p. 173. Gleig, *The Campaigns of the British Army,* pp. 96, 102–6.

CHAPTER SEVEN

1. Andrew Jackson, *Correspondence of Andrew Jackson,* ed. John Spencer Bassett (Washington: Carnegie Institution of Washington, 1927), II, 71, 87 (Monroe to Jackson, Oct. 10; Jackson to Claiborne, Oct. 31).
2. Charles Gayarré, *History of Louisiana: The American Domination* (New York: Wm. J. Widdleton, 1866), p. 364. Bernard Marigny, "Reflections on the Campaign of General Andrew Jackson in Louisiana in 1814 and '15," *Louisiana Historical Quarterly,* VI, 63. Jackson, *Correspondence,* II, 55–56 (Claiborne to Jackson, Sept. 20). John Spencer Bassett, *The Life of Andrew Jackson* (New York: Doubleday, Page & Co., 1911), I, 152, reports Lafitte to have gone to the mouth of Lafourche. Charles Gayarré in "Historical Sketch of Pierre and Jean Lafitte," *Magazine of American History,* X, 391, reports him at the German coast.
3. Gayarré, *History of Louisiana,* p. 354.
4. *Ibid.,* pp. 355–56, 366. W. C. C. Claiborne, *Official Letter Books of W. C. C. Claiborne, 1801–16,* ed. Dunbar Rowland (Jackson, Miss.: State Department of Archives and History, 1917), VI, 294.
5. Jackson, *Correspondence,* II, 87–88 (Jackson to Claiborne, Oct. 31).
6. *Ibid.,* II, 54–55, 75–76, 81 (Claiborne to Jackson, Sept. 19, Oct. 17, Oct. 24). W. C. C. Claiborne, *Official Letter Books,* VI, 297. A. Lacarriere Latour, *Historical Memoir of the War in West Florida and Louisiana* (Philadelphia: John Conrad & Co., 1816), appendix, pp. xxii–xxiv (General Orders, Militia GHQ, New Orleans, Sept. 8).

7. Nathaniel Claiborne, *Notes on the War in the South* (Richmond: Wm. Ramsay, 1819), p. 54 (the idle sailors). "Andrew Jackson and Judge D. A. Hall," *Louisiana Historical Quarterly*, V, 532, and James Parton, *Life of Andrew Jackson* (Boston: Houghton, Mifflin Co., 1860), II, 78, note (the British spy).

8. "Jackson and Hall," p. 556. W. C. C. Claiborne, *Official Letter Books*, VI, 285, 289. Jackson, *Correspondence*, II, 90–92 (Claiborne to Jackson, Nov. 5; Livingston to Jackson, Nov. 5).

9. Bassett, *The Life of Andrew Jackson*, I, 163. J. W. Fortescue, *A History of the British Army* (London: Macmillan Co., 1920), X, 150 (Cochrane's avidity).

10. Bassett, *The Life of Andrew Jackson*, I, 137–40. Marquis James, *The Life of Andrew Jackson* (New York: Bobbs-Merrill Co., 1938), pp. 194–98. Jackson, *Correspondence*, II, 92–95, 96–99 (various notes and Jackson to Monroe, Nov. 14). "Major Howell Tatum's Journal," ed. John Spencer Bassett, *Smith College Studies in History*, VII, 65–82.

11. Bassett, *The Life of Andrew Jackson*, I, 143. "Major Howell Tatum's Journal," pp. 87–88. Bassett says Jackson left Nov. 21; Tatum, p. 89, and John Henry Eaton, *The Life of Andrew Jackson* (Philadelphia: Samuel Bradford, 1824), p. 259, say Nov. 22

12. W. C. C. Claiborne, *Official Letter Books*, VI, 305, 313–14. Eaton, *The Life of Andrew Jackson*, pp. 269–70. Vincent Nolte, *The Memoirs of Vincent Nolte: Reminiscences in the Period of Anthony Adverse* (New York: G. Howard Watt, 1934), pp. 198–99.

13. John Spencer Cooper, *Rough Notes of Seven Campaigns* (Carlisle: G. & T. Coward, 1914), p. 130.

14. *Ibid.* John Henry Cooke, *A Narrative of Events in the South of France and of the Attack on New Orleans* (London: T. & W. Boone, 1835), pp. 89–93.

15. Cooke, *A Narrative of Events*, p. 97.

16. Cooper, *Rough Notes*, pp. 130–31.

17. George R. Gleig, *The Campaigns of the British Army at Washington and New Orleans* (London: John Murray, 1847), pp. 112–19. John Buchan, *The History of the Royal Scots Fusiliers: 1678–1918* (London: Thos. Nelson & Sons, 1925), p. 173.

18. Gleig, *The Campaigns of the British Army*, pp. 122–30, 205–6. Fortescue, *A History of the British Army*, X, 150.

19. William Surtees, *Twenty-five Years in the Rifle Brigade* (Edinburgh: Wm. Blackwood, 1833), pp. 327–30.

20. *Ibid.*, p. 330. Gleig, *The Campaigns of the British Army*, pp. 130–31, 132. Buchan, *The Royal Scots Fusiliers*, pp. 162–65.

21. Richard Johns and P. H. Nicolas, *The Naval and Military Heroes of Great Britain or Calendar of Victory* (London: Henry G. Bohn, 1860), pp. 73, 80–82. Buchan, *The Royal Scots Fusiliers*, p. 151 (Corporal Brown's reaction).

22. Buchan, *The Royal Scots Fusiliers*, pp. 162–65 (Bergen-op-Zoom).

Journal of the Society for Army Historical Research, VIII (1929), 124 (dress of the 93rd).

23. William James, *A Full and Correct Account of the Military Occurrences of the Late War between Great Britain and the United States of America* (London: Privately printed, 1818), II, 508–13 (Brooke to Bathurst, Sept. 17) (conduct of officers at Bladensburg). Latour, *Historical Memoir,* appendix, p. cxxxvi (names of commanders).

24. Field Marshal Arthur, Duke of Wellington, *Supplementary Dispatches, Correspondence, and Memoranda,* ed. (his son) The Duke of Wellington (London: John Murray, 1863), X, 395 (Keane's Journal of Operations).

25. Gleig, *The Campaigns of the British Army,* pp. 132–33, gives Nov. 25 and 26 as the dates of departure. Keane, in Wellington, *Supplementary Dispatches,* X, 395, gives Nov. 27. Surtees, *The Rifle Brigade,* p. 332, gives Nov. 29.

26. Alexander Dickson, "Artillery Services in North America in 1814 and 1815," *Journal of the Society for Army Historical Research,* VIII, 89 (the *Statira*). John Philippart, *The Royal Military Calendar* (London: A. J. Valpy, 1815), II, 122–23, and *The Dictionary of National Biography,* VII, 1148 (Gibbs).

27. Philippart, *The Royal Military Calendar,* II, 55–56. Field Marshal Arthur, Duke of Wellington, "Letter of the Duke of Wellington (May 22, 1815) on the Battle of New Orleans," *Louisiana Historical Quarterly,* IX, 6. *The Dictionary of National Biography,* XV, 83–84.

28. Dickson, "Artillery Services," p. 89. *The Dictionary of National Biography,* III, 342.

29. A. T. Mahan, *Sea Power in Its Relation to the War of 1812* (New York: Little, Brown & Co., 1905), II, 429–30, 434. Fortescue, *A History of the British Army,* X, 136.

30. "Major Howell Tatum's Journal," pp. 89–96.

CHAPTER EIGHT

1. "Major Howell Tatum's Journal," ed. John Spencer Bassett, *Smith College Studies in History,* VII, 96. Andrew Jackson, *Correspondence of Andrew Jackson,* ed. John Spencer Bassett (Washington: Carnegie Institution of Washington, 1927), II, 112–13 (Jackson to Coffee, Dec. 11). Several later accounts have stated that Jackson arrived Dec. 2.

2. W. C. C. Claiborne, *Official Letter Books of W. C. C. Claiborne, 1801–16,* ed. Dunbar Rowland (Jackson, Miss.: State Department of Archives and History, 1917), VI, 320–21. Jackson, *Correspondence,* II, 100 (Claiborne to Jackson, Nov. 16). Bernard Marigny, "Reflections on the Campaign of General Andrew Jackson in Louisiana in 1814 and

'15," *Louisiana Historical Quarterly*, VI, 64. Charles Gayarré, *History of Louisiana: The American Domination* (New York, Wm. J. Widdleton, 1866), p. 397.

3. Vincent Nolte, *The Memoirs of Vincent Nolte: Reminiscences in the Period of Anthony Adverse* (New York: G. Howard Watt, 1934), pp. 189–201 (Nolte's quarrels).

4. Jackson, *Correspondence*, II, 172 (Jackson to Col. Robert Hays, Feb. 17), speaks of his health. John Spencer Bassett, *The Life of Andrew Jackson* (New York: Doubleday, Page & Co., 1911), I, 166, and John Henry Eaton, *The Life of Andrew Jackson* (Philadelphia: Samuel Bradford, 1824), pp. 431–32, describe Jackson. "Major Howell Tatum's Journal," p. 96, Marigny, "Reflections on the Campaign," p. 82, and Alexander Walker, *Jackson and New Orleans* (New York: J. C. Derby, 1856), p. 17 (his arrival). Benson J. Lossing, *The Pictorial Field-Book of the War of 1812* (New York: Harper & Bros., 1868), p. 1024, puts his headquarters at 104 Royal Street.

5. Jackson, *Correspondence*, II, 51–54 (Committee of Safety to Jackson, Sept. 18).

6. Claiborne, *Official Letter Books*, VI, 297–98, 305–8, 310–12. Also Jackson, *Correspondence*, II, 81–82, 84–85, 100, 120–21 (Claiborne to Jackson, Oct. 24, Nov. 16, Dec. 20; McRea to Jackson, Oct. 27). The information about two troops of cavalry is from Alcée Fortier, *A History of Louisiana* (New York: Goupil & Co. of Paris, 1903), III, 166.

7. Bassett, *The Life of Andrew Jackson*, I, 147, 165. Jackson, *Correspondence*, II, 27, 66–67, 90 (Ross to Jackson, Aug. 15, Oct. 3; Claiborne to Jackson, Nov. 4).

8. A. Lacarriere Latour, *Historical Memoir of the War in West Florida and Louisiana* (Philadelphia: John Conrad & Co., 1816), p. 8. Jackson, *Correspondence*, II, 67 (Ross to Jackson, Oct. 3).

9. Marigny, "Reflections on the Campaign," p. 82, and W. O. Hart, "Mrs. Louise Livingston, Wife of Edward Livingston," *Louisiana Historical Quarterly*, V, 354 (Marigny's offer). "Andrew Jackson and Judge D. A. Hall," *Louisiana Historical Quarterly*, V, 558 (Jackson's suspicions of Claiborne). "Major Howell Tatum's Journal," p. 98 (the colored officers).

10. Marigny, "Reflections on the Campaign," p. 65.

11. Bassett, *The Life of Andrew Jackson*, I, 166; Latour, *Historical Memoir*, p. 52; Lossing, *The Pictorial Field-Book*, p. 1024; Walker, *Jackson and New Orleans*, pp. 74–75; Gayarré, *History of Louisiana*, p. 432. Nolte, *Memoirs*, p. 206, says Captain White's company was made up of Irishmen. Stanley Clisby Arthur, *The Story of the Battle of New Orleans* (New Orleans: Louisiana Historical Society, 1915), pp. 249–51, gives the roster of the battalion.

12. James Parton, *Life of Andrew Jackson* (Boston: Houghton, Mifflin Co., 1860), II, 30–31; Bassett, *The Life of Andrew Jackson*, I, 166–67.

13. "Major Howell Tatum's Journal," p. 96; Bassett, *The Life of Andrew Jackson,* I, 167; Jackson, *Correspondence,* II, 112–13 (Jackson to Coffee, Dec. 11); Walker, *Jackson and New Orleans,* 135–36.

14. Drawings of the Macarty mansion are in Lossing, *The Pictorial Field-Book,* p. 1037, and Arthur, *Battle of New Orleans,* p. 117; they vary, but both show a solid three-story mansion. Drawings of Villeré's house are in Lossing, *Pictorial Field-Book,* p. 1029, and Arthur, *Battle of New Orleans,* p. 95. One of Lacoste's is in Lossing, *Pictorial Field-Book,* p. 1031; one of Three-Oaks, behind Jackson's line, in Arthur, *Battle of New Orleans,* p. 81.

15. John Spencer Cooper, *Rough Notes of Seven Campaigns* (2nd ed.; Carlisle: G. & T. Coward, 1914), pp. 131–32.

16. John Henry Cooke, *A Narrative of Events in the South of France and of the Attack on New Orleans* (London: T. & W. Boone, 1835), pp. 98–100.

17. Cooper, *Rough Notes,* pp. 132–33. Cooke, *A Narrative of Events,* pp. 102–3.

18. Cooper, *Rough Notes,* p. 134.

19. Richard Johns and P. H. Nicolas, *The Naval and Military Heroes of Great Britain or Calendar of Victory* (London: Henry G. Bohn, 1860), *passim.*

20. William James, *A Full and Correct Account of the Military Occurrences of the Late War between Great Britain and the United States of America* (London: Privately printed, 1818), II, 508–13 (Brooke to Bathurst, Sept. 17).

21. Johns and Nicolas, *The Naval and Military Heroes of Great Britain,* pp. 210–12.

22. *Ibid.,* pp. 101–13.

23. George R. Gleig, *The Campaigns of the British Army at Washington and New Orleans* (London: John Murray, 1847), pp. 132–34. John Buchan, *The History of the Royal Scots Fusiliers: 1678–1918* (London: Thos. Nelson & Sons, 1925), p. 174.

24. For the British attitude toward the Louisiana coast, William James, *Military Occurrences,* II, 347.

25. *Ibid.,* p. 348. Field Marshal Arthur, Duke of Wellington, *Supplementary Dispatches, Correspondence, and Memoranda,* ed. (his son) The Duke of Wellington (London: John Murray, 1863), X, 395 (Keane's Journal of Operations).

CHAPTER NINE

1. Alexander Walker, *Jackson and New Orleans* (New York: J. C. Derby, 1856), p. 58.

2. A. Lacarriere Latour, *Historical Memoir of the War in West Florida and Louisiana* (Philadelphia: John Conrad & Co., 1816), p. 93. Field

Marshal Arthur, Duke of Wellington, *Supplementary Dispatches, Correspondence, and Memoranda,* ed. (his son) The Duke of Wellington (London: John Murray, 1863), X, 401 (Keane's Journal of Operations). William Surtees, *Twenty-five Years in the Rifle Brigade* (Edinburgh: Wm. Blackwood, 1833), pp. 334, 339.

3. Walker, *Jackson and New Orleans,* pp. 90–91. "Major Howell Tatum's Journal," ed. John Spencer Bassett, *Smith College Studies in History,* VII, 56, gives the *Sophia* eighteen guns. The duplication of the *Thames* as both thirty-two and transport is Walker's.

4. Augustus C. Buell, *History of Andrew Jackson* (New York: Chas. Scribner's Sons, 1904), II, 72–73. J. W. Fortescue, *A History of the British Army* (London: Macmillan Co., 1920), X, 150. Walker, *Jackson and New Orleans,* pp. 93–94.

5. George R. Gleig, *The Campaigns of the British Army at Washington and New Orleans* (London: John Murray, 1847), p. 143. Surtees, *The Rifle Brigade,* p. 339. Wellington, *Supplementary Dispatches,* p. 401 (Keane's Journal). "Unpublished Letter Relative to the Battle of New Orleans," *Publications of the Louisiana Historical Society,* IX, 77.

6. Wellington, *Supplementary Dispatches,* p. 395 (Keane's Journal).

7. Latour, *Historical Memoir,* pp. cxxxviii–cxxxix (Cochrane to Croker, Dec. 16). Wellington, *Supplementary Dispatches,* p. 395 (Keane's Journal).

8. "Major Howell Tatum's Journal," pp. 98–99. Latour, *Historical Memoir,* pp. 54–55, 187–89, 191. Andrew Jackson, *Correspondence of Andrew Jackson,* ed. John Spencer Bassett (Washington: Carnegie Institution of Washington, 1927), II, 111–12 (Jackson to Monroe, Dec. 10).

9. Jackson, *Correspondence,* II, 107 (Col. Hayne to Jackson, Dec. 1).

10. "Major Howell Tatum's Journal," pp. 100–1. Charles Gayarré, *History of Louisiana: The American Domination* (New York: Wm. J. Widdleton, 1866), pp. 383–84. Latour, *Historical Memoir,* p. 55.

11. Latour, *Historical Memoir,* pp. 56 (slaves at work), 64 (dragoons).

12. "Major Howell Tatum's Journal," p. 101.

13. Bernard Marigny, "Reflections on the Campaign of General Andrew Jackson in Louisiana in 1814 and '15," *Louisiana Historical Quarterly,* VI, 65. W. C. C. Claiborne, *Official Letter Books of W. C. C. Claiborne, 1801–16,* ed. Dunbar Rowland (Jackson, Miss.: State Department of Archives and History, 1917), VI, 324. Gayarré, *History of Louisiana,* p. 411. Latour, *Historical Memoir,* p. 71. Charles Gayarré, "Historical Sketch of Pierre and Jean Lafitte," *Magazine of American History,* X, 393. Marquis James, *The Life of Andrew Jackson* (New York: Bobbs-Merrill Co., 1938), p. 213 (Lafitte's mission to Barataria).

14. Gayarré, *History of Louisiana,* p. 405 (Juzan). Donald E. Everett, "Emigres and Militiamen: Free Persons of Color in New Orleans, 1803–15," *Journal of Negro History,* XXXVIII, 397, note, and Gayarré, *History of Louisiana,* p. 406 (Savary). Everett, pp. 396–97 (size of col-

ored battalion). Alcée Fortier, *A History of Louisiana* (New York: Goupil & Co. of Paris, 1903), III, 165 (the fact that Col. Fortier furnished his own men). John Spencer Bassett, *The Life of Andrew Jackson* (New York: Doubleday, Page & Co., 1911), I, 157 (Jackson's order to the paymaster).

15. Vincent Nolte, *The Memoirs of Vincent Nolte: Reminiscences in the Period of Anthony Adverse* (New York: G. Howard Watt, 1934), pp. 205–6.

16. J. Fair Hardin, "The First Great River Captain," *Louisiana Historical Quarterly,* X, 27.

17. Jackson, *Correspondence,* II, 85, note, 112–13, 113–14 (Jackson to Coffee, Dec. 11; Carroll to Jackson, Dec. 14). John Henry Eaton, *The Life of Andrew Jackson* (Philadelphia: Samuel Bradford, 1824), p. 292. James Parton, *Life of Andrew Jackson* (Boston: Houghton, Mifflin Co., 1860), II, 35–36.

18. W. C. C. Claiborne, *Official Letter Books,* VI, 369–83 (Claiborne's feelings).

19. Latour, *Historical Memoir,* pp. xxxv–xxxvi (Jones to Patterson, March 12).

20. *Ibid.,* pp. 58–59, xxxiv (Jones to Patterson), cxxxviii (Cochrane to Croker, Dec. 16).

21. *Ibid.,* pp. cxxxviii–cxxxix (Cochrane to Croker, Dec. 16), xxxvi (Jones's report), cxxxii–cxxxv (Court of Inquiry, which reports forty-five to fifty barges), cxl (Lockyer to Cochrane, Dec. 17). Fortescue, *A History of the British Army,* X, 152, reports forty-five barges.

22. Latour, *Historical Memoir,* pp. xxxiii-xxxv, cxl–cxliii (Jones to Patterson, March 12; Lockyer to Cochrane, Dec. 17).

23. John Spencer Cooper, *Rough Notes of Seven Campaigns* (2nd ed.; Carlisle: G. & T. Coward, 1914), p. 135.

24. Benson J. Lossing, *The Pictorial Field-Book of the War of 1812* (New York: Harper & Bros., 1868), p. 1013. Henry Adams, *History of the United States of America during the Second Administration of James Madison* (New York: Chas. Scribner's Sons, 1904), II, 288–92.

CHAPTER TEN

1. The description of the battle is based upon A. Lacarriere Latour, *Historical Memoir of the War in West Florida and Louisiana* (Philadelphia: John Conrad & Co., 1816), pp. xxxiii–xxxv, cxl–cxliii (reports of Jones and Lockyer), except where noted.

2. Alexander Walker, *Jackson and New Orleans* (New York: J. C. Derby, 1856), pp. 105, 108 (Lieutenant Tatnall), 105–6 (Spedden, Ferris, and McKeever). The order of capture is also given in Latour, *Historical Memoir,* pp. cxxxii–cxxxv (the Court of Inquiry's report).

3. Walker, *Jackson and New Orleans,* p. 107 (the American loss). Lockyer reports the British loss.

4. Walker, *Jackson and New Orleans,* pp. 138–39.

5. Latour, *Historical Memoir,* p. 82, describes the fishermen's normal activities.

6. *Ibid.,* p. 189 (Fort St. Philip).

7. Benson J. Lossing, *The Pictorial Field-Book of the War of 1812* (New York: Harper & Bros., 1868), has pictures of Claiborne (p. 1019), Plauché (p. 1024), and De la Ronde (p. 1030) in uniform. John Spencer Bassett, *The Life of Andrew Jackson* (New York: Doubleday, Page & Co., 1911), I, 166 (Jackson's dress). Charles Gayarré, *History of Louisiana: The American Domination* (New York: Wm. J. Widdleton, 1866), p. 532 (Lacoste). Stanley Clisby Arthur, *The Story of the Battle of New Orleans* (New Orleans: Louisiana Historical Society, 1915), has pictures of Coffee, Carroll, Livingston, Plauché (p. 69), and Morgan (p. 172).

8. Gayarré, *History of Louisiana,* pp. 392–94. Latour, *Historical Memoir,* pp. 68, 70.

9. Walker, *Jackson and New Orleans,* p. 138.

CHAPTER ELEVEN

1. Field Marshal Arthur, Duke of Wellington, *Supplementary Dispatches, Correspondence, and Memoranda,* ed. (his son) The Duke of Wellington (London: John Murray, 1863), X, 395 (Keane's Journal of Operations).

2. Wellington, *Supplementary Dispatches,* X, 752 (Peninsular prize money).

3. George R. Gleig, *The Campaigns of the British Army at Washington and New Orleans* (London: John Murray, 1847), p. 141, and William Surtees, *Twenty-five Years in the Rifle Brigade* (Edinburgh: Wm. Blackwood, 1833), pp. 336–37 (the voyage). A. Lacarriere Latour, *Historical Memoir of the War in West Florida and Louisiana* (Philadelphia: John Conrad & Co., 1816), pp. 255–56, and Gleig, *The Campaigns of the British Army,* p. 16, discuss "beauty and booty" as a slogan. Zachary F. Smith, *The Battle of New Orleans* (Louisville, Ky.: John P. Morton & Co., 1904), pp. 49–50, uses the phrase "lust and loot."

4. John Buchan, *The History of the Royal Scots Fusiliers: 1678–1918* (London: Thos. Nelson & Sons, 1925), pp. 172 (Cochrane's greed), 151 (Corporal Brown), 162–65 (Bergen-op-Zoom), 178 (summary).

5. Alexander Walker, *Jackson and New Orleans* (New York: J. C. Derby, 1856), p. 112. Gleig, *The Campaigns of the British Army,* p. 139. Surtees, *The Rifle Brigade,* pp. 337–38. Latour, *Historical Memoir,* p. clxi (Cochrane to Croker, Jan. 18).

6. Wellington, *Supplementary Dispatches,* p. 395. Norman McF. Walker, "The Geographical Nomenclature of Louisiana," *Magazine of American History,* X, 211, gives the origin of the name "Pea Island." Gleig, *The Campaigns of the British Army,* pp. 141–42, and Surtees, *The Rifle Brigade,* p. 337, describe the island.

7. Gleig, *The Campaigns of the British Army,* p. 142. Andrew Jackson, *Correspondence of Andrew Jackson,* ed. John Spencer Bassett (Washington: Carnegie Institution of Washington, 1927), II, 109–10 ("Diary of a British Officer").

8. Latour, *Historical Memoir,* pp. 64–65. Charles Gayarré, *History of Louisiana: The American Domination* (New York: Wm. J. Widdleton, 1866), pp. 404–5. John Brannan, *Official Letters of the Military and Naval Officers of the U.S., 1812–15* (Washington: Privately printed, 1823), p. 461 (Patterson to Jackson, Jan. 27).

9. "Major Howell Tatum's Journal," ed. John Spencer Bassett, *Smith College Studies in History,* VII, 100, 102, 111. Marquis James, *The Life of Andrew Jackson* (New York: Bobbs-Merrill Co., 1938), pp. 207–8. Latour, *Historical Memoir,* pp. 77, xlv (Jackson to Secretary of War, Dec. 27). Gayarré, *History of Louisiana,* p. 384.

10. John Spencer Bassett, *The Life of Andrew Jackson* (New York: Doubleday, Page & Co., 1911), I, 165, 170 (Coffee). Latour, *Historical Memoir,* p. 75, and Brannan, *Official Letters,* p. 462 (Patterson to Jackson, Jan. 27) (Shields and Morrell). Gayarré, *History of Louisiana,* p. 402 (Claiborne's speech to the legislature).

11. Gayarré, *History of Louisiana,* pp. 402–3.

12. Latour, *Historical Memoir,* pp. 75–6. Walker, *Jackson and New Orleans,* p. 111, puts the prisoners on the *Tonnant,* and pp. 109–11 describes Jones and Spedden.

13. Jackson, *Correspondence,* II, 109–10. Surtees, *The Rifle Brigade,* p. 338, makes exactly the same remark about the cold that the anonymous officer makes.

14. John Henry Cooke, *A Narrative of Events in the South of France and of the Attack on New Orleans* (London: T. & W. Boone, 1835), p. 122 (the attitude of the 21st toward the 93rd).

15. Latour, *Historical Memoir,* p. clx (Cochrane to Croker, Jan. 18).

16. Gayarré, *History of Louisiana,* p. 384 (blocking of Manchac). Latour, *Historical Memoir,* p. xlv (Jackson to Secretary of War, Dec. 27), and "Major Howell Tatum's Journal," p. 102, discuss the difficulties of getting the bayous blocked.

17. Latour, *Historical Memoir,* pp. 68, 141. Walker, *Jackson and New Orleans,* pp. 141–44. Benson J. Lossing, *The Pictorial Field-Book of the War of 1812* (New York: Harper & Bros., 1868), p. 1027.

18. Jackson's address is in Latour, *Historical Memoir,* pp. xxxvii–xxxix.

19. Walker, *Jackson and New Orleans,* p. 144.

20. Bassett, *The Life of Andrew Jackson,* I, 174.

21. Brannan, *Official Letters,* p. 462 (Patterson's report of Dec. 27). Walker, *Jackson and New Orleans,* p. 241.

22. Gayarré, *History of Louisiana,* p. 404 (dragoons). Latour, *Historical Memoir,* p. 130 (Villeré). "Major Howell Tatum's Journal," pp. 104–5, and Mrs. Dunbar Rowland, *Andrew Jackson's Campaign Against the British* (New York: Macmillan Co., 1926), p. 298 (new recruits). "A Massachusetts Volunteer at the Battle of New Orleans," *Louisiana Historical Quarterly,* IX, 30–31.

23. Latour, *Historical Memoir,* pp. 69, 122. Lossing, *The Pictorial Field-Book,* pp. 1027–28.

24. Latour, *Historical Memoir,* pp. 74, 189. "Major Howell Tatum's Journal," p. 105.

25. Marquis James, *The Life of Andrew Jackson,* p. 821, note, discusses this report.

26. Latour, *Historical Memoir,* p. 93, names some of the Spaniards from Pensacola. Walker, *Jackson and New Orleans,* p. 111, mentions Morrell's report. See also Latour, *Historical Memoir,* pp. cxxxvii–cxxxviii (Morrell to Latour, April 18).

27. Latour, *Historical Memoir,* p. clx (Cochrane to Croker, Jan. 18). Wellington, *Supplementary Dispatches,* X, 395. Walker, *Jackson and New Orleans,* p. 114.

CHAPTER TWELVE

1. "Major Howell Tatum's Journal," ed. John Spencer Bassett, *Smith College Studies in History,* VII, 105. John Spencer Bassett, *The Life of Andrew Jackson* (New York: Doubleday, Page & Co., 1911), I, 170.

2. For the dress of the Tennesseans, Alexander Walker, *Jackson and New Orleans* (New York: J. C. Derby, 1856), p. 154. For their coats, *Niles Weekly Register,* VII, 377.

3. A. Lacarriere Latour, *Historical Memoir of the War in West Florida and Louisiana* (Philadelphia: John Conrad & Co., 1816), p. clxxxviii (General Orders, Jan. 21).

4. W. C. C. Claiborne, *Official Letter Books of W. C. C. Claiborne, 1801–16,* ed. Dunbar Rowland (Jackson, Miss.: State Department of Archives and History, 1917), VI, 369–83.

5. "Report of the Committee of Inquiry on the Military Measures Executed against the Legislature," *Louisiana Historical Quarterly,* IX, 238.

6. Bernard Marigny, "Reflections on the Campaign of General Andrew Jackson in Louisiana in 1814 and '15," *Louisiana Historical Quarterly,* VI, 74–75.

7. Latour, *Historical Memoir,* pp. 78–79, 83. Walker, *Jackson and New Orleans,* p. 114 ("blue shirts and tarpaulins").

8. Latour, *Historical Memoir,* p. 83. Charles Gayarré, *History of Louisiana: The American Domination* (New York: Wm. J. Widdleton, 1866), p. 418.

9. Field Marshal Arthur, Duke of Wellington, *Supplementary Dispatches, Correspondence, and Memoranda,* ed. (his son) The Duke of Wellington (London: John Murray, 1863), X, 395 (General Keane's Journal of Operations). Latour, *Historical Memoir,* pp. cxliii, clx (Keane to Pakenham, Dec. 26; Cochrane to Croker, Jan. 18).

10. Wellington, *Supplementary Dispatches,* pp. 395–96.

11. Marquis James, *The Life of Andrew Jackson* (New York: Bobbs-Merrill Co., 1938), p. 821, note, has a theory about Villeré's failure to block the bayous.

12. Latour, *Historical Memoir,* pp. 78, 83. Gayarré, *History of Louisiana,* pp. 418–19.

13. Wellington, *Supplementary Dispatches,* p. 396. George R. Gleig, *The Campaigns of the British Army at Washington and New Orleans* (London: John Murray, 1847), pp. 145–46. Latour, *Historical Memoir,* p. cxliii (Keane to Pakenham, Dec. 26). William Surtees, *Twenty-five Years in the Rifle Brigade* (Edinburgh: Wm. Blackwood, 1833), p. 337 (the shivering West Indians).

14. Latour, *Historical Memoir,* pp. cxliii, clxi (Keane to Pakenham, Dec. 26; Cochrane to Croker, Jan. 18). Wellington, *Supplementary Dispatches,* p. 396. Gleig, *The Campaigns of the British Army,* p. 146. Surtees, *The Rifle Brigade,* p. 340. These accounts differ about the time of embarkation, varying from 10:00 A.M. to 2:00 P.M.

15. George R. Gleig, *The Campaigns of the British Army,* p. 146.

16. Latour, *Historical Memoir,* pp. 87–88.

17. Andrew Jackson, *Correspondence of Andrew Jackson,* ed. John Spencer Bassett (Washington: Carnegie Institution of Washington, 1927), II, 117, note. "Major Howell Tatum's Journal," p. 105. Benson J. Lossing, *The Pictorial Field-Book of the War of 1812* (New York: Harper & Bros., 1868), p. 1029. Bassett, *The Life of Andrew Jackson,* I, 67, describes Carroll.

18. Mrs. Dunbar Rowland, *Andrew Jackson's Campaign against the British* (New York: Macmillan Co., 1926), pp. 247, 299 (dragoons).

19. Latour, *Historical Memoir,* pp. 189–90 (Fort St. Philip), 84, and Charles Gayarré, *History of Louisiana,* p. 419 (pickets at the fishing village).

20. Walker, *Jackson and New Orleans,* pp. 119–20 (Keane and Cochrane watching from a schooner). J. W. Fortescue, *A History of the British Army* (London: Macmillan Co., 1920), X, 161, reports Pakenham's distrust of Cochrane.

21. Gleig, *The Campaigns of the British Army,* pp. 146–7. William Surtees, *The Rifle Brigade,* p. 340.

22. Walker, *Jackson and New Orleans,* pp. 122–23. Latour, *Historical*

Memoir, p. 84. Wellington, *Supplementary Dispatches,* p. 396 (Keane's Journal of Operations). Gayarré, *History of Louisiana,* pp. 419–20. Latour specifies five British barges.

23. Latour, *Historical Memoir,* pp. 85–86. William James, *A Full and Correct Account of the Military Occurrences of the Late War between Great Britain and the United States of America* (London: Privately printed, 1818), II, 360. Gayarré, *History of Louisiana,* p. 420. Walker, *Jackson and New Orleans,* pp. 123–24. Latour names Ducros as the one who was questioned by Keane, while Cochrane was questioning the others; they all answered the same.

24. Wellington, *Supplementary Dispatches,* p. 196. Gleig, *The Campaigns of the British Army,* pp. 148–49. Latour, *Historical Memoir,* pp. cxliii (Keane to Pakenham, Dec. 26), 85 (American pickets). Surtees, *The Rifle Brigade,* p. 342.

25. Gayarré, *History of Louisiana,* p. 421. Walker, *Jackson and New Orleans,* pp. 126–28. Lossing, *The Pictorial Field-Book,* p. 1029. Latour, *Historical Memoir,* p. 201, mentions Gabriel's brother without naming him; Walker supplies the name.

26. Latour, *Historical Memoir,* p. 91. Lossing, *The Pictorial Field-Book,* p. 1029. Walker, *Jackson and New Orleans,* p. 151. Latour mentions "Ducros" as the picket questioned by Keane; his relationship to "Captain Ducros" is not clear.

27. Latour, *Historical Memoir,* pp. 88–89. "Major Howell Tatum's Journal," p. 107, simply credits Latour with bringing the news.

28. Marquis James, *The Life of Andrew Jackson,* p. 820, note, has a theory about the bringing of the news. *Niles Weekly Register,* VII, 359–60 (Senator Fromentin to friend in Baltimore, Dec. 28) has an early account crediting Major Villeré with first bringing the news.

29. Latour, *Historical Memoir,* p. 89.

30. Wellington, *Supplementary Dispatches,* p. 396. Gleig, *The Campaigns of the British Army,* pp. 150–51. Walker, *Jackson and New Orleans,* p. 169. Fortescue, *History of the British Army,* X, 154–55.

31. Gleig, *The Campaigns of the British Army,* pp. 151–52. Bassett, *The Life of Andrew Jackson,* I, 183.

32. Latour, *Historical Memoir,* p. 89.

33. Latour, *Historical Memoir,* p. xlv (Jackson to Secretary of War, Dec. 27). "Major Howell Tatum's Journal," p. 111 (Carroll's position and Claiborne's advice).

CHAPTER THIRTEEN

1. George R. Gleig, *The Campaigns of the British Army at Washington and New Orleans* (London: John Murray, 1847), p. 152. A. Lacarriere Latour, *Historical Memoir of the War in West Florida and*

Louisiana (Philadelphia: John Conrad & Co., 1816), p. 90. William Surtees, *Twenty-five Years in the Rifle Brigade* (Edinburgh: Wm. Blackwood, 1833), pp. 344–45.

2. Latour, *Historical Memoir,* pp. xlvi (Jackson to Secretary of War, Dec. 27), 89. Vincent Nolte, *The Memoirs of Vincent Nolte: Reminiscences in the Period of Anthony Adverse* (New York: G. Howard Watt, 1934), p. 210.

3. John Spencer Bassett, *The Life of Andrew Jackson* (New York: Doubleday, Page & Co., 1911), I, 217. Latour, *Historical Memoir,* p. xliii (Patterson to Secretary of Navy, Dec. 28).

4. Marquis James, *The Life of Andrew Jackson* (New York: Bobbs-Merrill Co., 1938), p. 224. Latour, *Historical Memoir,* pp. 96–97. Andrew Jackson, *Correspondence of Andrew Jackson,* ed. John Spencer Bassett (Washington: Carnegie Institution of Washington, 1927), II, 128, note, gives a slightly different arrangement of the troops.

5. Latour, *Historical Memoir,* p. xliii (Patterson to Secretary of Navy, Dec. 28).

6. W. C. C. Claiborne, *Official Letter Books of W. C. C. Claiborne, 1801–16,* ed. Dunbar Rowland (Jackson, Miss.: State Department of Archives and History, 1917), VI, 369–83.

7. Charles Gayarré, *History of Louisiana: The American Domination* (New York: Wm. J. Widdleton, 1866), pp. 433–34. Latour, *Historical Memoir,* p. 101.

8. Gayarré, *History of Louisiana,* pp. 435–36. John Henry Eaton, *The Life of Andrew Jackson* (Philadelphia: Samuel Bradford, 1824), p. 344. Bassett, *The Life of Andrew Jackson,* I, 217. François-Xavier Martin, *The History of Louisiana* (New Orleans: James A. Gresham, 1882), p. 376, 381. The affidavit of T. L. Butler in Jackson, *Correspondence,* II, 210, note, places this visit "about the 1st."

9. Gleig, *The Campaigns of the British Army,* pp. 152, 154–5. Latour, *Historical Memoir,* p. 92.

10. Latour, *Historical Memoir,* p. xliii (Patterson to Secretary of Navy, Dec. 28). Gayarré, *History of Louisiana,* p. 424. Gleig, *The Campaigns of the British Army,* pp. 153, 155. Latour, *Historical Memoir,* p. cxliv (Keane to Pakenham, Dec. 26).

11. Latour, *Historical Memoir,* pp. 95–96. "Major Howell Tatum's Journal," ed. John Spencer Bassett, *Smith College Studies in History,* VII, 108. (Tatum does not mention the marines.)

12. Surtees, *The Rifle Brigade,* pp. 346–47. J. W. Fortescue, *A History of the British Army* (London: Macmillan Co., 1920), X, 157–60, however, gives the picket of the 95th considerable credit for holding its ground while that of the 85th fled.

13. Latour, *Historical Memoir,* p. cxliv (Keane to Pakenham, Dec. 26). Gleig, *The Campaigns of the British Army,* p. 154.

14. Gleig, *The Campaigns of the British Army,* pp. 156–57.

15. "Major Howell Tatum's Journal," pp. 108–9, cites the confusion of the 7th and 44th.

16. Gayarré, *History of Louisiana*, pp. 426–27. Latour, *Historical Memoir*, pp. 95–97. Eaton, *The Life of Andrew Jackson*, p. 318. Alexander Walker, *Jackson and New Orleans* (New York: J. C. Derby, 1856), pp. 171–73.

17. Latour, *Historical Memoir*, pp. 98–100. Gayarré, *History of Louisiana*, pp. 429–30. Walker, *Jackson and New Orleans*, pp. 174–76. Gleig, *The Campaigns of the British Army*, p. 157. Eaton, *The Life of Andrew Jackson*, pp. 313–15, has Coffee driving the British all the way to the levee.

18. Latour, *Historical Memoir*, p. xlvi (Jackson to Secretary of War, Dec. 27). "Major Howell Tatum's Journal," p. 110. Eaton, *The Life of Andrew Jackson*, p. 317.

19. "Major Howell Tatum's Journal," p. 109. Gayarré, *History of Louisiana*, p. 428. Eaton, *The Life of Andrew Jackson*, p. 317.

20. Gayarré, *History of Louisiana*, p. 427. Walker, *Jackson and New Orleans*, p. 172.

21. Walker, *Jackson and New Orleans*, pp. 176–77. Surtees, *The Rifle Brigade*, p. 351. *Niles Weekly Register*, VII, 375.

22. Latour, *Historical Memoir*, p. 99. Gayarré, *History of Louisiana*, p. 430. Eaton, *The Life of Andrew Jackson*, p. 321. Walker, *Jackson and New Orleans*, pp. 177–78. Eaton tells a rather elaborate story about Dyer.

23. James Parton, *Life of Andrew Jackson* (Boston: Houghton, Mifflin Co., 1860), II, 101, quoting a letter of John Donelson.

24. Latour, *Historical Memoir*, pp. 99, xlvi (Jackson to Secretary of War, Dec. 27), cxliv–cxlv (Keane to Pakenham, Dec. 26). Gayarré, *History of Louisiana*, p. 430. Walker, *Jackson and New Orleans*, pp. 178–79.

25. Latour, *Historical Memoir*, pp. cxliv–cxlv (Keane to Pakenham, Dec. 26).

26. *Ibid.*, pp. 101–2. Gayarré, *History of Louisiana*, pp. 434–35. "Report of the Committee of Inquiry on the Military Measures Executed against the Legislature," *Louisiana Historical Quarterly*, IX, 275.

27. Gleig, *The Campaigns of the British Army*, 157–60. Latour, *Historical Memoir*, p. cxlvi (Keane to Pakenham, Dec. 26).

28. Latour, *Historical Memoir*, p. 102. Gayarré, *History of Louisiana*, pp. 434–35. Bassett, *The Life of Andrew Jackson*, I, 182–83. Latour, *Historical Memoir*, p. xlvi (Jackson to Secretary of War, Dec. 27).

29. Latour, *Historical Memoir*, pp. xliii–xliv (Patterson to Secretary of Navy, Dec. 28).

30. *Ibid.*, p. lviii.

31. *Ibid.*, pp. clxx–clxxi, cxlv (Keane to Pakenham, Dec. 26). Field Marshal Arthur, Duke of Wellington, *Supplementary Dispatches, Cor-*

respondence, and Memoranda, ed. (his son) The Duke of Wellington (London: John Murray, 1863), X, 397. William James, *A Full and Correct Account of the Military Occurrences of the Late War between Great Britain and the United States of America* (London: Privately printed, 1818), II, 532–33.

32. Gleig, *The Campaigns of the British Army,* pp. 160–62.

CHAPTER FOURTEEN

1. Preamble to the Treaty of Ghent.

2. A. T. Mahan, *Sea Power in Its Relation to the War of 1812* (Boston: Little, Brown & Co., 1905), II, 412–13, 420. John Quincy Adams, *The Duplicate Letters, the Fisheries, and the Mississippi. Documents Relating to Transactions at the Negotiation of Ghent* (Washington: Davis and Force, 1822), pp. 17–18. Benson J. Lossing, *The Pictorial Field-Book of the War of 1812* (New York: Harper & Bros., 1868), pp. 1059–60. J. W. Fortescue, *A History of the British Army* (London: Macmillan Co., 1920), X, 151.

3. John Quincy Adams, *The Duplicate Letters,* pp. 17–24.

4. Henry Adams, *History of the United States of America during the Second Administration of James Madison* (New York: Chas. Scribner's Sons, 1904), II, 316. Mahan, *Sea Power,* II, 426, 431. John Quincy Adams, *The Duplicate Letters,* pp. 26–42.

5. The following description of the negotiations is from John Quincy Adams, *The Duplicate Letters,* pp. 42–53.

6. The Treaty of Ghent.

7. Lossing, *The Pictorial Field-Book,* p. 1063.

CHAPTER FIFTEEN

1. Field Marshal Arthur, Duke of Wellington, *Supplementary Dispatches, Correspondence, and Memoranda* (London: John Murray, 1863), X, 397 (General Keane's Journal of Operations). George R. Gleig, *The Campaigns of the British Army at Washington and New Orleans* (London: John Murray, 1847), p. 163.

2. Wellington, *Supplementary Dispatches,* p. 397. A. Lacarriere Latour, *Historical Memoir of the War in West Florida and Louisiana* (Philadelphia: John Conrad & Co., 1816), p. clxii (Cochrane to Croker, Jan. 18).

3. Alexander Dickson, "Artillery Services in North America in 1814 and 1815," *Journal of the Society for Army Historical Research,* VIII, 89–92.

4. Latour, *Historical Memoir,* pp. 112–13. Charles Gayarré, *History of Louisiana: The American Domination* (New York: Wm. J. Widdleton, 1866), p. 442. Alexander Walker, *Jackson and New Orleans* (New

York: J. C. Derby, 1856), pp. 222 (description of Macarty mansion), 211 (Jackson's words). Pictures of the mansion are in Marquis James, *The Life of Andrew Jackson* (New York: Bobbs-Merrill Co., 1938), pp. 192–93, and Benson J. Lossing, *The Pictorial Field-Book of the War of 1812* (New York: Harper & Bros., 1868), p. 1037. The outline of the swamps is described in "Major Howell Tatum's Journal," ed. John Spencer Bassett, *Smith College Studies in History*, VII, 112.

5. Latour, *Historical Memoir*, pp. 150–51. John Spencer Bassett, *The Life of Andrew Jackson* (New York: Doubleday, Page & Co., 1911), I, 184.

6. Latour, *Historical Memoir*, p. 113.

7. Gayarré, *History of Louisiana*, p. 436. James Parton, *Life of Andrew Jackson* (Boston: Houghton, Mifflin Co., 1860), II, 109. Nathaniel Claiborne, *Notes on the War in the South* (Richmond: Wm. Ramsay, 1819), p. 60. John Henry Eaton, *The Life of Andrew Jackson* (Philadelphia: Samuel Bradford, 1824), p. 329 (Kemper). Latour, *Historical Memoir*, pp. 110, xlvi (Jackson to Secretary of War, Dec. 27). *Niles Weekly Register*, VII, 356 (the pun on "coffee"), VII, 378 (the report on the colored troops).

8. Donald E. Everett, "Emigres and Militiamen: Free Persons of Color in New Orleans, 1803–15," *Journal of Negro History*, XXXVIII, 398. Gayarré, *History of Louisiana*, pp. 477–78. W. O. Hart, "Mrs. Louise Livingston, Wife of Edward Livingston," *Louisiana Historical Quarterly*, V, 355. Walker, *Jackson and New Orleans*, p. 222.

9. Latour, *Historical Memoir*, pp. xliii–xliv (Patterson to Secretary of Navy, Dec. 28).

10. *Ibid.*, p. 102. Gayarré, *History of Louisiana*, p. 435.

11. W. C. C. Claiborne, *Official Letter Books of W. C. C. Claiborne, 1801–16*, ed. Dunbar Rowland (Jackson, Miss.: State Department of Archives and History, 1917), VI, 369–83.

12. Walker, *Jackson and New Orleans*, p. 213 (Jackson's retort to Cochrane). *Niles Weekly Register*, VII, 316 (Cochrane's reply). Walker, *Jackson and New Orleans*, p. 195 ("castle"). Lossing, *A Pictorial Field-Book*, p. 1034. Gleig, *The Campaigns of the British Army*, p. 163 (British camp).

13. Gleig, *The Campaigns of the British Army*, pp. 164–65.

14. John Henry Cooke, *A Narrative of Events in the South of France and at the Attack on New Orleans* (London: T. & W. Boone, 1835), p. 120.

15. Dickson, "Artillery Services," p. 93. Richard Johns and P. H. Nicolas, *The Naval and Military Heroes of Great Britain or Calendar of Victory* (London: Henry G. Bohn, 1860), pp. 181–83 (formation). *The Journal of the Society for Army Historical Research*, VII, 1–7, 184; VIII, 32 (colors and dress of regiments). Cooke, *A Narrative of Events*, p. 168 (the color of the facings of the 85th). "Unpublished Letter Relative to the Battle of New Orleans," *Publications of the Louisiana His-*

torical Society, IX, 78. Gleig, *The Campaigns of the British Army,* p. 164.

16. Gleig, *The Campaigns of the British Army,* pp. 164–65.

17. Parton, *Life of Andrew Jackson,* II, 126–27.

18. William Surtees, *Twenty-five Years in the Rifle Brigade* (Edinburgh: Wm. Blackwood, 1833), pp. 353–54.

19. Dickson, "Artillery Services," p. 100.

20. Latour, *Historical Memoir,* pp. cxliii–cxlvi (Keane to Pakenham, Dec. 26).

21. William James, *A Full and Correct Account of the Military Occurrences of the Late War between Great Britain and the United States of America* (London: Privately printed, 1818), II, 364. Walker, *Jackson and New Orleans,* p. 212.

22. Walker, *Jackson and New Orleans,* p. 212.

23. Bassett, *The Life of Andrew Jackson,* I, 184. Gayarré, *History of Louisiana,* p. 456. Latour, *Historical Memoir,* pp. 121, 134. "Major Howell Tatum's Journal," p. 112. Vincent Nolte, *The Memoirs of Vincent Nolte: Reminiscences in the Period of Anthony Adverse* (New York: G. Howard Watt, 1934), p. 216. Walker, *Jackson and New Orleans,* p. 260. "A Contemporary Account of the Battle of New Orleans by a Soldier in the Ranks," *Louisiana Historical Quarterly,* IX, 14.

24. Bassett, *The Life of Andrew Jackson,* I, 191. Augustus C. Buell, *History of Andrew Jackson* (New York: Chas. Scribner's Sons, 1904), I, 402. Latour, *Historical Memoir,* p. 146. Lossing, *The Pictorial Field-Book,* p. 1042.

25. Latour, *Historical Memoir,* p. 117. Eaton, *The Life of Andrew Jackson,* p. 334. Gayarré, *History of Louisiana,* pp. 443, 480.

26. Walker, *Jackson and New Orleans,* p. 210.

27. Latour, *Historical Memoir,* pp. 114–15, 127. Gayarré, *History of Louisiana,* p. 443.

28. Latour, *Historical Memoir,* pp. 85, 113–14, 115–16, 128–29, 189–90. Gleig, *The Campaigns of the British Army,* pp. 167–68. Walker, *Jackson and New Orleans,* p. 243.

29. Latour, *Historical Memoir,* pp. 117–18, 122–23. "Major Howell Tatum's Journal," p. 114. W. C. C. Claiborne, *Official Letter Books,* VI, 383–87, 369–83.

30. Dickson, "Artillery Services," p. 98.

31. Latour, *Historical Memoir,* xliii (Patterson to Secretary of Navy, Dec. 28).

32. Gayarré, *History of Louisiana,* pp. 562–63. Marquis James, *The Life of Andrew Jackson,* p. 240. Eaton, *The Life of Andrew Jackson,* p. 347. François-Xavier Martin, *The History of Louisiana* (New Orleans: James A. Gresham, 1882), pp. 381–82.

33. Wellington, *Supplementary Dispatches,* p. 397. Gleig, *The Campaigns of the British Army,* p. 165. Dickson, "Artillery Services," pp. 95, 98.

34. Gleig, *The Campaigns of the British Army,* pp. 165, 167. Wellington, *Supplementary Dispatches,* p. 397. Dickson, "Artillery Services," pp. 95, 97.

35. Latour, *Historical Memoir,* p. xliii (Patterson to Secretary of Navy, Dec. 28).

36. Bernard Marigny, "Reflections on the Campaign of General Andrew Jackson in Louisiana in 1814 and '15," *Louisiana Historical Quarterly,* VI, 70. "Andrew Jackson and Judge D. A. Hall," *Louisiana Historical Quarterly,* V, 523 (Bradford), 534–35 (Plauché's men), 527–28 (Hiriart), 518 (Hiriart and Declouet). "Report of the Committee of Inquiry on the Military Measures Executed against the Legislature," *Louisiana Historical Quarterly,* IX, 266 (Duncan), 267 (Morgan and Declouet). Buell, *History of Andrew Jackson,* I, 361–63, uses the quoted phrases to describe the Creoles. Nolte, *Memoirs,* pp. 211 (Beale), 215 (the second regiment).

37. Latour, *Historical Memoir,* p. 113. Gleig, *The Campaigns of the British Army,* p. 165.

38. Dickson, "Artillery Services," p. 99. Latour, *Historical Memoir,* pp. xlvii–xlviii (Jackson to Secretary of War, Dec. 29; Henley to Patterson, Dec. 28).

39. Dickson, "Artillery Services," p. 99. Latour, *Historical Memoir,* pp. xlvii–xlviii.

40. Latour, *Historical Memoir,* p. 118. Gayarré, *History of Louisiana,* pp. 444–45. Walker, *Jackson and New Orleans,* p. 217.

41. Gleig, *The Campaigns of the British Army,* p. 166. Surtees, *The Rifle Brigade,* p. 355.

42. Gleig, *The Campaigns of the British Army,* p. 166. John B. B. Trussell, "Thunder by the River," *Field Artillery Journal,* XXXIX, 173–75. Wellington, *Supplementary Dispatches,* p. 397. Surtees, *The Rifle Brigade,* p. 388. Walker, *Jackson and New Orleans,* p. 225. Dickson, "Artillery Services," p. 100.

43. Latour, *Historical Memoir,* pp. 119–22. Bassett, *The Life of Andrew Jackson,* I, 185, differs slightly about the batteries.

44. "Major Howell Tatum's Journal," pp. 112, 114–15.

45. Dickson, "Artillery Services," p. 100.

46. Eaton, *The Life of Andrew Jackson,* p. 351. Parton, *Life of Andrew Jackson,* II, 147–48.

47. "Report of the Committee of Inquiry," pp. 274–75.

CHAPTER SIXTEEN

1. George R. Gleig, *The Campaigns of the British Army at Washington and New Orleans* (London: John Murray, 1847), p. 169. Alexander Dickson, "Artillery Services in North America in 1814 and 1815," *Journal of the Society for Army Historical Research,* VIII, 101. "General

Court-Martial for Trial of Brevet Lieutenant-Colonel Mullins," *Louisiana Historical Quarterly*, IX, 60, 61, 64 (Mullins' dress).

2. Gleig, *The Campaigns of the British Army*, p. 169.

3. Field Marshall Arthur, Duke of Wellington, *Supplementary Dispatches, Correspondence, and Memoranda*, ed. (his son) The Duke of Wellington (London: John Murray, 1863), X, 397 (General Keane's Journal of Operations). Charles Gayarré, *History of Louisiana: The American Domination* (New York: Wm. J. Widdleton, 1866), p. 445.

4. Alexander Walker, *Jackson and New Orleans* (New York: J. C. Derby, 1856), p. 227. John Brannan, *Official Letters of the Military and Naval Officers of the U.S., 1812–15* (Washington: Privately printed, 1823), p. 462 (Patterson to Secretary of Navy, Jan. 27).

5. Gleig, *The Campaigns of the British Army*, pp. 168–69. "Major Howell Tatum's Journal," ed. John Spencer Bassett, *Smith College Studies in History*, VII, 115.

6. Gleig, *The Campaigns of the British Army*, p. 169. William Surtees, *Twenty-five Years in the Rifle Brigade* (Edinburgh: Wm. Blackwood, 1833), p. 361. A. Lacarriere Latour, *Historical Memoir of the War in West Florida and Louisiana* (Philadelphia: John Conrad & Co., 1816), p. 119.

7. Walker, *Jackson and New Orleans*, p. 227.

8. "Report of the Committee of Inquiry on the Military Measures Executed against the Legislature," *Louisiana Historical Quarterly*, IX, 275–77.

9. Gleig, *The Campaigns of the British Army*, pp. 169–70. Wellington, *Supplementary Dispatches*, p. 397.

10. Dickson, "Artillery Services," p. 101. John B. B. Trussell, "Thunder by the River," *Field Artillery Journal*, XXXIX, 173.

11. "Major Howell Tatum's Journal," pp. 115–16.

12. Dickson, "Artillery Services," pp. 101–2. Latour, *Historical Memoir*, p. xlix (Patterson to Secretary of Navy, Dec. 29). Gayarré, *History of Louisiana*, p. 445. Surtees, *The Rifle Brigade*, p. 360.

13. Walker, *Jackson and New Orleans*, p. 232. Latour, *Historical Memoir*, p. lix. Vincent Nolte, *The Memoirs of Vincent Nolte: Reminiscences in the Period of Anthony Adverse* (New York: G. Howard Watt, 1934), p. 218.

14. Dickson, "Artillery Services," p. 102.

15. Gleig, *The Campaigns of the British Army*, p. 170.

16. Gayarré, *History of Louisiana*, p. 446. Latour, *Historical Memoir*, p. 123. Walker, *Jackson and New Orleans*, p. 231. "Major Howell Tatum's Journal," p. 115.

17. "Major Howell Tatum's Journal," p. 115.

18. "Report of the Committee of Inquiry," p. 264–66.

19. Latour, *Historical Memoir*, pp. xlix (Patterson to Secretary of Navy, Dec. 29), 123. Gayarré, *History of Louisiana*, p. 446. Walker, *Jackson and New Orleans*, p. 231.

20. "Report of the Committee of Inquiry," pp. 250, 264. Bernard Marigny, "Reflections on the Campaign of General Andrew Jackson in Louisiana in 1814 and '15," *Louisiana Historical Quarterly*, VI, 66.

21. "Report of the Committee of Inquiry," pp. 225, 226, 248, 252–53, 254–55. Marigny, "Reflections on the Campaign," p. 67.

22. Gleig, *The Campaigns of the British Army*, p. 171. Benson J. Lossing, *The Pictorial Field-Book of the War of 1812* (New York: Harper & Bros., 1868), p. 1038.

23. Gayarré, *History of Louisiana*, p. 446. "Major Howell Tatum's Journal," p. 116. Walker, *Jackson and New Orleans*, p. 231. Lossing, *The Pictorial Field-Book*, p. 1038.

24. Dickson, "Artillery Services," pp. 102–3.

25. James Parton, *Life of Andrew Jackson* (Boston: Houghton, Mifflin Co., 1860), II, 139.

26. "Major Howell Tatum's Journal," p. 116. Latour, *Historical Memoir*, p. 123. Gayarré, *History of Louisiana*, p. 446. John Henry Eaton, *The Life of Andrew Jackson* (Philadelphia: Samuel Bradford, 1824), p. 342. Walker, *Jackson and New Orleans* p. 231.

27. Gleig, *The Campaigns of the British Army*, p. 171.

28. Latour, *Historical Memoir*, pp. lix, clxxi, l (Patterson to Secretary of Navy, Dec. 29). Walker, *Jackson and New Orleans*, p. 233.

29. Latour, *Historical Memoir*, pp. l (Patterson to Secretary of Navy, Dec. 29), 124.

30. "Report of the Committee of Inquiry," pp. 250–51.

31. *Ibid.*, pp. 236, 238, 273–74.

32. Wellington, *Supplementary Dispatches*, p. 397. Gleig, *The Campaigns of the British Army*, p. 171. Surtees, *The Rifle Brigade*, pp. 361–62. Latour, *Historical Memoir*, pp. 125–26.

33. Lossing, *The Pictorial Field-Book*, p. 1063.

CHAPTER SEVENTEEN

1. Alexander Walker, *Jackson and New Orleans* (New York: J. C. Derby, 1856), p. 240.

2. *Ibid.*, pp. 295–96.

3. Marquis James, *The Life of Andrew Jackson* (New York: Bobbs-Merrill Co., 1938), p. 229. Andrew Jackson, *Correspondence of Andrew Jackson*, ed. John Spencer Bassett (Washington: Carnegie Institution of Washington, 1927), II, 125 (Livingston to Jackson, Dec. 25). A. Lacarriere Latour, *Historical Memoir of the War in West Florida and Louisiana* (Philadelphia: John Conrad & Co., 1816), pp. 129, 147. John Henry Eaton, *The Life of Andrew Jackson* (Philadelphia: Samuel Bradford, 1824), p. 356.

4. Latour, *Historical Memoir*, p. l (Patterson to Secretary of Navy, Jan. 2).

5. *Ibid.*

6. Field Marshal Arthur, Duke of Wellington, *Supplementary Dispatches, Correspondence, and Memoranda,* ed. (his son) The Duke of Wellington (London: John Murray, 1863), X, 397 (General Keane's Journal of Operations). John B. B. Trussell, "Thunder by the River," *Field Artillery Journal,* XXXIX, 173. Alexander Dickson, "Artillery Services in North America in 1814 and 1815," *Journal of the Society for Army Historical Research,* VIII, 104–5.

7. John Spencer Cooper, *Rough Notes of Seven Campaigns* (2nd ed.; Carlisle: G. & T. Coward, 1914), pp. 135–36. John Henry Cooke, *A Narrative of Events in the South of France and of the Attack on New Orleans* (London: T. & W. Boone, 1835), pp. 124, 157.

8. Dickson, "Artillery Services," p. 109. Wellington, *Supplementary Dispatches,* p. 398.

9. Dickson, "Artillery Services," pp. 109–12. Wellington, *Supplementary Dispatches,* p. 398. John Spencer Bassett, *The Life of Andrew Jackson* (New York: Doubleday, Page & Co., 1911), I, 187. Trussell, "Thunder by the River," p. 173. "Major Howell Tatum's Journal," ed. John Spencer Bassett, *Smith College Studies in History,* VII, 120. Walker, *Jackson and New Orleans,* p. 251. Charles Gayarré, *History of Louisiana: The American Domination* (New York: Wm. J. Widdleton, 1866), p. 455. Latour, *Historical Memoir,* p. 131. Benson J. Lossing, *The Pictorial Field-Book of the War of 1812* (New York: Harper & Bros., 1868), p. 1039. These accounts differ about the number of batteries and guns; I have followed Dickson.

10. Wellington, *Supplementary Dispatches,* p. 398. Dickson, "Artillery Services," pp. 107–8.

11. George R. Gleig, *The Campaigns of the British Army at Washington and New Orleans* (London: John Murray, 1847), pp. 172–73. "Major Howell Tatum's Journal," p. 120.

12. Gayarré, *History of Louisiana,* p. 465. Latour, *Historical Memoir,* pp. 126, 130, 148. François-Xavier Martin, *The History of Louisiana* (New Orleans: James A. Gresham, 1882), p. 382. Walker, *Jackson and New Orleans,* p. 241. Latour, *Historical Memoir,* p. clxxxvii (General Orders, Jan. 21).

13. Wellington, *Supplementary Dispatches,* p. 398. Dickson, "Artillery Services," p. 147. Gleig, *The Campaigns of the British Army,* p. 173. William Surtees, *Twenty-five Years in the Rifle Brigade* (Edinburgh: Wm. Blackwood, 1833), p. 364. Eaton, *The Life of Andrew Jackson,* p. 353.

14. Gleig, *The Campaigns of the British Army,* p. 173. Walker, *Jackson and New Orleans,* p. 255.

15. Wellington, *Supplementary Dispatches,* p. 398. Gayarré, *History of Louisiana,* p. 455. Latour, *Historical Memoir,* p. 132, 138, li (Patterson to Secretary of Navy, Jan. 2). A letter in *Niles Weekly Register,* VII, 360–61, has the fog clearing at 8:00 A.M.

16. James Parton, *Life of Andrew Jackson* (Boston: Houghton, Mifflin Co., 1860), II, 156. Latour, *Historical Memoir,* p. li (Patterson to Secretary of Navy, Jan. 2). Gayarré, *History of Louisiana,* p. 457. Gleig, *The Campaigns of the British Army,* p. 174. Walker, *Jackson and New Orleans,* p. 255.

17. Gayarré, *History of Louisiana,* p. 455. "Major Howell Tatum's Journal," p. 121. Walker, *Jackson and New Orleans,* p. 256.

18. "Major Howell Tatum's Journal," p. 121 (he mentions only one caisson destroyed). Latour, *Historical Memoir,* pp. 133–34. Gayarré, *History of Louisiana,* p. 456. Walker, *Jackson and New Orleans,* pp. 260–61.

19. Latour, *Historical Memoir,* p. li (Patterson to Secretary of Navy, Jan. 2).

20. Walker, *Jackson and New Orleans,* p. 260. Surtees, *The Rifle Brigade,* p. 366.

21. Walker, *Jackson and New Orleans,* p. 258.

22. Latour, *Historical Memoir,* p. 135. Gayarré, *History of Louisiana,* p. 457. Gleig, *The Campaigns of the British Army,* p. 174. "Major Howell Tatum's Journal," p. 120. Latour, *Historical Memoir,* p. li (Patterson to Secretary of Navy, Jan. 2). Wellington, *Supplementary Dispatches,* p. 398. Dickson, "Artillery Services," p. 149. Marquis James, *The Life of Andrew Jackson,* p. 239, contributes the information about the whisky.

23. Wellington, *Supplementary Dispatches,* p. 398. Walker, *Jackson and New Orleans,* pp. 266–67.

24. Dickson, "Artillery Services," pp. 149–50. "General Court-Martial for Trial of Brevet Lieutenant-Colonel Mullins," *Louisiana Historical Quarterly,* IX, 90. Gayarré, *History of Louisiana,* p. 458. Walker, *Jackson and New Orleans,* p. 267. Lossing, *The Pictorial Field-Book,* p. 1041.

25. Gleig, *The Campaigns of the British Army,* p. 174. "Unpublished Letter Relative to the Battle of New Orleans," *Publications of the Louisiana Historical Society,* IX, 77, 79.

26. Latour, *Historical Memoir,* pp. lix, clxxii.

27. Walker, *Jackson and New Orleans,* pp. 264–65.

28. Henry Adams, *History of the United States during the Second Administration of James Madison* (New York: Chas, Scribner's Sons, 1904), II, 364. Dickson, "Artillery Services," p. 148.

CHAPTER EIGHTEEN

1. Alexander Walker, *Jackson and New Orleans* (New York: J. C. Derby, 1856), p. 183. Augustus C. Buell, *History of Andrew Jackson* (New York: Chas. Scribner's Sons, 1904), II, 60–61, 84.

2. For troops movements, A. Lacarriere Latour, *Historical Memoir of the War in West Florida and Louisiana* (Philadelphia: John Conrad

& Co., 1816), pp. 136, 143; François-Xavier Martin, *The History of Louisiana* (New Orleans: James A. Gresham, 1882), p. 385; Charles Gayarré, *History of Louisiana: The American Domination* (New York: Wm. J. Widdleton, 1866), p. 480. Buell, *History of Andrew Jackson,* I, 423, and Latour, *Historical Memoir,* p. 138, report on the Kentuckians. Latour's Boisgervais line is described on pp. 124, 166; Kemper's trip is on p. 139; Patterson's activities are reported on pp. lx–lxi (Patterson to Secretary of Navy, Jan. 13).

3. J. Fair Hardin, "The First Great River Captain," *Louisiana Historical Quarterly,* X, 27–28.

4. Latour, *Historical Memoir,* pp. clxii–clxv (Cochrane to Croker, Jan. 18), lxix (Overton to Jackson, Jan. 19).

5. *Ibid.,* p. 162. Henry Adams, *History of the United States of America during the Second Administration of James Madison* (New York: Chas. Scribner's Sons, 1904), II, 367, 372. J. W. Fortescue, *A History of the British Army* (London: Macmillan Co., 1920), X, 164.

6. John Spencer Cooper, *Rough Notes of Seven Campaigns* (2nd ed.; Carlisle: G. & T. Coward, 1914), p. 136.

7. Pakenham's order for the attack is included in Field Marshal Arthur, Duke of Wellington, *Supplementary Dispatches, Correspondence, and Memoranda,* ed. (his son) The Duke of Wellington (London: John Murray, 1863), X, 399–400 (General Keane's Journal of Operations).

8. George R. Gleig, *The Campaigns of the British Army at Washington and New Orleans* (London: John Murray, 1847), p. 176. William Surtees, *Twenty-five Years in the Rifle Brigade* (Edinburgh: Wm. Blackwood, 1833), p. 369. "General Court-Martial for Trial of Brevet Lieutenant-Colonel Mullins," *Louisiana Historical Quarterly,* IX, 83.

9. "Major Howell Tatum's Journal," ed. John Spencer Bassett, *Smith College Studies in History,* VII, 122, and William Surtees, *The Rifle Brigade,* p. 356, report the annoyances in camp. Cooper, *Rough Notes,* p. 136, reports the carrying of ammunition by the soldiers.

10. Cooper, *Rough Notes,* p. 136. Alexander Dickson, "Artillery Services in North America in 1814 and 1815," *Journal of the Society for Army Historical Research,* VIII, 153.

11. Henry Adams, *History,* II, 295–310.

12. Latour, *Historical Memoir,* pp. 147–48, clxxxvii (General Orders, Jan. 21) (Jackson's artillery on the left bank), 126, 168, lx–lxi (Patterson to Secretary of Navy, Jan. 13) (the right bank). Walker, *Jackson and New Orleans,* p. 307, and John Spencer Bassett, *The Life of Andrew Jackson* (New York: Doubleday, Page & Co., 1911), I, 190 (controversy about the forward redoubt).

13. Latour, *Historical Memoir,* pp. 150–52. Marquis James, *The Life of Andrew Jackson* (New York: Bobbs-Merrill Co., 1938), p. 243, reports 5,172 men on the line according to morning reports.

14. Latour, *Historical Memoir,* pp. 167–68.

15. For the arrival and condition of the Kentuckians, "Major Howell Tatum's Journal," p. 122; Latour, *Historical Memoir*, pp. 141–42; Gayarré, *History of Louisiana*, p. 461; John Henry Eaton, *The Life of Andrew Jackson* (Philadelphia: Samuel Bradford, 1824), p. 360; James Parton, *Life of Andrew Jackson* (Boston: Houghton, Mifflin Co., 1860), II, 36. The contractor's whereabouts is the subject of Andrew Jackson, *The Correspondence of Andrew Jackson,* ed. John Spencer Bassett (Washington: Carnegie Institution of Washington, 1927), II, 124, 130–31 (Jackson to Holmes, Dec. 25; Jackson to Monroe, Jan. 3; Butler to Holmes, Jan. 6). Latour, *Historical Memoir*, pp. 141–42 (citizens' reactions). Nathaniel Claiborne, *Notes on the War in the South* (Richmond: Wm. Ramsay, 1819), p. 77 (the boys drilling and marching). Adair's method of getting arms is reported by Latour, *Historical Memoir*, p. 141; "Major Howell Tatum's Journal," p. 123; and Zachary Smith, *The Battle of New Orleans* (Louisville, Ky.: John P. Morton & Co., 1904), pp. 73–74.

16. Gayarré, *History of Louisiana*, p. 462 (patriotism of the citizens). Stanley Clisby Arthur, *The Story of the Battle of New Orleans* (New Orleans: Louisiana Historical Society, 1915), p. 232, tells of the marriage of the British surgeon Dr. Josiah E. Kerr to Mlle Manette Trudeau, a planter's daughter.

17. Latour, *Historical Memoir*, pp. 190–91, lxix (Overton to Jackson, Feb. 17). "Major Howell Tatum's Journal," p. 123.

18. Gayarré, *History of Louisiana*, pp. 459–60, and Latour, *Historical Memoir*, pp. 138–40 (the false alarms).

19. Smith, *The Battle of New Orleans*, pp. 73–74. Jackson, *Correspondence*, II, 192–95 (Adair to Jackson, March 20).

20. John Henry Cooke, *A Narrative of Events in the South of France and of the Attack on New Orleans* (London: T. & W. Boone, 1835), p. 216. Cooke, p. 176, calls New Orleans "the city of the swamps." For the dress and colors of the 7th and 43rd regiments, *Journal of the Society for Army Historical Research*, VIII, 242, and Cooke, *Narrative of Events*, p. 217.

21. Latour, *Historical Memoir*, p. clxii (Cochrane to Croker, Jan. 18). "General Court-Martial," p. 37.

22. Wellington, *Supplementary Dispatches*, pp. 399–400 (Keane's Journal). Keane reports 200 marines designated to cross in Thornton's force. David B. Morgan in "General David B. Morgan's Defense of the Conduct of the Louisiana Militia in the Battle on the Left Side of the River," *Louisiana Historical Quarterly*, IX, 18; Latour, *Historical Memoir*, p. cl (Lambert to Bathurst, Jan. 10); and Surtees, *The Rifle Brigade*, p. 370, report 400 marines. "Major Howell Tatum's Journal," p. 125, gives Keane's route. For the movement of the 44th, "General Court-Martial," p. 42; Cooke, *A Narrative of Events*, p. 244; Wellington, *Supplementary Dispatches*, p. 398; and Cooper's description of the assault on Badajoz, *Rough Notes*, p. 79.

23. "General Court-Martial," pp. 35–38, 66–67, 84, 90.

24. Buell, *History of Andrew Jackson,* II, 23. Walker, *Jackson and New Orleans,* pp. 322–23.

25. "General Court-Martial," pp. 55–56, 71–72.

26. Dickson, "Artillery Services," p. 159 (artillery labors). Fortescue, *History of the British Army,* X, 166, note (trouble with the canal).

27. Cooper, *Rough Notes,* pp. 138, 140.

28. Surtees, *The Rifle Brigade,* pp. 372–73.

29. Cooke, *A Narrative of Events,* pp. 224–25.

30. Vincent Nolte, *The Memoirs of Vincent Nolte: Reminiscences in the Period of Anthony Adverse* (New York: G. Howard Watt, 1934), p. 221, reports that the men lay on their arms.

31. Latour, *Historical Memoir,* p. lxi (Patterson to Secretary of Navy, Jan. 13). Jackson, *Correspondence,* II, 132 (Patterson to Jackson, Jan. 7). Andrew Jackson, "General Jackson's Last Letter from Chalmette prior to the Battle of New Orleans," *Publications of the Louisiana Historical Society,* I, Part II, 48–49. Latour, *Historical Memoir,* p. 150. For the Kentuckians and the guns at the armory, Smith, *Battle of New Orleans,* pp. 115–17; Benson J. Lossing, *The Pictorial Field-Book of the War of 1812* (New York: Harper & Bros., 1868), p. 1045; Gayarré, *History of Louisiana,* p. 481; and Latour, *Historical Memoir,* p. 170.

32. Latour, *Historical Memoir,* pp. 169, lxi (Patterson to Secretary of Navy, Jan. 13).

33. Buell, *History of Andrew Jackson,* II, 7–9.

CHAPTER NINETEEN

1. John Henry Eaton, *The Life of Andrew Jackson* (Philadelphia: Samuel Bradford, 1824), p. 366. "General Court-Martial for Trial of Brevet Lieutenant-Colonel Mullins," *Louisiana Historical Quarterly,* IX, 44. Alexander Walker, *Jackson and New Orleans* (New York: J. C. Derby, 1856), p. 325.

2. Alexander Dickson, "Artillery Services in North America in 1814 and 1815," *Journal of the Society for Army Historical Research,* VIII, 160. Field Marshall Arthur, Duke of Wellington, *Supplementary Dispatches, Correspondence, and Memoranda,* ed. (his son) The Duke of Wellington (London: John Murray, 1863), X, 400 (General Keane's Journal of Operations). A. Lacarriere Latour, *Historical Memoir of the War in West Florida and Louisiana* (Philadelphia: John Conrad & Co., 1816), pp. cl, clvii, clxii (Lambert to Bathurst, Jan. 20; Thornton to Pakenham, Jan. 8; Cochrane to Croker, Jan. 18). George R. Gleig, *The Campaigns of the British Army at Washington and New Orleans* (London: John Murray, 1847), p. 340. These accounts differ about the exact size of the force that crossed the river.

3. "General Court-Martial," p. 38, 47, 50, 65, 73.

4. Augustus C. Buell, *History of Andrew Jackson* (New York: Chas. Scribner's Sons, 1904), II, 18 (initial movement of the troops). William Surtees, *Twenty-five Years in the Rifle Brigade* (Edinburgh: Wm. Blackwood, 1833), p. 370 (position of the 93rd).

5. "Major Howell Tatum's Journal," ed. John Spencer Bassett, *Smith College Studies in History,* VII, 125 (positions of the columns on the field).

6. Gleig, *The Campaigns of the British Army,* p. 178. Wellington, *Supplementary Dispatches,* p. 400. Latour, *Historical Memoir,* p. clvii (Thornton to Pakenham).

7. Latour, *Historical Memoir,* p. 154. Buell, *History of Andrew Jackson,* II, 9–10.

8. Latour, *Historical Memoir,* p. 171. Zachary Smith, *The Battle of New Orleans* (Louisville, Ky.: John P. Morton & Co., 1904), pp. 98–100. Eaton, *The Life of Andrew Jackson,* p. 363. David B. Morgan, "General David B. Morgan's Defense of the Conduct of the Louisiana Militia in the Battle on the Left Side of the River," *Louisiana Historical Quarterly,* IX, 21.

9. Charles Gayarré, *History of Louisiana: The American Domination* (New York: Wm. J. Widdleton, 1866), p. 482. Latour, *Historical Memoir,* p. 170. "Major Howell Tatum's Journal," p. 129. Smith, *The Battle of New Orleans,* p. 100.

10. "General Court-Martial," pp. 45, 47–48, 55. Buell, *History of Andrew Jackson,* II, 11.

11. Buell, *History of Andrew Jackson,* II, 11 and 19, puts the British 600–700 yards from the line at this moment.

12. *Ibid.,* p. 11, puts Jackson with Carroll and Adair. Latour, *Historical Memoir,* p. 154, and Buell, *History of Andrew Jackson,* II, 11–12, 19, describe the signal rocket. "Major Howell Tatum's Journal," p. 125, describes the beginning of the march.

13. Latour, *Historical Memoir,* p. 148 (the order of firing). Buell, *History of Andrew Jackson,* II, 12, 13, and 15, and Vincent Nolte, *The Memoirs of Vincent Nolte: Reminiscences in the Period of Anthony Adverse* (New York: G. Howard Watt, 1934), p. 221, describe the appearance of the British fire.

14. "General Court-Martial," pp. 36, 55, 57–58, 82, 105.

15. John Henry Cooke, *A Narrative of Events in the South of France and of the Attack on New Orleans* (London: T. & W. Boone, 1835), pp. 233–34.

16. Buell, *History of Andrew Jackson,* II, 15–17. Latour, *Historical Memoir,* p. 155. Smith, *The Battle of New Orleans,* p. 77.

17. Latour, *Historical Memoir,* p. clvii (Thornton to Pakenham).

18. *Ibid.,* p. 155. James Parton, *Life of Andrew Jackson* (Boston: Houghton, Mifflin Co., 1860), II, 196, and Smith, *The Battle of New Orleans,* p. 78, describe the strange sound of the rifle volleys.

19. "Major Howell Tatum's Journal," p. 125.

20. Buell, *History of Andrew Jackson*, II, 21. "General Court-Martial," *passim.*

21. Latour, *Historical Memoir*, p. 158. Cooke, *A Narrative of Events*, p. 254. Gayarré, *History of Louisiana*, pp. 469–70. Walker, *Jackson and New Orleans*, pp. 333–35.

22. Latour, *Historical Memoir*, p. 158. "Major Howell Tatum's Journal," pp. 126–27. Gayarré, *History of Louisiana*, p. 470. Walker, *Jackson and New Orleans*, p. 335. Dickson, "Artillery Services," p. 163. Cooke, *A Narrative of Events*, p. 254. Surtees, *The Rifle Brigade*, p. 377. Cooke asserts that Rennie did not reach the breastwork, but the others have him dying on it. A letter in *Niles Weekly Register*, VII, 376, has Rennie killing two men with his pistols before being killed.

23. "A Contemporary Account of the Battle of New Orleans by a Soldier in the Ranks," *Louisiana Historical Quarterly*, IX, 11–12. Nolte, *Memoirs*, p. 221.

24. "General Court-Martial," pp. 51, 56.

25. Parton, *Life of Andrew Jackson*, II, 196, places this repulse 100 yards from the line.

26. Cooke, *A Narrative of Events*, pp. 235–38.

27. Latour, *Historical Memoir*, p. 171. Gleig, *The Campaigns of the British Army*, p. 180. Andrew Jackson, *Correspondence of Andrew Jackson*, ed. John Spencer Bassett (Washington: Carnegie Institution of Washington, 1927), II, 192–95 (Adair to Jackson, March 20). Gayarré, *History of Louisiana*, p. 484. François-Xavier Martin, *The History of Louisiana* (New Orleans: James A. Gresham, 1882), p. 385, and Eaton, *The Life of Andrew Jackson*, p. 374, have Morgan ordering the retreat. Morgan, "General Morgan's Defense," p. 19, claims the troops broke before he gave the order.

28. W. C. C. Claiborne, *Official Letter Books of W. C. C. Claiborne, 1801–16*, ed. Dunbar Rowland (Jackson, Miss.: State Department of Archives and History, 1917), VI, 369–83 (the governor's activities).

29. Latour, *Historical Memoir*, p. 155. Wellington, *Supplementary Dispatches*, p. 400. John Spencer Cooper, *Rough Notes of Seven Campaigns* (2nd ed.; Carlisle: G. & T. Coward, 1914), p. 139. Charles Gayarré, "Historical Sketch of Pierre and Jean Lafitte," *Magazine of American History*, X, 394 (Jackson and Dominique). Cooke, *A Narrative of Events*, p. 254, and Surtees, *The Rifle Brigade*, p. 377 (the retreat of Rennie's men).

30. "Major Howell Tatum's Journal," p. 125. "General Court-Martial," p. 45.

31. "General Court-Martial," pp. 42–43.

32. Buell, *History of Andrew Jackson*, II, 24.

33. "General Court-Martial," pp. 48 (Tapp), 39 (Debbeig), 70 (Johnson), 84 (Phelan), 52 (Knight). "Major Howell Tatum's Journal," p. 127.

34. Gayarré, *History of Louisiana*, p. 474.

35. Parton, *Life of Andrew Jackson,* II, 198. Cooke, *A Narrative of Events,* p. 252. Buell, *History of Andrew Jackson,* II, 29.

36. Walker, *Jackson and New Orleans,* pp. 330–31.

37. Latour, *Historical Memoir,* p. clviii (Thornton to Pakenham). Gleig, *The Campaigns of the British Army,* pp. 180–81. Eaton, *The Life of Andrew Jackson,* pp. 374–75.

38. Latour, *Historical Memoir,* pp. 171–72. Morgan, "General Morgan's Defense," p. 21. Jackson, *Correspondence,* II, 192–95 (Adair to Jackson, March 20).

39. Morgan, "General Morgan's Defense," pp. 22–23. Latour, *Historical Memoir,* p. lxiii (Patterson to Secretary of Navy, Jan. 13) has the Kentuckians breaking first.

40. Latour, *Historical Memoir,* pp. lxii–lxiii (Patterson to Secretary of Navy, Jan. 13).

41. *Ibid.,* p. clix (Thornton to Pakenham). Gleig, *The Campaigns of the British Army,* pp. 22, 181. "Major Howell Tatum's Journal," pp. 128–29, also describes this clash.

42. "General Court-Martial," p. 64, has the 21st passing Knight. The various testimony is conflicting about who first fired and who first took to the woods. Tatum reports several advances, pauses, and retreats.

43. "A Contemporary Account," pp. 12–14.

44. "General Court-Martial," pp. 84–100.

45. Cooper, *Rough Notes,* pp. 139–40.

46. Latour, *Historical Memoir,* pp. clxiii, clxvi (Cochrane to Croker, Jan. 18; Lambert to Earl Bathurst, Jan. 28). Neither specifically indicates that there was a quarrel. Dickson, "Artillery Services," p. 164, reports them in conference at Gibbs's headquarters.

47. Morgan, "General Morgan's Defense," p. 25. Gleig, *The Campaigns of the British Army,* pp. 181–82.

48. Henry Adams, *History of the United States of America during the Second Administration of James Madison* (New York: Chas. Scribner's Sons, 1904), II, 377–79. Morgan, "General Morgan's Defense," p. 25. Latour, *Historical Memoir,* pp. 173, 175. "Major Howell Tatum's Journal," pp. 127–28. Gayarré, *History of Louisiana,* p. 493. Jackson, *Correspondence,* II, 132–33 (Jackson to Morgan, Jan. 8). Some historians have the attack on the left bank completed before that on the right bank commenced. Latour is not clear about this, but Tatum indicates that the two actions were almost simultaneous.

49. W. C. C. Claiborne, *Official Letter Books,* pp. 369–83. Claiborne claims to have been at the Rodriguez line "dodging balls"; Davezac, with an endorsement by Doctor Ker, says the governor was sheltered (Jackson, *Correspondence,* II, 202–3).

50. Latour, *Historical Memoir,* p. 159. Wellington, *Supplementary Dispatches,* p. 400.

51. Cooper, *Rough Notes,* p. 141.

52. Cooke, *A Narrative of Events,* pp. 239–41.

53. Surtees, *The Rifle Brigade,* pp. 374–77.
54. Latour, *Historical Memoir,* pp. clxviii–clxix (Lambert to Bathurst, Jan. 28).
55. "A Contemporary Account," p. 15.
56. Jackson, *Correspondence,* II, 134, note (Coffee to Butler, Jan. 8).
57. Latour, *Historical Memoir,* p. clix (Thornton to Pakenham, Jan. 8). Gleig, *The Campaigns of the British Army,* p. 181. William James, *A Full and Correct Account of the Military Occurrences of the Late War between Great Britain and the United States of America* (London: Privately printed, 1818), II, 386. Dickson, "Artillery Services," p. 166. J. W. Fortescue, *A History of the British Army* (London: Macmillan Co., 1920), X, 173.
58. Surtees, *The Rifle Brigade,* pp. 379–80.
59. "Major Howell Tatum's Journal," p. 131. Latour, *Historical Memoir,* p. liv (Jackson to Secretary of War, Jan. 9). Dickson, "Artillery Services," p. 164. Walker, *Jackson and New Orleans,* pp. 355–57.
60. W. C. C. Claiborne, *Official Letter Books,* VI, 369–83. Latour, *Historical Memoir,* pp. 175–76. Gayarré, *History of Louisiana,* p. 493.
61. Gleig, *The Campaigns of the British Army,* p. 182.
62. Cooper, *Rough Notes,* p. 141. Surtees, *The Rifle Brigade,* p. 381.
63. Latour, *Historical Memoir,* pp. lix–lx.
64. *Ibid.,* pp. cliii-clvi. Dickson, "Artillery Services," p. 168, concurs on artillery losses. Wellington, *Supplementary Dispatches,* p. 400, reports a total British loss of 2,030. Buell, *History of Andrew Jackson,* II, 41, estimates it at 3,326.
65. Latour, *Historical Memoir,* p. 177, note. Gayarré, *History of Louisiana,* pp. 477–78, 487. Walker, *Jackson and New Orleans,* pp. 346–47. Morgan, "General Morgan's Defense," pp. 25–28. *Niles Weekly Register,* VII, 374–75, reports 40 carts and 10 boats.

CHAPTER TWENTY

1. A. Lacarriere Latour, *Historical Memoir of the War in West Florida and Louisiana* (Philadelphia: John Conrad & Co., 1816), p. lxiii (Patterson to Secretary of Navy, Jan. 13). James Parton, *Life of Andrew Jackson* (Boston: Houghton, Mifflin Co., 1860), II, 234.
2. Andrew Jackson, *Correspondence of Andrew Jackson,* ed. John Spencer Bassett (Washington: Carnegie Institution of Washington, 1927), II, 134 (Jackson to Lambert, Jan. 8). Latour, *Historical Memoir,* p. 178. Charles Gayarré, *History of Louisiana: The American Domination* (New York: Wm. J. Widdleton, 1866), p. 496. Alexander Walker, *Jackson and New Orleans* (New York: J. C. Derby, 1856), p. 357.
3. George R. Gleig, *The Campaigns of the British Army at Washington and New Orleans* (London: John Murray, 1847), p. 182. John Spencer Cooper, *Rough Notes of Seven Campaigns* (2nd ed.; Carlisle:

G. & T. Coward, 1914), p. 142. "Major Howell Tatum's Journal," ed. John Spencer Bassett, *Smith College Studies in History,* VII, 131–32. Jackson, *Correspondence,* II, 134, note (Coffee to Butler, Jan. 8).

4. Gleig, *The Campaigns of the British Army,* p. 182. Cooper, *Rough Notes,* p. 142. Walker, *Jackson and New Orleans,* p. 360. Vincent Nolte, *The Memoirs of Vincent Nolte: Reminiscences in the Period of Anthony Adverse* (New York: G. Howard Watt, 1934), p. 223. Alexander Dickson, "Artillery Services in North America in 1814 and 1815," *Journal of the Society for Army Historical Research,* VIII, 169.

5. Cooper, *Rough Notes,* p. 142.

6. Latour, *Historical Memoir,* pp. lxix–lxx (Overton to Jackson, Jan. 19).

7. *Ibid.,* pp. clxiii, clxvi (Cochrane to Croker, Jan. 18; Lambert to Bathurst, Jan. 28).

8. Benson J. Lossing, *The Pictorial Field-Book of the War of 1812* (New York: Harper & Bros., 1868), p. 1050. *Niles Weekly Register,* VII, 411.

9. Gleig, *The Campaigns of the British Army,* pp. 183, 202–6. John Henry Cooke, *A Narrative of Events in the South of France and of the Attack on New Orleans* (London: T. & W. Boone, 1835), pp. 258–61. William Surtees, *Twenty-five Years in the Rifle Brigade* (Edinburgh: Wm. Blackwood, 1833), pp. 387–88. J. W. Fortescue, *A History of the British Army* (London: Macmillan Co., 1920), X, 178, defends Pakenham's decision not to wait; p. 177 suggests that Cochrane should have been the one to be court-martialed.

10. Gleig, *The Campaigns of the British Army,* pp. 183, 191–92. Walker, *Jackson and New Orleans,* p. 367. Fortescue, *A History of the British Army,* X, 174.

11. Gayarré, *History of Louisiana,* p. 493. W. C. C. Claiborne, *Official Letter Books of W. C. C. Claiborne, 1801–16,* ed. Dunbar Rowland (Jackson, Miss.: State Department of Archives and History, 1917), VI, 369–83. Latour, *Historical Memoir,* pp. lxiv–lxv (Jackson to troops on the right bank, Jan. 8).

12. Latour, *Historical Memoir,* p. 192.

13. *Ibid.,* p. lxiii–lxiv (Patterson to Secretary of Navy, Jan. 13). Gleig, *The Campaigns of the British Army,* p. 185. Cooper, *Rough Notes,* p. 143. Cooke, *A Narrative of Events,* pp. 267–69. Surtees, *The Rifle Brigade,* pp. 383–84, and Dickson, "Artillery Services," p. 173, report the loss of both feet by Lt. D'Arcy.

14. Gleig, *The Campaigns of the British Army,* pp. 185–86.

15. Walker, *Jackson and New Orleans,* pp. 322–23. Cooke, *A Narrative of Events,* p. 240.

16. Field Marshal Arthur, Duke of Wellington, *Supplementary Dispatches, Correspondence, and Memoranda,* ed. (his son) The Duke of Wellington (London: John Murray, 1863), X, 400–1 (General Keane's Journal of Operations).

17. Latour, *Historical Memoir,* pp. 192–95, lxx (Overton to Jackson, Jan. 19).

18. *Ibid.,* pp. 179, lxiii (Patterson to Secretary of Navy, Jan. 13). Dickson, "Artillery Services," p. 170. John Henry Eaton, *The Life of Andrew Jackson* (Philadelphia: Samuel Bradford, 1824), p. 389.

19. Latour, *Historical Memoir,* pp. 195–96, lxx (Overton to Jackson, Jan. 19).

20. *Ibid.,* pp. 179–80, lxvi ("Provisional articles").

21. W. C. C. Claiborne, *Official Letter Books,* VI, 369–83.

22. Gleig, *The Campaigns of the British Army,* pp. 187–88. Cooper, *Rough Notes,* pp. 144–45. Cooke, *A Narrative of Events,* pp. 271–73. Surtees, *The Rifle Brigade,* pp. 385–86. Dickson, "Artillery Services," pp. 174–77. Cooke, p. 272, reports the soldiers' balancing by means of their guns. Parton, *Life of Andrew Jackson,* II, 268, and Surtees, p. 386, report the slaves.

23. Gleig, *The Campaigns of the British Army,* pp. 188–89. Cooper, *Rough Notes,* pp. 144–45. Walker, *Jackson and New Orleans,* pp. 379–80. Dickson, "Artillery Services," p. 176. Latour, *Historical Memoir,* p. lvi (Jackson to Secretary of War, Jan. 19).

24. Gleig, *The Campaigns of the British Army,* pp. 189–90. Surtees, *The Rifle Brigade,* p. 386.

25. Latour, *Historical Memoir,* p. 180. Gayarré, *History of Louisiana,* p. 497, reports sixty-six prisoners. Latour, *Historical Memoir,* p. lvii (Jackson to Secretary of War, Jan. 19). Latour, pp. 185–86, and Walker, *Jackson and New Orleans,* pp. 382–83, report Kemper's trip.

26. Latour, *Historical Memoir,* pp. 180–81. "Major Howell Tatum's Journal," p. 134.

27. Gleig, *The Campaigns of the British Army,* p. 190. Cooper, *Rough Notes,* p. 146.

28. Gleig, *The Campaigns of the British Army,* pp. 192–93. Surtees, *The Rifle Brigade,* pp. 391–93. Dickson, "Artillery Services," p. 216. Cooper, *Rough Notes,* pp. 146–48. Cooke, *A Narrative of Events,* p. 277, corroborates Surtees about the slaughtering of cattle and hogs. Cooper, pp. 147–48, describes the alligator incident. Surtees on p. 394 reports the capture of an alligator by the dragoons and on p. 403 describes the snake upsetting an officer. "Unpublished Letter Relative to the Battle of New Orleans," *Publications of the Louisiana Historical Society,* IX, 79 (the letter).

29. Latour, *Historical Memoir,* pp. clxxiii–clxxiv (Lambert to Bathurst, Feb. 14). Walker, *Jackson and New Orleans,* pp. 394–95. John Spencer Bassett, *The Life of Andrew Jackson* (New York: Doubleday, Page & Co., 1911), I, 210.

30. Latour, *Historical Memoir,* p. 199. Gayarré, *History of Louisiana,* pp. 506–10. Nolte, *Memoirs,* p. 226, reports that Mme Livingston placed the laurel crown on Jackson's head; thinking, perhaps, of Mark An-

tony and Julius Caesar, he accuses Livingston's wife of doing so "with studied enthusiasm" and Jackson of "somewhat unwillingly" putting the crown aside. But Stanley Clisby Arthur, *The Story of the Battle of New Orleans* (New Orleans: Louisiana Historical Society, 1915), p. 235, declares that it was Carolina Ker, sister of Dr. David Ker, who gave Jackson the crowns. Arthur names Madeline Zoe Cruzat and Celeste Duplessis as the two young girls and specifies eighteen as the number of young ladies representing states.

31. Latour, *Historical Memoir,* pp. lxxi–lxxiii (Address of Dubourg to Jackson, Jan. 23).

32. *Ibid.,* p. lxxiii (Jackson's reply).

33. Bassett, *The Life of Andrew Jackson,* I, 206. Latour, *Historical Memoir,* p. 204. Jackson, *Correspondence,* II, 85, note, and 130–31 (Jackson to Monroe, Jan. 3).

34. Lossing, *The Pictorial Field-Book,* pp. 1063–65.

35. Gleig, *The Campaigns of the British Army,* pp. 194–96. Cooke, *A Narrative of Events,* pp. 284–306. Surtees, *The Rifle Brigade,* p. 400. Cooper, *Rough Notes,* p. 147.

36. Surtees, *The Rifle Brigade,* p. 398. John Philippart, *The Royal Military Calendar* (London: A. J. Valpy, 1815), II, *passim.*

37. Gleig, *The Campaigns of the British Army,* p. 196.

38. Wellington, *Supplementary Dispatches,* X, 536–37. *Dictionary of National Biography,* X, 1154–55, XXII, 951. Field Marshal Arthur, Duke of Wellington, "Letter of the Duke of Wellington (May 22, 1815) on the Battle of New Orleans," *Louisiana Historical Quarterly,* IX, 6.

39. Walker, *Jackson and New Orleans,* p. 408. *Dictionary of National Biography,* III, 343–44, VI, 926–28. Lossing, *The Pictorial Field-Book,* p. 1032.

40. "General Court-Martial for Trial of Brevet Lieutenant-Colonel Mullins," *Louisiana Historical Quarterly,* IX, 109–10.

41. Wellington, *Supplementary Dispatches,* X, *passim.* Surtees, *The Rifle Brigade,* pp. 408–9 (the 95th). John Buchan, *The History of the Royal Scots Fusiliers: 1678–1918* (London: Thos. Nelson & Sons, 1925), pp. 197–220, 235–49, 291 ff (the 21st). Wellington, "Letter," p. 7.

42. Cooper, *Rough Notes,* pp. iv–v, 150–51.

43. Surtees, *The Rifle Brigade,* pp. 414–23.

44. Lossing, *The Pictorial Field-Book,* p. 937.

45. Walker, *Jackson and New Orleans,* pp. 267–72.

46. Lossing, *The Pictorial Field-Book,* pp. 1042–43 (Plauché), 1050 (Overton), 1043 (Carroll), 1045 (Adair). Zachary Smith, *The Battle of New Orleans* (Louisville, Ky.: John P. Morton & Co., 1904), pp. 172–73 (Slaughter). Mrs. Dunbar Rowland, *Andrew Jackson's Campaign against the British* (New York: Macmillan Co., 1926), pp. 397–98 (Hinds).

47. Charles Gayarré, "Historical Sketch of Pierre and Jean Lafitte,"

Magazine of American History, X, 395–96. Alcée Fortier, *A History of Louisiana* (New York: Goupil & Co. of Paris, 1903), III, 170. Lossing, *The Pictorial Field-Book,* p. 1043.

48. Walker, *Jackson and New Orleans,* pp. 286–94. Fortier, *History of Louisiana,* III, 171.

49. Lossing, *The Pictorial Field-Book,* pp. 1025 (Patterson), 1027 (Livingston). W. O. Hart, "Mrs. Louise Livingston, Wife of Edward Livingston," *Louisiana Historical Quarterly,* V, 355–56 (Livingston). "The Nicholls Family in Louisiana," *Louisiana Historical Quarterly,* VI, 16 (Nicholls).

50. Donald E. Everett, "Emigres and Militiamen: Free Persons of Color in New Orleans, 1803–15," *Journal of Negro History,* XXXVIII, 398–401.

51. W. C. C. Claiborne, *Official Letter Books,* VI, 347. Nathaniel Claiborne, *Notes on the War in the South* (Richmond: Wm. Ramsay, 1819), p. 91.

52. Bernard Marigny ("Reflections on the Campaign of General Andrew Jackson in Louisiana in 1814 and '15," *Louisiana Historical Quarterly,* VI, 69) is the apologist. Marquis James, *The Life of Andrew Jackson* (New York: Bobbs-Merrill Co., 1938), pp. 254–55, for the two letters quoted. Jackson, *Correspondence,* II, 163 (Dubuchet to Jackson, Feb. 11) (request of the dragoon captain).

53. Augustus C. Buell, *History of Andrew Jackson* (New York: Chas. Scribner's Sons, 1904), II, 42–43 (I have altered his statement). Marigny, "Reflections on the Campaign," p. 66, answers him. Nolte, *Memoirs,* pp. 219, 223–24 (accusations against Duncan, Duplessis, Claiborne, and Livingston).

54. "Andrew Jackson and Judge D. A. Hall," *Louisiana Historical Quarterly,* V, 521.

55. François-Xavier Martin, *The History of Louisiana* (New Orleans: James A. Gresham, 1882), pp. 391–93. Parton, *Life of Andrew Jackson,* II, 309–11, reprints Louaillier's letter. "Andrew Jackson and Judge D. A. Hall," p. 530.

56. Marigny, "Reflections on the Campaign," pp. 71–72. Latour, *Historical Memoir,* p. 205.

57. Bassett, *The Life of Andrew Jackson,* I, 148, 226–27. Martin, *History of Louisiana,* pp. 404–5. "Andrew Jackson and Judge D. A. Hall," pp. 545–50.

58. "Andrew Jackson and Judge D. A. Hall," p. 526 (Plauché's remarks). Nolte, *Memoirs,* p. 230 (description of Davezac). "Andrew Jackson and Judge D. A. Hall," p. 532, indicates Davezac's and De la Ronde's defense of Jackson. Marquis James, *The Life of Andrew Jackson,* pp. 257–58, and Nolte, *Memoirs,* p. 238, discuss Mrs. Jackson. "Andrew Jackson and Judge D. A. Hall," p. 550 (Jackson's actions at the trial). Martin, *History of Louisiana,* p. 410, and "Andrew Jackson

and Judge D. A. Hall," p. 519 (the Baratarians' reaction). "Andrew Jackson and Judge D. A. Hall," p. 522, reports Jackson's refusal of the money. Gayarré, *History of Louisiana*, p. 625, quotes him. "Andrew Jackson and Judge D. A. Hall," p. 562 (Jackson's words about Hall).

59. W. C. C. Claiborne, *Official Letter Books*, VI, 351.

✵ ✵

Bibliography

Note: The official letters cited in the footnotes are published in one or more of the following: Appendixes to Latour and William James; Brannan; *Niles Weekly Register;* Jackson, *Correspondence;* U.S. Congress, *American State Papers, Military Affairs.* I have cited only one source for each letter.

Adams, Henry. *History of the United States of America during the Second Administration of James Madison.* Vol. II. New York: Chas. Scribner's Sons, 1904.

Adams, John Quincy. *The Duplicate Letters, the Fisheries, and the Mississippi. Documents Relating to Transactions at the Negotiation of Ghent.* Washington: Davis and Force, 1822.

Adams, Reed McC. B. "New Orleans and the War of 1812," *Louisiana Historical Quarterly,* XVI (1933), 221–34, 479–503, 681–703; XVII (1934), 169–82, 349–63, 502–23.

"Andrew Jackson and Judge D. A. Hall," *Louisiana Historical Quarterly,* V (1922), 509–70.

Armstrong, John. *Notices of the War of 1812.* 2 vols. New York: Wiley & Putnam, 1840.

Arthur, Stanley Clisby. *The Story of the Battle of New Orleans.* New Orleans: Louisiana Historical Society, 1915.

Bassett, John Spencer. *The Life of Andrew Jackson.* 2 vols. New York: Doubleday, Page & Co., 1911.

Brannan, John. *Official Letters of the Military and Naval Officers of the U.S., 1812–15.* Washington: Privately printed, 1823.

Brackenridge, H. M. *History of the Late War.* Philadelphia: James Kay, Jr., 1839.

Buchan, John. *The History of the Royal Scots Fusiliers: 1678–1918.* London: Thos. Nelson & Sons, 1925.

Buell, Augustus C. *History of Andrew Jackson.* 2 vols. New York: Chas. Scribner's Sons, 1904.

Claiborne, Nathaniel Herbert. *Notes on the War in the South.* Richmond: William Ramsay, 1819.

Claiborne, W. C. C. *Official Letter Books of W. C. C. Claiborne, 1801–16,* ed. Dunbar Rowland. Vol. VI. Jackson, Miss.: State Department of Archives and History, 1917.

"Contemporary Account of the Battle of New Orleans by a Soldier in the Ranks, A," *Louisiana Historical Quarterly,* IX (1926), 11–15.

Cooke, John Henry. *A Narrative of Events in the South of France and of the Attack on New Orleans.* London: T. & W. Boone, 1835.

Cooper, John Spencer. *Rough Notes of Seven Campaigns.* 2nd ed. Carlisle: G. & T. Coward, 1914. (Originally published 1869.)

Dickson, Sir Alexander, K.C.B. "Artillery Services in North America in 1814 and 1815." Introduction and notes by J. H. Leslie. *Journal of the Society for Army Historical Research,* VIII (1929), 79–113, 147–78, 213–27.

Dictionary of National Biography, The.

Eaton, John Henry. *The Life of Andrew Jackson.* Philadelphia: Samuel Bradford, 1824.

Everett, Donald E. "Emigres and Militiamen: Free Persons of Color in New Orleans, 1803–15," *Journal of Negro History,* XXXVIII (October, 1953), 377–402.

Fortescue, J. W. *A History of the British Army.* Vol. X. London: Macmillan Co., 1920.

Fortier, Alcée. *A History of Louisiana.* 4 vols. New York: Goupil & Co. of Paris, 1903.

Gayarré, Charles. "Historical Sketch of Pierre and Jean Lafitte," *Magazine of American History,* X (July–December, 1883), 284–98, 389–96.

———. *History of Louisiana: The American Domination.* New York: Wm. J. Widdleton, 1866.

"General Court-Martial for Trial of Brevet Lieutenant-Colonel Mullins," *Louisiana Historical Quarterly,* IX (1926), 33–110. (Originally published Dublin: Wm. Espy, 1815.)

Gleig, George R. *The Campaigns of the British Army at Washington and New Orleans.* London: John Murray, 1847.

Hardin, J. Fair. "The First Great River Captain," *Louisiana Historical Quarterly,* X (1927), 25–67.

Hart, W. O. "Mrs. Louise Livingston, Wife of Edward Livingston," *Louisiana Historical Quarterly,* V (1922), 352–56.

Jackson, Andrew. *Correspondence of Andrew Jackson,* ed. John Spencer Bassett. Vol. II (May 1, 1814–Dec. 31, 1819). Washington: Carnegie Institution of Washington, 1927.

———. "General Jackson's Last Letter from Chalmette prior to the Battle of New Orleans," *Publications of the Louisiana Historical Society,* I, Part II (1895), 48–49.

James, Marquis. *The Life of Andrew Jackson.* New York: Bobbs-Merrill Co., 1938.

James, William. *A Full and Correct Account of the Military Occurrences of the Late War between Great Britain and the United States of America.* Vol. II. London: Privately printed, 1818.

Johns, Richard, and P. H. Nicolas. *The Naval and Military Heroes of Great Britain or Calendar of Victory.* London: Henry G. Bohn, 1860.

Journal of the Society for Army Historical Research, The. Vols. VII and VIII (1928–29).

Kendall, John S. "Old New Orleans Houses," *Louisiana Historical Quarterly,* XVII (1934), 680–705.

King, Grace. *Creole Families of New Orleans.* New York: Macmillan Co., 1921.

Latour, A. Lacarriere. *Historical Memoir of the War in West Florida and Louisiana.* Translated from the French by H. P. Nugent. Philadelphia: John Conrad & Co., 1816.

Lossing, Benson J. *The Pictorial Field-Book of the War of 1812.* New York: Harper & Bros., 1868.

Mahan, A. T. *Sea Power in Its Relations to the War of 1812.* 2 vols. Boston: Little, Brown & Co., 1905.

Marigny, Bernard. "Reflections on the Campaign of General Andrew Jackson in Louisiana in 1814 and '15," translated by Grace King, *Louisiana Historical Quarterly,* VI (1923), 61–85. (Original French version, New Orleans: J. L. Sollee, 1848.)

Martin, François-Xavier. *The History of Louisiana.* New Orleans: James A. Gresham, 1882.

"Massachusetts Volunteer at the Battle of New Orleans, A," *Louisiana Historical Quarterly,* IX (1926), 30–31.

McClellan, Edwin N. "The Navy at the Battle of New Orleans," *U.S. Naval Institute Proceedings,* L (December, 1924), 2041–60.

Morgan, David B. "Genl. David B. Morgan's Defense of the Conduct of the Louisiana Militia in the Battle on the Left Side of the River," *Louisiana Historical Quarterly,* IX (1926), 16–29.

Morse, Edward Clarke. "Capt. Ogden's Troop of Horse in the Battle of New Orleans," *Louisiana Historical Quarterly,* X (1927), 381–82.

"The Nicholls Family in Louisiana," *Louisiana Historical Quarterly,* VI (1923), 5–18.

Niles Weekly Register, Vols. VII and VIII (September, 1814–September, 1815).

Nolte, Vincent. *The Memoirs of Vincent Nolte: Reminiscences in the Period of Anthony Adverse.* Translated from the German. New York: G. Howard Watt, 1934. (Originally published in the U.S., 1854.)

Parsons, Edward Alexander. "Jean Lafitte in the War of 1812," *Proceedings of the American Antiquarian Society,* L, Part 2 (October, 1940), 205–24.

Parton, James. *Life of Andrew Jackson*. 3 vols. Boston: Houghton, Mifflin Co., 1860.

Philippart, John. *The Royal Military Calendar*. Vol. II. London: A. J. Valpy, 1815.

"Report of the Committee of Inquiry on the Military Measures Executed against the Legislature," *Louisiana Historical Quarterly*, IX (1926), 223–80. (Originally published New Orleans: Roche Bros., 1815.)

Roosevelt, Theodore. *The Naval War of 1812*. 4th ed. New York: G. P. Putnam's Sons, 1889.

Rowland, Mrs. Dunbar. *Andrew Jackson's Campaign against the British*. New York: Macmillan Co., 1926.

Smith, Zachary F. *The Battle of New Orleans*. (Filson Club Publications, No. 19.) Louisville, Ky.: John P. Morton & Co., 1904.

Soniat, Meloncy C. "The Faubourgs Forming the Upper Section of the City of New Orleans," *Louisiana Historical Quarterly*, XX (1937), 192–211.

Surtees, William. *Twenty-five Years in the Rifle Brigade*. Edinburgh: Wm. Blackwood, 1833.

Tatum, Howell. "Major Howell Tatum's Journal," ed. John Spencer Bassett, *Smith College Studies in History*, VII (1921–22), Nos. 1, 2, 3.

Trussell, John B. B., Jr. "Thunder by the River," *Field Artillery Journal*, XXXIX (July–August, 1949), 173–75.

U.S. Congress. *American State Papers. Class V, Military Affairs*. 7 vols. Washington: Gales & Seaton, 1832–61.

"Unpublished Letter Relative to the Battle of New Orleans," *Publications of the Louisiana Historical Society*, IX (1917), 76–80.

Walker, Alexander. *Jackson and New Orleans*. New York: J. C. Derby, 1856.

Walker, Norman McF. "The Geographical Nomenclature of Louisiana," *Magazine of American History*, X (July–December, 1883), 211–22.

Wellington, Field Marshal Arthur, Duke of. *Supplementary Dispatches, Correspondence, and Memoranda*, ed. (his son) The Duke of Wellington. Vol. X. London: John Murray, 1863.

———. "Letter of the Duke of Wellington (May 22, 1815) on the Battle of New Orleans," *Louisiana Historical Quarterly*, IX (1926), 5–10.

Whittington, G. P. "Dr. John Sibley of Natchitoches, 1757–1837," *Louisiana Historical Quarterly*, X (1927), 467–92. (Reprints Sibley's Journal of July–October, 1802.)

☼ ☼

Index

Abercromby, General, 66
Adair, John, 37, 115, 209, 216, 217, 219, 225, 232, 233, 269
Adams, John Quincy, 153, 155, 157, 160
Adams, William, 153, 160
Aetna, 82, 210
Albuhera: battle of, 6, 29, 77, 211, 267
Alceste, 81, 263
Aldea Ponte: battle of, 6, 29
Alexandria: battle of, 28, 65-66, 110
Alligator, 89, 93-94
America: preparing for invasion, 31; invasion of, 34; leaders in, 35-39; Lafitte's service to, 46; Keane's knowledge of, 66; Castlereagh's expectations, 81; allegiance of fishermen to, 98; honoring Jackson, 265. *See also* United States
American artillery: at Fort Bowyer, 53; at Fort St. Philip, 85, 129, 209, 218; at Fort St. John, 114, 129; at Petites Coquilles, 106, 129; on Dec. 23, 137, 140, 147-48, 166; at Gentilly, 175; on Dec. 28, 180, 184, 185, 187-88, 189, 190, 191, 192; water battery, 198, 201, 202, 203, 205, 214-15, 226, 230, 232, 234, 238, 242, 243, 253, 257, 259; on Jan. 1, 201, 202, 203, 204, 206; increased, 209, 210; on Jan. 8, 214-15, 230, 232, 234, 235, 245, 250; shelling British, 257. *See also* Baratarians
American cavalry, 58, 73, 122, 246, 270; Ogden's, 73, 99, 216; Feliciana,

73, 86, 113, 114, 137, 138-39; Attakapas, 121. *See also* Mississippi Dragoons
American regiments:
7th: before the siege, 75, 86; at Fort St. Philip, 85, 218; on Dec. 23, 137, 140, 144, 148; between battles, 164, 180, 225; on Jan. 8, 216
44th: before the siege, 73, 75, 86; on Dec. 23, 140, 144, 146, 148; at Rodriguez, 166, 173, 180; on Jan. 8, 216
Americans: conduct of in War of 1812, 4, 44, 55, 56, 138; in Louisiana, 14, 15, 17, 18-19, 45, 50, 51, 57-58, 72, 112, 272; attitude of British toward, 81, 176-77
American sailors, 48-49, 115, 179, 184, 193, 201
American troops: activity of, 32, 84, 87, 111, 112, 113, 114, 219, 225-26; attitude of Wellington toward, 70; composition of, 88; number of, 115-16, 131; at Fort St. Philip, 129; on the line of defense, 175, 180, 214-15; celebrations of, 195, 206-7; delivering British dead, 254; in victory parade, 263-64. *See also* Battles of the New Orleans campaign
American war. *See* War of 1812
Anaconda, 82, 163
Anaya, Don Juan de, 120
Anchorage, British, 83, 92, 97, 103, 109, 163, 169, 199, 208-9, 255, 258
Annapolis, 265

Index

Jackson, Andrew (*continued*)
58; health, 52, 72; and Louisianans, 52, 57-58, 74, 88, 99-100, 101-2, 112, 142, 270-73; goes to New Orleans, 70, 71, 72; and legislature, 71, 74, 107-8, 189-91, 193-94; hears of British arrival, 90, 134-35; declares martial law, 113; and Tennesseans, 118, 119, 128; on Dec. 23, 137, 139-40, 146, 147, 148, 149, 150-51, 166; builds breastworks, 164, 168, 173; and British wounded, 167; repartee with Cochrane, 168; feared, 176, 177, 194, 195, 256; between battles, 173-75, 197, 209-10, 214-16, 219, 225-26, 260; on Dec. 28, 184, 185, 188, 191, 192, 193; orders parade, 201; on Jan. 1, 202, 204-5; comments on Kentuckians, 209, 256; and Shreve, 209-10; on Jan. 8, 229, 232, 233, 239, 240, 241, 246, 249-50; on Jan. 9, 253, 256; honored, 263-65, 269, 312-13n30; mentioned, 69, 83, 92, 116, 127, 162, 230, 243, 247, 262, 268
Jackson, Mrs. Andrew, 37, 273
Jackson, Mississippi, 269
Jackson Square. *See* Place d'Armes
Jamaica, 56, 57, 62, 63, 64, 65, 68, 192, 266
Jefferson, Thomas, 14-15, 17, 18, 102
Johnson, Sailing-Master (U.S.N.), 90, 91
Johnston, Lieutenant-Colonel (44th), 221-22, 223, 228, 240
Jones, Thomas apCatesby (U.S.N.): on lakes, 37, 89, 90; at Barataria, 49; in battle, 91-92, 93-96; wounded, 96, 109
Jourdan canal, 216, 246, 259
Jumonville plantation, 113, 123, 126, 134, 135, 142, 150, 175, 177, 180, 192, 206, 248
Juzan, Captain (Choctaws), 87

Keane, Major General John: plans for, 29, 78, 212; early career, 34, 65-66; en route, 56, 65, 68, 79, 92; plans, 67-68, 80, 81, 83, 91, 105, 117, 124-25; at Pea Island, 110, 115-16; landing troops, 129, 131, 132, 135; on Dec. 23, 143, 146, 149, 151; afterward, 162-63, 168; relinquishes command, 169-70; and difficulties of invasion, 171-72; on Dec. 28, 179, 181, 183, 184, 187, 188; between battles, 195, 211, 224; on Jan. 1, 199; on Jan. 8, 220, 229, 231, 235-36, 241; wounded, 241; mistakes of, 255; Journal of, 258; honored, 266; later career, 266
Kemper, Reuben, 38, 120, 166, 174, 175, 209, 262, 269
Kentucky, 13, 31, 37, 269
Kentucky troops: en route, 86, 115, 209; arrival and condition of, 216-17; on Rodriguez line, 217, 219; on right bank, 225-26, 230, 238, 242-43, 246, 256; during battle, 230, 233, 236, 238-39, 244; after the battle, 253
Ker, Carolina, 312-13n30
Ker, Dr. David, 309n49, 312-13n30
Kerr, Lieutenant (U.S. artillery), 214
Kerr, Josiah, 218
Kingston, Jamaica, 63, 64
Knight, Lieutenant (44th), 223, 228, 233, 240, 244-45

Labatut, General (Corps of Veterans), 191
Lacoste, Pierre, 38, 88, 100, 114, 121, 129, 174, 175
Lacoste canal, 136
Lacoste plantation, 126, 134, 135, 136, 137, 138, 140, 144, 147, 175, 180
Lafayette, 18
Lafitte, Jean, 21, 32, 38, 83, 269, 282n2; approached by British, 40-47; volunteers, 46, 48, 87; in army, 87, 114, 121, 193, 197, 246
Lafitte, Pierre, 21, 32, 38, 44, 47, 114, 139, 193
Lafon (Engineer), 86, 99, 175, 259
Lafourche, 13, 52, 73, 86, 114, 209
Lake Borgne, 12, 39, 73, 80, 83, 85, 86, 89, 93, 97, 105, 107, 111, 122, 126, 129, 131, 163, 168, 212, 213, 255, 256, 262
Lake Champlain, 154
Lake Pontchartrain, 12, 14, 48, 50, 70, 73, 80, 85, 86, 99, 102, 106
Lambert, Major General John: plans for, 29, 212; early career, 35, 79; en route, 68, 92, 199, 210; personality, 78; at camp, 211, 224; on Jan. 8, 229, 239, 241, 245; in command, 245, 249-50, 252, 253, 256, 257, 260, 262; criticized, 255; later events, 263, 266; honors, 266
Lane, Captain (rockets), 181
Latour, A. Lacarrière: on Jackson's staff, 72, 139, 230; making maps, 73; building fortifications, 86, 99,